THE CATHOLIC ETHICIST
IN THE LOCAL CHURCH

CATHOLIC THEOLOGICAL ETHICS IN THE WORLD CHURCH

James F. Keenan, Series Editor

Since theological ethics is so diffuse today, since practitioners and scholars are caught up in their own specific cultures, and since their interlocutors tend to be in other disciplines, there is the need for an international exchange of ideas in Catholic theological ethics.

Catholic Theological Ethics in the World Church (CTEWC) recognizes the need to appreciate the challenge of pluralism, to dialogue from and beyond local culture, and to interconnect within a world church not dominated solely by a northern paradigm. In this light, CTEWC is undertaking four areas of activity: fostering new scholars in theological ethics, sponsoring regional conferencing, supporting the exchange of ideas via our website (catholicethics.com), and publishing a book series.

The book series will pursue critical and emerging issues in theological ethics. It will proceed in a manner that reflects local cultures and engages in cross-cultural, interdisciplinary conversations motivated by mercy and care and shaped by shared visions of hope.

THE CATHOLIC ETHICIST IN THE LOCAL CHURCH

Edited by

ANTONIO AUTIERO

LAURENTI MAGESA

TOGETHER IN GOD'S MISSION OF MERCY

Founded in 1970, Orbis Books endeavors to publish works that enlighten the mind, nourish the spirit, and challenge the conscience. The publishing arm of the Maryknoll Fathers and Brothers, Orbis seeks to explore the global dimensions of the Christian faith and mission, to invite dialogue with diverse cultures and religious traditions, and to serve the cause of reconciliation and peace. The books published reflect the views of their authors and do not represent the official position of the Maryknoll Society. To learn more about Maryknoll and Orbis Books, please visit our website at www.maryknollsociety.org.

Library of Congress Cataloging-in-Publication Data

Names: Autiero, Antonio, editor.
Title: The Catholic ethicist in the local church / edited by Antonio Autiero,
    Laurenti Magesa.
Description: Maryknoll : Orbis Books, 2018. | Series: Catholic theological
    ethics in the world church series 6 | Includes bibliographical references
    and index.
Identifiers: LCCN 2017049710 (print) | LCCN 2017055630 (ebook) |
    ISBN 9781608337408 (e-book) | ISBN 9781626982741 (pbk.)
Subjects: LCSH: Christian ethics—Catholic authors.
Classification: LCC BJ1249 (ebook) | LCC BJ1249 .C19185 2018 (print) |
    DDC 241/.042—dc23
LC record available at https://lccn.loc.gov/2017049710

CONTENTS

Part III: Fields of Conflicts

ACKNOWLEDGMENTS

Twenty-five scholars from different parts of the world, of different ages, and differently involved in the work of theological ethics have taken the floor to construct the arguments contained in this book. We acknowledge each of them and express our deepest gratitude. In the spirit of the CTEWC Network, they have offered reflections and narratives on their social, cultural, and ecclesial contexts.

To the members of the CTEWC Planning Committee—and, most especially, James F. Keenan, SJ—thank you for inspiring the theme of this book; to some of them, thanks for the patient accompaniment and effective work in comprehensively revising the material of this book.

For editing the manuscript, we are grateful to Margaret Loughman, a student at Boston College, USA. Her editorial help has contributed to the quality of the book. We also want to thank fellow students Rachel Duquette, Liam Haffey, and Jack McErlean for their assistance with the manuscript.

Last but not least, our appreciation, as usual, goes to Orbis Books, our publisher.

INTRODUCTION

Antonio Autiero and Laurenti Magesa

This volume is the last of the series of books published in recent years, at the initiative of the Planning Committee of Catholic Theological Ethics in the World Church (CTEWC).

After the first world conference on theological ethics in Padua (2006) and the second in Trent (2010), the importance of creating a network of moral theologians around the world became clear. This network has particular significance because it expresses the importance of dialogue and exchange on the central issues that concern ethical discourse in today's world. To serve this need of engaging in conversations, the CTEWC series of books addresses crucial topics such as migration, sustainability, feminist ethics, the relationship between the Bible and morality, and the historical evolution of moral theology. Moreover, the list of contributors to each volume is significant: ethicists from each continent are invited to address aspects of the subject studied by offering their particular cultural and context-specific perspectives. In this way, the series may be seen as a chorus of about 150 ethical voices rising from the various continents in synergy with each other.

This last volume of the CTEWC series focuses on particular aspects of the relationship between different contexts and cultures by aiming to articulate the profile of the Catholic ethicist in the context of the local church.

The book comprises theological voices from five continents of the world. These voices reflect on the identity of the moral theologian, not from an abstract, universally defined point of view, but in light of their concrete experiences of being present and active in their local churches.

Each topic addressed in this volume is dictated by the ecclesiological turning point that characterized the Second Vatican Council. For theological ethicists, the emphasis on the church, locally situated and embodied, together with the consciousness that the ecclesial experience is not lost in the indefinite vagueness of a universal horizon but finds its reality and concreteness in the vital context of local cultures, promotes a new self-understanding of their ecclesial profile and roles.

In this volume, the classic theme of the ecclesial vocation of the theologian—and particularly of the moral theologian—is discussed in various contributions that highlight a paradigm shift that affects, first, the spatial location of the theologian (both universal and local). Second, this paradigm shift concerns the relational interactions of the theologian by showing how theological ethicists belong to and are shaped by their cultures, their people, and their church. The reality surrounding each theologian asks to be understood and interpreted in the light of the local

1

culture and social context. In doing this, theological ethicists are engaged in the historical hermeneutic of their people and their church. Third, in their reflective, foundational capacity, theologians also articulate the heritage and wisdom of general and universal ethics through what emerges from the life story of local churches. This approach leads to a reflective hermeneutic attitude based on life experiences, which is the needed background to understand current ethical challenges and respond to them. Finally, this reflective-hermeneutic way of proceeding is able to appreciate the heritage of general ethical principles and the needed deliberations in particular situations without considering deductive wisdom as the sole decisional and regulatory source. Rather, the reflective-hermeneutic approach interacts in dynamic ways with concrete experiences, and the emerging ethical sensitivity that characterizes different cultures and contexts.

The book is divided into three parts. In the first, key questions that help to define the relationship between ecclesiology and theological ethics are posed. One such question concerns the relationship between the universal church and the particular churches, and how this relationship influences the definition of multiple subjects (i.e., women and men, laity and clergy), issues, tasks, and challenges. What is the authority of the moral "magisterium" in the particular churches? How should "moral education" be understood in relation to the particular culture of a local community? From Latin America, **Elio Gasda** and **Maria Isabel Gil Espinosa** discuss the "people of God" as a relevant theological category that shapes the ecclesiology of communion and its implications for theological ethics. The importance of the magisterium in the church and its relationships with theologians is discussed, in different contexts, by **Vimal Tirimanna** and **Antonio Autiero**. These contributions highlight the need to articulate anew the ecclesial vocation of theological ethicists today. Moreover, as **Kenneth R. Himes** suggests, Catholic social teaching should be reconsidered and contextualized in a church that is both local and universal. Finally, the pneumatological (**Laurie Johnston**), anthropological (**Pablo A. Blanco**), and ethical (**Daniel J. Fleming**) aspects of a Vatican II ecclesiology further enhance this foundational part of the volume.

The second part contains more applied and practical reflections, focusing on concrete life in the local communities and on the moral issues that emerge. A multifaceted picture of the conditions of social and ecclesial life in the various continents is presented: from Africa (**Laurenti Magesa, Anthonia Bolanle Ojo**) to Asia (**Nhu Y-Lan Tran**); and from Latin America (**Claudia Montes de Oca Ayala, Aldo Marcelo Cáceres**) to Europe (**Roman Globokar, Konrad Glombik,** and **Grégoire Catta**). The figures and roles of theological ethicists, their social community, and local authorities, as well as their academic and ecclesial membership are examined.

The emergence of local conflicts and proposed strategies to address and resolve them are the subjects of the third part of the book. Topics include issues in bioethics (**Haruko K. Okano**) and criminal justice (**George Kodithottam**); the challenges of political violence (**Anne Celestine Achieng Oyier-Ondigo**) and terrorism (**Elias Omondi Opongo**); issues concerning disability (**Mary Jo Iozzio**); the relevance of feminist contributions (**Barbara Hilkert Andolsen**); and expanding current digital challenges (**Jana Marguerite Bennett**). Finally, the active engagement of Catholic nongovernmental organizations within the Belgian civil society exemplifies possible new types of commitment for theological ethicists, as **Ellen Van Stichel** indicates.

In the Epilogue, **Lindsay Marcellus**, a young ethicist, critically examines the current landscape in North American theological ethics in order to focus on new sensitivities and new ways of carrying out the work of the Catholic ethicist.

In this volume, the reader is invited to enter not only into multifaceted and diverse ethical contexts but also to appreciate their profound unity. The variety of concrete living conditions in local churches is inseparable from the unity of inspiration that embodies a way of "being and doing" theological ethics shaped by Jesus's gospel and a passionate concern for all human beings, for their joys and hopes and for their griefs and anxieties (see *Gaudium et spes*, no. 1).

Part I

Foundational Aspects

THEOLOGICAL ETHICS
AND THE *PEOPLE OF GOD*

Profile, Tensions, and Perspectives

Elio Gasda

Introduction

The ministry of theologians has existed since the early church (1 Cor. 12:28; Eph. 4:11; Acts 13:1; James 3:1). Its tensions with the hierarchy date back to the first centuries of Christianity.

For example, recall the issues presented by Gnosticism and Arianism. Those theological positions helped the church to clarify the faith. The *munus* (duty, or gift) of the theologian was defined by the tradition as "faith seeking understanding" (St. Anselm). Theology deepens understanding by articulating faith in different forms of thinking, languages, and symbolic expressions. Christian action happens in everyday life. Theology and the magisterium are a second act, that is, they do not exhaust all the mystery, dynamism, and prospects of the people of God. Theology seeks to capture and interpret people's questions, anxieties, and needs. A theological ethic that is separate from people's reality does not correspond to the theologian's ministry and condemns theology to pastoral irrelevance.

Theological reflection is not limited to its insertion into ecclesial structure. Theology is a science within the academic framework composed of a diversity of interlocutors. Economics, politics, culture, technology, and genetics, as well as other religions, considerably influence Christians' moral behavior. Therefore, it is normal to have tensions between real life and the moral education generated by a bimillenarian tradition.

Roma locuta; causa finita est? (Rome has spoken; the matter is finished?) What can be seen as irreformable in Catholic morals? Can a pontificate consider a teaching as definitive, but not dogmatic, even if the same question remains open for its successors? The problem is aggravated when only a few voices, those closer to the magisterium, are heard and when the theological foundations are replaced by the authority of the office and by the Stoic argument of *natural law*. In these cases, theologians can adopt a double standard: they disagree in private but agree in public—*the silent schism of theology.*

7

Where is the problem? Thomas Aquinas distinguished two teaching ministries: the bishops—*magisterium cathedrae pastoralis*—and the theologians—*magisterium cathedrae magistralis*. The episcopal magisterium makes doctrinal decisions, and the theologians' magisterium rests on scientific research. However, since the nineteenth century, the pontifical authority has been strengthened with the promulgation of the doctrine of papal infallibility and the exclusion of pontifical universities from participating and voting in ecumenical councils, causing serious damage to theological reflection.

Conflict of Ecclesiologies

Hierarchology of the First Vatican Council

Much of the tension in the relationship between theological ethics and the magisterium concerns the ecclesiological issue, which was partially resolved in the Second Vatican Council. The church retains precouncil remnants, in which an ecclesiology composed of two types of believers prevailed, the learning and the teaching church. The priests had full authority, and the multitude of the faithful meekly obeyed the hierarchy. In this model, theology was a function derived from and dependent on the hierarchy. The First Vatican Council institutionalized an ecclesiology based on the idea of *societas perfecta,* inspired by nominalism, whereby the essence of society derives from the powers that govern it: a perfect and absolutely independent society, with full legislative, judicial, and coercive powers, whose characteristics are visibly identifiable. Like *societas inaequalis hierarchica* (unequal society), the church is centered on the pontiff and his Roman curia. Ecclesiology becomes a hierarchology to the extent that only the legal, vertical, and uniform vision of the church is noticeable. The First Vatican Council's emphasis on the regulatory function of the ecclesial authority concerning moral issues limited theology to the role of supporting the doctrine of the magisterium on Catholic behaviors.

The First Vatican Council reduced Catholic morals to disciplinary codes, covering all fields of action and research. The popular understanding of papal infallibility regards the pontiff as the voice of Christ, who must be obeyed in matters of sexual, cultural, and family morality. He is the "internal norm" of theological activity. The criterion of ecclesiality is measured by fidelity to the magisterium. Theology is exercised more by delegation than by competence. This domestication of theology is due to the church's aversion to modernity. Moralist theologians are guided by the magisterium to fight the modernism represented by liberalism and socialism, by secularization and the secular state. An antimodernist magisterium usurps the function of the theologian in order to defend its own positions.

Theology becomes prisoner to papal infallibility. The *Pastor Aeternus* Constitution immunizes the magisterium from all forms of distinct thought. The theory of infallibility has imposed itself as a formal principle of moral theology and doctrinal support. This model finds its complement in the *Dei Filius* Constitution. The two documents are consistent in their assertion of authority as a central element of Catholic morals. In the *Dei Filius* preamble, the "seduction of new ideas" is cited as one of the mistakes Catholics must fight against. The mystery of Revelation, seen as incompatible with modernity, is understood as a set of doctrines absolutely and unconditionally defined without appeal by the pontifical authority based in Rome.

Hierarchology extends to theology. Catholic morals are reduced to a set of obligations and commandments. Moral theology is left to play the role of *ancilla* (servant), demonstrating how the theories of the magisterium are supported in the scriptures and the tradition. Most moralists merely limit themselves to reflecting and defending the categories of the pontifical magisterium. One of the most serious consequences of this is the moralists' self-disqualification. The pastoral authority regulates the theological exercise and invades its internal dynamics, that is, its epistemology. Confronted with an unresolved theological–moral issue, judgment is immediately passed by authority, thus obstructing investigation.

Ecclesiology of Communion—Second Vatican Council

The Second Vatican Council renewed ecclesiology by overcoming the idea of a *societas perfecta* church and embracing the church as mystery and sacrament (*Lumen gentium [LG]*, chap. I). Instead of a church identified with the hierarchy, the Council emphasized a church of the people of God, based on communion (*LG*, chap. II). Instead of an ecclesiocentric church, it supported a servant church, open to the world and to the signs of the times (*Gaudium et spes [GS]*, nos. 4, 11, 44). Instead of a triumphalist church, it urged for a pilgrim church, servant of humankind (*LG*, chap. VII). The world and history are the places of God's self-communication. Being church-in-the-world belongs to the theological constitution of the church itself. The respectful dialogue with cultures enriches both the church and cultures.

The mystery of the church, icon of the Trinity, is inexhaustible. It is the people of God, the body of Christ, and the Temple of the Holy Spirit, composed by all who receive the gift of faith and are incorporated into the "body of Christ" by baptism. This is the foundation of the church's unity as well as of the plurality of charisms. The mission of Christ, priest, king, and prophet, continues in each baptized person. This is the sacramental character of the church. The various functions manifest the presence of the same Spirit.

The Council has adopted a new methodology. The doctrinal statements of general character are no longer the starting point of the reflection but the gospel and human experience. The church is a humble interlocutor "without always having at hand the solution to particular problems" (*GS*, no. 33). With the same objectivity, it states, "Let the layman not imagine that his pastors are always such experts, that to every problem which arises, however complicated, they can readily give him a concrete solution, or even that such is their mission" (*GS*, no. 43). It confirms the change of focus in the church–society relationship and emphasizes the role of the laity. In the respectful encounter of the church with society, controversies are normal and positive.

The theological ministry is a charism of the Spirit at the service of the people of God. Vatican II returned morals and ethics to the field of theology as an autonomous science meeting the requirements of an interdisciplinary, critical–theoretical knowledge that seeks to bear its fruit in charity (*Optatam totius,* no. 16). It is an investigation guided by the light of the gospel and by human experience (*GS*, no. 46). *Sapientia christiana* (art. 39.1.1) emphasizes the freedom in the teaching of theology, and its scientific character has been legally recognized in *Codex Iuris Canonici* 218: "Those who are engaged in the sacred sciences have a just freedom of inquiry and of expressing their opinion prudently on matters in which they possess expertise, while observing the submission due to the magisterium of the church." The renovation suppressed the *clericalization* of theology and the monopoly of priests-teachers entrusted by the magisterium to teach in seminaries and religious institutes. When it regained its status, theology no longer was the *ancilla* of the magisterium.[1]

The distinction between a *teaching* and a *learning* church has also been overcome. The people of God must take part in the reflections and deliberations on moral issues. All theology is contextualized by the experience of the people. All human experience is subject to the interpretation of knowledge marked by the historical context, ideological vision, language, and methodology of the researcher. Formulations are always provisional. Theological ethics is a science with all the possibilities of human knowledge. Its scientific character makes it necessarily critical, because every interpretation is an approximation of the experience. It is natural for there to be a "conflict of interpretations" (Paul Ricoeur). Moral problems cannot be solved with irrevocable decisions that are made unilaterally and presented in a catechism.

The ecclesiological renovation rescues the concept of *sensus fidelium* and one of the most valuable gifts of the Spirit: discernment.[2] Automatic responses or a priori prohibitions do not respond to the new issues faced by the faithful. The plurality of ideas is welcome, given the uncertainties. The fundamental obedience of the theologian and the magisterium is to the good of the people of God. According to Cardinal Ratzinger, "The Pope is not an absolute monarch whose thoughts and desires are law. On the contrary, the Pope's ministry is a guarantee of obedience to Christ and to his Word. He must not proclaim his own ideas, but rather constantly bind himself and the Church to obedience to God's Word."[3]

In Brazil, a synthesis between the *hierarchology* and *ecclesiology of communion* of the Second Vatican Council has not yet been achieved. The juxtaposition of these two ecclesiologies interferes directly with theological ethics. Renovation does not take place in a spirit of serenity. Tensions were present in the time of Paul VI and even more so with John Paul II and Benedict XVI. The Latin American church was one of the few that managed to move forward on the Second Vatican Council's proposal. The reception of the Council in the CELAM (Latin American Episcopal

Council) Conference in Medellín (1968) was crucial to the advancement of theological ethics in Brazil. With Pope Francis, a Latin American, some of these tensions have been resolved.

Points of Tension

One of the tasks of theological ethics is to address the anguish and concerns of the people of God, especially the poor and the oppressed. The biblical categories of the orphan, the poor, the widow, and the stranger are redefined in the vulnerable subjects that cry out for recognition of their human dignity: workers, women, gays, blacks, refugees, migrants, indigenous peoples, and new family configurations. The poor, the marginalized, and the downtrodden are concepts that go beyond the socioeconomic context by pointing to the dimensions of sexual identity, moral, cultural, and gender discrimination. Focusing on the issues raised by these alterities also implies the emergence of new tensions with the magisterium, especially on the ethics of human reproduction and sexuality, on gender issues, and on new family configurations.

In tensions regarding human sexuality, the distancing has intensified since Paul VI's 1968 encyclical *Humanae vitae*. Disciplinary decrees on sexuality are no longer accepted by many faithful. Fertility and contraception, second-marriage couples, and civil unions of people of the same sex are addressed differently by the magisterium and theological ethics. Pope Francis's apostolic exhortation *Amoris laetitia* (*AL*; 2016) eased tensions. The magisterium has a vision of sexuality marked by stoicism, a pre-Christian philosophical current, in which sexual acts are linked to procreation, never to pleasure and affection. A physicalist reading of *natural law* is still used as a paradigm for judging sexual behaviors. The civil union between two people of the same sex, necessary from a legal and social point of view, is condemned by the magisterium.

Discourses about sexuality emerge in historic moments as attempts to control sexual practices. The application of new theories to theology causes a breach in universal discourse. Among a polyphony of theological voices, the provisional character of positions should be taken into consideration in order to respect people's individual experiences. Different meanings have been given to sexual relations in different historical, cultural, and political periods. A theological construction that is open to the emergence of new sexual–affective identities, such as homoaffective relationships, can inspire a new sexual ethic, not derived from a heteronormative and procreative understanding, but supported by the appreciation of human beings in their entirety.

There are many tensions around the issue of women. The process of deconstruction of the patriarchal, kyriarchal, and androcentric ideologies points to the recognition of a female identity beyond biological sex. Gender perspectives identify the social distinction linked to recognition as man or woman within socially established standards. Gender studies are present in most Brazilian universities and refer to the forms of cultural construction of masculine and feminine attributes, and the institutions and daily practices that constitute social relations.

Theories, such as that of gender, are used to reflect on social relations, but the magisterium condemns them as ideology. Theological ethics, on the other hand, considers them a field of science that investigates cultural behavior patterns in light of sexuality. Gender identity is one of the organizing principles of social life, and is at the root of many situations of injustice and violence. Gender equality advocates rights and equal opportunities for men and women and stresses the need for the emancipation of women not only in the workplace but also in politics and in the church, under equal conditions with men. Women are individuals with full rights and must have the power to exercise those rights.

New family settings are the third focus of tension. The family is an ancient pre-Christian institution that carries evolution in its conceptualization and config-uration. In Brazil, family relationships have expanded beyond the patriarchal, matrimonial, and patrimonial model. Models founded on affection, the redefinition of gender roles in the workplace, and affective relationships have begun to emerge.

Even though families have never been the same, the magisterium, based on a physicalist interpretation of *natural law*, insists on imposing a uniform family model, namely, that ordinary families are only those in which, by marital contract, a man and a woman commit themselves to each other until death and engage in sexual intercourse solely for the purpose of procreation. According to *Humanae vitae*, the two meanings of the conjugal act, unitive and procreative, are inseparable. Sexual relationships between a man and a woman outside of a marriage context are irregular and a serious offense against the natural order desired by God. It does not matter if there is love, faithfulness, and respect in the extramarital union; according to the judgment of the magisterium, this situation will always be irregular.

For theological ethics, the meaning of family goes beyond procreation and the conjugal act. Based on the anthropology of Vatican II, theological ethics points to a more holistic and comprehensive understanding of the concept of family, and takes into consideration relational, affective, psychological, and spiritual aspects. A new vision of sexual anthropology and new studies on women, gender roles, and new family settings are demands of the people of God that preconciliar methods and paradigms can neither interpret nor respond to.

Epistemological Conflict

Theological ethics plays the role of mediator, both between the church and society and between the church and science. It aims to render ecclesial thinking intelligible to science and to present the advances, discussions, and demands of science and society to the church. Therefore, its epistemology is necessarily distinct from doctrinal teaching discourse. Mainly through a physicalist reading of *natural law*, the Rome-based pontifical magisterium perpetuates the logic of Western moral discourse. That would explain the difficulty in recognizing a theological reflection outside the borders of Rome. Theological ethics reflects this logic when it repro-duces a Romanized Christianity that has little to do with the cultures of native peoples and Afro-descendants. How can one reflect on the construction of the Latin American moral subject while relying upon European assumptions? Should Western Europe be the only genuine locus of knowledge production?

Since the establishment of European epistemic hegemony, modernity has become the sign of cultural superiority over other civilizations.[4] The fact that Brazil occupies a subordinate position in the geopolitics of knowledge and in the decision-making levels of the Catholic Church hinders the advancement of reflection in the areas of tension mentioned above. A theology still beholden to the magisterium, with its paradigms and methodology, is consistently unable to inter-pret all the wealth of experience of the Brazilian people. Theologians swing between occasional manifestations of autonomy and the defense of a Romanized moralism based on the paradigm of a physicalist interpretation of *natural law*.

According to Enrique Dussel, modernity is not merely an intra-European phenomenon, but rather a worldwide one. It affects the peripheral colonized world of the sacrificed Indians, the enslaved blacks, the oppressed women, and the despised popular culture. The presentation of Christianity in its Greco–Roman form as the religion par excellence prevents us from viewing in other cultures and religions an aspiration to truth. Some Latin American ethicist bishops and theologians studied in Europe and adopted the Romanized epistemology of the magisterium. In very few cases, such as liberation theology, it has been possible to produce a perspective that has not been influenced by colonizing biases. Eurocen-trism has cast its shadow on moral theology in many ways.

The Entire Church Is Both Learner and Teacher

The fundamental principle of a liberating education can help to overcome this tension: "no one teaches another, nor is anyone self-taught; people teach each other, mediated by the world."[5] The separation between teaching and learning perpetu-ates the distinction between the *ecclesia docens* and the *ecclesia discens*. The whole church is, at the same time, learner and teacher. The removal of this distinction by the Second Vatican Council allowed for the participation of the people of God in developing the moral teaching of the church. Bishops and theologians are now also apprentices, not only the laity. Nobody can teach what they have not learned. Learning is a necessary condition for effective teaching. The teaching of bishops and theologians should not come primarily from catechisms and documents, but rather from the experience and wisdom of the people. This particularly applies to moral teachings.

Paulo Freire's principle is inspiring for a renewed theological ethics.[6] People consider their religious and cultural traditions to be part of their identity. Discourse will be superficial without a deep knowledge of popular identity. Delving into the density of the human condition makes the theologian realistic in the most acute sense of the term. God communicates Godself in this anthropological–cultural reality; there are many signs of the Kingdom of God among people, cultures, and religions.

The epistemological turn leads theology to open itself up to other epistemic and cultural experiences. Theological ethics is a science that produces knowledge for other audiences besides the ecclesial institution. The magisterium is not its sole interlocutor. Theological discourse is a public discourse. Considering the academy and society[7] as its interlocutors implies assuming a more dialogical epistemology with the world. In this quest, theology encounters the academic thought that investigates the negative impacts of Eurocentrism on religion, culture, and moral behavior.[8] Decolonizing, for theological ethics, means going beyond the Romanized forms of knowledge based on binary constructions such as male/female, black/white, rich/poor, or heterosexual/homosexual. It reveals new codes for interpreting human experience.

Border and Transcultural Theology

In Brazil, theological ethics opens to forms of knowledge that take into consideration possibilities perceived by Eurocentrism as primitive, mythical, exotic, and profane. This opening to border thinking, or modes of thinking from the margins, helps to recover different kinds of experiences and to overthrow the paradigms and schemas of the magisterium. This methodological option breaks with the obligation of understanding all human behaviors through the lenses of Romanized Christianity. Western rationality operates by looking from top to bottom, with the underdeveloped peoples of the Southern Hemisphere, such as those of Brazil, at the bottom. This vision, burdened with stereotypes, perceives the other not as an equal, but as a stranger who requires salvation and mercy.[9]

To consider the people of God, the academy, and society as *places of knowledge* leads to a non-Eurocentric theological ethics: a kind of border thinking that is more suitable to dialogue with emerging subjects and their demands. The Cartesian *I think therefore I am* gives way to a new proposition: *I am where I think.*[10] Feminist, gender, ethnic, Asian American, native people, African American, and queer studies cannot continue to be treated from a Eurocentric perspective. In accordance with Romanized morality, social relations are based on a monocultural model, to the detriment of other models based on plurality and diversity. Eurocentrism and the recognition process of the subjective, social, and ecclesial dignity of the other are part of the same process of *Romanized monoculturalism.*

Theological ethics in Brazil has begun to develop itself through methods other than those of the European tradition. Why would the symbolic–narrative form of Amerindians and Afro-descendants be less appropriate than European thought? Why should we not open ourselves to the influences of other cultural traditions in order to reflect Christian praxis? They contain signs of the ethics of the Kingdom. God's saving action takes place in the whole creation, in the multiplicity of cultures and religions. There are more forms of expression of Jesus's ethics than that which is focused on the doctrine of the magisterium. Yielding to the temptation of summarizing into a single synthesis the diversity of human behavior does not account for the universality of the gospel.

The profile of theological ethics is cross-cultural since cultural traditions offer an ethic that demands to be interpreted with respect. In search of a method, ways of interpreting the life, history, and mystery of the people are investigated. Symbols and narratives strive to overcome the fixation of Western theology on its dogmatic formulas, and to open up to other experiences of God, other languages, behaviors, and values. These skills help to dissolve the linear horizon, to question the perspective from above, and to construct more inclusive subjectivities that propose images of the world in terms of faith and morals. This line of thinking critically examines the constant repetition of norms and their rationale in order to build a theology in harmony with the plural identity of the Brazilian people and to think of differences as positive. Dialogue among cultures allows people to respect human rights. The moral transformation of people that makes them respect themselves and others doesn't happen without dialogue. This is the only way to participate in the debate on the big issues that really matter to people.

All border thinking is necessarily critical. Tensions with hierarchy are inevitable. However, who would claim that tensions are not welcome when they are for the greater glory of God and for the abundant life of God's sons and daughters?

Perspectives:
A Theological Ethic for a Church on Its Pilgrim Way

Theological ethics is coming out of the restorationist quagmire enforced by John Paul II and Benedict XVI, where censorship of thought and research was constant. There are many affinities between the current pontificate of Francis and the theological ethics produced in Brazil, and a healthy and respectful atmosphere between theology and the magisterium. Unlike the hierarchical ecclesiology that took place under his predecessors, the model of communion now prevails. The theological–pastoral orientation takes into consideration the experience of the church in Latin America. The inculturation of the gospel and the church's call to reach those who are at the existential and social borders becomes a theological–pastoral imperative. Pope Francis's influence in the orientation proposed to the universal church is perfectly in tune with the spirit of Vatican II. Magisterium and theology want a welcoming church rather than a berating one: a church with less bureaucracy and more participation. In this regard, the sensitivity to women's ecclesial and social role has rekindled the hope for a less patriarchal church government. Francis's request for a study on the possible restoration of the ministry of women deacons points to a fuller integration of women in decision making.

One of the most relevant points of convergence is the recognition of the authority of the faithful's conscience and its implications in moral life. "Not all doctrinal, moral or pastoral discussions have to be resolved through magisterial interventions. . . . In each country or region, it is possible to search for more incul-turated solutions, attentive to the traditions and local challenges" (*AL*, no. 3). Rigid and demanding doctrinal principles can be beautiful in theory and please the hier-archy, but they do not respond to the reality of the people of God. To address this issue, the International Theological Commission released the study *Sensus Fidei in the Life of the Church* (2014), which draws attention to the laity's role in the devel-opment of moral education. A deeper appreciation of the *sensus fidei* leads the church to become more participatory and less clerical. The magisterium assumes the concept of discernment as a category of moral decision that is thoroughly addressed by theological ethics.

The family theme is another point of dialogue between the magisterium and theological ethics. The papacy wants to relinquish a repressive sexual and family morality in favor of an ethic based on the reality of new family forms. The solution to "irregular situations" relies on careful discernment. The category of "complexity" arises and is used to oppose the simplifications of the church's preconciliar wing that does not tolerate the postures of the current pontificate on moral issues.

The struggle for recognition and citizenship of the LGBT population brings great challenges to theological ethics and the teaching of the magisterium. In gestures and words, Pope Francis demonstrates greater acceptance of the faithful who are members of the LGBT community.

New doctrinal approaches, the institution of proceedings (such as the preparation and completion of the Synod of Bishops on the family), and the exhortation to theologians to discuss border issues and deal with the conflicts that affect all, are fostering more liberating perspectives within theological ethics. Even if the discourse is ambiguous regarding gender issues, the emphasis on complementarity and respect for diversity makes it possible to have a more advanced reflection on the regulatory implications for sexual–affective relation-ships that are nonheterosexual.

In Brazil, theological ethics distinguishes itself by proclaiming its option for the poor, the wronged, the socially and culturally excluded, and the discriminated. It is practicing the culture of encounter, so distant from xenophobia, discrimi-nation, and intolerance. In this encounter, the general does not invalidate the particular. Nothing is dissolved, everything is integrated. "The world's peoples want to be the artisans of their own destiny. They want their culture, their language, their social processes, and their religious traditions to be respected."[11]

Immersed in the rawness of human torment, the current teaching expands the common heritage of Latin American liberation theology and changes the focus on sexual ethics to a focus on social ethics. In conjunction with liberation theologians and theological ethicists, the church is breaking free from the obsession with sexu-ality to instead prioritize social justice and to denounce the idolatry of capital. The magisterium and theological ethics both want a poor church for the poor.

Notes

1. Bernard Häring, *É tudo ou nada: mudança de rumo na Teologia Moral e restauração* (Aparecida, Brazil: Santuário, 1995).

2. Richard Gaillardetz, *By What Authority? Primer on Scripture, the Magisterium, and the Sense of the Faithful* (Collegeville, MN: Liturgical Press, 2003).

3. Joseph Ratzinger, *Convocados en el caminho de la fe* (Madrid: Ediciones Cristiandad, 2004), 223–48, at 240.

4. Walter Mignolo, *Desobediencia epistémica. Retórica de la modernidad, lógica de la colonialidad y gramática de la decolonialidad* (Buenos Aires: Ediciones Signo, 2010).

5. Paulo Freire, *Pedagogy of the Oppressed* (New York: Continuum, 2005), 80.

6. Ibid.

7. Cf. David Tracy, *The Analogical Imagination: Christian Theology and the Culture of Pluralism* (New York: Crossroads, 1981), chap. 1.

8. Frantz Fanon, *Os Condenados da terra* (Rio de Janeiro: Civilização Brasileira, 1968).

9. Pablo Richard, *Força ética e espiritual da teologia da libertação: No contexto atual da globalização* (São Paulo: Paulinas, 2006); Juan Luís de León Azcarate, "La demonización del otro, un viaje de ida y vuelta. Demonización indígena de los españoles en el siglo XVI," *Religión y Cultura* 60, no. 270–71 (2014): 363–82.

10. Mignolo, *Desobediencia epistémica.*

11. Pope Francis, *Discurso no II Encontro Mundial dos movimentos populares,* Santa Cruz de la Sierra, July 9, 2015.

Pending Tasks of Moral Theology in the Framework of an Ecclesiology of Communion

Maria Isabel Gil Espinosa

The essence of the church is in its mission of service to the world, in its mission to save it in totality, and to save it in history, here and now. The church is in solidarity with the hopes and joys, with the anguish and sorrow of men.

—Monsignor Oscar Romero

In the context of this volume, reflections on some pending tasks of moral theology will be developed in an ecclesiological atmosphere. For this reason, we must first identify which model of church we are located in, where we are as we reflect upon those pending tasks. Second, after making clear where we are located as church, we will determine some tasks of moral theology that are still pending today.

In Which Church Model Are We Located?

In speaking of church we know that we are not referring to a single model or concept of church, neither throughout history nor even today. However, the Second Vatican Council will give us the key to a new ecclesial sense[1] of communion, of participation as the people of God,[2] as body of Christ,[3] and as church of the poor, and it is in this sense a new ecclesiology. The Council undoubtedly intended a change of horizon in which new perspectives were opened for a special theology of the church. We see this especially in *Lumen gentium* (Dogmatic Constitution on the Church) and in *Gaudium et spes* (Pastoral Constitution on the Church in the Modern World).

As we have indicated, the Council presents an ecclesiology that indicates its goal toward communion:

The Church is in Christ as a sacrament, or as a sign and instrument of intimate union with God and of the unity of the whole human race; it proposes to present, with more precision, to its faithful and to the whole world its nature and its universal mission, abounding in the doctrine of the preceding councils. The conditions of our time make this duty of the Church more urgent, namely, that all men, who today are most closely united by multiple social, technical, and cultural ties, also achieve full unity in Christ.[4]

And in the line of a Pauline ecclesiology, the church is presented as the body of Christ:

And just as all the limbs of the human body, though many, yet form one body, so do the faithful in Christ (1 Cor 12:12). Also in the constitution of the body of Christ the diversity of members and offices is in force. Only one is the Spirit, which distributes its varied gifts for the good of the Church according to his wealth and the diversity of ministries (1 Cor 12:1–11) . . . It produces and urges charity among the faithful, unifying the body by itself and with its virtue and the internal connection of the members. Therefore, if one member suffers in something, with him all the others suffer; or if one member is honored, the other members enjoy jointly (1 Cor 12:26).[5]

Therefore, this figure of the body of Christ that manifests the nature of the church and emphasizes the aspects of community, relationship, bond, solidarity, and encounter is the symbolism that underlies the mystery of communion.[6] In this same vein *Lumen gentium* presents, in its second chapter, the church with the image of the people of God:

The condition of this people is the dignity and freedom of the children of God, in whose hearts the Holy Spirit dwells as in a temple. It has by law the new command to love as Christ himself loved us (Jn 13, 34). This people . . . instituted it to be a communion of life, charity and truth.[7]

Undoubtedly, this definition of the church as the people of God marks the entire ecclesiology of *Lumen gentium* and emphasizes its communal character.

Likewise, the church of the poor is another of the ecclesial titles that has had great relevance in the development of a theology of the church from Vatican II; the issue of poverty, as Estrada says,

is analyzed from the same revelation, studying its implications for the treaty of God, . . . ecclesiology . . . can be said to have become a constituent element of the image of the Christian God, of the mission of Christ . . . and of the very constitution of the Church in its ministerial and sacramental structure.[8]

In short, the ecclesiology of communion, understood as the body of Christ, the people of God, and the church of the poor, is the central and fundamental idea of the Council, and it cannot be reduced to organizational matters or to an approach that simply refers to the poor as a marginal concern,[9] because as *Gaudium et spes* states, poverty is a constitutive part of the church's being and mission:

> The joys and hopes, the sorrows and the anguishes of the men of our time, especially of the poor and of those who suffer, are both joys and hopes, sorrows and anguishes of the disciples of Christ. There is nothing truly human that does not find echo in its heart . . . The Church therefore feels intimate and truly supportive of the human race and its history.[10]

Theological Elements of an Ecclesiology of Communion

This section identifies some theological foundations of an ecclesiology of communion. Much of contemporary theology has assumed the understanding of God as God has revealed Godself in history, that is, as a God who is communion, a community of three persons. As Gonzalo Zarazaga states,

> "The economic Trinity is the immanent Trinity" means precisely that God has not revealed himself fundamentally through doctrinal knowledge or by making known his metaphysical essence, but has donated himself, to give himself personally to men, in history, as He himself is: Father, Son and Holy Spirit.[11]

If this is so, then we can affirm that the interpersonal communion of love is the essence of the being of God. This has implications for our understanding of ourselves as intrinsically relational beings and also for our understanding that the essence of the church cannot be understood outside of the concept of communion. That is, we can only affirm that we are authentically Christians if we live the Trinitarian faith. This is because the communion to which that Trinitarian God invites us is the communion that God is, since we have been created in the image and likeness of God.

The Cappadocian Fathers also understood the Christian God as a Trinitarian God. Quoting Gregory of Nazianzus, Ware notes,

> When I say God, I think Father, Son, and Holy Spirit, says Saint Gregory of Nazianzus. For him, the doctrine of the Trinity is not only a possible way of thinking about God. It is the only way. The one God of the Christian Church can only be conceived as a Trinity. Outside from the unity in the diversity of the Father, the Son and the Holy Spirit, one cannot know God in the fullness of truth and reality of his being. There is no authentic Christian experience that is not, explicitly or implicitly, a Trinitarian

experience. In this way, Gregory's approach is not abstract, but personal. In his understanding, God is not a theoretical concept, it is not a philosophical axiom or postulate but a living communion of three persons or hypostasis inseparably joined together in a union of mutual love.[12]

The foundation of this communion is the Christian God who has revealed himself in Jesus and who has wanted to become part of our history. Without the concept of communion, it is not possible to speak of God because that is the essence of his being.

In the Christian tradition it is affirmed that we have been created in the image and likeness of God, and that affirmation must be interpreted to mean that we have been created in the image of God as Trinity. Hence our most genuine vocation is to reproduce the eternal *perichoresis* that unites the Father, the Son, and the Holy Spirit. Every form of community is intended to become the communion that is God. Faith in the Trinitarian God cannot leave us indifferent to human rights, poverty, and injustices; we cannot remain indifferent to any kind of suffering, because God is a mystery of shared love. Believing in the Trinitarian God, which is relational, has far-reaching implications for the realities of our world.[13]

In short, the mystery of the Trinity as communion is the source of the existence of the communion church.[14] For this reason, the church is not simply an institution but a mode of existence, a way of being. The mystery of the church, even in its institutional dimension, is deeply united to the being of the human person, the world, and God. The ecclesial being is united to the very being of God. It is a form of relationship, an event of communion. However, in order for the church to offer this form of existence, it must itself be an image of God's form of existence. The being of God is a relational being; without the concept of communion, it will not be possible to speak of the being of God, because communion is an ontological category.[15]

From these observations, we can deduce that the local church cannot be reduced to a species of separated ghettos, because their essence is communion. In this sense, Saint Paul emphasizes that sharing the bread and the cup of the Lord incorporates the believers in such a way that they form one body, the body of Christ (1 Cor 10–18), and the body of Christ is the church. Therefore, it is not an artificial, false, or forced communion, but a vital communion such as that which exists between the limbs of the body.

Moral Theology in the Framework of a Communion Church

In the previous section some clues were proposed that provide understanding of the true essence of the church and thereby help present the theological framework of an ecclesiology of communion—people of God, body of Christ, church of the poor—not simply as titles, but rather as characteristics that are inherent to the church. Within this framework of a theology of the church some pending tasks in today's moral theology will be located.

However, before addressing these tasks, it is necessary to keep in mind that, although contemporary theology has been elaborating these reflections from the revelation of God as self-donation (*Dei verbum*, no. 2), the truth is that the Trinitarian mystery of a communion God says very little to Christians in practical life, and the affirmation of a triune God has had very few real-world implications. It can be said that for many Christians the Trinitarian postulate has a mere ornamental function and that it could practically be dispensed with.[16] Or, as Rahner would say, if the Trinitarian axiom were dispensed with in theology, in practice nothing would happen.[17]

Undoubtedly, a distorted understanding of the Trinitarian God has had serious consequences for ecclesiology and for moral theology. For the most part, the understanding of church has been based on a Christological monism. As a result, its apostolic dimension has been emphasized above all, and its institutional, hierarchical, and ministerial character underlined in its ecclesiology.[18]

Thus, the theological foundation of some ecclesiologies is not the Trinitarian God, the Christian God *revealed* in Jesus, or the communion church (people of God, body of Christ, church of the poor). Instead, the emphasis of these ecclesiologies is on the church's hierarchical, juridical, and institutional nature. However, according to the theological elements already analyzed, we can say that the core of the church is both communion and community; in other words, the church is local and, eucharistic or not, it is the Christian community.[19] In this sense Estrada says:

> The reification and materialization that is lived in the second millennium also has consequences for ecclesiology. The church is juridized and materialized on the basis of its mysterious character. It is no longer called the body of Christ (this denomination now passes to the Eucharist to underline the real presence of Christ). Theological reflection on the Eucharist and, in general, the treatise on sacraments unfolds without a treatise on ecclesiology that frames them and impregnates them. Ecclesiology and Eucharist are separated and the visible, the legal, and the corporate are imposed to the church.[20]

This represents a serious difficulty because, in fact, in some cases, when referring to the communion church (people of God, body of Christ, church of the poor), allusion is only being made to empty titles, to a discourse devoid of content. This is because, in reality, it is the hierarchical and ministerial institution that is actually working. Undoubtedly, this flawed ecclesiology will have implications for the role that moral theology must play in the church and the tasks it must perform. This is why, as stated at the outset, it is important to ask ourselves in which model of church we are located, and from where we identify the pending tasks for moral theology today.

Another difficulty that may prevent us from understanding the church as communion is a dualistic understanding of reality that divides it into the sacred and the profane. Such an understanding could lead to a closed ecclesiocentrism that is solely concerned with the administration of the sacred reality. It will consequently perceive threats in everything that does not appear to belong to this sacred universe—that is, everything that is secular, temporal, civil, and profane. However, the historical and existential world to which Vatican II refers (or, as Pope Francis would say, the existential peripheries) is also the theological place in which this Trinitarian God reveals Godself.

Therefore, a theology that takes seriously the self-communication of God as Father, Son, and Holy Spirit, in a communion of love, must go far beyond a dualistic viewpoint and must resist the temptation to reduce its raison d'être to the administration of "the divine" with contempt for that which is human. This ecclesiology must take history seriously as a history of salvation, and must put effort into building the Kingdom of God here and now. It must be a church that is conscious of the social and political dimension of faith and that feels responsible for history, because it understands that this is also a theological place and a sacred reality.

From the difficulties mentioned it is clear why, on the one hand, when the church is referred to, it is not understood as a single model or concept and, on the other hand, why it is necessary to ask within which ecclesiological framework moral theology is situated and to try to identify its function and, consequently, the tasks that it has pending today. Of course, there are other important implications and questions that flow from an ecclesiology of communion that incorporates people of God, body of Christ, and church of the poor. For example, what is the function of the sacraments, of the liturgy, of prayer, etc.? These are questions we cannot answer in this brief reflection, but rather we will focus now on the central question of the function and pending tasks of moral theology in the context of an ecclesiology of communion, in the concept of communion church as described in this essay.

Some Pending Tasks

According to the above, the first pending task for moral theology today is determining its function within the proposed ecclesiology of communion as people of God, body of Christ, church of the poor. This is because, unquestionably, and in the context of these theological foundations, its function can no longer be reduced, as in the past, to counting and measuring sins, especially the sexual sins of the laity. It is clear that in the context of an ecclesiology of communion–people of God, the confessional can no longer be the only function and purpose of moral theology.

Moral theology must review its function within an ecclesiology of communion. Indeed this is asked for by the Council when it asks that moral theology, like other theological disciplines, be renewed by a more living contact with the mystery of Christ and the history of salvation (*Optatam totius*, no. 16). In this context it emphasizes that "special care should be taken in perfecting moral theology, whose scientific exposition, more nourished by Sacred Scripture,[21] explains the greatness of the vocation of the faithful in Christ, and the obligation that they have to bear fruit in charity for the life of the world."[22] Here the Council is indicating what it believes the main function of moral theology should be in a communion–people of God ecclesiology. It is to show the greatness of the vocation of the faithful in Christ and the obligation to bear fruit in charity. Thus, its function is situated in a call-and-response scheme and not in the old law-compliance mode. It is a moral theology that is situated in the following of Christ and in the fundamental option, and its call is not directed exclusively to clergy and the religious, but rather to all, because the call to holiness is universal.[23] Following Jesus is a right of the whole people of God.

As a consequence of this, a second task arises. It is an urgent and necessary task to desexualize moral theology[24] and to reorient it away from the exclusive focus it seems to have on sacramental consumerism. Similarly, moral theology has the pending task of revising the operative concept of sin in order to ensure that it has more coherence with an ecclesiology of communion. This will involve an orientation toward the vocation of the faithful in Christ, orienting the whole people of God to a fundamental, positive option for Christ and explaining to them that the call to holiness is universal, and that all of the people, because of their faith in a God who is communion, have a duty to produce fruits of justice and solidarity in accordance with a communion church.

Following the ecclesiological horizon proposed by Vatican II in *Gaudium et spes*, moral theology, in coherence with the aforementioned function, has today a third task pending, which is that its reflection and its praxis cannot be outside of "the joys and the hopes, the sorrows and anguish of the men of our time, especially of the poor and of those who suffer."[25] It cannot be, as Pope Francis would say, outside the existential peripheries of human beings of our time.

In this sense we can see that there are truly alarming realities around us, such as the abuse of human rights; the scandal of refugees, displaced, and immigrants because of wars; and the internal conflicts in many countries where millions of human beings are dispossessed of all of their belongings. This is a reality that cries out to heaven.[26] Similarly, the figures on world hunger, not metaphorical hunger but real hunger, of people living on less than one or two dollars a day, are chilling.[27] Along the same lines are the modern forms of slavery in which, according to the International Labor Organization,

> Nearly 21 million people are victims of forced labor: 11.4 million women and girls, and 9.5 million men and boys. About 19 million victims are exploited by individuals or private companies and more than 2 million by the State or rebel groups. Of those exploited by individuals or companies, 4.5 million are victims of forced sexual exploitation. Forced labor in the private economy generates illegal annual profits of $150 billion per year. Domestic work, agriculture, construction, manufacturing and entertainment are among the most affected sectors. Migrant workers and indigenous peoples are especially vulnerable to forced labor.[28]

These data show the task that moral theology today has pending, if it wants to fulfill its role in the framework of a communion church. One wonders at the sense of scandal that this shocking reality evokes within some ecclesial sectors, relative to the scandal provoked by the eighth chapter of *Amoris laetitia* on the possibility posed by Pope Francis that remarried divorced people may approach the sacraments. Yet these serious violations of human rights and dignity do not seem to generate the same level of concern and, even more seriously, seem at times to bear no relation to faith in the God in whom the church says to believe (Matt 25).

However, Vatican II does conceive of the church as communion, body of Christ (*Lumen gentium*, no. 7), people of God (*Lumen gentium*, chap. 2), and church of the poor. This was the spirit proclaimed by John XXIII in his radio message a month before the opening of the Second Vatican Council, which stated, "For underdeveloped countries the Church presents itself as it is and wants to be, as the Church of all, as the Church of the poor in particular."[29] This is the spirit of the Covenant of the Catacombs,[30] and in the same sense, is the ecclesiological approach of Pope Francis, who from the first moment of his pontificate stated, "How I would like a poor church and for the poor!"[31] This was the way in which the efforts of Monsignor Oscar Romero were focused, when he affirmed that "the essence of the Church is in its mission of service to the world, in its mission to save it in totality and to save it in history, here and now. The Church is in solidarity with the hopes and joys, with the anguish and sorrows of men."[32] Moreover, we know that these were not just words, but were manifested in concrete actions that cost him his life. Thus, if moral theology wants to be faithful to its role within an ecclesiology of communion, it cannot avoid these tasks.

A fourth pending task of moral theology, according to its role in the context of an ecclesiology of communion, is to give the conscience its rightful place according to the teaching of the church and particularly in *Gaudium et spes*:

> In the depths of his conscience, man detects a law which he does not impose upon himself, but which holds him to obedience. Always summoning him to love good and avoid evil, the voice of conscience when necessary speaks to his heart: do this, shun that. For man has in his heart a law written by God; to obey it is the very dignity of man; according to it he will be judged. Conscience is the most secret core and sanctuary of a man. There he is alone with God, Whose voice echoes in his depths. In a wonderful manner conscience reveals that law which is fulfilled by love of God and neighbor. In fidelity to conscience, Christians are joined with the rest of men in the search for truth, and for the genuine solution to the numerous problems which arise in the life of individuals from social relationships. Hence the more right conscience holds sway, the more persons and groups turn aside from blind choice and strive to be guided by the objective norms of morality. Conscience frequently errs from invincible

ignorance without losing its dignity. The same cannot be said for a man who cares but little for truth and goodness, or for a conscience which by degrees grows practically sightless as a result of habitual sin.[33]

Giving conscience its proper place would prevent wasting so much energy in useless discussions that seem not to be within the framework of a communion church, but rather are focused on defending other interests.

In the framework of a communion church, a fifth task that is related to the place of the laity and women in the church must be mentioned. In this case, discrimination based on status or gender is in conflict with human rights. Therefore, this is a matter that moral theology should be concerned about if it wants to be faithful to its role in an ecclesiology of communion. I want to clarify that I am not limiting this discussion to participation in ordained ministry.

A sixth pending task of moral theology today has to do with taking seriously the problems of an integral ecology. For brevity's sake, I will not further develop this point, but the encyclical *Laudato si'* does address the kinds of tasks that are pending in this branch of ethics.

Conclusion

Only a few of the pending tasks of moral theology today are mentioned above;[34] the work will be much deeper if moral theology really wants to situate itself on the horizon of an ecclesiology of communion.

In looking at moral theology, the question arises as to whether something similar to that which happened with the sacraments occurred, namely, that its reflection and praxis were developed outside of an ecclesiology of communion, and within a framework of a more legal, hierarchical, and institutional church, rather than a communal one.

Undoubtedly, the topics mentioned above are, on the one hand, important sources of moral discernment; on the other hand, these sources of moral discernment are pointing to the important challenges for moral theology today and its pending tasks. Similarly, for the church, these cannot be marginal matters if it is the case that the church is a communion in the image and likeness of our Trinitarian God. This church is a church where all, men and women, clergy and laity, have the same vocation in Christ, and therefore have the same dignity and are deserving of the same consideration and respect. It is a church that cannot be indifferent to the joys and hopes, the sadness and the anguish of the men and women of our time, especially the poor and those who suffer the most.

Notes

1. Cf. John Paul II, Speech at the Cathedral of Mexico, January 26, 1979.
2. *Lumen gentium*, chap. 2.

3. Ibid., nos. 7, 23, 26, 28, 30, 48, 50.

4. Ibid., no. 1.

5. Ibid., no. 7.

6. Alberto Parra, "Ecclesiology of Communion in Puebla," *Theologica Xaveriana* 29 (1979): 125.

7. *Lumen gentium*, no. 9.

8. Juan Antonio Estrada, *From the Mystery of the Church to the People of God* (Salamanca, Spain: Sigueme, 1988). 239.

9. Salvador Pié-Ninot, "Ecclesia in et ex ecclesiis (LG 23)," *Catalan Journal of Theology* 22 (1997): 75–76.

10. *Gaudium et spes*, no. 1.

11. Gonzalo Zarazaga, "Towards a Trinitarian Anthropology," in *Trinitarian Anthropology for Our Peoples* (Bogotá: CELAM, 2014), 55.

12. Kallistos Ware, "The Holy Trinity: Model of Being Person in Relationship," in *Relationality in the Physical Sciences and in Theology*, ed. John Polkinghorne (Estella/Navarra, Spain: Divine Word, 2013), 141.

13. Ibid., 161–64.

14. Ioannis Zizioulas, *The Ecclesial Being: Person, Communion, Church* (Salamanca, Spain: Sígueme, 2003), 90.

15. Ibid., 29–32.

16. Estrada, *From the Mystery of the Church*, 145.

17. Karl Rahner, "Doctrine of God," in *Writings of Theology* IV (Madrid: Taurus, 1962), 107.

18. Estrada, *From the Mystery of the Church*, 121–22.

19. Ibid., 145.

20. Ibid., 150–51.

21. With exegesis *Dei verbum*, no. 12.

22. *Optatam totius*, no. 16.

23. *Lumen gentium*, no. 40.

24. *Let the accent not just be around sexual matters.*

25. *Gaudium et spes*, no. 1.

26. According to the UN High Commission for Refugees report, up to December 31, 2016, 65.6 million people were forcibly displaced. See http://www.acnur.org/recursos/estadisticas/.

27. The Food and Agriculture Organization defines hunger as a synonym for chronic malnutrition: 1.3 billion poor people live in extreme poverty; more than 60 percent of the world's population suffers from malnutrition, a major consequence of extreme poverty. See http://www.fao.org/hunger/es/.

28. http://www.ilo.org/global/topics/forced-labour/lang--es/index.htm.

29. Tuesday, September 11, 1962. See https://w2.vatican.va/content/john-xxiii/es/messages/pont_messages/1962/documents/hf_j-xxiii_mes_19620911_ecumenical-council.html.

30. On November 16, 1965, when the Second Vatican Council was finishing, about forty bishops, encouraged by Dom Helder Camara, celebrated a Mass in the Catacombs of Santa Domitilla where they made the Covenant of the Catacombs for a poor church and of the poor. Xabier Pikaza and José Antunes da Silva, eds. *The Covenant of the Catacombs: The Mission of the Poor in the Church* (Estella/Navarra, Spain: Divine Word, 2015).

31. Pope Francis. Press Conference before the International Media, March 16, 2013. See https://es.zenit.org/articles/francisco-quiero-una-iglesia-pobre-y-para-los-pobres/.

32. Monsignor Oscar Romero, *The Political Dimension of Faith from the Option for the Poor: An Ecclesial Experience in El Salvador, Central America*. Speech on receiving the honorary doctorate by the University of Louvain, February 2, 1980, fifty days before his assassination. See http://servicioskoinonia.org/relat/135.htm.

33. *Gaudium et spes*, no. 16 (footnotes omitted).

34. See other tasks in James F. Keenan, "Emerging Topics on Theological Ethics," *Theologica Latinoamericana Digital Encyclopedia*, http://theologicalatinoamericana.com/?p=462.

"The Theology of the End of the World"

Rethinking Theological Ethics from the Existential Peripheries

Pablo A. Blanco

Introduction

There are many who miss emeritus Pope Benedict XVI's theological wisdom, but is Bergoglio less of a theologian than Ratzinger? Is his theology shallower? What kind of dialogue does his theology hold with reality?

For instance, when Francis refers to mercy, he talks about the confessional; when describing how grace should reach everybody, he talks about "customs"; and when he refers to the wounds of the world, he talks about the church as a "field hospital." These examples lead us to the analysis and identification of the original aspects of Francis's theological thinking that I call "the theology of the end of the world."

It is appropriate to clarify that the reference to a theology of the end of the world is not made in an eschatological sense like parousia, that is, the end time, but rather in a political–geographical–cultural–historical sense, associated with a way of thinking and acting originating in the world's peripheries, using Pope Francis's own words on the day he was elected: "You know that it was the duty of the Conclave to give Rome a Bishop. It seems that my brother Cardinals have gone to the ends of the earth to get one."[1]

What is more, this aspect of the theology of the end of the world implies a particular hermeneutics that is essentially pastoral: it is not about theology becoming praxis, but about the possibility of finding praxis in theological categories and keys. So, to say "theology of the end of the world" is not just to point to a geographical place (which could be well expressed by using the preposition *from*); it refers also to an original understanding, it remarks upon these theological novelties, and it names its own theological identity.

This new theological reading of reality challenges theological ethics to go beyond mere theories, toward a fundamental aspect of incarnation derived from the theology of the end of the world set out by Pope Francis. Indeed, his great contribution to theological understanding is the idea that any theology of change is an "incarnational" theology. We will return to this notion of "incarnational" theology in a later section.

Theology of the End of the World: A Third Way?

The Catholic and non-Catholic worlds are won over by Pope Francis's way of acting. From the beginning of his pontificate until today, countless gestures of this Argentine and Latin American pope can be identified.

What is a gesture? It is a verbal or nonverbal expression coming from an individual, whose interpretation and symbolisms transcend its seeming superficiality, aimed at questioning "another one," a singular or collective subject.

These questions are necessary. In some ecclesiastical environments, Pope Francis lacks the theological wisdom expressed by emeritus Pope Benedict XVI. The latter's outstanding presence, his careful language, and his German intellectual sharpness and coherence contrast with Pope Francis's unpredictable and—to some—gangling figure, his simple language, and his questioning of everyday-life situations. It has become evident that Francis is in his element with the simple homeless, but it would be a mistake to think that he would be out of his element with distinguished and select experts in the most refined kinds of knowledge.

It would be fitting to remember now that, in the New Testament, it is pointed out that there are two ways to do theology. On the one hand, we have Saint Paul's "speculative theology." And then we have, in another context, the "narrative theology" of the gospels. That is to say, there is the philosophical speculation, which is characteristic of the Hellenistic culture (and of Paul), and there is the historical account, which is characteristic of the biblical tradition.

Can we affirm that Ratzinger is in his element with the speculative theology, whereas Bergoglio is in his element when he comes down from the analytical heights, from the speculation of the "being," to the concrete and tangible "happening"?

As time went by, theology was systematized and organized in treatises (which are still studied in seminaries and taught in catechism courses), and Paul's speculative theology turned out to be more determinative than the narrative theology of the gospels.[2] And so—for example—people are taught more about the theology of redemption preached by Paul than about Jesus's testimonial and prophetic presence.

It is evident that the speculative way of thinking appeals to certain minds because of its depth and its analytic determination—but are gestures less thick and deep than the act of thinking? Is there any gesture more irrefutable, from the theological point of view, than incarnation itself?

If our analysis ended at this point, we could venture that maybe with Pope Francis we find a new "theology of the gestures." Nevertheless, we would be overlooking the "pastoral" aspect behind each of the pope's actions, where we can perceive a certain way of reading God's presence in the world and an indication of how the ministers and the faithful should act before that presence.

When Pope Francis decided to make his first pastoral visit to the island of Lampedusa (Italy), where leisure ships coexist with poor and desperate immigrants who have set sail to try to reach European soil, he provided not only a "gesture" but also a theological and pastoral perspective about the place of the poor and our responsibility as laypeople in the world.

That is why we can affirm that, between the speculative and narrative theologies, Francis is forging a "third way": a pastoral theological option. This pastoral theology has its origins in some Fathers of the Church that have made eminent contributions like John Chrysostom (347–407) and Pope Gregory the Great (540–604). However, its "systematic reflection" aspect is newer, in relation to other areas of theology.

Indeed, the Second Vatican Council's *pastoral* Constitution *Gaudium et spes* (1965) inaugurates the development of pastoral theology as a systematic reflection on the church's actions, as an open gate to evangelization (preaching, and teaching of the catechism) in everyday life (through sacraments, and all pastoral activities) to uncover truths from the sacred scriptures, from systematic and dogmatic theology, and from the people of God's lived reality.

This new theological praxis "coordinates theory and practice in the field of reality, thus bringing together: action and contemplation, teaching and studying, pastoral care and theology."[3] This pastoral theological line coming from the Council will be picked up especially by the Latin American magisterium.

Theology of the End of the World: Sources, Roots, and Inspirations

The Latin American-inspired pastoral theology option developed at the heart of popular movements, the ecclesiastical communities, and pastoral theological debates about the reception of the universal magisterium—Vatican II—in Latin America by the end of the 1960s.[4]

According to Scannone,[5] "for some scholars, the baptism certificate of the real Latin American theology was the Second Vatican Council," as a theological perspective that called forth the voice and experience of local churches and the value of peoples' cultures, incorporating them into the church's daily tasks.

At this point, an Argentine theological line also comes up: the "theology of the people" inspired by Argentine theologian Father Lucio Gera's thoughts on the relationship the people of God has with the peoples (especially the Latin American and Argentine peoples), their culture, and their religion.

According to Scannone, that theological line "favored the category of People of God over other post-Council categories like 'community' or 'communion', not only because of its biblical roots and council reaffirmation, but also because it highlights the historical, personal, communal, and social moments of the Church,[6] . . . as places where the signs show, to which the People of God must answer pastorally in its evangelizing mission."[7]

The importance of mentioning this Latin American view lies in its historical–cultural perspective. The people of God is the subject of a common history (memory, conscience, and historic project) and culture, understood as an ethos (ethical core of shared values) that shapes a common lifestyle (a particular relationship with the world, other men, and the transcendent mystery) that is expressed in institutions and frameworks of life and coexistence.[8]

It is necessary also for pastors and theologians (Puebla's document talks about a "pastoral vision of reality") to read history and people's sociohistorical situation from a prophetic point of view, and to perceive the people of God and their interrelationships from an understanding made in faith.

In view of the above, we can sense that in Pope Francis's theological thinking, there are influences and categories from the "theology of the people," a fundamental aspect of incarnation, and a particular pastoral hermeneutics of an essentially Latin American character or inspiration.

On one hand, the hermeneutic part refers to a dynamic reading of the "signs of the times," in which the social happenings are symbols or texts that must be interpreted instead of being objectively described and explained.

On the other hand, we can sense that Latin American inspiration in the great reception of Pope Francis's pastoral theology, which has been accepted by a large portion of the church, especially in Latin America: "Francis lives our Latin American pastoral style in the closeness to the people, the warmth in manners, the simple way of preaching. He expresses the grammar of simplicity in his life and his ministry . . . by means of an affectionate, symbolic, gestural, and festive culture."[9]

Francis's theological thinking may not be, then, the direct implementation of the "theology of the people," but a new, broader, Latin American theological perspective that understands the "theology of the people" by dialoguing with it. I call this new perspective a theology of the end of the world; "end of the world" both as a political–geographical–cultural–historical reference and for its constituent "peripheral" theological elements in relation to dominant theological paradigms. It is a particular theology that is a meeting point for kerygmatic, pastoral, cultural, and sociostructural aspects.

Lastly, it is necessary to underline in the Latin American perspective the nonindividual, nonindividualist character of both its faith in Christ and its communal and social openness. The Second Vatican Council establishes this relation: "Thus it is evident to everyone, that all the faithful of Christ of whatever rank or status, are called to the fullness of the Christian life and to the perfection of charity; by this holiness as such a more human manner of living is promoted in this earthly society."[10]

From this point of view, it is not about theology becoming praxis, but about the possibility of reading praxis in categories and theological keys.

As stated earlier, Pope Francis's great contribution to theological understanding is that any theology of change is an "incarnate" theology. Western society in particular is lacking in incarnate theology. As Saint John Paul II points out, "The theological dimension is needed both for interpreting and solving present-day problems in human society."[11]

We will now evaluate what I consider to be the Latin American–inspired interpretative keys that make up the theology of the end of the world and that can be used as a guide to rethink theological ethics.

Theology of the End of the World: Four Theological Places

Since the middle of the twentieth century, among the Latin American bishops, there has been a progressive realization about the common problems and wishes of the whole believing people of Latin America that demands common pastoral considerations and answers.

This continuing process has as unquestionable reference the various meetings (conferences) of the Latin American Episcopate, whose documents, taking the Second Vatican Council as source, have been able to give their hallmark to the categories, worries, and reflections derived from the universal magisterium. A part of that hallmark has been the different theological perspectives that have arisen in Latin America.

In Pope Francis's pastoral theological perspective, we can identify four theological "places" resulting from interpreting the Latin American magisterium.

History as a Theological Place

The event of incarnation in itself, theoretical foundation of pastoral theology and hermeneutic criterion of the Christian praxis, is not a limited and isolated event. Its singularity is the same singularity as God's, acting in history for human salvation. This Christological setting reminds the church that it is church-in-the-world. It is incarnation as intrinsic law of the Christian faith.

History, therefore, becomes a theological place and an object of reflection, where Christ and history become "Word."[12] The term *history* refers to the ethical experience, a structuring characteristic of the human person as a whole.

As said in Medellín (1968),[13] people and their communities are inserted in economic–human–historical systems and institutions that are crystallized in "unfair structures that characterize the Latin American situation."[14] This assertion is made again by Francis: it is the "evil crystallized in unjust social structures, which cannot be the basis of hope for a better future."[15]

These international domination structures "decisively determine the underdevelopment of the peripheral peoples."[16] The "structures of economic, political, and cultural dependence"[17] are "oppressive structures, derived from the material abuse and the power abuse, from exploiting workers or from the injustice of the transactions."[18]

Nevertheless, "Christ's resurrection everywhere calls forth seeds of that new world; even if they are cut back, they grow again, for the resurrection is already secretly woven into the fabric of this history, for Jesus did not rise in vain."[19]

The People as a Theological Place

Latin America, apart from being a geographical reality, is a community of peoples with its own history, specific values, and similar problems.[20]

According to Scannone,[21] San Miguel's Document has been crucial to the implementation of Medellín's lessons (1968) in Argentina by our Episcopate. The document, which was greatly influenced by the COEPAL (Episcopal Pastoral Commission), states that

> The Church is to distinguish its liberating or saving action to the people's view from its interests, because, as the people is subject and agent of the human history, which is closely related to the history of Salvation, . . . the signs of the times are present and distinguishable in the events typical of said people or in the events affecting said people. . . .Therefore, the actions of the Church should be directed not only towards the people but also, and mainly, from the people.[22]

As theologian Lucio Gera says, the people of God "is inserted in history and walks with the peoples in history."[23] The "theology of the people" understands the "world" not in an abstract way and just objectively, but in a concrete way and subjectively, just like the history and the reality of the peoples.

Without disregarding scientific intervention, wisdom prevails both in the people and, theologically, in the people of God as it knows the people and it recognizes the signs of the times in it, in its way, by the light of faith and the anointing of Jesus, God's saint. A type of knowledge "by inherence" (human and theological) emerges.

An example of convergence with the "theology of the people" is given in *Evangelii gaudium* when, quoting Puebla's[24] and Aparecida's[25] documents, it comes to the conclusion that "the people continuously evangelizes itself," and "the Gospel has been inculturated in a people."[26]

When Pope Francis talks about the people of God, he refers to its "multifaceted harmony,"[27] which is due to the diversity of cultures that enrich it. When he talks about the people, he uses the image of the polyhedron to emphasize the plural unity of the irreducible difference within.

The Poor as a Theological Place

The poor are a place of revelation and conversion for theology and for the church, but they are also a historical and universal reality.[28]

In Medellín (1968), bishops make a commitment that requires solidarity with each poor person.[29] This solidarity means "to take their problems and struggles as our own, speak up for them." Speaking up for them is neither quieting the voice of the poor nor interpreting it; it refers to "denunciating injustice and oppression, in the Christian fight against the unbearable condition with which the Poor person frequently puts up, the will to enter into dialogue with those responsible for this situation."[30]

Medellín (1968) tried to reply by turning to the gospel, to the "deaf clamor . . . of millions of men, asking their pastors for a liberation that is not given by anyone."[31] In Puebla (1979), it was pointed out that in order to live and announce the demand of Christian poverty, the church should review its structures and the life of its members, especially the pastoral agents, with a view to an effective conversion.[32]

And in Pope Francis's words, "For the Church, the option for the poor is primarily a theological category rather than a cultural, sociological, political, or philosophical one. . . . This is why I want a Church which is poor and for the poor."[33] Aparecida's document (2007)—in whose final writing Bergoglio participated—reveals the face of the poor, focusing not only on their misery, neglect, exploitation, hunger, scarcity, and humiliation but also on their inner poverty, based on a lack of dignity hindering the development of their true vocation: "Anything related to Christ is related to the poor and everything related to the poor claims Jesus Christ."[34] The preferential option for the poor is not just another decision in Christian life; it is what characterizes it.[35]

Culture as a Theological Place

"The word 'culture' indicates the particular way in which, in a people, men develop their relationship with nature, among themselves, and with God."[36] Culture is a way of making the question about the meaning of personal existence. In this respect, it is the open search for truth, which is renewed in each generation, and it is a reflection of how people and society think of themselves and their destiny.[37] Language, history, and the attitudes of the people before the fundamental events of existence, like being born, loving, working, dying, like the attitude they adopt before the greatest mystery, the mystery of God, express and reflect that culture.[38]

"People," from the perspective of culture, bring together the ideas of communion and participation, on the one hand, and the ideas of communal and diversified organization, on the other hand.[39] As a dimension of plural unity (and not of division and conflict, like the class dimension), this makes it possible to conceive of the ecclesiastical communion, which respects differences.

One of the interpretational signs for that integration—understood as a dialogue among cultures and as God's showing Godself in culture—is the concept of "popular religiosity." While the church recognizes its limits, it also points out that "we can see in the expression of popular religiosity, an enormous reserve of authentically Christian virtues, especially related to charity . . . by which the people . . . expresses its faith in a simple, emotional, collective way."[40]

Popular religiosity is valuable as the externalization of a confident clamor for justice, liberation, and redress, and also as a concrete exercising of fraternity and reciprocity among one another.[41]

Francis says that "genuine forms of popular religiosity are incarnate, since they are born of the incarnation of Christian faith in popular culture. For this reason they entail a personal relationship . . . with God, with Christ, with Mary . . . [they] are fleshy, they have a face. They are capable of fostering relationships and not just enabling escapism."[42]

The evangelizing role of the church reaches culture, because it is the setting where all human activity takes place, aiding it on its journey in search of truth and also in the selfless search for peace.[43]

The "novelty" of the exclusion is also because of a cultural background: an individualist culture that imposes itself. Such a culture is based on the consumerism that leads to indifference to others and to a lack of responsibility to them. It considers people an object of consumption that is discarded when its use does not provide the "expected benefits."[44]

The action emerging from the evangelizing conscience, restoring the weave of social relationships with the testimony that is denunciation and announcement, arrives in Aparecida (2007) with the proposal of creative evangelization that implies determinedly participating in building new ways to manage the economy and public affairs, along with the responsibility for extending that participation not only to the educational sphere but also to the construction of awareness and presence in the new Areopagus of culture.

It is therefore necessary to make progress on the evangelization of culture.[45]

Theology of the End of the World: Two Interpretive Dimensions

Pope Francis's pastoral theological option is based on two interpretative "dimensions" that cross and identify the Latin American magisterium: the Marian dimension and the dimension of the missionary discipleship.

The Marian Dimension

The gospel becomes incarnated in a reality and originalities typical of our characteristically Latin American history and culture, which talk to the people (male and female) inhabiting the continent. With our Mother's apparition in Guadalupe with her mestizo face, Mary inculturates herself and becomes our Mother and one with all her children.[46] Inculturation is not a simple assessment of a culture in its current state. It is not an anthropological concept but a theological one. The simplest definition of inculturation is the "dialogue between the Christian faith and cultures."

Mary personifies God's preferential option for the poor, God's triumph where there is weakness and God's support of the suffering, especially those suffering the injustice of those who hold power. The Christian people, with their characteristic sense of faith, perceive that Mary is Mother of the people, advocate of the poor, a people's woman who knew, like the people themselves, suffering and oppression. In

Mary's tenderness, the people have always looked for the great sign of her maternal and merciful face, and of the closeness between the Father and Christ.

The Marian dimension presupposes a bond of proximity and commitment between the presence of what is divine and human existential experience before life and history. Mary's maternal figure sums up the discipular answer of the Latin American church.

As indicated by the document of Puebla, "without Mary the Gospel becomes disincarnated, is disfigured and transformed into ideology, into spiritual rationalism."[47]

Coming back from Sweden, Pope Francis affirmed that "in Catholic ecclesiology there are two dimensions to think about: the 'petrine' dimension, which is from the Apostles—Peter and the apostolic college, which is the pastoral activity of bishops—as well as the 'marian' dimension, which is the feminine dimension of the Church. The Church does not exist without this feminine dimension, because she herself is feminine. There is no Church without this female dimension, because she is female."[48]

There is a "Marian" style in the evangelization work of the Latin American church: "Whenever we look to Mary, we come to believe once again in the revolutionary nature of love and tenderness. In her we see that humility and tenderness are not virtues of the weak but of the strong who need not to treat others poorly in order to feel important themselves."[49]

The Dimension of the Missionary Discipleship

The preferential option for the poor signifies the Latin American church's option as expressed by Medellín (1968). It is a choice derived from following the poor and suffering Christ, who expressed himself as denunciation, claim for justice, conscience of the coresponsibility before serious situations, and finally as the duty to participate in the transformation of the structures of sin and in the construction of the Kingdom of God.

That is why being disciple and being missionary go hand in hand. Being disciple is being missionary: "any disciple is missionary, as Jesus makes him part of his mission, and at the same time he ties him to Him as friend and brother. Then, the same way He is witness of the Father's mystery, the disciples are witnesses of the Lord's death and resurrection until He comes back. Completing this task is not optional, but an integral part of the Christian identity, because it is the testimonial extension of the vocation itself."[50]

The mission does not require a particular kind of enlightenment, nor is it a call for a few chosen ones, because those who know and love their Lord experience the need to share with others the joy of being sent, of going to the world to announce Jesus Christ, to make love and service a reality in those who need it the most: to sum up, to build the Kingdom of God. In turn, "the mission and the discipleship are inseparable, so it must not be understood as a stage subsequent to the instruction, though it is carried out in different ways depending on the disciple's own vocation and on the moment of human and Christian maturing on which the person is."[51]

On the other hand, that vocation is not solitary; it is essentially communitarian. A missionary disciple participates in communion with our Christian brethren with whom we share faith, but at the same time the disciple is inserted in a community where he or she specifically belongs and where the missionary disciple is called to be a way of changing reality.

Faith challenges us to leave our confinement—where we feel comfortable —in order for us to be more fully human. "There is no discipleship without communion. . . . Faith sets us free from the isolation of the self, because it takes us to the communion. This means that it is a constituent dimension of the Christian event to belong to a specific community, where we can live a permanent discipleship and communion experience."[52]

That new approach is taken once again by Francis in *Evangelii gaudium*, by stating that "we no longer say that we are 'disciples' and 'missionaries' but rather that we are always 'missionary disciples.'"[53]

Rethinking Theological Ethics from the Theology of the End of the World

In light of the above, it is clear that theological ethics should not study reality by intending only to extend an ethical view through it but by trying to find out how much God is present in that reality—even if just seminally. The challenge of theological ethics is getting to those theological places and dimensions presented by the theology of the end of the world, and to the many actions aimed at transforming reality (often from peripheral or nonhegemonic situations) and spotting the "seeds of the Word" (e.g., present evangelical values) there showing God's presence.

The concept of the "seeds of the Word" is rooted in patristic theology, particularly in writings from the second century (in Saint Justin, for example), but it only reappears in Christian and Catholic theology after eighteen centuries of silence. The Medellín Conference, in its document on popular pastoral care, uses it to guide the pastoral actions within the popular religiosity problem: "it is precisely part of the Church's evangelizing work to discover in religiosity the 'secret presence of God,' the 'sparkle of the truth illuminating us all,' the Word's light, present even before Incarnation or apostolic preaching."[54]

The Puebla Conference, in its chapter on Evangelization of Culture, states, "Cultures are not a deserted field, lacking authentic values. And the evangelization of the Church is not a process of destruction, but a process of consolidation and strengthening of those values; a contribution to the growth of the 'seeds of the Word' present in the cultures."[55]

The Aparecida Conference[56] affirms that "as disciples of Jesus Christ, incarnate in the life of all peoples we discover and recognize from the faith the 'seeds of the Word' present in the traditions and cultures of the peoples."

These quotations are not intended to be exhaustive, but rather to illustrate how the concept of the "seeds of the Word" has had a great impact on the postcouncil Catholic theology that nourishes Pope Francis's theological–pastoral option, which can in turn be helpful in rethinking theological ethics.

Final Reflection

Highlighting the Latin American roots of Pope Francis's pastoral theological option does not mean we should forget the ecclesiological perspective and the universal character that his magisterium inspires and conveys, and that make this option a gift for the church and the world.

Furthermore, the Holy Spirit that renews all things[57] also raises that particular perspective to a new "end of the world"—this time as Epiphany—in all peoples' vocation for peace and unity under the sign of communion and mercy, of which Francis has become witness, messenger, and builder: "the communion with Christ impels us to go out to the men and women of our day, to offer them the concrete sign of mercy."[58]

Notes

1. H. H. Francis, *Apostolic Blessing "Urbi Et Orbi"* (Vatican City, March 13, 2013).

2. Cf. Heinrich Schlier, *La carta a los Gálatas* (Salamanca, Spain: Sígueme, 1975), 124–37; Günther Bornkamm. *Pablo de tarso* (Salamanca, Spain: Sígueme, 1979), 16–17; Comments of Ernst Haenchen, *Die Apostelgeschichte* (Gottingen, Germany: Vandenhoeck & Ruprecht, 1965): "at the same time Paul's theological value is emphasized, his historical value is relativized." Charles Kingsley Barrett, *Paul: An Introduction to His Thought* (London: Chapman, 1994), 7, recognizes St. Lucas as a popular historian but inferior to Paul as a theologian. The study of the historiography of the gospels has not yet been satisfactorily carried out, as it is recognized by Gerhard Schneider, *Die Apostelgeschichte, I Teil*; versión italiana: *Gli atti degli apostoli*, Parte prima (Brescia, Italy: Paideia Editrice, 1985), 170.

3. Emilce Cuda, "Francisco: Entre la teología de la liberación y la teología del Pueblo," *Catholic Theological Ethics in the World* 2 (2013), http://www.catholicethics.com/forum-submissions/francisco-entre-la-teologa-de-la-liberacin-y-la-teologa-del-pueblo.

4. Rafael Luciani, "La opción teológico-pastoral del Papa Francisco," *Revista Perspectivas Teológica* 48, no. 1 (2016): 81–115.

5. Juan Carlos Scannone SJ, "Perspectivas eclesiológicas de la 'teología del pueblo' en la Argentina," in *Ecclesia tertii millenni advenientis,* ed. F. Chica, S. Panizzolo, and H. Wagner (Casale Monferrato, Italy: Piemme, 1997), 686–704.

6. That is, moments at the core of societies that express their cultural and social identity of dynamism and search from a Christian horizon.

7. Scannone, "Perspectivas eclesiológicas," 687.

8. Ibid.

9. Carlos María Galli, "La teología pastoral de Evangelii gaudium en el proyecto misionero de Francisco," *Revista Teología* 114 (August 2014): 30.

10. *Lumen gentium*, no. 40.

11. *Centesimus annus*, no. 55.

12. Cf. *Evangelii gaudium*, no. 247.

13. Latin American Bishops' Council, *Final Document of the Second General Confer-ence of the Episcopate* (Medellín: CELAM, 1968).

14. Ibid., 1, 2.

15. *Evangelii gaudium*, no. 59.

16. Latin American Bishops' Council, *Final Document of the Second General Confer-ence*, 10, 3.15.

17. Ibid., 10, 1.2.

18. Ibid., 6.

19. *Evangelii gaudium*, no. 278.

20. Latin American Bishops' Council, *Final Document of the Second General Confer-ence*, 6, 16.

21. Scannone, "Perspectivas eclesiológicas."

22. Argentine Episcopal Conference, "Declaración del Episcopado Argentino," in *Documento de San Miguel* (Buenos Aires: Paulinas, 1972).

23. Scannone, "Perspectivas eclesiológicas," 693.

24. Latin American Bishops' Council, *Final Document of the Third General Conference of the Episcopate* (Puebla, Mexico: CELAM, 1979), 450.

25. Latin American Bishops' Council, *The Final Document of the Fifth General Confer-ence of the Episcopate* (Aparecida, Brazil: CELAM, 2007), 264.

26. *Evangelii gaudium*, no. 122.

27. Ibid., nos. 116–17.

28. The poor refer not to an individual and isolated subject, immersed in the condi-tions and structures that delimit them and define them as such, but to a collective subject "the poor" who share the same situation of oppression, marginalization, or exclusion, under social and structural conditions that delimit and define them. The plural also expresses the multiple poverty situations that are not tied only to materialistic poverty, Latin American Bishops' Council, *The Final Document of the Fifth General Conference*, 402.

29. Cf. Latin American Bishops' Council, *Final Document of the Second General Conference*, 3, 14.

30. Ibid., 3, 10.

31. Ibid., 14, 1.2.

32. Latin American Bishops' Council, *Final Document of the Third General Conference*, 1157.

33. *Evangelii gaudium*, no. 198.

34. Latin American Bishops' Council, *The Final Document of the Fifth General Confer-ence*, 393.

35. Cf. ibid., 394.

36. *Gaudium et spes*, no. 53b.

37. Cf. Latin American Bishops' Council, *Final Document of the Fourth General Conference of the Episcopate* (Santo Domingo, Dominican Republic: CELAM, 1992), 222.

38. Cf. ibid., 229.

39. Scannone, "Perspectivas eclesiológicas," 695.

40. Latin American Bishops' Council, *Final Document of the Second General Confer-ence*, 6, 2-3.

41. Cf. Latin American Bishops' Council, *Final Document of the Third General Conference*, 452.

42. *Evangelii gaudium*, no. 90.

43. Cf. Latin American Bishops' Council, *Final Document of the Fourth General Conference*, 203.

44. Cf. Latin American Bishops' Council, *Final Document of the Fifth General Conference*, 46.

45. Cf. Latin American Bishops' Council, *Final Document of the Third General Conference*, 409–19.

46. Cf. ibid., 446.

47. Ibid., 301.

48. H. H. Francis, *Apostolic Journey to Sweden: In-Flight Press Conference* (Sweden to Rome, November 1, 2016).

49. *Evangelii gaudium*, no. 288.

50. Latin American Bishops' Council, *Final Document of the Fifth General Conference*, 144.

51. Ibid., 278.

52. Ibid., 156.

53. *Evangelii gaudium*, no. 120.

54. Latin American Bishops' Council, *Final Document of the Second General Conference,* 6.5.

55. Latin American Bishops' Council, *Final Document of the Third General Conference*, 401.

56. Latin American Bishops' Council, *Final Document of the Fifth General Conference*, 529.

57. Cf. Apocalypse 21.5.

58. H. H. Francis, "Mercy as the Instrument of Communion," *Catechesis of the Pope* (Rome, August 17, 2016).

"All Who Saw It Began to Grumble"

Reflections on Accompaniment and
Conscience *Trans*formation

Daniel J. Fleming

He entered Jericho and was passing through it. A man was there named Zacchaeus; he was a chief tax collector and was rich. He was trying to see who Jesus was, but on account of the crowd he could not, because he was short in stature. So he ran ahead and climbed a sycamore tree to see him, because he was going to pass that way. When Jesus came to the place, he looked up and said to him, "Zacchaeus, hurry and come down; for I must stay at your house today." So he hurried down and was happy to welcome him. All who saw it began to grumble and said, "He has gone to be the guest of one who is a sinner." Zacchaeus stood there and said to the Lord, "Look, half of my possessions, Lord, I will give to the poor; and if I have defrauded anyone of anything, I will pay back four times as much." Then Jesus said to him, "Today salvation has come to this house, because he too is a son of Abraham. For the Son of Man came to seek out and to save the lost."

—Luke 19:1–10

In this essay, I analyze what I refer to as conscience *trans*formation, which I posit as a specifying term within the category of conscience formation. Conscience transformation refers to those instances wherein one undergoes some form of moral *metanoia*, which is distinct from the normal developmental sense of conscience formation. Such a category is relevant for those who have a formed conscience, though not in a way that corresponds with the Good. The purpose of this essay is to propose principles for how the church may best effect conscience transformation in local contexts. I argue that such can be found in Pope Francis's discussion of *accompaniment*. I begin with a brief comment on the category of conscience transformation, distinguishing it from the broader category of conscience formation, and then engage in an exegesis of the story of Jesus and Zacchaeus, found in Luke's Gospel, which I argue provides a paradigm for conscience transformation. Next, I read Pope Francis's exhortations

Evangelii gaudium and *Amoris laetitia* and draw out their focus on accompaniment, identifying key features of this, and arguing that they set conditions for conscience transformation. I link these to the story of Jesus and Zacchaeus. I then discuss recent findings from Darcia Narvaez, a leading researcher in the field of moral psychology, which provide scientific support for the model of conscience transformation that is found in this story. Finally, I summarize key features of accompaniment and discuss their implications for moral theology in local contexts.

On Conscience *Trans*formation

I have chosen to utilize the terminology of conscience *trans*formation within this essay because it points to a subset of the phenomenon of conscience *formation* (or moral development, in current scientific literature, which will be dealt with below).[1] Implicit in discussions of conscience formation is a paradigm that sees persons as on a developmental journey that begins in infancy and culminates in adulthood. On this view, conscience formation is that process which develops one's conscience in a manner that gradually moves it toward maturity, cultivating greater degrees of the kind of freedom that allows a person to "act according to a knowing and free choice that is personally motivated and prompted from within, not under blind internal impulse nor by mere external pressure."[2] However, the term conscience *formation* does not adequately capture what intervention might be necessary to effect a transformation in a conscience that is already formed, but in a manner that does not correspond to the Good. This may have happened through exposure to misinformation about the Good, poor examples, the influence of cultural norms and ideologies, socialization within a situation of structural sin, or it could refer to a conscience that has grown "practically sightless as a result of habitual sin."[3] That such a conscience can change to align with the Good reveals what is meant by conscience transformation, a term that I would suggest is closely aligned with the phenomenon captured by the Greek *metanoia*, meaning to have a change of heart. This is a pattern that we see frequently in the gospels when Jesus encounters sinners, and it is also a pattern that has been attracting interest in the field of moral education, to which we will return below.

Jesus and Zacchaeus

A paradigmatic example of conscience transformation occurs in chapter 19 of Luke's Gospel in the story of Jesus and Zacchaeus.[4] Several features of this text are relevant in discerning its meaning for the discussion at hand. Broad features of the story are familiar: Zacchaeus, a *chief* tax collector, would have been a member of the community who was at best tolerated and at worst despised for the genesis of his wealth: tax collection for the Roman empire.[5] As Green notes, in this story, "Luke dismisses the usual, stereotypical categories by which one's status before God is predetermined, including even those surprising ones that might have been suggested in Luke's narration."[6] What emerges instead is an episode in which all of the clichés about who is "out" and who is "in" are undermined. The audience within the story is made to experience this surprise. It is significant that the formula "*all* who saw it began to grumble and said, 'He has gone to be the guest of one who is a sinner'" is used. This indicates a more general suspicion of Zacchaeus among the community, including the disciples, rather than only the Scribes and Pharisees who are specified where Luke uses similar formulas elsewhere (e.g., 5:30, 7:34, 7;39, 15:2).[7] Zacchaeus was no more popular than an investment banker would be following the global financial crisis.

The positioning of the story and its links to other elements in the Gospel are also relevant.[8] It follows directly from the story of Jesus healing a blind man as he entered Jericho (18:35–34) and, prior to that, the story of the rich aristocrat who asks Jesus, "What must I do to inherit eternal life?" (18:18–23). Regarding the former, there is a relevant link with the Zacchaeus story inasmuch as, like the blind man, Zacchaeus could not "see" Jesus at first (19:3; cf. 18:36–37).[9] The blind man was literally healed and able to see, this being linked to his salvation (18:42), and subsequent following of Jesus (18:42). Similarly, Zacchaeus is able to see, both literally by climbing the tree (19:4) and more broadly through recognizing who Jesus is and by committing to the demands that discipleship will place on him (19:8), with the formula of salvation repeated again by Jesus in 19:9.[10] Furthermore, the Greek word used to identify Zacchaeus as a chief tax collector in 19:2 (ἀρχιτελώνης) creates a parallel between Zacchaeus and the rich man in 18:18, who is referred to as a "ruler" (ἄρχων).[11] In this case the parallel becomes a contrast in the stories: unlike the rich man, Zacchaeus is able to commit to the rigorous demands of Jesus (cf. 18:23, 19:8) and thus exemplifies his transformation. Of importance here, too, is that the precise nature of Zacchaeus's response to Jesus, in claiming that he will pay back fourfold to anyone who he may have cheated (19:8), demonstrates a technical knowledge of the law, though one that we assume, by his standing in the community and his job, has not been enacted by Zacchaeus previously.[12]

That the story also mentions the Son of Man who "came to seek out and to save the lost (ἀπολωλός)" in 19:10 links it to the ἀπολωλός image in the story of the lost sheep, the lost coin, and the prodigal son from chapter 15 of the Gospel.[13] This connection allows for an interpretation of the story as one of salvation that aligns with the motif of the lost being found.[14] This, argues Green, also links the story to (for example) Ezekiel 34, in which God and David "seek out the lost of Israel, those mistreated at the hands of Israel's leaders, and shepherd them."[15] Green goes on to say that "in seeking hospitality with one spurned as a socio-religious outcast, then, Jesus is simply fulfilling the divine will."[16] These points are further illustrated through a thematic analysis of the Zacchaeus story alongside other elements in the Gospel, which include references to table fellowship (5:27–32 and 15:1–32). In view of such analysis, Hamm argues that the story is best understood as a "climactic example" of *metanoia* within the Gospel, and observes the following pattern of this phenomenon through each of the examples: first table fellowship with the lost (including Jesus's defense of such fellowship when opposed), transformation, image of salvation, and then rejoicing.[17]

It is the "table fellowship" element of the Zacchaeus story that I wish to focus on here, for it appears as a precondition for the kind of transformation that Zacchaeus experiences in the story. That Jesus engages in such fellowship with sinners is the source of concern for those around him—the proximity of Jesus to sinners is construed as if he somehow approves of their sin: in our time, we might wonder if Jesus would be accused of material cooperation with Zacchaeus—"how was the money which paid for this meal obtained?!" However, Jesus consistently defends himself against these critiques, and utilizes the "lost and found" motif to do so. The overall implication is that when one is lost, it is fellowship that becomes the condition of possibility for being found. Or, to switch to the language that I will use for the remainder of this essay, when one's conscience is formed but in a direction other than that of the Good, it is accompaniment that is the condition of possibility for transformation. I will argue in the next section that in *Evangelii gaudium* and *Amoris laetitia* Pope Francis follows a similar methodology.

Accompaniment in
Evangelii Gaudium and *Amoris Laetitia*

In both *Evangelii gaudium* (*EG*) and *Amoris laetitia* (*AL*), Francis spends a significant amount of time developing the theme of the "art of accompaniment," which, he suggests, "teaches us to remove our sandals before the sacred ground of the other (cf. *Ex* 3:5)" and has the purpose of "making present the fragrance of Christ's closeness and his personal gaze."[18] The gaze of Christ is further explicated in the *Relatio* from the 2014 Synod, later cited in *AL*, which notes that Christ "looked upon the women and men whom he met with love and tenderness, accompanying their steps in truth, patience, and mercy as he proclaimed the demands of the Kingdom of God."[19] Such accompaniment corresponds with the characteristics of Jesus's table fellowship inasmuch as it is "steady and reassuring, reflecting our closeness and our compassionate gaze which also heals, liberates, and encourages growth in the Christian life."[20]

EG sets a direction for Francis's understanding of accompaniment, which is then expanded in *AL*. Accompaniment, in *EG*, is an essential aspect of making the joy of the gospel present to the world. It moves those within the church to the fringes, beyond being bystanders to being actively involved with those to whom they minister.[21] As such, it involves sharing in another person's journey, which, to be genuine, has to acknowledge and enter into solidarity with the complexity of the human condition and its developmental characteristics.[22] Held together, these features begin to have relevance for the moral pedagogy of the church:

> One who accompanies others has to realize that each person's situation before God and their life in grace are mysteries which no one can fully know from without. The Gospel tells us to correct others and to help them

to grow on the basis of a recognition of the objective evil of their actions (cf. Mt 18:15), but without making judgments about their responsibility and culpability (cf. Mt 7:1; Lk 6:37). Someone good at such accompaniment does not give in to frustrations or fears. He or she invites others to let themselves be healed, to take up their mat, embrace the cross, leave all behind and go forth ever anew to proclaim the Gospel. Our personal experience of being accompanied and assisted, and of openness to those who accompany us, will teach us to be patient and compassionate with others, and to find the right way to gain their trust, their openness and their readiness to grow.[23]

Such an approach further extends Francis's reminder about church teaching regarding subjective moral culpability earlier in the document, holding this together with a developmental understanding of the person (i.e., the possibility and hope that people develop and change over time) and, *a fortiori*, a theology of moral growth that emphasizes that "a small step, in the midst of great human limitations, can be more pleasing to God than a life which appears outwardly in order but moves through the day without confronting great difficulties."[24]

The groundwork established in *EG* for understanding accompaniment is developed and applied substantially in *AL*. While the focus of *AL* is particular inasmuch as it is concerned with the family, its moral pedagogy can be distilled and applied more generally.[25] This is especially the case when it comes to accompanying those who are living in situations that do not correspond with church teaching, and thus (potentially) find themselves at the fringes of the community, or, at a minimum, the target of the kind of "grumbling" that Zacchaeus received in his time.

In relation to this, first, in general terms, *AL* shares with *EG* an understanding of accompaniment that recognizes the complexity of the human person, subjective considerations when it comes to sin, and the possibility of moral development.[26] It frames this within the hope articulated in the *Relatio synodi* that "God's indulgent love always accompanies our human journey; through grace, it heals and transforms hardened hearts, leading them back to the beginning through the way of the cross."[27] More specifically, for those whose lives do not correspond with the church's moral teaching, Francis pushes for a response of accompaniment, which does not assume separation from the community too quickly (as did the crowd in the Zacchaeus story). Instead, it looks toward the model of accompaniment outlined above, noting that this does not represent a weakening of faith or lack of resolution for moral principles, but rather provides an authentic expression of charity and opens up the possibility of an encounter with Christ.[28]

These principles are distilled in their relevance for moral theology at the end of *AL*'s chapter 8, and are worth quoting in full:

The teaching of moral theology should not fail to incorporate these considerations, for although it is quite true that concern must be shown for the integrity of the Church's moral teaching, special care should always be shown to emphasize and encourage the highest and most central values of the Gospel, particularly the primacy of charity as a response to the completely gratuitous offer of God's love.[29]

Francis then goes on to note:

> At times we find it hard to make room for God's unconditional love in our pastoral activity. We put so many conditions on mercy that we empty it of its concrete meaning and real significance. That is the worst way of watering down the Gospel. It is true, for example, that mercy does not exclude justice and truth, but first and foremost we have to say that mercy is the fullness of justice and the most radiant manifestation of God's truth. For this reason, we should always consider "inadequate any theological conception which in the end puts in doubt the omnipotence of God and, especially, his mercy."[30]

And he draws these points together by suggesting:

> This offers us a framework and a setting which help us avoid a cold bureaucratic morality in dealing with more sensitive issues. Instead, it sets us in the context of a pastoral discernment filled with merciful love, which is ever ready to understand, forgive, accompany, hope, and above all integrate. That is the mindset which should prevail in the Church and lead us to "open our hearts to those living on the outermost fringes of society."[31]

Francis is acutely aware of how this approach might be critiqued and spends a substantial amount of the exhortation providing a defense of its implications. This defense is not the central concern of this essay; however, it is worth noting briefly its key features. First, it holds that moral development is a gradual process and that, correlatively, in the development of one's conscience one's capacity to conform with the objective good may be lesser or greater depending on one's own situation and stage of development.[32] The necessary consequence of this observation is that the function of a conscience that is *on a journey of moral development* includes both recognizing what is objectively good and also recognizing

> with sincerity and honesty what for now is the most generous response which can be given to God, and come to see with a certain moral security that it is what God himself is asking amid the concrete complexity of one's limits, while yet not fully the objective ideal.[33]

That this is recognized implies that the church, in the context of its accompaniment in concrete relationships, needs to affirm the goodness of such responses and the persons who make them.

This leads to the second critique that Francis anticipates, namely, that in reaching out in this way, the church may be seen either to be cooperating with wrongdoing, compromising its own teaching, occasioning theological scandal, or some combination of these.[34] The following synthesizes Francis's response (note that the quote is taken from a section of *AL* that itself quotes *EG* twice; see the footnote for further details):

> I understand those who prefer a more rigorous pastoral care which leaves no room for confusion. But I sincerely believe that Jesus wants a Church attentive to the goodness which the Holy Spirit sows in the midst of human weakness, a Mother who, while clearly expressing her objective teaching, "always does what good she can, even if in the process, her shoes get soiled by the mud of the street". The Church's pastors, in proposing to the faithful the full ideal of the Gospel and the Church's teaching, must also help them to treat the weak with compassion, avoiding aggravation or unduly harsh or hasty judgements. The Gospel itself tells us not to judge or condemn (cf. Mt 7:1; Lk 6:37). Jesus expects us to stop looking for those personal or communal niches which shelter us from the mael- strom of human misfortune, and instead to enter into the reality of other people's lives and to know the power of tenderness. Whenever we do so, our lives become wonderfully complicated.[35]

One can see here Francis addressing the same concern raised by those who grum- bled at Jesus's accompaniment of Zacchaeus: if part of the church's mission is seeking out those who are lost, *of course* that is going to involve her shoes "getting soiled by the mud of the street." For Francis, the higher value of mercy—what Keenan refers to as Francis's maximal interpretation of moral demand[36]—warrants muddy feet: it is more important to find and love those who are lost than it is to attain an image of purity. And it is clear, too, that Francis sees *this* approach as the precondition for the kind of moral development he hopes for in *EG* and *AL*. It is an approach that sees people gradually moving toward what is Good in the context of close and loving relationships with the church and those who minister in its name. I would argue that this *especially* includes those for whom conscience *transformation* rather than conscience *formation* is the correct category. Note the similarities with the paradigm analyzed above in the story of Zacchaeus: in the story, first table fellowship, then transformation; in Francis, first accompaniment, then transformation.

Moral Psychology and the Possibility of Conscience Transformation

Elsewhere in his writing, Francis has encouraged a disposition of openness to the insights of the sciences for the work of theology, and the case at hand is no different: conscience formation (and transformation) is a human phenomenon that receives significant attention within the sciences, especially those concerned with moral development and education.[37] I have argued elsewhere for the necessity of engaging with such insights for any of the church's discussions about conscience formation, and that argument underpins the ensuing discussion.[38] The central questions in this section follow: What insights might the sciences offer into the conditions that allow for conscience transformation? And, how do they relate to the "art of accompaniment" as developed above? To put it another way, is there some scientific support for an approach of accompaniment? I focus here on the disciplines of moral education and moral psychology, particularly the work of Darcia Narvaez, to analyze these claims.[39]

At the outset, it is important to note that despite some neodeterminist tendencies in current moral psychology, by and large there is agreement within this discipline and its aligned discipline of moral education that moral development can occur (that is, that our moral dispositions are not only the consequence of prerational factors, such as biology and genetics, though they might include these) and also that moral transformation is possible (that is, that a person's moral disposition can change, even when deeply ingrained).[40] Within these parameters, Narvaez's theoretical approach has received a substantial amount of attention for its integration of current scientific insights and contact with Aristotelian moral philosophy, thereby making it an appropriate dialogue partner for the current study.

Narvaez's approach rests on the foundations of evolutionary biology, which hold that humans are an evolved species who share essential traits with their ancestors while also having evolved beyond these, especially in our capacity for reason. Applying these insights to the human brain, Narvaez argues that the brain, too, should be seen as the result of evolution, possessing more "primal" systems that are shared with all living creatures (such as those associated with fight or flight as well as the seeking out of food), mediate systems that are shared with our closest evolutionary ancestors (such as the capacity for relationship and empathy), and advanced systems that are found in humans alone (such as our capacity for abstract reason).[41] What is significant in Narvaez's approach is her argument that all three systems *continue* to function in the human brain, and may be more or less dominant depending on contextual considerations and developmental history. Thus, reason does not *replace* its more primal antecedents: it builds on, expresses, and, in some cases, directs them.

Narvaez gives a name to each of these systems and the kind of disposition they lead to when they are dominant: the first system is the *safety* system, which when dominant expresses itself in concerns for safety; the second system is the *engagement* system, which when dominant expresses itself in concerns for sociality and engagement; the third system is the *imagination* system. This latter system is associated with the most recent parts of the human brain to evolve, which underpin our capacities for deliberative reason and decision making. The first two systems—safety and engagement—are mutually exclusive, meaning that if one is dominant in the brain at a particular time the other will not be. The third system works in tandem with whichever more primal system is dominant at a given time, an observation that provides in Narvaez's work a richer vision of virtue that can explain why persons who are virtuous in *most* circumstances may change in a context wherein their safety, rather than engagement, system is dominant.[42] In Narvaez's approach, optimal moral functioning in the human brain occurs when the engagement and imagination systems work in tandem: this provides the resources the brain needs to cultivate capacities such as mercy and compassion, as well as the creativity required for complex and principle-based moral reasoning.[43] Far from a perspective that proffers "reason alone" as the starting point for morality, Narvaez's findings illustrate that reason works in tandem with prerational systems that underpin its operations.[44]

Narvaez posits that each of the more primal systems has triggers that make it more dominant: where a person feels threatened in any way or is lacking for the basic necessities of life, the safety system will be dominant and will steer the imagination system's functioning towards narratives and rationales that support it. On a simple level, one can see the evolutionary value of this: if my life is in danger, it is as well that my brain works in such a way to protect it. Further, if there is something that will genuinely put my life in danger, then it is as well that my rational brain supports it with narratives that help me to avoid it (understanding that it is dangerous to walk alone at night in a strange city would be an example of this). Where the disposition becomes problematic is when it is activated on the basis of *apparent* but not *real* threat. This is where one's upbringing is important (bad experiences in childhood may lead the system to be active more often) or one's ideologies (such as racism or nationalism) can reinforce the safety mind-set's operations.[45] What occurs in such instances is a rigid inflexibility in worldview, and a lack of capacity to consider value sets other than those that reinforce the safety mind-set.[46] In short, when the safety system is active, moral development is thwarted, and the possibility of moral transformation is greatly lessened.[47] The lesson for this work: conscience transformation is undermined when the safety mind-set is triggered in persons, whether by experiencing persecution, exclusion, fear, or any form of threat.

The engagement system, on the other hand, is triggered in contexts with characteristics like those described above in the discussion of accompaniment. Where mercy, compassion, and care are the dominant values in a context, a person's safety system remains dormant, leading to the flourishing of the higher functions made possible in the engagement system.[48] Lest this be misread as an argument for leaving aside the more demanding aspects of morality in favor of a "watered-down" care ethic, Narvaez's argument is that the brain actually functions better in such contexts and is thus better able to deal with the more rigorous problems presented by the moral life.[49] This finding is also supported in other studies that analyze the most effective contexts for education to occur.[50]

Most significantly for the argument of this essay, it is such engagement-supportive contexts that best allow for both conscience formation and conscience transformation. Put concretely—a person whose conscience has been formed in a way that does not align with the good is in the best position to change if they find themselves in an environment characterized by mercy, compassion, and care. Correlatively, any sense of threat, persecution, exclusion, or fear will undermine this. If this approach is applied to the story of Zacchaeus, we could posit that the grumblings of his community—likely well known to Zacchaeus—had precisely the opposite effect of what they intended. Rather than providing motivation for him to change, they in fact could have undermined this possibility. In contradistinction, the approach of Jesus—which begins with accompaniment—provides the essential conditions required for Zacchaeus to be able to change. According to Narvaez's research, then, the approach illustrated above in the example of Zacchaeus and in Francis's "art of accompaniment" provides the best conditions of possibility for the transformation of conscience to occur.

Always Do What Good You Can, Even If in the Process Your Shoes Get Soiled By the Mud of the Street[51]

To this point, I have argued that accompaniment—a term that has been elucidated through the story of Zacchaeus and the writings of Pope Francis—is an essential condition for conscience transformation. To synthesize, I would posit these as the features of any such accompaniment, which can then elucidate appropriate moral responses in local contexts, a key role for the moral theologian:

1. Its primary disposition is mercy, which arises out of a hope and trust in God's grace and its capacity to reach all people;
2. This disposition leads to a motivation to seek out those who are "lost" and accompany them;
3. Such accompaniment recognizes that the formation (and transformation) of conscience is a developmental process, and one that takes place gradually—it thus rejoices in "small steps" and what good can be done, even where these are only part of the way toward an objective ideal;
4. Accompaniment does not mean the suspension of moral judgment, nor does it undermine the church's moral teaching and holds this as its ultimate goal, but it also acknowledges that the delivery—and reception—of such teaching to those whose consciences are aligned elsewhere needs to be set within the context of mercy and moral development;
5. It has the courage to withstand the grumbling of those who would say that the one accompanying "has gone to be the guest of one who is a sinner" (Luke 19:7) and its response is articulated according to the "lost and found" narrative;
6. It is willing to accept that in its work, its "shoes may be soiled."

If we in the church are serious about conscience transformation for those whose consciences are aligned away from the Good, then my argument is that this model is essential in our contact with them. Its application is necessarily contextual, and will rely on the prudence and courage of moral theologians in local contexts for it to be exercised.

To close, in *EG*, and later again in *AL*, Francis argues:

> Jesus wants us to touch human misery, to touch the suffering flesh of others. He hopes that we will stop looking for those personal or communal niches which shelter us from the maelstrom of human misfortune and instead enter into the reality of other people's lives and know the power of tenderness. Whenever we do so, our lives become wonderfully complicated.[52]

And he is right on this last point, for it does make things much more complicated. What relationships with which groups might Catholics be prompted to cultivate out of this model of accompaniment that we may have felt unable to in the past for fear of soiling our good reputation? What kinds of services will Catholic organizations look to provide out of this model of accompaniment that might previously have been avoided because they took us to the margins and into difficult ethical terrain? What kind of advocacy might the church and her organizations be willing to engage to promote this model of accompaniment, and out of the insights garnered from it, in seeking to be a voice for those who are lost? And finally, what might such a model mean for the study and practice of moral theology: will it change, for example, the role that categories such as material cooperation play in our moral discernment, or how they will apply?

These complex questions require much further investigation, and it is my position here that this model of accompaniment provides a context wherein such investigation can occur. No doubt it will lead to some grumbling, and perhaps also some soiled shoes, but this leads to the wonder Francis speaks about and, as he makes clear, the highest value of mercy demands this of us.

Notes

1. On this terminology, and the validity of considering conscience formation alongside insights in moral development psychology, see Daniel J. Fleming, "From Theory to Praxis: Challenges and Insights for Conscience Formation Today," in *Doing Asian Theological Ethics in a Cross-Cultural and an Interreligious Context*, ed. Yiu Sing Lúcás Chan, James F. Keenan, and Shaji George Kochuthara (Bengaluru, India: Dharmaram Publications, 2016), 291–304.

2. *Gaudium et spes (GS)*, nos. 16, 17. Such development is true both on the level of moral reasoning and also on the level of emotional development, a point which will be explored further below.

3. *GS*, no. 16.

4. The inclusion of such an exegesis at the outset of this work follows from the encouragement for all forms of theology, including theological ethics, being underpinned and nourished by its proper "soul," sacred scripture, in *Optatam totius*, no. 16.

5. Joel B. Green, *The Gospel of Luke* (Grand Rapids: William B. Edrmans, 1997), 668–69.

6. Ibid., 667.

7. Luke Timothy Johnson, *The Gospel of Luke* (Collegeville, MN: Liturgical Press, 1991), 285; Green, *The Gospel of Luke*, 671. Green also suggests that this disposition toward Zacchaeus could account for his experience of the crowd being an obstacle in his attempts to "see" Jesus. Green, *The Gospel of Luke*, 670.

8. Green, *The Gospel of Luke*, 666.

9. Ibid., 667.

10. Johnson notes the difference between the two words translated for salvation in these passages, σέσωκέν in 18:42 and σωτηρία in 19:9, though he argues that there is a thematic link between them. Johnson also points out that the use of σωτηρία points back to a prophecy in Luke's infancy narrative (1:69, 71, 77), which prefaces the birth of Jesus; see Johnson, *The Gospel of Luke*, 286. This gives the impression that this story in particular exemplifies a motif that is present earlier in the text.

11. Johnson, *The Gospel of Luke*, 285; Green, *The Gospel of Luke*, 666–67.

12. See Johnson, *The Gospel of Luke*, 286.

13. Dennis Hamm, "Luke 19:8 Once Again: Does Zacchaeus Defend or Resolve?" *Journal of Biblical Literature* 107, no. 3 (1988): 436.

14. Green, *The Gospel of Luke*, 673.

15. Ibid.

16. Ibid.

17. Hamm, "Luke 19:8 Once Again," 436–37.

18. *EG*, no. 169.

19. *Relatio synodi*, no. 12; *AL*, no. 60.

20. *EG*, no. 169.

21. *EG*, no. 170.

22. *EG*, no. 171.

23. *EG*, no. 172.

24. *EG*, no. 44.

25. Within this document it should be noted that Francis cautions against taking pastoral considerations of individuals' specific situations and making them into general principles; see *AL*, no. 304. However, that is not the methodology I am using here: my focus is on accompaniment as a general principle in Francis's writings and how its features might be understood and applied elsewhere, as against studying features of a specific pastoral response in context and universalizing those.

26. See as general examples, *AL*, nos. 223, 241–42.

27. *Relatio synodi*, no. 14; cited in *AL*, no. 62.

28. See *AL*, no. 243; cf. *Relatio synodi*, no. 51.

29. *AL*, no. 312.

30. Ibid. The first quote in this paragraph is taken from the International Theological Commission's document *The Hope of Salvation for Infants Who Die without Being Baptized* (April 19, 2007), no. 2. Keenan notes the significance of Francis's comment regarding the "watering down" of the gospel here: "In the past, 'watering down' usually referred to how pastoral practices could dilute doctrinal teaching; here the pontiff inverts its use to warn against an overzealous interpretation of doctrine that could compromise the Gospel message

of mercy." James F. Keenan, "Receiving *Amoris Laetitia*," *Theological Studies* 78, no. 1 (2017): 194–95.

31. *AL*, no. 312, cf. also *AL*, nos. 327, 334. The quote is taken from Francis's Papal Bull, *Misericordiae vultus*, no. 15.

32. Francis notes that this gradualism is an important part of St. John Paul II's *Familiaris consortio*, no. 34.

33. *AL*, no. 303. Here, Francis goes on to state that "In any event, let us recall that this discernment is dynamic; it must remain ever open to new stages of growth and to new decisions which can enable the ideal to be more fully realized."

34. *AL*, no. 334.

35. *AL*, no. 308. The first quote is taken from *EG*, no. 44. The second is taken from *EG*, no. 270.

36. *EG*, no. 242.

37. Ibid.

38. See Fleming, *From Theory to Praxis: Conscience Formation Today*.

39. In what follows I draw extensively on Narvaez's most recent major publication, *Neurobiology and the Development of Human Morality: Evolution, Culture, and Wisdom* (New York: W. W. Norton, 2014). This work draws on the same theoretical body that has been developed in earlier publications, including in Darcia Narvaez, "Building a Sustaining Classroom Climate for Purposeful Ethical Citizenship," in *International Research Handbook of Values Education and Student Wellbeing*, ed. Terence Lovat, Ron Toomey, and Neville Clement (Dordrecht, the Netherlands: Springer Publishing, 2010), 659–74; Darcia Narvaez, "Neurobiology and Moral Mindset," in *Handbook of Moral Motivation: Theories, Models, Applications*, ed. Karen Heinrichs, Fritz Oser, and Terence Lovat (Rotterdam: Sense Publishers, 2013), 323–42; Darcia Narvaez, "Triune Ethics: The Neurobiological Roots of Our Multiple Moralities," *New Ideas in Psychology* 26, no. 1 (2008): 95–119; Darcia Narvaez and Jenny L. Vaydich. "Moral Development and Behaviour under the Spotlight of the Neurobiological Sciences," *Journal of Moral Education* 37, no. 3 (2008): 289–312.

40. For an overview of this research, see John C. Gibbs, *Moral Development & Reality: Beyond the Theories of Kohlberg, Hoffman, and Haidt* (Oxford: Oxford University Press, 2014). See also William Damon and Anne Colby, *The Power of Ideals: The Real Story of Moral Choice* (Oxford: Oxford University Press, 2015). The current neodeterminist movement in moral psychology is represented by Jonathan Haidt, "The Emotional Dog and Its Rational Tail: A Social Intuitionist Approach to Moral Judgment," *Psychological Review* 108, no. 4 (2001): 814–34, and, more recently, Jonathan Haidt, "Moral Psychology Must Not Be Based on Faith and Hope," *Perspectives on Psychological Science* 5, no. 2 (2010): 182–84.

41. Narvaez, *Neurobiology and the Development of Human Morality*, 211.

42. Ibid., 205.

43. Narvaez, "Neurobiology and Moral Mindset," 328.

44. In this, Narvaez's approach shares features of Jean Porter, *Nature as Reason: A Thomistic Theory of the Natural Law* (Grand Rapids: William B. Eerdmans, 2005); and Stephen J. Pope, *Human Evolution and Christian Ethics* (Cambridge: Cambridge University Press, 2007).

45. This broad point is made in Narvaez, "Triune Ethics: The Neurobiological Roots of Our Multiple Moralities," 105.

46. Narvaez, *Neurobiology and the Development of Human Morality*, 211.

47. Ibid., 183.

48. See Narvaez, "Neurobiology and Moral Mindset," 328.

49. For summaries of this research, see Darcia Narvaez, "Building a Sustaining Class-room Climate for Purposeful Ethical Citizenship," in *International Research Handbook of Values Education and Student Wellbeing*, ed. Terence Lovat, Ron Toomey, and Neville Clement (Dordrecht, the Netherlands: Springer Publishing, 2010); Narvaez and Vaydich, "Moral Development and Behaviour under the Spotlight of the Neurobiological Sciences."

50. As summarized in Terence Lovat et al., *Values Pedagogy and Student Achievement: Contemporary Research Evidence* (Dordrecht, the Netherlands: Springer, 2011).

51. Cf. *EG*, no. 44.

52. *EG*, no. 270, cited also in *AL*, no. 308.

Pneumatology, Diversity, and the Role of Moral Theology Today

Laurie Johnston

Where, in the complexity and chaos of a globalizing world, is the Holy Spirit speaking to us and inviting us to grow today? So many of the challenges facing the church and theologians today are about how to relate identity and diversity, communion and difference. In Europe, some would open the door to more refugees, and others caution about losing their identity to the "Islamization" of Europe. In the United States, African Americans ask if their lives even matter when their murders by police go unpunished; meanwhile many whites in the United States voted for Trump because he sought to protect American culture from immigrants. And the church faces questions of identity as well, as more and more young people in the United States identify as "none" when asked to describe their religious affiliation. Many recent doctrinal debates arise from basic questions about where we draw the boundaries of Christian identity and praxis. When we encounter challenges like these, a first reaction is often simply to avoid them. And yet often it is precisely by confronting our challenges that we grow, both as individuals and as a church. This task of confronting challenges, with an eye toward discerning the work of the Holy Spirit, is part of our role as theologians in seeking to serve both the local and universal church.

The theologian Yves Congar provides a powerful example of facing contemporary challenges with hope and with a sense that they may be ways the Holy Spirit is calling us to grow. In one of the most striking passages in *True and False Reform in the Church*, Congar describes the ways that theological and ethical developments can come via challenges posed by the world to the church:

> It might even happen that underneath the questions which the world poses to the Church, there is God interrogating his own, standing at the door and knocking with the blows of realities and events, those teachers to whom he sometimes hands us over.[1]

Yet the "blows of realities and events" in the world are difficult to receive and interpret; many of the key debates within local churches today arise precisely from differing perspectives on how to respond: are these "realities and events" the work of the Holy Spirit, calling the churches to reform and fidelity, or are they merely signs of sin and societal corruption? And when these blows and realities are experienced primarily by one or more local churches, how should the church universal respond?

A deeper understanding of pneumatology can aid in this discernment—not by simplifying matters, but by helping us to deal better with the complexity. Yes, the Holy Spirit ensures the unity of the church and is the guarantor that the faith of the apostles will not vanish from the earth. The sense of the Holy Spirit as a steadying force, making the church secure and consistent, is an important way of understanding the church's role as a comforter and guide for Christians trying to navigate a confusing and chaotic world. And yet often our understanding of the Holy Spirit is far too safe and tame. After all, the Holy Spirit is also the guarantor of the catholicity—and therefore diversity—within the church. It is precisely a renewed faith in the Holy Spirit that can help us navigate the many ethical challenges posed today by questions of identity, community, and diversity. Migration, interreligious relations, inequality, or violence—all of these problems require an ability to understand how to relate to the "other": an "other" who may very well represent the invitation of the Spirit in our particular contexts.

The Holy Spirit is the spirit of unity, but not of uniformity. At Pentecost, we see that the Holy Spirit's very first activity is an outward motion toward a multiplicity of languages and cultures. As Yves Congar has written in his masterful work *I Believe in the Holy Spirit*:

> The Church was established in the world by Pentecost, which gave it a vocation to universality, which was to be achieved not by means of a uniform extension, but by the fact that everyone understood and expressed the marvels of God in his own language (Acts 2:6–11). Through the mission and gift of the Holy Spirit, the Church was born universal by being born manifold and particular . . . The Church overcame Babel, not by a return to a uniformity that existed before Babel, but by proclaiming an implantation of the same gospel and the same faith in varied and diverse cultural soils and human places.[2]

Thus, from the very beginning, those experiencing the gift of the Holy Spirit were engaged in an encounter with difference. And even when it was a joyful, almost inebriating encounter, it has also been a perplexing one. Whether it was astonishment over the linguistic miracle on the day of Pentecost or the confusion and resistance that quickly emerged after the conversion of Cornelius, it is clear that humans have often found the work of the Holy Spirit to be disconcerting and even disruptive. "God is a God not of disorder but of peace," Paul tells us in 1 Corinthians. And yet just as with the Corinthians, our experience of the Spirit is not always orderly—it is often surprising, perhaps even chaotic. In fact, the Spirit can be so disruptive that we often face temptation to try to wrangle it ourselves, which is why Paul must also warn people not to quench this Spirit (1 Thess. 5:19). The Holy Spirit is thus a challenge for theologians, particularly ethicists, who would like to codify and generalize, put human experiences, behaviors, virtues into categories. But we must also be sensitive to the unceasingly diversifying work of the Spirit. The task of theologians in local churches is to recognize the catholic, overflowing work of the Spirit and describe it in a way that ultimately also builds up the unity of the church.

A Recurring Temptation:
The Attempt to Control the Gift of the Holy Spirit

A first point to note about pneumatology is that Christians always face a temptation to control and domesticate the Holy Spirit. Even writing about the Holy Spirit is dangerous in this regard, and so I approach this essay with some trepidation. Our efforts to specify the work of the Holy Spirit risk simply being overrun by the Spirit, who is always ahead of us, blowing where the Spirit wills. Karl Barth, in an essay on "The Holy Ghost and the Christian Life," points out that if there is anything the Holy Spirit does, it is that the Spirit removes our presumptions about making claims about "what is or is not Christian life." As he puts it, "Ought not a serious consideration of the office of the Holy Ghost to the pardoned sinner to have this small result, at least, viz.: to make it more difficult in the future for such an adjective as ['Christian'] to drip from our lips and our pen?"[3] Of course, the effort to understand the nature of "Christian" life is precisely the task of moral theology, and thus cannot be avoided. But intellectual humility must remind us to be cautious about claiming to own the adjective "Christian," or claiming to own the work of the Holy Spirit.

The temptation to *control* and to *own* is a frequent one in human life; as Adam Kotsko argues, it is possible to see the fundamental human sin as an attempt to own what should rightly be received only as *gift*. Drawing upon the discussion of the Holy Spirit in Augustine's *De Trinitate*, Kotsko writes that

> the fall into sin is precisely the fall into desire as a fall into acquisitiveness or attempted ownership, and it is within this horizon that the Holy Spirit appears as a disruption—that is, as a gift in the strictest sense. Perhaps, then, one may understand the idea of the Holy Spirit as 'everlastingly gift' (5.17) to mean that the Holy Spirit as *communio* of the Father and the Son is eternally able to disrupt and undermine the human economy of property and regulated exchange.[4]

Like Simon Magus in Acts, humans even seek to *own* the Holy Spirit, though the Spirit's role as gift undermines any such possibility. The Spirit is not the property of the church alone, as is quickly clear in the case of Cornelius and his household: "the Holy Spirit falls on the Gentiles even without the mediation of baptism (Acts 10:44), disrupting even the expectations of the church, which was facing its own temptation to exercise proprietary rights over the gift of God."[5] Thus every human attempt to possess, control, and impose order is a betrayal and, furthermore, will ultimately be frustrated by that very Spirit whom we are attempting to control.

Relinquishing Control of Our Own Identity:
Whiteness as an Obstacle to Experiencing the Spirit

Not only does the Holy Spirit disrupt our sense of ownership, but also disrupts our very sense of our own identity. Willie James Jennings explains how the Christian vocation is a vocation to reconstrue our identity in dialogue with the other peoples and cultural groups in whom the Holy Spirit is present. This requires a genuine openness to difference, to learning from the other, and to having one's own identity reconfigured in light of that learning. But as Jennings writes, Christian missionaries, in alignment with colonialism and imperialism,

> produced a deeply deformed vision of making disciples in the New World, a distorted form which marks the Christianity we have inherited. That distorted form was executed through what I call a pedagogical imperialism. The missionary entered the New World imagining it shaped by fundamental social, cultural, and intellectual deficiency ... Christians entered the worlds of indigenous peoples in unrelenting evaluative mode, as eternal teachers with eternal students. We may call this cultural paternalism (as some historians have), but that term really does not get at the tragedy here ... This is a Christianity and Christian theology encased in evaluative mode.
>
> Whiteness was at play here. The possibilities of authentic Christian performance, authentic Christian life and knowledge, were gauged by the possibilities of being white, becoming white, and/or imitating whiteness ... Indigenous Christian life was never in the position of teacher, never in the position of really altering Western ways of life, never in the position of offering the Word of God to the missionary; the divine word could only go to work on those subject to the missionary. This asymmetrical theological relationship ... rendered not only the Christians of the New World mute but also closed off the Christian church of the West to the expansion of its own Christian identity inside new places and newly encountered identities of God's creatures in the world.[6]

In this sense, whiteness has quenched the Spirit, constraining much of the church's ability to experience what God has in store. In fact, Jennings argues, what Christians are called to is a relinquishment of our own identity and a willingness to let the Holy Spirit de-center the culture and people we have been born into. Like the first Gentile Christians, we must encounter Christianity as outsiders, becoming part of a community that is *not* ours by natural birth. We can do this only by moving away from what Jennings calls the "evaluative mode" of the missionary and into a mode of receptiveness and openness to difference, to the "other." Such an understanding of Christianity is quite radical:

> What would it mean for Christian theology to be a life form that generates a constellation of practices that invite people into multiple kinds of

alignment, alignments that cover a lifetime and are never closed, never settled, but rather always show openness to the creation? It would mean that we seek to enter the trajectory of Gentile Christian existence not as an act of theological retrieval, but as the continuation of that unfinished project of the Spirit always working ahead of us. What would it mean to be in that fundamental posture of the *Gentile-become-Christian*, that is *one of wishing to learn*, one who will seek to perform Christian identity inside ways of life not naturally her own . . . one in which *we are required* by the very nature of faith (mixed with desire) to enter deeply into different ways of life and to perform Christianity within the cultural logics of people different from us.[7]

Jennings's argument poses a serious challenge to white Christians in the United States and other contexts where white privilege and a sense of whiteness as normative prevent us, as white people, from becoming fully Christian, being truly "made new." Like the young rich man whose attachment to his wealth prevents him from becoming a disciple, an attachment to white privilege becomes an obstacle to experiencing the fullness of Christian life by learning from "the other." As Congar wrote many decades ago, "For a very long time, the 'other' was not sufficiently recognized as different and diverse, and the profound values concealed by that diversity were not appreciated."[8] This loss of profound values is a handicap for Christian life, but also a handicap for theologians. The inherited tradition of white normativity and white superiority continues to limit our theological insights.

As Jennings points out, it is precisely a kind of comfort with difference, an ability to genuinely encounter the other *as other* which is essential for us to do theology well. He writes, "Theology's 'enactment' . . . requires flexibility, adaptability, and translatability. Unfortunately, the colonial trajectory of Christianity robbed us of centuries of practice in doing this work of discipleship. Rather, this was the work of indigenous peoples having to accommodate their lives to a stable, often rigid, often unyielding, colonizing Christianity."[9] Thus, white Christians must learn from their far-more-experienced sisters and brothers about what it means to allow one's identity to be radically de-centered by the call of Christ and the disruptive power of the Holy Spirit. Only then can their—our—theology avoid the legitimization of white supremacy. Only then can genuine intimacy and unity in the Spirit become possible.

A Spirituality That Embraces Difference: *Laudato Si'* and the Beauty of Diversity

How can we cultivate not only a theology but also a spirituality that embraces the multiplicitous work of the Holy Spirit? This is particularly important for Christians in local churches who are grappling with how to respond to the religious and cultural "other." One way to approach this spiritual task is to draw upon the approach of Pope Francis in *Laudato si'*. There he explains that we must engage both the natural world and the human community with attentiveness to biodiversity and cultural diversity. "The human environment and the natural environment deteriorate together," he says, and so we must care for both, together. We must move away from a sense of ownership, whether of the land, of slaves, or even of the work of the Spirit. Instead, a deepened sensitivity toward the integrity of the natural world and the beauty of biodiversity can help us become more appreciative of human differences and the ways that they, like the natural world, can reveal the work of the Holy Spirit. Thus *Laudato si'* offers an aesthetic and ethical model for how we might genuinely appreciate the work of the Spirit in the world today.

In *Laudato si'*, Pope Francis laments the fact that global climate change is causing many species to become extinct. This is compounded by the ways that agribusinesses push toward monocultures—single species that can be grown efficiently and in large numbers, often through the aid of genetic modifications and large quantities of chemical pesticides. In the name of efficiency, farming moves toward standardization and uniformity, which then helps to satisfy the demands of a consumer economy shaped by patterns of conformity. This loss of biodiversity has serious practical consequences, given that many disappearing organisms may have offered important scientific insights or even cures for diseases. Reliance on just a few crop varieties is dangerous, too, as new pests or diseases may be able to wipe out vast quantities quite suddenly, instead of encountering many different species, some of which might offer greater resistance. But even beyond the practical problems, a loss of biodiversity is tragic simply because it means a loss of the beautiful, creative diversity in our world. Pope Francis writes, "Because of us, thousands of species will no longer give glory to God by their very existence, nor convey their message to us. We have no such right."[10]

Against such forces of exploitation, compulsive uniformity, monotony, and rigidity, Pope Francis calls for an appreciation of the richness of the world's biodiversity:

> We are called to recognize that other living beings have a value of their own in God's eyes: 'by their mere existence they bless him and give him glory', and indeed, 'the Lord rejoices in all his works' (*Ps* 104:31) . . . Each creature possesses its own particular goodness and perfection . . . Each of the various creatures, willed in its own being, reflects in its own way a ray of God's infinite wisdom and goodness. Man must therefore respect the particular goodness of every creature.[11]

This sense of the beauty of multiplicity and difference also extends, in Pope Francis's argument, to human cultures:

> A consumerist vision of human beings, encouraged by the mechanisms of today's globalized economy, has a levelling effect on cultures, diminishing the immense variety which is the heritage of all humanity. Attempts to

resolve all problems through uniform regulations or technical interventions can lead to overlooking the complexities of local problems which
demand the active participation of all members of the community . . .
Many intensive forms of environmental exploitation and degradation not
only exhaust the resources which provide local communities with their
livelihood, but also undo the social structures which, for a long time,
shaped cultural identity and their sense of the meaning of life and community. The disappearance of a culture can be just as serious, or even more
serious, than the disappearance of a species of plant or animal. The imposi-
tion of a dominant lifestyle linked to a single form of production can be
just as harmful as the altering of ecosystems.[12]

Thus the same forces of homogenization that threaten biodiversity also pose a
threat to the beautiful diversity of humankind. The ability to eat at a McDonald's
in nearly any country in the world may be convenient and familiar, but it poses a
threat to local cuisines, local businesses, and local communities.

This call for reverence toward the beautiful multiplicity of species and cultures
poses challenges for us, however. As humans, we often value familiarity, sameness,
comfort, and uniformity. Difference can be challenging and uncomfortable. Our
tolerance for complexity is limited, and there are many aspects of modern life which
strain that tolerance. The variety of media at our disposal and the dizzying assault
of tragic news stories can produce compassion fatigue. For those who are privileged
enough to have the option, there is a constant temptation to simply "check out." As
a David Sipress cartoon quipped, "My desire to be well-informed is currently at odds
with my desire to remain sane."[13] All of this means that for Christians today, a key
moral task is to increase our capacity to tolerate complexity, and our ability to love
the world and our fellow humans in it in all of their beautiful diversity, while at the
same time trusting in the Holy Spirit as the guarantor of the unity of the church.

Conclusion: From Pneumatology to Moral Theology

A key task for moral theologians is to help individuals, communities, and the
church as a whole to nurture an ability to love that moves beyond the desire to
control and toward an increased appreciation for the complexity that is the inevitable fruit of the Holy Spirit. Pope Francis's exhortation *Amoris laetitia* provides a
powerful example of how to respond to moral issues with a deep sense of the fruitful
catholicity that the Holy Spirit brings. He knows that there are those who would
insist on greater clarity of moral doctrine and clear dividing lines between who is
"in" or "out." Yet he argues that "Unity of teaching and practice is certainly necessary in the Church, but this does not preclude various ways of interpreting some
aspects of that teaching or drawing certain consequences from it. This will always be
the case as the Spirit guides us towards the entire truth."[14] While he has in mind the
moral questions around those who are in "irregular" marital situations, one could easily

imagine this referring to the long-standing tradition in the church of recognizing both pacifism and the just war tradition as being valid moral stances for Christians with regard to warfare. Or, when it comes to questions about who should receive baptism, Rowan Williams has written that such doctrinal and pastoral debates can actually represent "the Spirit at work in the community's puzzlement at its own existence and character." As Williams explains,

> Thus, for example: if I belong to a congregation which . . . operates what is sometimes called an 'indiscriminate' baptismal policy, my puzzlement may be to do with how a symbol of commitment (immersion, initiation) has become divorced from its natural function in relation to a visible and continuous belonging to a particular group. If I belong to a congregation which baptizes selectively, my puzzlement will be over the way in which a symbol of acceptance (adoption, incorporation) is seen to operate as a symbol of exclusion, stipulating conditions to be satisfied before acceptance is possible. Either case may generate puzzlement at what the Church is meant to be. Both ought therefore to provoke some interrogation of the basic Christian confession: what does commitment to Christ involve us in? Are we more concerned to see our mission as implying prophetic demand, a summons to 'own' one's faith in public risk and visible involvement? Or are we concerned with mission as gratuitous affirmation of wounded, frustrated or marginalized people—the risk being, so to say, God's rather than ours? Both queries lead us to a fresh engagement with the events which have in the first place created a community in which such questions are worth asking . . . And if there is not one answer to the question which can be established to everyone's satisfaction . . . that matters far less than the fact of a shared acknowledgement of the worthwhileness of the question and of the mode—which might be called 'trustful interrogation'—in which it is explored. So my thesis is that any such puzzlement over 'what the Church is meant to be' is the revelatory operation of God as 'Spirit' insofar as it keeps the Church engaged in the exploration of what its foundational events signify.[15]

Thus, an attempt to resolve such a question prematurely can be regarded as a form of quenching the Holy Spirit. We must instead be content with a certain amount of mystery or puzzlement when it comes to our Christian community. Perhaps there is a hint about the holiness of this mystery in the story about King David taking a census of the Israelites. Was it a failure to be open to holy puzzlement that drove King David to "number the people," as we read in 2 Samuel 24? Though God allowed David to proceed with the census, "afterwards, David was stricken to the heart because he had numbered the people. David said to the Lord, 'I have sinned greatly in what I have done. But now, O Lord, I pray you, take away the guilt of your servant; for I have done very foolishly.'"[16] In our day of public opinion surveys, membership polls, and "big data" mining—all forms of "numbering the people" into tidy categories—a sense of the mystery of the Holy Spirit at work in our community is difficult to preserve, indeed.

Part of why Pope Francis is so cautious about pursuing a high degree of doctrinal clarity or defining the boundaries of Christian identity is that he has a great deal of faith in the work of the Holy Spirit in the lives of people:

> As for the way of dealing with different "irregular" situations, the Synod Fathers reached a general consensus, which I support: "In considering a pastoral approach towards people who have contracted a civil marriage, who are divorced and remarried, or simply living together, the Church has the responsibility of helping them understand the divine pedagogy of grace in their lives and offering them assistance so they can reach the full-ness of God's plan for them," something which is always possible by the power of the Holy Spirit.[17]

And, it is not just that the Holy Spirit offers help to these people in their own lives; the Spirit also has gifts to bring to everyone else *through* these people: "On those in irregular situations: They are baptized; they are brothers and sisters; the Holy Spirit pours into their hearts gifts and talents *for the good of all*."[18] Thus, we are to receive the gifts of the Holy Spirit precisely from those people whose lives appear to challenge the normal categories of church teaching. As he goes on to say, "I understand those who prefer a more rigorous pastoral care which leaves no room for confusion. But I sincerely believe that Jesus wants a Church attentive to the goodness which the Holy Spirit sows in the midst of human weakness."[19]

Pope Francis clearly calls us today to practice mercy as "entering into the chaos of another," as James Keenan has defined it, with faith that the Holy Spirit meets us precisely there. Jesus, he writes, "expects us to stop looking for those personal or communal niches which shelter us from the maelstrom of human misfortune, and instead to enter into the reality of other people's lives and to know the power of tender-ness. Whenever we do so, our lives become wonderfully complicated."[20] If we are surprised by that complexity, we should not be. An experience of the other, of disloca-tion, of feeling one's own identity to be called into question, of being overwhelmed and perplexed by the call of Christ—these are to be seen as normal for Christians, because these are precisely the sensations that the Holy Spirit often provokes. The role of the comforter is not to remove us from this discomfort, but to help us understand how it draws us toward the love and truth that await us in the eschaton.

Notes

1. "Il peut même arriver que . . . sous les questions que le monde pose à l'Eglise, ce soit Dieu qui interroge les siens, se tenant à la porte et frappant à coups de faits et d'événements, ces maîtres qu'il nous donne parfois de sa main." Yves Congar, *Vrai et fausse réforme* (Paris: Les Éditions du Cerf, 1950), 141. My translation.

2. Yves Congar, *I Believe in the Holy Spirit* (Chestnut Ridge, NY: Crossroad Publising, 1997), 2:25–26.

3. Karl Barth, *The Holy Ghost and the Christian Life*, trans. R. Birch Hoyle (London: Frederich Muller, 1938), 70.

4. Adam Kotsko, "Gift and Communio: The Holy Spirit in Augustine's De Trinitate," *Scottish Journal of Theology* 64, no. 1 (2011): 1–12 at 11, doi:10.1017/S003693061000102X.

5. Ibid., 12.

6. Willie James Jennings, "Disfigurations of Christian Identity: Performing Identity as Theological Method," in *Lived Theology: New Perspectives on Method, Style, and Pedagogy*, ed. Charles Marsh, Peter Slade, and Sarah Azaransky (New York: Oxford University Press, 2017), 67–83, at 79–80.

7. Ibid., 82–83.

8. Congar, *I Believe in the Holy Spirit*, 2:25.

9. Jennings, "Disfigurations," 83.

10. *Laudato si'*, no. 33.

11. *Laudato si'*, no. 69, citing the *Catechism of the Catholic Church*, 2416 and 339.

12. *Laudato si'*, nos. 144–45.

13. David Sipress, "How to Stay Sane as a Cartoonist in Trumpland," *The New Yorker*, February 3, 2017.

14. *Amoris laetitia*, no. 1.

15. Rowan Williams, "Trinity and Revelation," *Modern Theology* 2, no. 3 (1986): 207–8.

16. 2 Samuel 24:10.

17. *Amoris laetitia*, no. 297.

18. *Amoris laetitia*, no. 299, emphasis added.

19. *Amoris laetitia*, no. 308, citing *Evangelii gaudium*, no. 45.

20. *Amoris laetitia*, no. 308, citing *Evangelii gaudium*, no. 270.

CATHOLIC SOCIAL TEACHING IN A CHURCH THAT IS BOTH LOCAL AND UNIVERSAL

Kenneth R. Himes

Twenty years ago, Terence McGoldrick in the US journal *Theological Studies* provided a survey of how various episcopal conferences (ECs) around the globe were conveying Catholic social teaching (CST).[1] Using a research catalogue developed at the Institute of Moral Theology at the University of Fribourg in Switzerland, the author reviewed the social teaching of ECs on five continents from 1891 to 1991. Apparent was that after Vatican II a variety of ECs took up questions related to peace and social justice, addressing them from their own experience as local churches.[2] This was due to many factors, but certainly one was the growing realization among many bishops that such local church leadership was integral to their episcopal role. Assessing the evidence, McGoldrick observed, "the sheer number of statements in recent years attests" to a conviction that bishops around the world have come to see that using CST to comment upon social issues within their locales is a significant part of their duties.[3]

A decade and a half later, the author returned to the topic to provide an update on what ECs were doing with regard to CST. He determined that ECs "have become more sophisticated over the last 15 years: with fewer statements and more activism" that has led to an "effective model aimed at structural social transformation."[4] While noting many advances in CST due to the activism of various ECs, McGoldrick also claimed, "globally, the number of EC statements has significantly decreased since 1998," adding that many of the episcopal statements "are more like calls to action or position statements than in-depth teaching statements."[5]

Part of the reason for the decline in major teaching documents is owed to the strategy of activism adopted by many ECs, whereby the preferred focus is to organize resources at the local church level in order to engage in social transformation through political participation and on-the-ground social change. However, there is another factor cited by McGoldrick: "the decline in the number of statements in recent decades is also due to opposition in some quarters of the Catholic hierarchy."[6] The pastoral activism by ECs "side-steps questions raised about the magisterial authority of EC statements."[7]

Teaching CST at the Local Church Level

No EC was more path breaking in articulating the meaning of CST for a local church than the Latin American EC (CELAM). The documents that emerged from the bishops' meeting at Medellín, Colombia, in 1968 put the Latin American church on a new pastoral trajectory, while inspiring and influencing many of the faithful around the world. Other ECs were also inspired to take up the challenge of developing statements that were theologically substantive efforts at naming and reflecting upon their local situation. Among the other ECs at the forefront of issuing major statements was that of the US bishops.

From its origins during World War I through its various name and organizational changes, the EC of the US bishops had consistently given the social mission of the church a prominent place in its work. The bishops believed an important task for the conference was to identify the social agenda as it arose from the local or national scene.[8] Something new, however, was introduced with the pastoral letters on war and peace and on economic justice, both formulated in the 1980s.[9] Those documents were significant not only for the content of the teaching but equally so for the process by which they came to be written.

Behind the entire exercise of the development of the pastoral letters was a fundamental premise that, especially in matters of social teaching, the nation's bishops had an important role in naming and speaking to the issues of the moment that the church ought to address. Out of a somewhat spontaneous reading of the signs of the times in 1980, a proposal was formulated to review and articulate Catholic teaching on modern warfare. Thus, what came to be called the Bernardin committee—so named because of its chairman, Joseph Bernardin of Chicago—was created to draft a statement.[10] In a similar manner, the decision to write an economics pastoral was made after floor discussion on a statement about Marxism raised the need to assess capitalism from the perspective of CST. It was Rembert Weakland of Milwaukee, the chairman of the committee, who proposed within the committee that what was needed was an assessment of a specific economy; thus, the letter became not a document about capitalism in general, but a pastoral letter on the US economy.

The bishops had a standard approach for developing teaching documents, with two options available.[11] One option is that a document emerges out of the standing committees of the conference, with permanent staff and invited experts involved as well. A draft is developed and once the committee approves, it is distributed to other bishops and even some outside experts, theological or otherwise, for comment and suggestions. The committee then revises the document in light of the feedback received and the text is formally submitted to the entire conference for discussion, possible emendation, and, hopefully, final approval. The second option is to develop an ad hoc committee to play the role that the standing committee plays in the first option. Both of the pastoral letters on war and peace and the US economy employed the second option.

During the course of developing the first pastoral, the Bernardin committee initiated some new elements into the standard procedures. Because of the intense interest in the topic at the time, when the Reagan administration was assuming power with expectations of more assertive, even bellicose, foreign and national security policies, the list of consultants went way beyond the usual number and kind of invited experts. The committee also met far more often than was originally planned as the drafting process took months longer than initially anticipated. A second innovation, that was unplanned, occurred when the first confidential draft was leaked to the religious and secular press. The draft text evoked widespread reaction and many unsolicited comments seeking to shape its revision. From that point on the Bernardin committee decided to disseminate subsequent drafts publicly, and the second and third drafts were subjected to extensive critique and commentary by an array of interested parties ranging far beyond ecclesiastical circles.

It was clear that by these actions something new was emerging in the life of the US church. Archbishop John Roach of St. Paul, MN, president of the EC at the time the Bernardin committee was active, voiced the belief that there was a new maturity in the relationship between the US bishops and the Vatican, a maturation that would lead to a deeper sense of collegiality within the episcopacy. It would lead the nation's bishops to "interpret the teaching of the Pope to the American church but also interpret the experience and insights of the American church to the Pope."[12] Roach's successor as president of the conference, James Malone of Youngstown, OH, had a similar view: "Together as a national hierarchy, we have found a new and collegial method of teaching . . . For the first time, the church has taught not simply through a finished product, but through the process that led to the finished document."[13] Through the process of extensive consultation, public discussion, and multiple draft texts, the US bishops in the first half of the 1980s became one of the most recognized and influential voices in public discussion on social issues within the nation.

Debating the Role and Function of the Local Church

While many saw the trends toward consultation with the laity, collaboration with theologians and other experts, and increased collegiality among the bishops as providing an example of a postconciliar ecclesiology coming to life, there were concerns expressed in various quarters, including the Vatican. In meetings, public statements, and dicastery documents, the Vatican raised questions on a number of matters. The following were among them: What is the level of authority attributed to these EC documents? Who is the audience for the documents? Is the role of the EC to encourage debate or to clarify and propose official teaching? Does the blending of different levels of authority in a teaching document confuse the faithful? What is the relationship of an individual bishop's teaching authority in his diocese to the teaching of the EC?[14] What has been described as a "bombshell" came at the Vatican meeting held in the spring of 1983 that brought together representatives of European and US ECs to discuss the peace pastoral. At that gathering the head of the Congregation for the Doctrine of the Faith, Joseph Ratzinger, posed several propositions for discussion, with the first being that an EC does not have a *mandatum docendi*.[15] In time, the debate further evolved to ask about the role of the local church and its relationship to the universal church.[16]

The Vatican's clear desire to rein in what it saw as the ECs overly active role in proposing teaching, as well as the various processes used to formulate that teaching, led to further debate that carried over into preparations for the 1985 synod. Finally, at that extraordinary synod, which celebrated the twentieth anniversary of the closing of Vatican II, there was a call to clarify the issues surrounding the role of the local and regional churches and the teaching authority of ECs. Such clarification was not quick to come, however, and it was only in 1998 that John Paul II issued his apostolic letter *Apostolos suos* (On the Theological and Juridical Nature of Episcopal Conferences).[17] On the theological principle of whether an EC can teach, the answer given was "yes." However, that *mandatum* may only be exercised under three conditions: (1) it must be a statement approved at a plenary session, not through committees; (2) it must be a statement approved by a unanimous vote; or (3) by a two-thirds vote that is then given a formal *recognitio* by the Holy See.[18]

Francis Sullivan has pointed out that these conditions do not really advance the understanding of the teaching role of ECs. First, by requiring a unanimous approval it effectively means that the EC has the authority that each bishop gives to it by his individual mandate. Second, by requiring the papal *recognitio* the universal magisterium makes up for the lack of authority that the two-thirds majority has to promulgate its teaching as authoritative. In effect, the conditions imposed by John Paul II supported the earlier view of Ratzinger that there is no intermediate level of teaching located in an EC but only two acceptable levels of teaching: the universal college or individual diocesan bishop.[19]

Richard Gaillardetz has noted, "there is a certain irony" that although John Paul II contributed many insights to CST, "he was cautious in recognizing complementary ecclesial processes through which the bishops and all the Christian faithful could contribute to the development of that teaching."[20] The squelching of the US bishops' process for developing pastoral letters, the limitations on ECs in the exercise of teaching authority, not to mention the decline of the episcopal synod as an effective instrument of collegiality all occurred under John Paul II.

Benedict XVI continued the centralization of the teaching office and the emphasis on the universal magisterium that had marked the papacy of John Paul II. With the onset of the papacy of Francis, however, it appears that a new openness to local or regional church teaching has arrived. It may be useful, therefore, to return to earlier developments during the papacy of Paul VI that offered guidance for the role of the local church in teaching, especially in the area of CST.

Another Perspective within the Tradition

To commemorate the eightieth anniversary of Leo XIII's *Rerum novarum*, Paul VI sent an apostolic letter to Cardinal Maurice Roy, president of both the Pontifical Commission *Justitia et Pax* as well as the Council of the Laity. In paragraph four of Paul's text, we find what has been called the "magna carta" of the local church. Having noted the many and dramatically diverse settings in which the modern church finds itself, the pope wrote three startling sentences:

> In the face of such widely varying situations it is difficult for us to utter a unified message and to put forward a solution which has universal validity. Such is not our ambition, nor is it our mission. It is up to the Christian communities to analyze with objectivity the situation which is proper to their own country, to shed on it the light of the Gospel's unalterable words and to draw principles of reflection, norms of judgment and directives for action from the social teaching of the Church.[21]

I refer to these sentences as startling because the pope first acknowledges a problem with formulating a single teaching that is apt for the universal church. Then Paul VI announces that such a teaching is not even the mission of the papacy. Finally, the pope endorses the duty of the local church to both read its own particular historical situation and formulate an appropriate response. Implicit in the papal reasoning is the role of subsidiarity in social teaching, acknowledging the limitations of the papacy to address the wide assortment of contexts in which the church must teach and minister.

The originality of Paul's message must not be overlooked. When John XXIII encouraged the use of Cardinal Cardijn's method of see–judge–act, it was specifically with reference to the application of social norms to particular situations.[22] In *Octogesima adveniens*, however, there is a different use of the Cardijn method.

> The starting point is reflection on the local situation by the local Christian community. The community then becomes the locus of dialogue between the situation and its traditions, namely Scripture and social teaching, in order to bring about action. The process is not application of ahistorical principles to situations, but dialogical discernment for action, emerging from concrete situations and Christian traditions.[23]

For John, the Cardijn method was used to apply the social principles; the principles were the starting point, which were used to judge the particular situation as analyzed by the local community. Paul assigned all three steps of the Cardijn method to the local community. As Elsbernd has persuasively argued in her analysis of paragraph four, the "social teaching itself is historically constituted via a dialogical development in Christian communities between the resources of their traditions and their specific situation prior to discernment for action."[24] Understanding Paul's approach means acknowledging that the local churches participate in the actual development of social teaching and do not simply receive a universal teaching that is given them to apply.[25]

Paul had first-hand experience of global diversity and the complexity of local situations as a consequence of his papal travels: Israel in 1964, the United States in 1965, India in 1966, Turkey and Portugal in 1967, Medellín in 1968, and Uganda in 1969. "These encounters with the People of God, their poverty, and their misery profoundly moved Paul VI, as his Wednesday audience reflections attest."[26] Beyond the innovation in methodology proposed by Paul, the papal journeys also seemed to encourage his thinking about the importance of the local church and ECs in the formulation and promotion of CST. He explicitly limited the papal role and in its place endorsed the responsibility of the local church for the social mission of the Christian community. Paul's attendance at the CELAM Conference held in Medellín appears to have been a key moment, for there the pope saw a model of collegial discernment and decision making by which a local church that was largely overshadowed at Vatican II found its voice and adapted the insights of *Gaudium et spes* to its own situation.

At Vatican II there was an experience of what Brad Hinze has called "a triadic vision of the Church as a community of dialogue and communication." The triad referred to "bishops, theologians, [and] the entire people of God in dynamic relationships of learning and teaching."[27] Obviously, the Second Vatican Council was built upon the collegial activity of bishops, but there was also a vital and essential collaboration with theologians and other *periti* upon whom the bishops relied for scholarly insight. Regarding the interaction of these two groups—bishops and scholars—consulting with the laity, the Council provided a rationale more than established a practice.

Gaudium et spes began a new way of understanding the church's engagement with the world. Church teaching, especially its social teaching, was not to begin with a deductive reasoning process that applied universal principles to specific situations. Rather, the entire people of God has "the duty of scrutinizing the signs of the times and of interpreting them in the light of the gospel."[28] Later in the same document, the bishops wrote,

> The laity should also know that it is generally the function of their well-formed Christian conscience to see that the divine law is inscribed in the life of the earthly city. From their priests they may look for spiritual light and nourishment. Let the laity not imagine that their pastors are always such experts, that to every problem that arises, however complicated, they can readily give a concrete solution or even that such is their mission. Rather, enlightened by Christian wisdom and giving close attention to the teaching authority of the Church, let the laity take on its own distinctive role.[29]

As the bishops went on to discuss the mission of the church as one of evangelization that entails giving expression to the revelation of Christ in a manner apropos to each nation, there was recognition that this required "a living exchange . . . fostered between the Church and the diverse cultures of people." Furthermore, "to promote such an exchange, the Church requires special help . . . With the help of the Holy Spirit, it is the task of the entire People of God, especially pastors and theologians, to hear, distinguish, and interpret the many voices of our age, and to judge them in the light of the divine Word."[30]

Part II of the Pastoral Constitution is composed of five particular areas that the Council called "some problems of special urgency." The remarks in each of the five areas begin with a look at the signs of the times. The document's "emphasis on the signs of the times illustrates a more historically conscious methodology at work" than is to be found in earlier official social teaching.[31] The classical consciousness of neo-Thomist natural law would begin with an exposition of human nature and then draw normative principles to be applied.

The vision of the Council indicates that the formulation of CST is a dynamic and historically conscious process that will function very differently than deductively reasoning from established norms to specific application. Instead it is a process that ought to engage the entire church in attending to the "signs of the times" appropriate to given contexts and discerning within those settings what it is that the Spirit of Christ calls upon disciples to do. The process would entail what Hinze calls "the *three modes of acting in relationships—collegiality* among bishops; *collaboration* between bishops and theologians; *consultation* among bishops, theologians, and the entire People of God."[32] One might add that in the area of moral matters, particularly CST, the consultation with laypeople is especially important since they have a range of lived experience within the modern world often unavailable to the clerical hierarchy.

Undoubtedly, *Gaudium et spes* is the conciliar document that has most influenced the church's social teaching in the contemporary era. In the years following the Council, the papal encyclical *Populorum progressio* in 1967 and the 1971 synod statement *Justitia in mundo* show clear evidence of the influence of methodology and content of the Pastoral Constitution. Yet for the advancement of CST it was the apostolic letter *Octogesima adveniens* (A Call to Action) that most clearly reflected the themes of collegiality, collaboration, and consultation, along with the method of a historically conscious discernment process that advocates beginning with the local and particular.[33]

Resources for a Revived Process

In this final section of the essay I would like to note several elements of the Catholic tradition that can advance our understanding of the importance of consultation, collaboration, and collegiality for the ongoing renewal of CST.

Discernment Requires Consultation

God's historical revelation in the person of Jesus Christ and the ongoing gift of the presence of the Spirit is a gift to all the members of the church. Thus, baptism, not ordination, becomes the key sacramental experience for the Christian believer to receive revelation. The Spirit's gifts to the church are multiple and not restricted to one segment of the faith community. It is for all in the ecclesial community to enter into an ongoing process of discernment, one that calls upon each member of the faithful to gain "a greater penetration of what its Christian commitment implies for life."[34] By underscoring the importance of the role of every church member, the Council was not disavowing the idea that some among the faithful are called to fill certain offices, including that of teacher. Rather, what is being envisioned is, "the church as a community of religious and moral discernment in which a dialogue exists between the proposition and explication of Christian faith and its implications by authoritative teachers and the reception of that teaching by the church community—which also possesses the gifts of the Spirit."[35] In order for that dialogue to happen, however, there had to be a renewed appreciation for the role of the *sensus fidelium* in the life of the church.

Following Antonio Autiero, we may call the *sensus fidelium* the "collective consciousness of the faith"[36] as grasped, lived, and believed by the church's membership. It is not to be understood as a reality put in opposition to the magisterium, but a reality that is to be integrated into the magisterium so that the official teachers of the church may authentically proclaim and teach the faith of the church. Seen this way, the division of the church into a teaching church and a learning church is simply inadequate since all are learners. Those who hold the office of teacher "are first of all believers, who have themselves learned the Christian faith from the Christian community."[37] They did not receive insight into the faith by private revelation, but rather through their participation in the lived faith of the ecclesial community.

And those who were cast by preconciliar ecclesiology into the role simply of learners are indeed teachers, though not in the sense of a "reflective knowledge of the mysteries of faith which deploys concepts and uses rational procedures to reach its conclusions."[38] Rather, we are dealing with those faith-filled disciples who have a sense (*sensus*) or instinct for the faith so that when confronted by the truth of the gospel they respond with a spontaneous affirmation rooted in their love and desire for God. It is an example of knowledge through connaturality that Aquinas and other medieval scholastics discussed. Again, Autiero maintains, "the community that authentically opens up to the breath of the Spirit and that is converted . . . acquires competence in the knowledge of moral demands and conducts a rational internal 'conversation' in order to evaluate the significance of the moral experience that it has acquired."[39]

The conciliar viewpoint sees the official teachers being stimulated in their discernment by the entire community resulting in "a new, perhaps modified proposition of the Christian faith and its implications."[40] The roles of teacher and learner are more fluid than the earlier approach envisioned, with a magisterium assisted by the Holy Spirit performing its role within the context of a community of disciples, inspired by the same Spirit, who give lived expression to the faith.

Reading the Signs of the Times Requires Collaboration

One of the hallmarks of the event that was Vatican II was the way that bishops worked with and relied upon the *periti* who had been invited. Rahner, Ratzinger, Congar, De Lubac, Häring, Fuchs, Murray, Pavan, Küng, Schillebeeckx, Chenu, Weigel, and Laurentin were just some of the scholars whose expertise was relied upon by the bishops during the Council. Appreciation for the role that theologians and others played in bringing the Council to a successful conclusion carried over into the way that ECs utilized academic expertise in CELAM's meetings at Medellín and Puebla, as well as the US EC's drafting of the pastoral letters.

Some in the Vatican expressed concern that the consultation process followed by the US bishops, with its frequent and public collaboration with experts, "could give the impression that the bishops were deficient in their knowledge of social justice and thus their teaching authority would be diminished."[41] In truth, the opposite seems to have been the case, that it was precisely because the Bernardin and Weakland committees had involved scholars and practitioners in fields such as theology, national security, economics, and public policy that the pastoral letters had the credibility that they did. Collaboration had not diminished but enhanced the teaching authority of the ECs.

Because of the nature of CST, bringing the wisdom of the tradition into dialogue with historically contingent data and conditions in specific and diverse contexts, it is necessary to engage in collaborative efforts with scholars and others who can provide insight for developing moral teaching. As bishops enter into the arenas of social, political, and economic life, they must turn their attention to lay experts in particular in order to formulate teaching. In doing so CST develops as a body of wisdom precisely because it is being brought into dialogue with diverse and complex situations.

As Elsbernd and others have emphasized, *Octogesima adveniens* was not proposing a method of ethical reasoning in which local churches simply applied already formulated teaching to a specific situation. Rather, the method espoused by Paul VI included the wisdom and experience of the local churches in the actual formulation of CST. The latter is a "complex and living tradition that cannot be understood apart from the communities that nurture it and embody its principles—even before it is applied."[42] Reading the signs of the times demands a profound engagement with all those disciplines and local church communities of faith praxis who have wisdom to share about what is happening in the world and where the presence of God's spirit may be seen to be at work. Collaboration is essential to the ongoing evolution of CST.

Universality Requires Collegiality

Francis has spoken of *synodality* as the way forward for the church. "It is precisely this path of synodality which God expects of the Church of the third millennium."[43] A church that practices synodality is one that listens, realizing "that listening is more than simply hearing. It is a mutual listening in which everyone has something to learn."[44] For Francis the idea of synodality is not only in support of the episcopal synod but is meant to convey an enhanced episcopal collegiality, greater decentralization of governance, and stronger ties to the grassroots of the church.

This project of Francis's is not novel but deeply traditional. By the second century there were bishops meeting in local councils and regional councils. For more than a century, there were such gatherings before the onset of a Christian emperor made it possible to hold the first ecumenical council in 325, and it is evident that in many of the earliest general councils it was the emperor not the Bishop of Rome who played the primary role.[45] Yet even after the advent of general councils, regional councils continued for many centuries with several making major contributions to doctrinal development, for example, Carthage in 418, Orange II in 529, and Toledo III in 589. The Council of Trent even called for regular provincial councils to be held, although this did not become a regular practice throughout the church. Still, in the US there were seven regional and three plenary councils held between 1829 and 1884.[46] By the outset of Vatican II, there were more than forty ECs established, and at the Council itself, "the role of the conferences became more important, as the bishops regularly gathered in them to discuss the questions that were coming up in the conciliar debates."[47] Indeed, *Lumen gentium* states that ECs can make a "manifold and fruitful contribution" to the reality of collegiality.[48]

Walter Kasper has made the case that "the local church is neither a province nor a department of the universal church; it is the church at a given place." At the Extraordinary Synod of 1985 the claim was made that "communion was the central and foundational idea of the Second Vatican Council."[49] The establishment of ECs becomes a concrete illustration and experience of communion within the episcopal body. It is not to be understood as a rival to the universal college of bishops headed by the bishop of Rome. Properly understood, the role of the ECs and other expressions of collegiality at intermediate levels enriches the teaching of the universal college. When the worldwide church is able to receive input from all the varied and diverse settings of the local churches it compensates for the danger of a universalism that glosses over differences and overlooks the experience of those in a marginal or minority position.[50] Benefiting from the experience, reflection, and pastoral activity of local churches as they encounter the "hopes and fears, griefs and anxieties of the people of this age"[51] helps the universal teaching office to be authentically catholic. In *Evangelii gaudium* and *Laudato si'*, Francis often cited teaching documents of a variety of ECs, providing testimony to how the universal church can learn from the local churches.

One can readily imagine a process whereby various ECs or other conjoint episcopal groups gather and assess the situations in their own churches. Papal teaching meant to be an expression of the universal church could build upon such episcopal teaching and offer a draft of a text to solicit input from local churches. The consultation process should engage the local and universal church both for local church documents and universal church documents. The church universal can provide important feedback and a broader range of experience and reflection to the local church, while the local church can offer a closer attentiveness to the diversity, uniqueness, and specificity of a local community's experience. In this way, the structures of synodality can strengthen universal teaching by making it more historically conscious, more inductive and empirical, and more likely to be a reflection of how the Spirit is moving throughout the entire body of Christ.

Notes

1. Terence McGoldrick, "Episcopal Conferences Worldwide on Catholic Social Teaching," *Theological Studies* 59, no. 1 (1998): 22–50.

2. Throughout the essay, I use the expression "local church(es)" to include either an individual diocese or an association of dioceses in a regional or national conference.

3. McGoldrick, "Episcopal Conferences Worldwide," 24.

4. Terence McGoldrick, "Episcopal Conferences Worldwide and Catholic Social Thought, in Theory and Praxis: An Update," *Theological Studies* 75, no. 2 (2014): 377.

5. Ibid., 382.

6. Ibid., 383.

7. Ibid., 385.

8. The centrality of the social mission for the early years of the conference is evident in Elizabeth McKeown, "The National Bishops' Conference: An Analysis of Its Origins," *Catholic Historical Review* 66 (October 1980): 565–83, and Joseph McShane, *"Sufficiently Radical": Catholicism, Progressivism and the Bishops Program of 1919* (Washington, DC: Catholic University Press, 1986), esp. chap. 2.

9. The two letters to which I will refer in this section are *The Challenge of Peace: God's Gift and Our Response* (Washington, DC: National Conference of Catholic Bishops, 1983) and *Economic Justice for All* (Washington, DC: National Conference of Catholic Bishops, 1985).

10. For background on the creation of the committee, see James Castelli, *The Bishops and the Bomb* (New York: Image Books, 1983), 13–25.

11. In the following paragraphs, I draw upon the narrative found in Bradford Hinze, "Developing a New Way of Teaching with Authority," in *Unfailing Patience and Sound Teaching: Reflections on Episcopal Ministry*, ed. David Stosur (Collegeville, MN: Liturgical Press, 2003), 165–96.

12. As quoted in Thomas Reese, "American Bishops and Their Agenda," *America,* December 17, 1983, 393.

13. James Malone, "The Church: Its Strengths and Its Questions," *Origins* 16, no. 23 (1986): 395.

14. I summarize here a number of points treated by Hinze, "Developing a New Way of Teaching," 174–80. The Vatican concerns about the process and style of teaching utilized by the US bishops only became more grave during the aborted drafting of a pastoral letter on women in the church, which was begun after the economics pastoral.

15. The characterization of Ratzinger's intervention as a "bombshell" is from Francis Sullivan, "The Teaching Authority of Episcopal Conferences," *Theological Studies* 63, no. 3 (2002): 476.

16. See, for example, Walter Kasper, "On the Church," *America*, April 23–30, 2001, 184, http://www.americamagazine.org/issue/333/article/church, and Joseph Ratzinger, "The Local Church and the Universal Church," *America*, November 19, 2001, 18, http://www.americamagazine.org/issue/351/local-church-and-universal-church. For an analysis, see Kilian McDonnell, "The Ratzinger/Kasper Debate: The Universal Church and Local Churches," *Theological Studies* 63, no. 2 (2002): 227–50.

17. http://w2.vatican.va/content/john-paul-ii/en/motu_proprio/documents/hf_jp-ii_motu-proprio_22071998_apostolos-suos.html.

18. *Apostolos suos*, nos. 22–23.

19. Sullivan, "Teaching Authority of ECs," 486–87.

20. Richard Gaillardetz, "The Ecclesiological Foundation of Modern Catholic Social Teaching," in *Modern Catholic Social Teaching: Commentaries and Interpretations*, 2nd ed., ed. Kenneth Himes (Washington, DC: Georgetown University Press, 2017). I am quoting from the as yet unpublished manuscript.

21. Paul VI, *Octogesima adveniens* (A Call to Action), no. 4.

22. The explicit mention of the Cardijn method is found in *Mater et Magistra* (Christianity and Social Progress), no. 236. The explanation of how the individual is to apply the social teaching to practical issues is nos. 226–41.

23. Mary Elsbernd, "What Ever Happened to *Octogesima Adveniens*?" *Theological Studies* 56, no. 1 (1995): 43.

24. Ibid.

25. This is in accord with one of the conclusions drawn by participants in an expert seminar on Catholic Social Thought and the Movements held at Leuven in 2010. For a report on the seminar, see Johan Verstraeten, "Catholic Social Thought and the Movements: Towards Social Discernment and a Transformative Presence in the World," *Journal of Catholic Social Thought* 10, no. 2 (2013): 231–40.

26. Elsbernd, "What Ever Happened?" 41.

27. Hinze, "Developing a New Way of Teaching," 181.

28. *Gaudium et spes* (Pastoral Constitution on the Church in the Modern World), no. 4.

29. Ibid., no. 43.

30. Ibid., no. 44.

31. Charles Curran, *Catholic Social Teaching, 1891–present* (Washington, DC: Georgetown University Press, 2002), 59.

32. Hinze, "Developing a New Way of Teaching," 181.

33. Curran, *Catholic Social Teaching*, 60.

34. John Boyle, *Church Teaching Authority* (South Bend, IN: University of Notre Dame Press, 1995), 109.

35. Ibid., 168.

36. Antonio Autiero, "The *Sensus Fidelium* and the Magisterium from the Council to the Present Day: Moral-Theological Reflections," in *The Sensus Fidelium and Moral Theology*, ed. Charles E. Curran and Lisa A. Fullam, eds. (Mahwah, NJ: Paulist Press, 2017), 193–213, at 195.

37. Boyle, *Church Teaching Authority*, 168.

38. Autiero, "The *Sensus Fidelium* and the Magisterium," 199.

39. Ibid., 203.

40. Boyle, *Church Teaching Authority*, 168.

41. Rembert Weakland, "*Economic Justice for All* Ten Years Later," *America*, March 22, 1997, 9.

42. McGoldrick, "Episcopal Conferences: An Update," 401.

43. Francis, "Address Commemorating the 50th Anniversary of the Institution of the Synod of Bishops," (October 17, 2015), http://w2.vatican.va/content/francesco/en/speeches/2015/october/documents/papa-francesco_20151017_50-anniversario-sinodo .html.

44. Ibid.

45. Charles Curran, *The Development of Moral Theology: Five Strands* (Washington, DC: Georgetown University Press, 2013), 157.

46. Sullivan, "Teaching Authority of ECs," 472–73.

47. Ibid., 474.

48. *Lumen gentium* (Dogmatic Constitution on the Church), no. 23.

49. Kasper, "On the Church."

50. Curran, *Catholic Social Teaching*, 118–19.

51. *Gaudium et spes*, no. 1.

CONTEXT AND MORAL TEACHING

The Crucial Importance of the Magisterium of the Local Church

Vimal Tirimanna

Introduction

Can the universal magisterium unilaterally give moral teachings that would be relevant and applicable for all the specific, concrete situations of the church spread all over the world? What is the role of the local church in formulating moral teachings within a specific context? In an effort to respond to these questions, this essay will first examine the importance of the context (the circumstances) that surrounds a moral agent. Then, it will highlight that it is the local church that is better acquainted with regard to the concrete contexts that surround moral agents in different local churches/contexts than a centralized Roman magisterium that acts in the name of the universal magisterium.[1] To illustrate this fact, we will enumerate a few moral issues for which concrete Catholic moral teachings have to invariably take seriously the diverse local contexts if they are to be relevant and meaningful. Vatican II[2] ecclesiology that stressed the role of the local church in moral teachings will be discussed next, followed by a very brief account of what hindered the realization of such Vatican II indications during the past few decades. I will conclude with a brief discussion of the need for Rome to be in continuous dialogue with the local churches, and vice versa, in the process of searching for moral truth,[3] especially in formulating Catholic moral teachings, which in turn demands some radical ecclesial/canonical structural changes to suit the ecclesiology of Vatican II.

Moral Theology and Context

Traditional Catholic moral theology has always given importance to the circumstances that surround the acting human agent who performs a human act in determining its morality. Although in the post–Vatican II era the importance of moral circumstances has in general taken a back seat mainly due to the stress (by the hierarchical magisterium) on moral object (perhaps, as an antidote to the prevalent trends of subjective individualism and relativism),[4] the church/theologians never completely overlooked the vital importance of the circumstances that surround a moral agent. The many contextual theologies that arose during this same period are a witness to this fact.[5]

A moral agent is always a contextualized person, a person from within a particular context, a person who is surrounded by a set of particular circumstances: hence, the importance attributed to circumstances in traditional fundamental moral theology. Moreover, the acting moral agent himself/herself is a unique human being with his/her unique character, upbringing, experiences in life, way of perceiving reality, knowledge, ability to use reason, emotional life, etc. Consequently, the different acting moral agents have very different worldviews.

At the same time, we cannot forget that the world we live in is diverse not only geographically but also culturally. Courau and Mendoza-Alvarez express our lived diversity as follows:

> Our planet is made up of very diverse cultural and religious universes. What happens when they face one another? How do they meet and engage in dialogue when their rational approach and apprehension of the world are unique? What happens when a Chinese person receives a European thought, a European discourse, of which the structures of language and reasoning have been constructed and elaborated over centuries? And conversely? More generally, how do we think and communicate in a particular culture, in a specific religious tradition, in a determined world? How do we make ourselves understood by others? Can we understand them?[6]

These questions are so common in our contemporary globalized world that they are of fundamental importance also for the moral teachings of the church. That is to say, the acting moral agents (with their particular worldviews), as well as the moral contexts in which they live and act, are diverse and never uniform. This was evident especially during the consultations for the two recent Synods on Family.[7] As such, no general single moral law/norm could ever cover all the particular contexts in the world, as the Aristotelian–Thomistic moral tradition had always upheld:

> The more you descend into the detail the more it appears how the general rule admits of exceptions, so that you have to hedge it with caution and qualifications. The greater the number of conditions accumulated the greater the number of ways in which the principle is seen to fall short.[8]

Necessarily and realistically, such norms/laws (principles) need to have their particular variances and nuances in diverse contexts. The traditional fundamental moral concept of *epikeia* results from this understanding. This not only calls for but also paves the way for a diversity of the expression of the same moral teachings in varying local contexts. What we mean here is surely not a question of subjective relativism with regard to morality or a type of situation ethics but the realistic demands of the diversity of moral agents and the diversity of circumstances that surround the contexts in which they live and act. This is precisely what Pope Paul VI wrote in 1971 after calling attention to "a wide diversity among the situations in which Christians—willingly or unwillingly—find themselves according to regions, socio-political systems and cultures":[9]

> In the face of such widely varying situations it is difficult for us to utter a unified message and to put forward a solution which has universal validity. Such is not our ambition, nor is it our mission. It is up to the Christian communities to analyze with objectivity the situation which is proper to their own country, to shed on it the light of the gospel's unalterable words and to draw principles of reflection, norms of judgment and directives for action from the social teaching of the Church.[10]

Some four decades later, his successor Pope Francis would repeat the same thought many a time. For example, in 2016, with regard to the discernment of "irregular situations" of marriage, he wrote, "If we consider the immense variety of concrete situations such as those I have mentioned, it is understandable that neither the Synod nor this Exhortation could be expected to provide a new set of general rules, canonical in nature and applicable to all cases."[11] Three years earlier he had written, "It is not advisable for the Pope to take the place of the local Bishop in the discernment of every issue which arises in their territory. In this sense, I am conscious of the need to promote a sound 'decentralization.'"[12]

Nuances and Variations in
Moral Teachings of the Local Church

The world as God has created it is diverse. Diversity, in fact, is the hallmark of God's creation; hence, diversity is what we experience in the reality in which we live and act. However, one needs to note that diversity does not defy unity though it surely does defy uniformity. That is why one cannot afford to forget that genuine unity in our lived reality is never uniformity but unity in diversity. This realistic fact is applicable also to moral teachings of the church from which emanate moral norms/laws for the believers. As such, while one needs to appreciate the role played by Rome in ensuring and maintaining the unity of faith and morals, one also should not be rigid but flexible in matters that are not essential for the Catholic faith, especially at the local, concrete level—the level of formulation and application of moral teachings. In this regard, Pope Francis writes,

> When we adopt a pastoral goal and a missionary style which would actually reach everyone without exception or exclusion, the message has to concentrate on the essentials on what is most beautiful, most grand, most appealing and at the same time most necessary. The message is simplified,

while losing none of its depth and truth, and thus becomes all the more forceful and convincing. (*EG*, no. 35)

This is in harmony with the famous rule of thumb of St. Augustine: *In essentials unity, in what is secondary freedom and in all things charity*. In fact, Vatican II itself taught of the existence of "a 'hierarchy' of truths, since they vary in their relation to the fundamental Christian faith."[13] This applies to "the whole corpus of the Church's teaching, including her moral teaching" (*EG*, no. 36). Moreover, Vatican II taught that "the deposit of faith or the truths are one thing and the manner in which they are enunciated, in the same meaning and understanding, is another."[14] Commenting on this teaching, McCormick shows how it is more relevant to teachings in moral theology:

> If there is a distinction between the deposit of faith and its formulation at a given time, this is a fortiori true of the behavioral implications of this deposit. For behavioral implications are even more dependent on the contingencies of time and place. To restate the Council's distinction in theological shorthand, we may and must distinguish between the substance of a moral teaching and its formulation.[15]

In his exhaustive study on the different Christian communities of the first century as evident in the New Testament texts, Raymond Brown highlights the absence of any sense of uniformity among them in the expression of their one faith in the One Lord Jesus Christ.[16] Rather, he points out the diversity of living in the Christian communities (churches) even within the single city of Ephesus itself.[17]

Vatican II also made a clear reference to the adaptation of one faith to suit different contexts when it said, "the heritage handed down by the apostles was received with differences of form and manner, so that from the earliest times of the Church it was explained variously in different places, owing to diversities of genius and conditions of life."[18] The same Council also taught that "the lawful variety that can exist in the Church must also be taken to apply to the differences in theological expression of doctrine."[19] Moreover, according to the conciliar teachings, bishops have to confirm their flocks "in a *living* faith,"[20] and so, to "present Christian doctrine *in a manner adapted to the needs of the times*, that is to say, in a manner that will respond to the difficulties and questions by which people are especially burdened and troubled."[21] Taking such clear conciliar indications, initially, quite a number of bishops and regional/local episcopal conferences embarked on a journey to reassert their legitimate teaching authority in their respective spheres of competence. For example, the Latin American bishops (through their continental episcopal conference, the CELAM) tried to apply the universal church teaching on *signs of the times* to their lived contexts of poverty and degradation; thus emerged the concept of "the preferential option for the poor" at Medellín in 1968.[22] Similarly, taking into account the living realities of Asia, generations of Asian bishops since the 1970s have been advocating a threefold dialogue (a "triple dialogue") as the most effective evangelical method on their continent: with ancient cultures (*inculturation*), living religions (*interreligious dialogue*), and the teeming millions of poor (*option for the poor*).[23] Accordingly, any general Western/Roman model of evangelization cannot be imposed on so socioculturally diverse a continent as Asia as experience itself has shown for centuries. This basic norm of missiology (i.e., contextual adaptation of the means of evangelization), which had been accepted by the official church for some decades now (though resisted by Rome earlier[24]) is also applicable in moral theology.[25] Simply put, the moral context, that is, the circumstances that surround a farmer in an Asian village, is very different from that of a businessman living in the city of New York. As such, the church's moral teachings need to be adapted (of course, without diluting the deposit of faith) according to the local contexts, and the best agent to do this obviously is the local church, headed by its local bishop(s). Given below are a few illustrations to show how local contexts demand nuances and variances in moral teaching:

- In both Asia and Africa, marriage is still regarded very highly and a vast majority of people still marry either civilly or in the church. The same cannot be said with regard to considerable numbers of people living in the developed regions where "living together" has almost become the accepted norm. Could the churches in those vastly different contexts merely propose the ideal teaching on marriage as if such concrete local variances of looking at married life did not matter?[26]

- It is well known that many African societies uphold the value of fertility of a married couple.[27] Among the many sociocultural values attributed to such a stance is that the parents depend on their children later in life when they are old. Since the civil laws do not make provisions for nursing homes, hospices, and other welfare facilities for the elders as they do in many Western developed societies, the full responsibility of caring for their elderly parents often falls on the children: hence, the value of fertility in a marriage, and consequently, the value of having as many children as possible. This is in total contrast to the currently prevalent trend in many Western/developed societies (Europe and North America), especially in a country like Italy, where the annual birth rate in 2015 was just eight babies born for every 1,000 residents, the lowest in the European Union.[28] If so, how can a universally valid general moral teaching on the importance of fertility be applied without any relevant nuancing/stressing in a country like Italy and in a country in Africa (where fertility is a prime value), that is, in two fundamentally different local contexts? Similarly, can the local church in a country like Bangladesh (where the birth rate is still very high), afford to formulate the teachings on the importance of fertility in the same way as the local church in Italy (where the birth rate is very low) would do?

- Quite a number of people in Asia and Africa often die due to violence, wars, malnutrition, lack of basic human needs, environmental disasters, etc., rather than due to euthanasia, refusal of treatment, or termination of artificial means of nourishment/hydration in a hospital context as happens in many developed countries and urban cities all over the world. Could the traditional pro-life issues of the church be highlighted with the same vigor (without any nuancing or adaptation) in both these vastly different realities?

- Then, there are specific socioeconomic issues on which the local churches in different societies have the duty to mobilize their faithful to bring them to the notice of those responsible in the governments of the respective countries. In an urban city in Europe, North America, Japan, or China, it may be the excessive pollution of the environment due to large-scale industries, whereas in a rural village in Sri Lanka or Tanzania, it may be the deforestation, so that the respective governments would act to combat them for the sake of the common good.

- In the sphere of social justice, many local churches in developing countries will have to put their accent on the moral evil of corruption because it is rampant in most of those societies. The churches in most of the developed countries may not need to stress this issue with the same intensity in their moral teachings.

- The use of condoms is very common in most societies today *in order to prevent births*. In the HIV/AIDS-rampant societies in Africa, while the respective churches will still have to stress the moral evil of the use of condoms when used as a contraceptive, could they not recommend in some cases the use of condoms as "the lesser evil" *when used to prevent the spread of that deadly disease*?

These few selected illustrations should suffice to convince the reader that while all the local churches should teach the same moral doctrine in communion with the universal church, each local church also should have its own nuances and variations in the same teachings, according to the pastoral needs of their particular contexts. This is precisely what Pope Francis says: "Different communities will have to devise more practical and effective initiatives that respect both the Church's teaching and local problems and needs" (*AL*, no. 199). In concrete terms, then, the bishops in charge of the local churches ought to have the space and the freedom (and of course, the willingness!) to exercise their own teaching role by themselves and through local/regional episcopal conferences for those teachings to be relevant and effective. Although this is common sense, surprisingly, it is not that commonly held within many circles of the Catholic Church as we will see in what follows in this essay. The current ecclesial structures that have not been adapted according to Vatican II's communion ecclesiology (communion between the universal and local churches) are inadequate to cater to such obvious pastoral demands.

Unfortunately, today in some quarters of the church in general—and among the influential decision makers within the church in particular—there is also a lurking fear that such recognition of the role of the local church in moral matters would eventually end up in subjective relativism. They seem to forget Pope Francis's warning: "Excessive centralization, rather than proving helpful, complicates the church's life and her missionary outreach" (*EG*, no. 32). Francis also notes that diversity "might appear as undesirable and leading to confusion" for those "who long for a monolithic body of doctrine guarded by all and leaving no room for nuance" (*EG*, no. 40). In fact, an unwarranted or undue fear psychosis is precisely the base of the majority of irrational and nonpastoral criticisms leveled against the pastoral solutions suggested by Pope Francis in his *Amoris laetitia* (especially those in chapter 8) wherein the local churches are called to play a leading role in accompanying, discerning, and integrating those who are estranged from the church due to their varying marriage situations.[29] Of course, for someone who has a sense of the history of the church, the true meaning of Christian morality (as an inner personally responsible morality based on one's properly formed conscience) that the pope suggests is not a problem at all. Moreover, for anyone who really believes in the special role of the Holy Spirit in formulating church doctrine, the unwarranted and obsessive fears of subjective relativism, and the consequent need for paternalistic protection of every believer, would not arise. Last but not least, if we consider the historical fact that in the early church (which had no central hierarchical teaching authority as we have today), there was no formidable threat of such subjective relativism that destroyed the one faith in Jesus Christ, then we ought to notice how unrealistic such fears are today.

The Indispensable Role of the Hierarchical Magisterium in Church Teachings

Christian tradition has always upheld that the bishops are the successors of apostles.[30] And it was to the apostles that Jesus Christ entrusted the explicit authority to bind and loose, which also surely includes the authority to teach what Christ imparted on them during his earthly ministry (Matt. 16:13–19; John 20:19–23). Thanks to this teaching role of the "successors of apostles" with the never-ending assistance of the Holy Spirit, not only is the essence of what Jesus lived and taught preserved, but the same is interpreted authentically for each passing age of history.[31] In this sense, one of the main graces bestowed on the church by Christ is its hierarchical magisterium.[32] One needs to note here that what follows from the gospels is the fact that all the apostles were given the authority, though Peter was given the explicit authority to be "the rock" or the head of the community of believers that also includes the apostles. As such, today, the church teaches that it is the entire College of Bishops (the successors of apostles) who together in communion with their head (Successor of Peter or the Bishop of Rome) have Christ's explicit mandate to teach.[33] Of course, as a successor of the apostles, each bishop,

too, has the right and duty to teach authoritatively but always in communion with
the head of the College of Bishops, namely, the Bishop of Rome.[34]

The Crucial Importance of the
Hierarchical Magisterium of the Local Church in
the Moral Discernment of the Faithful

The term *local church* has many meanings even within the Roman Catholic
Church in the theological and canonical parlance. For our purposes in this essay,
it means either the individual diocese or an individual episcopal conference that
consists of an assembly of dioceses. Following Vatican II teachings, Pope Francis has
shown that the local church "is the Church incarnate in a certain place, equipped
with all the means of salvation bestowed by Christ, but with local features" (*EG*,
no. 30). When in communion with the universal church (the Bishop of Rome),
the bishops of the local churches do exercise their teaching authority, individually
and together in their respective episcopal conferences. After all, Vatican II reversed
the pre–Vatican II trend to identify only the pope as the "vicar of Christ" and the
bishops as "vicars of the Pope."[35] The Council explicitly taught that the bishops, too,
are "vicars and ambassadors of Christ," and that they should not be "regarded as
vicars of Roman Pontiffs."[36] In *LG*, no. 27, we read that as "vicars and ambassadors
of Christ," bishops "have the sacred right and the duty before the Lord to make laws
for their subjects, to pass judgment on them and to moderate everything pertaining
to the ordering of worship and the apostolate." Moreover, bishops as successors of
the apostles are "preachers of the faith" and "authentic teachers, that is, teachers
endowed with the authority of Christ" (*LG*, no. 25). It is precisely such teachings of
the local churches through their bishops that obviously would be capable of taking
into account directly the particular contexts that surround the faithful within a
given particular church.

Local Magisterium of the Bishop

As things stand today, in the Catholic ecclesial structures, a diocese or a local
church ("a particular church") is entrusted to a diocesan bishop. Within such a local
church, the bishop's duty of teaching is described as follows: "In exercising their
duty of teaching—which is conspicuous among the principal duties of bishops—
they should announce the Gospel of Christ to men, calling them to a faith in the
power of the Spirit or confirming them in a living faith" (*CD*, no. 12).

So, among the principal duties of a bishop is to teach his flock in "calling them
to faith" and in "confirming them in a *living faith*." The faith they are to inculcate
has to be relevant to the latter: "The bishops should present Christian doctrine in
a manner adapted to the needs of the times; that is to say, in a manner that will
respond to the difficulties and questions by which people are especially burdened
and troubled" (*CD*, no. 13).

Local Magisterium of the Episcopal Conferences

Vatican II defined an "episcopal conference" as follows: "An episcopal conference is, as it were, a council in which the bishops of a given nation or territory jointly
exercise their pastoral office to promote the greater good which the Church offers
mankind, especially through the forms and methods of the apostolate fittingly
adapted to the circumstances of the age" (*CD*, no. 38.1). And *CD*, no. 18, says,

> Episcopal conferences, especially national ones, should pay special atten-
> tion to the very pressing problems concerning the above-mentioned
> groups. Through voluntary agreement and united efforts, they should look
> to and promote their spiritual care by means of suitable methods and insti-
> tutions. They should also bear in mind the special rules either already laid
> down or to be laid down by the Apostolic See which can be wisely adapted
> to the circumstances of time, place, and persons.

Thus, Vatican II, following the ancient church tradition, especially that of the
first few centuries, wished to restore not only the due competence of a bishop in his
teaching role as a successor of the apostles but also the competence of the regional/
national conferences of bishops in their teaching roles.

Setbacks for Vatican II Reforms on the
Teaching Authority of the Local Church

However, the reforms voted upon so enthusiastically by the Council Fathers to
strengthen the role of the local bishops in their particular churches were not to see
their full daylight during the five decades that have already passed since Vatican II.
This was due mainly to obstacles from the Roman Curia and from the reluctance or
the reticence of the bishops themselves to implement those reforms.

Obstacles from the Roman Curia

Legrand convincingly points out how the Vatican II reforms mentioned above
could not, as a whole, see the daylight during the post–Vatican II era.[37] To begin
with, though the Council considered the bishops to be "vicars and ambassadors of
Christ" rather than "vicars of the Roman Pontiff," the revised Code of Canon Law
published in 1983 is silent on these radical conciliar changes, and, in Canon 331,
the Code reserves the title "vicar of Christ" only for the pope.[38] Although Canons
368 (implicitly) and 753 (explicitly) of the same Code are in line with the Council's
vision of bishops as teachers of faith within their local churches, whatever efforts
that were undertaken in the aftermath of the Council[39] to decentralize the teaching
authority in the church simply fizzled out because they were tried within the same
old pre–Vatican II monarchical juridical model of the church.[40] Moreover, in his

well-researched essay, Faggioli demonstrates how during the post–Vatican II era, the Roman Curia regained its central role thanks mainly to Pope John Paul II and the then-head of the Congregation for the Doctrine of the Faith (CDF), Cardinal Ratzinger, who would later become Pope Benedict XVI.[41] The episcopal conferences that were made obligatory by the Council—where they were not already in existence—were granted "only a modest role of coordinating pastoral work."[42] Cardinal Ratzinger's oft-repeated assertion "A bishops' conference as such does not have a *mandatum docendi*. This belongs only to the individual bishops or to the college of bishops with the pope"[43] was gradually developed further by the Roman Curia. It culminated in 1998, when Pope John Paul II (with his *motu proprio* in the apostolic letter, *Apostolos suos*) stipulated that in order for the doctrinal declarations of an episcopal conference to be counted as of authentic magisterium, and to be published in the name of the conference itself, such declarations must be unanimously approved by the member bishops or receive the *recognitio* of the apostolic see if approved in plenary assembly by at least two-thirds of the member bishops.[44] According to Sullivan, there is no historical precedent for this requirement that a conciliar decree must have been unanimously approved for it to be published in the name of a council.[45] He also points out how, in the post–Vatican II period, the teaching of Pope John Paul II and the stipulations from Cardinal Ratzinger coincided in saying that the "teaching authority is properly held at only two levels: the universal level (the pope and the whole college of bishops with him), and the local level (the individual bishops)."[46] Sullivan goes on to say,

> This conclusion would imply that there is a basic theological difference between episcopal conferences and the regional councils of the early church that, by their exercise of teaching authority, played an important role in the faithful handing on and development of Christian doctrine. I do not see on what grounds one can judge that there is a basic theological difference between those regional councils and episcopal conferences.[47]

Thus, it appeared as if Rome (with the able assistance of the Curia) had reversed what the Council Fathers explicitly wished, that is, the reform of the Curia and restoration of the legitimate role of the bishops as heads of their local churches. Interestingly but ironically, during the same post–Vatican II era, some Vatican dicasteries seem to have usurped a certain degree of teaching authority for themselves, which of course has no roots either in the conciliar teachings on the magisterium or in the tradition. For example—as Sullivan himself points out—in its *Donum veritatis* of 1990, the CDF describes its own newfound "magisterial" function.[48] In this regard, Legrand gives the example of a German priest who asked the Holy See what he should do with regard to the issue of allowing young girls to serve Mass just as their brothers do. Instead of referring the priest either to his own vicar general or the local bishop, or the respective episcopal conference, two curial dicasteries reportedly resolved the problem, "in four or five stages, by reference to universal norms."[49] Legrand also gives the example of how the Indonesian episcopal conference had to submit their liturgical translations "to Rome for approval by people who neither speak nor understand our languages."[50] Needless to say, such recentralization of the Curia's role was a severe blow to the reforms intended by Vatican II to enhance the teaching role of the bishop/s in the local church.

Reluctance/Reticence of the Local Bishops Themselves

Ironically, the second major obstacle to strengthening the teaching role of the local bishops has been the somewhat puerile attitude of the vast majority of the bishops themselves. Either to evade personal responsibility or to please the Roman authorities (by being overtly docile to Rome), quite a number of bishops in the last three decades or so have been somewhat reluctant to shirk their overdependence on Rome. Examples of this sort of episcopal attitude coincide with the writer's own personal experiences. Imagine a cardinal-archbishop (who was also the president of a certain local episcopal conference) categorically saying that he simply could not "allow" any ecumenical dialogue in the area that came under the particular conference "unless and until Rome gives clear-cut concrete guidelines as to how to conduct such dialogues"! Similarly, a number of bishops also found it hard to accept that it is they who now will have to take responsibility in declaring nullity in some of the matrimonial nullity procedures when Pope Francis wished to expedite such processes through his two documents in August 2015.[51] Then, there is the other common illustration of quite a number of bishops asking the writer himself why Rome has not given clear-cut guidance in *AL* on the pastoral treatment of individual cases of the divorced and remarried Catholics, especially with regard to their possible reception of the Eucharist. As a matter of fact, one of the main criticisms against *AL* coming from quite a number of bishops has precisely to do with this particular point, that is, they have not been given clear-cut guidelines to be followed.

Ironically, it is this sort of overdependence on Rome on the part of the bishops of the local churches that reinforces the undue interference of the Roman Curia in the local churches. In this sense, one cannot level the blame squarely on the Roman Curia for usurping the authority of local bishops to teach. Such abdication of their rights and duties as teachers of faith by local bishops is not only irresponsible but also is a positive blocking of the functioning of the Holy Spirit in the local churches entrusted to their pastoral care. After all, they are the "vicars of Christ," the shepherds, through whom the Lord guides his respective flocks entrusted to them.

Conclusion

Authentic magisterial teachings consist of a healthy communion, a healthy dialogue between the universal and the particular churches. The words *being in communion* would today surely amount to "two-way traffic," that is, to a serious and sincere dialogue between the local and the universal churches. What is called for, therefore, is not the ignoring or the unilateral silencing of the local church (even when such a church is in error!) but being in dialogue with that church. After all, as Avery Dulles pointed out, there is no direct wire of an omniscient magisterium to the Holy Spirit with regard to truths of revelation.[52]

It is the local churches/local bishops who are best equipped to attend to the particular nuances and variations in the universal moral teachings in view of their particular circumstances or contextual factors: hence, the vital importance of reaffirming their crucial role in assisting the faithful in their concrete moral discernment processes. While one needs to appreciate the important role the Roman Curia is called upon to play in serving the pope and the local bishops in their communion or dialogues with each other, one simply cannot endorse any usurping of the teaching role of the local bishops by the Curia. This is because in the church, the unique role of teaching on faith and morals is explicitly and traditionally reserved for the pope in communion with the bishops, and vice versa. Equally unacceptable is the somewhat common, current tendency among quite a number of bishops to abdicate their teaching authority in their respective local churches. These realities feed into each other in a vicious cycle, in the process effectively blocking the divinely ordained teaching role of the local bishops within their churches. However, reaffirmation of the role of local bishops in teaching cannot be achieved realistically and successfully within the present ecclesial–canonical structures that still belong to the pre–Vatican II monarchical model of papacy. Hence, there is a need for new ecclesial–canonical structures that would effectively break the vicious cycle of the Roman Curian tendency to usurp the teaching role of the bishops, on the one hand, and the reluctance of the local bishops to assert and assume their right and duty to teach, on the other hand.

Thanks to the advent of Pope Francis, it seems that the vision of Vatican II for the church is gradually being resurrected. His stress on the need for structural reforms of the church, his appointing a group of nine cardinals representing all the continents of the world as a special advisory group, and his launching of a two-year synodal process to discern issues on family and marriage, a process in which the authentic, ancient role of synods was reinforced, etc., are all signs of a returning to the Vatican II ecclesiology of communion. But most of all, his insistence during the recent synodal process that bishops speak without fear, with *parresia* and *sub petro et cum petro*, clearly indicates his sincere determination in promoting a communion ecclesiology where all bishops have a say in the teaching office of the church. His unprecedented use of the statements of various local episcopal conferences in his three main official documents to date (*Evangelii gaudium*, *Laudato si'*, and *Amoris laetitia*) as sources (in the form of footnotes) also affirms the important role the episcopal conferences ought to play in the office of teaching. However, such efforts cannot remain merely as part of the personal agenda of Pope Francis—they ought to be continued even after him, in order to be faithful to Vatican II's intentions: hence, the need to initiate appropriate structural changes (beginning with a reform of canon law that is truly attuned to Vatican II's ecclesiology) that would ensure the continuity of an ecclesiology that is truly based on the communion of bishops with the pope with regard to teaching, which in turn would pave the way for the teaching of local churches, in and through local bishops and episcopal conferences.

Notes

1. At the very outset, I would like to highlight that there exists a clear-cut but subtle distinction between "the universal Church" and "the Roman Curia" which is naively overlooked very often when one deals with the universal magisterium, which strictly is to do with the Bishop of Rome teaching in communion with the College of Bishops spread all over the world. Such overlooking has also contributed to the diluting of the teaching competence of the local magisterium in the Catholic Church.

2. In this essay, the term *Vatican II* is used to refer to the Second Vatican Council.

3. Of course, in the search for moral truth, the dialogue ought to be not only with the local churches but also with non-Catholic Christians, other religions, various sciences, etc. The limited space of this essay would not allow me to consider these in detail.

4. See, for example, Pope John Paul II's encyclical letter *Veritatis splendor*.

5. Cf. Stephen B. Bevans, *Models of Contextual Theology* (Maryknoll, NY: Orbis Books, 1992).

6. Thierry-Marie Courau and Carlos Mendoza-Àlvarez, "Editorial," *Concilium* 1 (2017): 7.

7. Cf. Pope Francis, *Amoris laetitia (AL)*.

8. Thomas Aquinas, *Summa Theologiae*, I-IIae, q.94, art.4, in *St. Thomas Aquinas, Summa Theologiae*, ed. Thomas Gilby (Cambridge: Blackfriars, 1966), 28:89.

9. Pope Paul VI, *Octagesima adveniens*, no. 3.

10. Ibid., no. 4.

11. *AL*, no. 300.

12. Pope Francis, *Evangelii gaudium (EG)*, no. 16.

13. *Unitatis redintegratio*, no. 11. In this essay, all the documents of Vatican II are taken from Austin P. Flannery, ed., *Documents of Vatican II* (Grand Rapids, MI: William B. Eerdmans, 1975).

14. *Gaudium et spes*, no. 62.

15. Richard A. McCormick, *The Critical Calling: Reflections on Moral Dilemmas Since Vatican II* (Washington, DC: Georgetown University Press, 1989), 137.

16. Cf, Raymond E. Brown, *The Churches the Apostles Left Behind* (New York: Paulist Press, 1984).

17. Ibid., 22–23. See also ibid., 29.

18. *Unitatis redintegratio*, no. 14.

19. *Unitatis redintegratio*, no. 17.

20. *Christus dominus*, no. 12. The italics are mine.

21. *Christus dominus*, no. 13. The italics are mine.

22. Cf. Juan Carlos Scannone, "*Gaudium et Spes* and the Unfinished Agenda of Vatican II," *Origins* 45, no. 35 (2016): 595.

23. Cf. Gaudencio Rosales and C. G. Arevalo, *For All the Peoples of Asia: Federation of Asian Bishops' Conferences—Documents from 1970 to 1991* (Quezon City, the Philippines: Claretian Publications, 1992), 14–15.

24. For example, the missionary efforts of inculturation in the sixteenth and seventeenth centuries by the well-known Jesuits Matteo Ricci in China and Roberto de Nobili in India were firmly opposed by Rome.

25. Cf. Vimal Tirimanna, "FABC and Doing Moral Theology in Asia," in *Doing Asian Theological Ethics in a Cross-Cultural and Interreligious Context*, ed. Yiu Sing Lucas Chan, James F. Keenan, and Shaji George Kochuthara (Bangalore, India: Dharmaram Publications, 2016), 21–33.

26. This is precisely the point to which Pope Francis makes reference in *AL*, no. 36: "At times we have also proposed a far too abstract and almost artificial theological ideal of marriage, far removed from the concrete situations and practical possibilities of real families."

27. I have come to know more and more of this fact thanks to my students from Africa in Rome.

28. Cf. https://www.thelocal.it/20160708/italy-has-the-lowest-birth-rate-in-the-eu-report.

29. Cf. *AL*, no. 8.

30. Cf. *Lumen gentium* (*LG*), nos. 18, 20, 22. *CD*, nos. 2, 4, 6, and 8.

31. Cf. *Dei verbum*, nos. 8–10.

32. What we mean by "magisterium" in this essay is "the hierarchical teaching office" in the church exercised in communion by the pope and the bishops. For further details of this concept, see Francis A. Sullivan, *Magisterium: The Teaching Authority in the Church* (New York: Paulist Press, 1983).

33. Cf. *LG*, nos. 19, 24–25; *CD*, nos. 2, 4.

34. Cf. *LG*, nos. 24–25.

35. Cf. Richard R. Gaillardetz and Catherine E. Clifford, *Keys to the Council: Unlocking the Teaching of Vatican II* (Collegeville, MN: Liturgical Press, 2012), 115–16.

36. Cf. *LG*, no. 27.

37. Cf. Hervé Legrand, "Forty Years Later: What Has Become of the Ecclesiological Reforms Envisaged by Vatican II?" *Concilium* 4 (2005): 57–72.

38. Ibid., 62–63.

39. For example, the special Pontifical Commission appointed for the revision of the Code of Canon Law so that the revision would be in harmony with Vatican II teachings adopted as one of its main principles of revision: the principle of subsidiarity (Principle No. 5) according to which "greater weight should be given to particular legislation, even at the national and regional levels, so that the unique characteristics of individual churches will become apparent." Cf. John A. Alessandro, "General Introduction," in *The Code of Canon Law: A Text and Commentary*, ed. James A. Coriden et al. (New York: Paulist Press, 1985), 6.

40. Cf. Legrand, "Forty Years Later," 59–65. See also Charles E. Curran, *The Catholic Moral Tradition Today: A Synthesis* (Washington, DC: Georgetown University Press, 1999), 227.

41. Cf. Massimo Faggioli, "The Roman Curia at and after Vatican II: Legal-Rational or Theological Reform?" *Theological Studies* 76, no. 3 (2015): 562–67. Interestingly, Dulles notes how the same theologian, Ratzinger, argued in 1965 that National Episcopal Conferences are "genuine though partial realizations of collegiality." See Avery Dulles, "The Teaching Authority of Bishops' Conferences," *America* 148, June 11, 1983, 453–54.

42. Legrand, "Forty Years Later," 60.

43. "Rome Consultation on Peace and Disarmament: A Vatican Synthesis," *Origins* 12 (1983): 692.

44. Cf. Pope John Paul II, "The Theological and Juridical Nature of Episcopal Conferences," *Origins* 28 (1998): 157.

45. Cf. Francis A. Sullivan, "Development in Teaching Authority Since Vatican II," *Theological Studies* 73, no. 3 (2012): 573.

46. Ibid., 574.

47. Ibid.

48. Cf. The Congregation for the Doctrine of the Faith, *Donum Veritatis* (Vatican City: Libreria Editrice Vaticana, 1990), 18. As already pointed out above, according to official teachings, as "successors of apostles," only the pope in communion with the College of Bishops (and vice versa) hold the official teaching competence in the Church.

49. Hervé Legrand, "Roman Primacy, Communion between Churches, and Communion between Bishops," *Concilium* 5 (2013): 69.

50. Ibid. In this regard, one cannot forget the usurping role played by the Roman Curia in the recent translation of the New English Missal, over and above the bishops of the local churches wherein English is used at the eucharistic celebration.

51. Cf. Motu Proprio, *Mitis index dominus Iesus* (August 15, 2015) and Motu Proprio, *Mitis et misericors Iesus* (August 15, 2015).

52. Avery R. Dulles, "Conscience and Church Authority," in *Conscience: Its Freedom and Limitations*, ed. William C. Bier (New York: Fordham University Press, 1971), 253–54.

ON THE ECCLESIAL VOCATION OF THE MORAL THEOLOGIAN

Some Significant Shifts of Emphasis

Antonio Autiero

In recent decades, in the aftermath of the Second Vatican Council, we can observe a recurrent attention to the theme of the relationship between the magisterium and theology. This is repeatedly formulated as a focus on the "ecclesial vocation" of the theologian, and obviously, this decisively concerns the moral theologian, too. In this essay, I shall look more deeply at the modulation of this theme and examine whether there are shifts of emphasis that are significant for understanding the place of the moral theologian in the real context of the church and of society.

Historical Soundings

The ecclesial dimension of theology highlights the relationship between theology and the church's magisterium. This relationship is not new. It has its roots in traditions that certainly developed from more ancient times.[1] The recognition of the specific task of the church's magisterium—to guard, transmit, and interpret the content of the revealed message—is indisputably given in the church's self-understanding from its origins onward. The "apostolicity" of the church (that is to say, the fact that it is founded on the role played by the apostles and on the apostolic succession) means that the one who exercises the function of guide and teacher in the church is assured of the presence and action of the Holy Spirit, who inspires, assists, and protects the teacher in the exercise of the authority to teach in an unfalsified manner the content of the faith, namely, God's self-revelation in Jesus Christ.

This function took on a particular importance when, with scholasticism, the foundations were laid for a true and genuine scientific theology, which found a home in the nascent university institutions of the thirteenth century, where it entered into a relationship with other forms of knowledge. Above all, this scientific theology demonstrated the need to ensure that the contents of the faith had a logical foundation and that their understanding did not contradict the reason. The recurrent motif in Anselm of Canterbury (1033–1109) of a *fides quaerens intellectum* (a "faith that yearns for intelligibility"), and its reflections in similar expressions such as *intellectus fidei* ("intelligence of the faith") or *credo, ut*

94

intelligam ("I believe in order to understand"), do not always produce a symbiosis that is necessarily irenic and devoid of tensions between the scientific activity of theology and the authoritative exercise of the church's magisterium. In the context of the Reformation in the sixteenth century, there emerges a new awareness of the competence in believing and in teaching—a competence that is attributed to all the faithful. This generates a deeper understanding of the *sensus fidei* and the *sensus fidelium,* with very important consequences also for the question of the relationship between magisterium and theology.[2]

It must, however, be recognized that the demand made by the Reformation did not succeed in acquiring the same importance in the Catholic understanding of the relationship that we are describing here. On the contrary, the perspective that gradually crystallized led to an unbalanced development of this relationship. With the Council of Trent (1545–63), there began a process of unification of the theological approaches, at the cost of the pluralism of the schools. The magisterium thus tended to favor one theological school over the others and to make it the dominant theology that could be taught everywhere in the world. Another factor also played an important role: the dogmatic definition by the First Vatican Council in 1870 of the supreme and universally binding teaching authority of the pope (infallibility). The interlocking of these two tendencies led to a difficult epoch for theology, which often encountered mistrust and suspicion. Errors were listed and deviations that were considered illegitimate were condemned—as with the *Syllabus complectens praecipuos nostrae aetatis errores* ("Syllabus containing the principal errors of our times"), published by Pius IX in 1864—and all this was done at the expense of theology. The Syllabus condensed an openly antimodern vision of the church. It was only the Second Vatican Council that succeeded in adequately balancing and correcting this vision.[3]

The Years of the Second Vatican Council

The conciliar renewal could not have happened without the contribution of theology, which had already been at work for many decades with an impetus of renewal that, while not wishing to diminish the importance of the magisterium, also wanted to free itself from the state of marginality and subjugation in which it was confined. The ground was prepared for the Second Vatican Council, at which the presence of the theologians played a determinative and constantly expanding role, first by the Tübingen School[4] and later by the *Nouvelle Théologie,*[5] in different epochs and with different approaches.

The participation of the theologians as experts of the Council and as advisers to the individual conciliar fathers, as well as their activity in drawing up the documents, are striking signs of the recovery of the dignity of theology and of the recognition, also on the part of the magisterium, of its inalienable task and its essential value as a factor in the life of the church. This, however, does not eliminate the awareness that tensions and contrasts can emerge and that these need to be resolved with equilibrium and wisdom. In this way, it becomes ever clearer that theology, as a reality that belongs essentially to the church, lives on the basis of its double configuration: on the one hand, it evaluates, receives, and elaborates the affirmations by the magisterium, while on the other hand, it is called to carry out its scientific task, with a rational foundation, namely, the historical reconstruction and the critical and hermeneutical in-depth analysis of the questions that are to be tackled. The theologians who were present at the Council—but in general, anyone who works as a theologian—live this "double fidelity," conscious of its importance but also of the necessity of mediations and of "compromises."

A classic comment in this regard was made by Joseph Ratzinger, at that time a theologian and an expert at the Council. Writing about the approval of *Dei verbum,* he underlined the constructive contribution by the theologians in their mediation and collaboration. They were regarded as true and genuine partners of the magisterium, and it was acknowledged that they had the right and the duty to carry out their theological work as a scientific work, as a synthesis of what fidelity to the ecclesial tradition requires. This meant the recognition of theology as a critical science with a responsibility for the proclamation of the gospel in the world.

> But the basic compromise that . . . undergirds [*Dei verbum*] is more than a compromise. It is a very important synthesis: the text links fidelity to the ecclesial tradition with the assent to critical science, and thereby opens up, in a new way, the path for faith in today's world. The text does not renounce Trent and Vatican I, but nor does it mummify what happened in the past, since it is aware that fidelity in spiritual matters can be realized only through a continually renewed assimilation.[6]

The climate of trust that permeated the relationship between magisterium and theology, and that brought to light the ecclesial character of theology, was generated by a threefold orientation that occupied a central position at the Council.

In the first place, there was an ecclesiological orientation that was abandoning the traditional juridical categories, which had seen in the church a "perfect society" with a hierarchical structure. The new theological grammar of the pioneers of the Council,[7] which was taken over by the conciliar fathers, finds its center in the combination of other categories, such as the "people of God," the "body of Christ," and "fraternal *communio.*"[8] With various accents, but with a powerful convergence of their intentions, the theologians of that time developed the bases of an ecclesiology of communion, which the Council fully adopted.[9] It is interesting to note that the church had never previously produced such a profound work of reflection on itself, in its totality as a people under way, as the body of Christ, and as fraternity in communion. But this self-reflection by the church did not lead to a self-referential concentration on itself. We cannot speak here of an "ecclesiocentrism" heightened by the interests of the hierarchy that excluded, marginalized, or domesticated other voices in the church, especially those of the theologians. On the contrary, the conciliar ecclesiology made a determinative contribution, thanks also to theological research, and to a better understanding and discovery of the relative and relational character of the church itself.

It is here that we grasp the second orientation of the Council: it positions the church at the center of the substantial relationship with the Word and sends the church to its mission in the world. This means that among the conciliar documents with the title "Constitution," the primacy belongs, not to *Lumen gentium,* but to *Dei verbum.* Nor is *Lumen gentium* itself a self-contained document, but one that points to *Gaudium et spes,* in which it finds its fulfillment. The option of regarding the theology of revelation as the "first theology" (*theologia prima*), with primacy over ecclesiology,[10] contains an explosive charge that also affects the rethinking of the ecclesial vocation of the theologian. This option is expressed in terms of listening to the Word and of obedience to the Word, an obedience that is common to all believers, from the pope to the last of the faithful. Corresponding to the relativization of ecclesiology, therefore, there is a radicalization in the meaning of the encounter with the Word, which is heard in faith, celebrated in the liturgy, understood thanks to theological mediation, and put into action in one's life. The centrality of *Dei verbum* generates what we may call (with Christoph Theobald) the "vertical axis" of the hermeneutic of the Council.[11] This permits us to grasp that magisterium and theology have a common origin, namely, the primacy of the Word, and that they express a mission that is interlinked, not opposed. This mission converges in the service of the Word, and it is not regulated by the logic of power and the conflict between competences.

The combination of these two orientations that we have described generates a third, which is directly pertinent to the work of theology: a methodological orientation. Awareness of the insufficiency of the theological methodology, which had been adopted by the traditional theology of the schools until before the Council, had reached saturation levels. The limitations of the inductive structure of theological reflection were all too obvious. Theology was required to make plausible whatever the magisterium had declared in the form of binding assertions. The theologian was seen as a disseminator of knowledge relative to the contents of the faith that were elaborated and proclaimed by the magisterium. There was no lack of essentialist and abstract concentrations, formulations that were static and remote from real life. Ultimately, it was not only the role of theology and the profile of the theologian that suffered under asphyxiating forms that were devoid of contact with reality; the message of the faith itself made no impact on life.

The renewal came about via the question of theological methodology. The important contributions came from synergies of a variety of theological milieus at the time of the Council. In particular, the road that various theologians took together, which issued in the publication of a new systematic theology with the emblematic title *Mysterium salutis,* played a determinative role.[12] This marks a shift in the perspective: the salvation-historical perspective inspires a new working method and thus also delineates anew the profile of the theologian, his place in the church, and his relationship to the magisterium. Instead of the deductive method, we find a method that is authenticated by the structure of relationship. The starting point of this method is the conviction, well expressed programmatically by Karl Rahner, that theology (or dogmatics, as he put it) is based on the endeavor to gain a critical, and thus scientific, understanding of the contents of the faith—an understanding that must be at the service of people's real lives. It corresponds, not to the need felt by a theoretical curiosity, but rather to the request for salvation that is inherent in the human being.[13]

Theology is at the intersection of two poles, that of understanding the message and that of illuminating the mystery of the human being to whom the message is destined. The correlation between the essential factor (the truth of the faith) and the existential factor (the *conditio humana* in the real context of history) forms the new basis of theological work. It takes up provocative questions from various theological approaches at the time of the Council. On the one hand, we find the provocative demand that we look at the human being in an adequate manner. As the one for whom the message is destined, the person must be understood in the condition as a "hearer of the Word" (to borrow the metaphor employed by Karl Rahner as the title of his book).[14] A fundamental theological anthropology develops from the conviction that "God's revelation does not increase our knowledge by means of things that we could have learned otherwise. By means of the grace of hearing and understanding, it deepens knowledge about the profundities of human existence. In other words, it radicalizes, in a certain sense, the self-understanding of the human being."[15]

Correlation, as a methodology for theology and as a vital space for the role of the theologian in the church, is made more specific in the approach taken by Paul Tillich, namely, "the theology of culture."[16] For Tillich, "correlation establishes an interdependence between two independent factors: the existential questions and the theological answers . . . The 'theological circle' in which the theologian is located when he does theology is not a geometrical circumference with one single center, but rather an ellipse with two centers: existential questions and theological answers."[17] Accordingly, a double fidelity and a double competence are demanded of the theologian. This ecclesial vocation is carried out on the two radii of the foci of the ellipse.

To know and to reflect on human experience are not accessories. They are essential to the theologian's work. A look at experience enriches the idea of correlation: this is the contribution by Edward Schillebeeckx, especially in his thinking in the second period of his theological activity.[18] The question of meaning enters into the circuit of correlation and gives specific accents to the nature of the human being's questions and of the answers that faith can give. In this way, the method of correlation acquires a particular hermeneutical modulation that not only makes possible a better understanding of human experience, but also expands this experience, so that the human being becomes present to the world and to history, which the person must actively transform.[19]

This brief sketch has focused on the period of the Council. We can conclude by saying that there emerges an interesting, lively, and renewed role of theology and a profile of the identity of the theologian, whose ecclesial vocation is carried out in a double fidelity, in the service of the Word and of the human being. The tension between magisterium and theology is a creative tension characterized by a reciprocal stimulus and a fundamental reciprocal enrichment.

The Period after the Council

The lively theological activity in the period of the Council created an open climate of trust in the relations between magisterium and theology in the years immediately after the Council, too. The ecclesial vocation of the theologian did not need to be discussed too often, since it was perceived to be connatural and spontaneous. Attention concentrated rather on clarifying the epistemological status of theology, above all its rootedness in divine revelation. Accordingly, its relationship to the magisterium is not one of contrast, but of convergence, as Paul VI emphasized in his address on October 1, 1966, to the International Congress on the Theology of the Second Vatican Council, where he spoke of a "common root,"[20] namely, the revelation that is entrusted to the entire church. The International Theological Commission intervened in 1975 with a document containing twelve theses on the relationship between magisterium and theology. The discourse is structured in such a way that it lists the points in common as well as the diversity of the tasks and functions of each.[21] A shift in language already begins here, thanks to the preoccupation of giving greater centrality to the patrimony of the truths of the faith that must be guarded, protected, and spread.

With regard to the relationship between magisterium and theology, there now began an erosion of the trusting status that held in the Council years. Individual actions of suspicion and accusations against some theologians prompted the question whether that spirit of reciprocal collaboration was being lost. Otto Hermann Pesch speaks of a "restoration" in the 1970s and 1980s, with a gradual departure from the spirit of the "laborious compromise" of which Joseph Ratzinger had written in his commentary on *Dei verbum,* quoted above. Now theology was to be obligated to an internal and external obedience vis-à-vis the official teaching of the church, even if this teaching was not yet formally proclaimed as dogma. There was increasing evidence of a transition from the conciliar collaboration to a juxtaposition between magisterium and theology.[22] In the institutional apparatus of the ecclesiastical hierarchy, there was a growing consciousness of a

> right to investigate, to guide, and to control that went so far as to put scientific theology deliberately under observation . . . From the formal and material point of view, the ecclesiastical magisterium becomes the internal norm of theological work, that is to say, the proximate and general norm

of the truth . . . Theology, therefore, can be practiced only by a mandate that is delegated . . . in a particular manner by the pope.[23]

The ecclesial character of theology, and more precisely of the theologian, are measured more in terms of obsequiousness to the magisterium than in terms of recognizing the role of the theologian, the function of theology, and its necessary freedom of scientific research. This climate is undoubtedly dominated also by the discussion of the reception of the Second Vatican Council and by the antinomy between a hermeneutic of reform and a "hermeneutic of continuity."[24] It makes a particular impact on moral-theological matters and restructures for the moral theologian the question of the ecclesial vocation of the theologian and the relationship to the magisterium. The analyses of a growing fundamentalism on topics of moral theology[25] demonstrate the delicate nature of this question and indicate the tensions between moral theologians and the magisterium, which were a very specific issue at the time of the encyclical *Veritatis splendor* (1993).[26]

A few years earlier, on May 5, 1990, the Congregation for the Doctrine of the Faith had issued the Instruction *Donum veritatis,* on the ecclesial vocation of the theologian.[27] The first thing to be noted in this text is the transition from a discourse about theology to a discourse about the theologian. The central point is thus no longer (as in the 1975 document) the epistemological question of theology as a science, but the personal and communal profile of the person in the church who works as a professional theologian. By speaking of the theologian, not of theology, *Donum veritatis* gives the central place "to the person, not to his work, while admitting that, in the dynamism of the ecclesial communion, the *personal* dimension of the theologian converges on the *structural* and *institutional* dimension."[28] In the triangular relationship between faith, magisterium, and theology, and in view of the fact that the faith discloses itself to human adherence and human intelligence in a way that is always new and always more ample, the work of the theologian is recognized to be not only legitimate but also necessary. The theologian's ethos accompanies him/her in a readiness to be open, to accept the newness of understanding, of deeper investigation, and of the actualization of the contents of the faith. And since the revelation is given to the church as a whole, the Instruction recognizes the primacy of the community, even with regard to the function of the pastors and theologians (*Donum veritatis*, no. 14). It affirms that the theologians have the task of a double mediation: from the community to the magisterium, and from the magisterium to the community. Both of these movements—but genetically speaking, the first more than the second—confront the theologian with the necessity of belonging to the community of believers and being anchored therein. The theologian must understand and interpret the community's life of faith, its petitions for salvation, and its attempts to respond to the challenges of the age. This presupposes a reflective equilibrium that integrates the understanding of the faith and the understanding of the believer's existence, an equilibrium that is lost and ends up without orientation if the attention is directed principally to the individual truths of the faith, in their material object (*fides quae creditor*).

The existence of this risk is confirmed by the opening words of the Instruction, where we read: "The truth which sets us free is a gift of Jesus Christ" (*Donum veritatis*, no. 1). The truth shifts here to doctrine, to the truth about him.[29] The objective aspect of the faith becomes predominant, and this leads to a concentration on the doctrinal, theoretical, and veritative dimension. But *Dei verbum* teaches us that revelation is not the handing over to the human being of truths that concern God, but rather the invitation to enter into a relationship with him, in Jesus Christ, by the power of the Holy Spirit (no. 2).

This shift toward the truths that are to be believed also helps us to understand the most relevant consequences for the ecclesial vocation of the theologian and for the relationship to the magisterium. In this matter, *Donum veritatis* displays obvious weaknesses that we wish to recall briefly. Above all, as Dietmar Mieth observes, in this document "the authority of the magisterium is underlined with an extraordinary force, and limits are set to the thinking of theologians who do not conform."[30] The freedom of research in theology is subject to restrictive and severe conditions, so that the room for dissent and the articulation of a creative energy in the theologian's work are limited. And this leads to the request that one take a good "ecumenical" grip of the Instruction itself.[31]

Our analysis up to this point has shown how complex it is to speak of the "ecclesial vocation" of the theologian. The implications of this formula, with the various modulations of theological discourse, are decisive, as is the consciousness of the church and of belonging to the church, on the part both of the individual theologian and of the academic theological community. Now, we wish to examine what today's theological and ecclesial climate contribute to this question. In particular, we shall look at the profile of the moral theologian and at his/her ecclesial vocation, as these emerge in the pontificate of Pope Francis from *Evangelii gaudium* (*EG*; 2013) and *Amoris laetitia* (*AL*; 2016).

Shifts of Emphasis Today

The relationship between the proclamation of the gospel and the transmission of the doctrine about the matters of faith is modulating in a new way. The former has primacy over the latter. Francis draws inspiration for his pontificate from this principle of the radicality of the gospel, and he opens up new paths for theology too. All human beings "have a right to receive the Gospel. Christians have the duty to proclaim the Gospel without excluding anyone. Instead of seeming to impose new obligations, they should appear as people who wish to share their joy, who point to a horizon of beauty and who invite others to a delicious banquet" (*EG*, no. 14). We find here a basis for evangelization and a heuristic principle for the praxis of serving the gospel and serving humanity. At the same time, we are oriented toward a profound understanding of the necessary attention to the particularities of life, to the diversity of cultures, and to the concreteness of the existential conditions of those to whom the proclamation is addressed. This generates an image of the church that lives communion over against the horizon of the diversities and the differences, and the theologian too must know how to take this on board.[32]

EG, which is a genuine "exercise in contextual theology,"[33] indicates the horizon of meaning over against which we can rethink the church in terms of the local church. This is an important return to the conciliar ecclesiology, which lives from the primacy of the Word, and which enables us also to grasp the equilibrium between the universal church and the local church.[34] When he encourages us to reflect on the local church (*EG,* no. 30), the pope also finds the point of contact with the ecclesial value of the theologian. In *EG,* no. 40, and especially in *EG,* no. 133, the ecclesiality of the theologian is seen as situated in the context of the local church, in dialogue with its world and its culture. For the moral theologian, this shift of emphasis demands and produces a sensitivity and a particular competence in reading the features of the history of the persons and the people who make up the theologian's own church, in order to envisage creatively the responses to the question about meaning and to the existential questions that are proper to one's own culture. Theological investigation and ethical research are motivated, not by Roman centralism, but by fidelity to the history of the people who live in a local church. And the judgment on theology that emerges is not made principally by institutions with the task of verification and control, but rather by the believing people who are capable of expressing themselves with *parrhêsia* and of evaluating whether a theology is capable of transforming life.

For the moral theologian, taking seriously the existence and the experience of concrete persons in the fragility of their histories means participating in a privileged manner in the life of the church, in which the moral theologian shares the reception of the gospel and faith in the God who is close at hand. *AL* translates all this into a concrete language, when it takes on a double theological option of great importance: "love as the primary law, and mercy as the fruit of love."[35] This means that the metaphor of the church as a "field hospital" (*AL,* no. 291) is not sentimental rhetoric. On the contrary, it is the hermeneutical refinement of the look at reality; it points out the horizon of life and of the understanding of the church that calls the moral theologian to leave behind the logic of judgment and to enter into the pragmatism of the triad of "accompanying, discerning, and integrating weakness" (*AL,* nos. 291–312). And this is fidelity to the moral ideals, while warning conscientiously and responsibly against absolutizing these ideals (*AL,* nos. 36–38).

Conclusion

The profile of the moral theologian today, and his/her place in the local church, are definitively constructed on the labor in solidarity that entails interpreting existence, penetrating the richness of the gospel, accompanying believing existence, and rationally mediating solutions to conflicts. When we observe the style of Pope Francis's pontificate, we see that his path and the path of the moral theologian have all these things in common.

It is precisely this awareness that can generate the hope of rediscovering the climate of trust in the relationship between magisterium and theology that existed in the times and the places of the Second Vatican Council.

Notes

1. Herbert Vorgrimler, "Lehramt," in *Neues Theologisches Wörterbuch* (Freiburg: Herder, 2000), 380–81, offers a concise and incisive historical summary. On the specific relationship between the magisterium and moral theology, see Alfons Riedl, "Lehramt und Moraltheologie," in *Theologie und Hierarchie*, ed. Josef Pfammatter (Zurich: Benzinger, 1988), 79–110; Josef Schuster, *Ethos und kirchliches Lehramt. Zur Kompetenz des Lehramtes in Fragen der natürlichen Sittlichkeit* (Frankfurt a.M.: Knecht, 1984).

2. I refer here to my essay: "The *Sensus Fidelium* and the Magisterium from the Council to the Present Day: Moral-Theological Reflections," in *The Sensus Fidelium and Moral Theology*, ed. Charles E. Curran and Lisa A. Fullam (Mahwah, NJ: Paulist Press, 2017), 193–213.

3. Josef Ratzinger, *Principles of Catholic Theology* (San Francisco: Ignatius Press, 1987), 381, does not hesitate to say that the Council, and in particular *Gaudium et spes,* "serves as a counter syllabus and, as such, represents, on the part of the Church, an attempt at an official reconciliation with the new era inaugurated in 1789."

4. It is usual to distinguish various phases of the Tübingen School, in relation to the work of renewal by the Protestant and Catholic theologians at various periods. For the contribution made by Catholic theology, see Josef R. Geiselmann, *Die katholische Tübinger Schule: Ihre theologische Eigenart* (Freiburg, Germany: Herder, 1964).

5. For a very useful account, see Rosino Gibellini, *La teologia del XX secolo,* 2nd ed. (Brescia, Italy: Queriniana, 1993), 173ff.

6. See Josef Ratzinger, "Kommentar zu dei verbum," in *Lexikon für Theologie und Kirche* (Freiburg, Germany: Herder, 1967), EII:497–528, 571–83, at 503.

7. The contribution of Yves Congar was decisive. See his "Si può definire la Chiesa?" in *Santa Chiesa. Saggi ecclesiologici* (Brescia, Italy: Morcelliana, 1967), 38–39. For Congar, the category of the people of God is central. However, in view of the limitations that this category can contain, it must be integrated with that of the body of Christ: "Under the new covenant, the covenant of the promises that are realized by the incarnation of the Son and by the gift of the Spirit, the people of God receives a status that can be expressed only in the category of the body of Christ," in "La Chiesa come popolo di Dio," in *Ecco la Chiesa che amo!* (Brescia, Italy: Queriniana, 1969), 39.

8. See Severino Dianich, *Ecclesiologia. Questioni di metodo e una proposta* (Cinisello Balsamo, Italy: Ed. S. Paolo, 1993), chaps. 6–9.

9. One specific contribution to the elaboration of the category of communion arrived much earlier than the Council itself. It goes back to the German social philosopher and theologian Friedrich Pilgram (1819–90), a convert to Catholicism. Thanks also to his sensitivity to social issues, he foresaw the Second Vatican Council and elaborated the idea of a church in the form of a "communion of human beings with God and with one another": *Physiologie der Kirche* (Mainz, Germany: 1860). This book was republished as a paperback in 2012 by Nabu Press. See also Bernhard Casper, "Pilgram," in *Lexikon für Theologie und Kirche*, 3rd ed. (Freiburg, Germany: Herder, 2006), 8:302–303.

10. See Ormond Rush, *The Eyes of Faith: The Sense of the Faithful and the Church's Reception of Revelation* (Washington, DC: Catholic University of America Press, 2009); and Ormund Rush; "Sensus Fidei: Faith 'Making Sense' of Revelation," *Theological Studies* 62, no. 2 (2001): 231–61, where he proposes a hermeneutical approach to the understanding of the *sensus fidei*.

11. Christoph Theobald, *Dans les traces de la constitution Dei verbum du concile Vatican II* (Paris: Du Cerf, 2009).

12. Johannes Feiner and Magnus Loehrer, eds., *Mysterium Salutis. Grundriss heilsge-schichtlicher Dogmatik* (Einsiedeln, Switzerland: Benziger, 1965–1976). This work consists of seven volumes in the original German edition; it was translated into numerous languages, and is the real signal of the renewal of twentieth-century systematic theology.

13. See Karl Rahner, "Saggio di uno schema di dogmatica," in *Saggi teologici* (Rome: Edizioni Paoline, 1965), 51–111.

14. Karl Rahner, *Hörer des Wortes* (Munich: Kösel Verlag, 1963).

15. Herbert Vorgrimler, *Karl Rahner. Gotteserfahrung in Leben und Denken* (Darmstadt, Germany: Primus Verlag, 2004), 204.

16. Paul Tillich, *Theology of Culture* (New York: Oxford University Press, 1959).

17. Gibellini, *La teologia del XX secolo,* 97.

18. See Edward Schillebeeckx, *God, the Future of Man* (London: Sheed and Ward, 1969).

19. In this semantic broadening of the methodology of correlation, one can find inter-esting points of contact between Schillebeeckx's theology of experience and the political theology of Johann Baptist Metz, as well as links to the "new critical theory" of Jürgen Habermas. On this, see Gibellini, *La teologia del XX secolo,* 347ff.

20. "At vero illud maximi momenti est, quod Magisterio et Theologiae communis est radix, scilicet divina Revelatio, quae per Spiritum Sanctum catholicae Ecclesiae tradita est," in *Acta apostolicae sedis* (*AAS*) 58 (1966): 889–96, at 890.

21. International Theological Commission, *The Ecclesiastical Magisterium and Theology* (Rome: 1975).

22. Otto H. Pesch, *Das zweite vatikanische Konzil: Vorgeschichte, verlauf, ergebnisse, nachgeschichte* (Würzburg, Germany: Echter Verlag, 1993), 207.

23. Ibid., 288. Pesch's statements are backed up by the relevant studies by Max Seckler, which he duly cites.

24. This expression was used by Benedict XVI in his address to the College of Cardi-nals and the members of the Roman Curia on December 22, 2005. It contains "a double message . . . On the one hand, the disparagement of the Council is rejected. And on the other hand, the Council as an event of renewal is relativized": Stephan Goertz, Rudolf Hein, and Katharina Klöcker, "Zur Genealogie und Kritik des Katholischen Fundamentalismus: Eine Einführung," in *Fluchtpunkt Fundamentalismus? Gegenwartsdiagnosen Katholischer Moral* (Freiburg, Germany: Herder, 2013), 11–76, at 39 n. 11.

25. The essay by Franz Böckle, "Fundamentalische Positionen innerhalb der Katho-lischen Moraltheologie," in *Die verdrängte Freiheit. Fundamentalismus in den Kirchen*, ed. Hermann Kochanek (Freiburg, German: Herder, 1991), 137–54, is highly relevant here.

26. "The encyclical, especially the third chapter, with the Pope's impressive and striking warnings that one must accept even harsh sacrifices for the moral good, makes the reader sadly conscious of how deep the rift of alienation and incomprehension between

magisterium and theology has become in recent years": Walter Kerber, "Veritatis Splendor," in *Stimmen der Zeit* 12 (1993): 793–94.

27. *AAS* 82 (1990): 1550–570 (quotation below from the official English translation).

28. Angelo Antón, "I teologi davanti all'Istruzione *Donum veritatis*. Il compito della teologia tra 'ecclesialità' e 'scientificità' e il suo rapporto col magistero ecclesiastico," *Gregorianum* 78, no. 2 (1997): 224.

29. There is something similar in the discourse of Benedict XVI to the members of the International Theological Commission on December 7, 2012: "This gift . . . establishes in the believer a kind of supernatural instinct that has a vital connaturality with the object of faith itself."

30. Dietmar Mieth, "Ein Dokument voller Widersprüche," *Streitgespräch um Theologie und lehramt. Die Instruktion über die Kirchliche berufung des Theologen in der Diskussion*, ed. Peter Hünermann and Dietmar Mieth (Frankfurt a.M.: Knecht, 1991), 118–137, at 118.

31. This question is discussed by Reinhard Frieling, "Instrumentalisierte Freiheit der Theologie? Bemerkungen eines Evangelischen Theologen zur Römischen 'Instruktion über die Kirchliche berufung des Theologen' (Mai 1990)," *Zeitschrift für Theologie und Kirche* 88 (1991): 121–38.

32. "The pursuit of ecclesial communion in diversity or difference rather than in uniformity of ideas and practices demands a deeper understanding of the relationship between faith and culture, one that grasps the *dynamic* character of this relationship and the inescapable need for ongoing dialogue between the Gospel proclamation and the cultures including the culture of secular modernity": Allan F. Deck, *Francis, Bishop of Rome: The Gospel for the Third Millennium* (New York: Paulist Press, 2016), 71.

33. Gerard Wehlan, "Evangelii gaudium come 'teologia contestuale': aiutare la Chiesa ad 'alzarsi al livello dei suoi tempi,'" *Evangelii gaudium: il testo ci interroga. Chiavi di lettura, testimonianze e prospettive*, ed. Humberto M. Yánez (Rome: G&BP, 2014), 23–38, at 23.

34. See Ormond Rush, "Sensus Fidelium und Katholizität. Ortskirche und Universalkirche im gespräch mit Gott," in *Die Wechselseitige rezeption Zwischen Ortskirche und Universalkirche. Das Zweite Vatikanische Konzil und die Kirche im osten Deutschlands*, ed. Myriam Wijlens (Würzburg, Germany: Echter Verlag, 2014), 151–60.

35. Stephan Goertz and Caroline Witting, "Un punto di svolta per la teologia morale? Contesto, ricezione e ermeneutica di *Amoris laetitia*," in *Amoris laetitia. Un punto di svolta per la teologia morale?* ed. Stephan Goertz and Caroline Witting, Italian edition by Antonio Autiero (Milan: San Paolo, 2017), 13–79, at 64ff.

Part II

Contexts and Perspectives

THE ROLE OF THE MORAL THEOLOGIAN IN THE VIETNAMESE CHURCH

Nhu Y-Lan Tran

The moral theologian is a member of society, so his/her work is certainly conditioned by concrete historical and cultural contexts. Grasping the local church's situation is key to understanding the role of the moral theologian. The first section in this essay describes the difficult situation of the local church and some challenges in sociopolitical ethics in Vietnam, a small communist country in Southeast Asia. The second section shows how the moral theologian may hopefully contribute more creatively and effectively to the church and to society.

The Context of the Local Church

A Church Persecuted for Its Perceived "Foreignness"

Catholicism came to Vietnam in the sixteenth century, brought by Western missionaries along with the new wave of European commercial ventures. Hence, from its beginnings, Catholicism was seen as a Western religion that was tied to foreign powers. Fearful that those who followed Western religions would deny their ancestors, as well as not be faithful to the Royal Court, the kings promulgated decrees banning Catholicism from 1625 to 1886.[1] Innumerable arrests, imprisonments, and killings were executed across the country over four centuries. About 130,000 Vietnamese Catholics shed their blood to witness to their faith. But the saying of Tertullian that "the blood of the martyrs is the seeds of Christians" proved once more to be true, as the number of Vietnamese Catholics has increased rapidly.[2]

The persecution has continued in various forms until now, with a brief respite during the French colonization period from 1887 to 1954. The persecution has affected the local church in its practice of faith. After the unification of the country in 1975, the communist government confiscated the church's social and cultural institutions (such as schools and hospitals in South Vietnam) and restricted the activities of the clergy and religious.[3] Despite many difficulties, the church has enjoyed a good reputation among the inhabitants because of its charitable activities. In recent years, Catholics have been permitted to manage kindergarten schools.

Today, the government still regards Catholics as second- or third-class citizens.[4] Since the collapse of the communist-ruled states in Eastern Europe in 1989, the government has started an "open door policy," and has shown a more positive attitude toward respecting people's faith beliefs. Nonetheless, threats of violence, coercion, and harassment still exist,[5] and the church has had almost no voice in Vietnamese society.

A People Divided by Two Ideologies

The past decades saw the confrontation between North Vietnam's communist movement for national unification and South Vietnam's republican democracy, a confrontation that involved American military forces and brought the nation into a long and grueling war.[6] The devastating consequences of war destroyed infrastructures, hindered intellectual progress, harmed the people's physical health, and above all inflicted lasting mental, emotional, and spiritual wounds.[7] Even now, a large number of people in North and South Vietnam, as well as Vietnamese abroad, cannot look beyond the war[8] and find it difficult to imagine a future in which peace, forgiveness, and cooperation could exist.

The Need to Reconstruct an Ethic of Integral and Authentic Development

A reconstruction of the basic ethics of being human, that is to say, how the full and authentic development of the human person can be and ought to be, is a major challenge as Vietnam undergoes industrialization. The industrialization model currently being pursued in Vietnam is not sustainable. Many industrial factories are releasing harmful chemical wastes in common drainages and rivers, thereby threatening long-term public health.[9] In early April 2016, in the Middle Region, the country's worst environmental disaster affected millions of people. Formosa Ha Tinh Steel, a unit of Taiwan's Formosa Plastics that runs an $11 billion steel plant, sullied more than 200 km (125 miles) of coastline, killing more than 100 tons of fish and devastating the environment, jobs, and economies of four provinces. The Middle Region is expected to take a decade to completely recover from this environmental disaster.[10]

Excessive exploitation of agricultural lands is gradually exhausting arable resources.[11] Thousands of hectares of forests have been destroyed, ironically, even by officials who are responsible for forest protection. Flash floods and heavy floods follow the destruction of forests.[12] As of this writing, Phu Yen Province's government has approved the destruction of nearly 116 hectares of protective forest in order to build a golf course.[13]

Moreover, unabated toxicity in the food supply is an urgent concern. Many vegetables and fruits are contaminated with toxic chemicals that farmers use to stimulate their agricultural products to grow better and faster, as well as to keep their freshness or lengthen their shelf life.[14] Commercial ethics and the rights of consumers still appear to be alien to Vietnam. Farmers and traders disregard the dangers toxic foods pose to public health; they are concerned instead with maximizing profits and interests.

The Degradation of Ethics in the Educational System

The educational philosophy of Vietnam as manipulated by incompetent officials has emphasized pragmatism. Shaping the ethical sentiments and moral character of younger generations is only a secondary consideration. The pragmatic desire to attain economic and material goals with whatever means, and at whatever cost,[15] is omnipresent in education[16] and in the society as a whole. Consequently, many young people go abroad to study and do not want to return.

Role of Moral Theologians

Inculturation and Relationship to the Magisterium

In his inspiring article, "Ecclesia in Asia: Challenges for Asian Christianity,"[17] Peter Phan, a noted Vietnamese American theologian, rightly raises the need for Asian churches themselves to do theology. This is necessary for Christianity to shed its image as a foreign religion and to be intelligible in the Vietnamese context. Inculturation means a twofold process of "insertion of the gospel into a particular culture" and "introduction of the culture into the gospel."[18] Concretely, the Vietnamese church should consider the basic principles of Catholic faith and morality, and examine how these can work in the context of Vietnamese culture and values. The Vietnamese culture, in turn, may enrich the meaning of the gospel.[19] The fruit of inculturation is "the transformation of the culture from within by the gospel and the enrichment of the gospel by the culture with its new ways of understanding and living it."[20]

Redemptorist priest Vimal Tirimanna, the Sri Lankan theologian, rightly lamented that most Asian theologians have walked along "the beaten track of the classical Western moral theology" (neoscholasticism), a theology that sees faith as assent to a body of truths and dogmas and uses philosophy to explain them.[21] Meanwhile, Asian theology today begins with experience of the faith and dialogues with sociology, psychology, and anthropology, along with Asian resources for analyzing reality.[22] As the Second Vatican Council acknowledges, it is "thanks to the experience of past ages, the progress of the sciences, and the treasures hidden in the various forms of human culture, [that] the nature of the human person is revealed and *new roads to truth are opened*." Theologians have taken up the challenge of finding diverse ways of theologizing in a plurality of contexts and cultures.[23]

On the part of the pope and the universal church, when they exercise authority, they should extend collegiality to other churches in teaching moral issues, in order to respect the work of the Holy Spirit in each local church. It is the pope and the bishops who hold official teaching authority. The teaching role of theologians is "professional," rather than authoritative. This privilege and the assistance of the Holy Spirit do not exempt the pope and bishops from the tasks of ongoing learning and self-training as well as exchange with theologians and other laypersons in order that the pope and bishops have sufficient foundation and information for their discernment, and can avoid errors as much as possible.

Phan criticizes the use of the terms *faithful* and *obedient* to express the relationship between the local church and the pope, and instead prefers collegiality and solidarity. For him, the term *faithful* should be exclusively reserved to the relationship between Jesus Christ and believers. I think that this is a very delicate yet important distinction for the Vietnamese church to consider as it seeks to establish a good, creative, and fruitful relationship with the pope and the universal church.

Phan is right when he suggests that the terms *obedient* and *faithful* in the Asian context could imply the obedience of mandarins toward the liege lord in a feudal regime.[24] However, we need to modify the meaning of these terms in accordance with the context of our modern society. Faithfulness has been a great and treasured virtue of Vietnamese Confucian morality. It is one among the Confucian "Ngũ thường": Nhân, lễ, nghĩa, trí, tín (five cardinal virtues: benevolence, courteousness, righteousness, prudence, and faithfulness). Faithfulness is also the basis of five Confucian relationships, namely, between homeland–citizens,[25] parent–child,[26] husband–wife, brother–sister, and friend–friend. How can the Vietnamese reject such a cardinal virtue in their relationship with the universal church? The Vietnamese owe obedience and faithfulness not in the feudal, but ecclesial context, that is, faithfulness to Christ himself who gave Peter and his successors the authority to lead peoples.

The risky point in Phan's criticism is the danger of separation from, and against, the pope and the universal church when conflict appears. Conflicts are unavoidable in the context of today's culture of pluralism, individualism, and liberalism. The aim is not to destroy authority but to find out how to use authority in a constructive, loving, and serving way as Jesus does. Admittedly, this is a weighty challenge for both parties. In the pilgrim condition of the church, and given the pluralism in today's world, the pope's authority is necessary to avoid chaos. To be sure, the other extreme to be avoided could be overcentralization and dictatorship. The universal church must avoid falling into these extremes. Paul Lakeland, for instance, reserves the role of doctrinal teaching to the pope and the college of bishops but they will do so as "the voice of the whole community, not separated from it."[27] Moral theologians' disagreement with magisterial teaching on some issues can be constructive. The moral theologian can listen to the experience and voices of Christians and articulate these perspectives as contributions to the progress of moral theology.[28]

Both faithfulness and collegiality are cornerstones for establishing unity in diversities and among local churches, the universal church, and the pope.

Searching for Ethical Responses to National Issues

The moral theologian is to seek ethical responses to the nation's challenges and to help the church in executing its mission in the world. The moral theologian helps the local church to find answers to the socioeconomic, religious, and moral issues confronting the nation.

However, with the dictatorship of the communist government in Vietnam, it is hard or even dangerous for the church and moral theologians to protest against the government's violation of human rights. However, "even a worm will turn." Sometimes people have demonstrated to protest government injustice, but the government rapidly suppresses the rallies by force.[29] Most of the time, though, the moral theologian's activities have been limited to within the church, parishes, and theology institutes. What the moral theologian could do in the meantime is to raise public awareness of human dignity and human rights. Inside Vietnamese secular society there rests a number of good-willed and wealthy people who want to contribute to the development of the country through the renewal of the educational system. I think that Catholic moral theologians may collaborate with these good-willed people to guide young generations toward the authentic flourishing of humanity.

Dialogue with Communists and Peoples of Other Faiths

Our pope sets an example for Vietnamese moral theologians to engage in dialogue with the communists and people of other faith. Since starting his papacy in 2013, Pope Francis has been a restless voice of reason and decency when tackling the world's challenging issues. While President Trump has been calling for building walls, Francis insists that those who build walls and not bridges are not Christians. When some Western politicians called for accepting only Christian refugees, the pope welcomed Muslim refugees in Rome and washed their feet in the ceremony on Holy Thursday. He also reminds Christians that Jesus himself was a refugee. While others warned about the threat of refugees to Europe's identity, Pope Francis sees this crisis as an "opportunity to grow." In his address to the US Congress in September 2015, the pope said that instead of fear for the refugees' chaos, we should listen to the refugees' stories, look at their weak bodies, and do our best to respond to their urgent needs. As to the question of whether Islam is a religion of peace or violence, Pope Francis has many times insisted that terrorism has no religion. Therefore, when Pope Francis recently visited Egypt and addressed Muslim-majority societies, he brought with him the best of Christianity.[30] I believe that Pope Francis is paving a new way of dialogue, which is very important in the Vietnamese context as well. Furthermore, in the dialogue with people of other religions or atheists, the language of virtues, humanity, and authentic human flourishing may build a bridge between Catholicism and other people. When I have talked about ecological ethics to both Christian and non-Christian students, I evoke in them love for the country, the dignity of human life, and the virtue of treasuring the lives of creatures. Those are common virtues for all Vietnamese, regardless of religious and political positions.

Transforming Male-Dominated Church Institutions

According to an unofficial statistic, the number of theologians in Vietnam is less than one hundred persons among around eight million Catholics. Of these, one can count the number of moral theologians on the fingers of one hand. I received my doctorate in moral theology in 2006 from Weston Jesuit School of Theology,

MA, USA, and became Vietnam's first Catholic woman moral theologian. To this day, I am still the only Catholic woman moral theologian in Vietnam.

The Vietnamese church has accepted women theologians; a number of them have been invited to teach at different theology institutes across Vietnam (except major seminaries). In 2007, the invitation for me to teach in the Vietnamese Jesuit Scholasticate was historic. The then-director told me, "This is the first time in Vietnamese Jesuit tradition that a woman professor enters our institute to teach Jesuits." This privilege is truly groundbreaking, and signals a shift in the Vietnamese church regarding the teaching role of women.[31] Today there is another woman biblical theologian who has been invited to teach in the Jesuit Scholasticate. There seems to be a pressure, and corresponding efforts on the part of the Vietnamese church, to involve more women in major seminary teaching in Vietnam. In 2014, I was honored to be the first woman professor at St. Joseph Major Seminary of Ho Chi Minh archdiocese in its 150-year history. Seminarians have welcomed me warmly, expressed their gratitude for my teaching, and their joy at having "a cool wind" in their formation. I have also taught in other theologates such as the Dominican Center of Studies, Franciscan Scholasticate, Salesian Don Bosco Theology Institute, De La Salle Theology Institute, and Theology Institute for Men Religious. These theologates receive students from different religious congregations. My students respect me as their professor and also see me as their mother, sister, and friend. I find that the students appreciate my professional competence as well as my feminine characteristics of caring, delicateness, generosity, and tenderness. During my studies in the United States, I experienced my professors' loving devotion for their students. In turn, I devote my life to students following the examples of my professors, first and foremost, James Keenan, the American Jesuit, to whom I owe my success today as a valuable female moral theologian in Vietnam. My passionate contribution to the church is an expression of my gratitude toward my parents, professors, benefactors, and congregation.

Moreover, I am the only woman theologian member of the Committee for the Doctrine of the Faith in Vietnam, which is directly under the Catholic Bishops' Conference of Vietnam (CBCV). Along with my work as a medical doctor and teacher of theology, I collaborate with the bimonthly journal *Hiệp Thông* (Communion), an official journal of the CBCV. Some of the bishops are getting to know me. These bishops, a great number of priests, and Catholic believers express their confidence in the logic, clarity, and convincing arguments of my medical–bioethical and sexual writings that are based on scientific facts and theological reasoning. Last year, the director of St. Joseph Major Seminary in Saigon invited me to give a seminar on chastity for all the priest formators of three dioceses.

Nowadays, more and more women religious embark in higher theological study abroad, and hopefully they will engage in the training of both religious men and women and seminarians. I engage in moral teaching with love for the church, and with my competences and wisdom. I am joyful to be a woman theologian who passionately contributes to the formation of future priests so that they may become good pastors (cf. John 21:15–18). However, a large number of priests still harbor the patriarchal mind-set. The local church has been traditionally patriarchal and hierarchical. I often remind my students that priesthood is a free gift from God, and that in the Catholic Church, Jesus himself has shown that leadership must be understood as service and not domination, and that priests should respect and listen to women's voices.

Conclusion

Moral theologians in Vietnam are challenged to counter the representation of Christianity as a Western religion through inculturation, to promote dialogue between different faiths and ideologies, to search together with peoples of good will for ethical responses to national concerns, and to transform church structures from within. In this process, the magisterium as official teaching authority must listen closely to the voices of Vietnamese theologians and laity.

Notes

1. J. B. An Dang, "Vietnamese Catholics under Communist Iron Grip," http://viet-catholic.net/News/Html/59371.htm.

2. Catholic Bishops' Conference of Vietnam (CBCV), "History of the Catholic Church in Vietnam," http://cbcvietnam.org/history/history-of-the-catholic-church-in-vietnam.html.

3. An Dang, "Vietnamese Catholics under Communist Iron Grip."

4. Cf. Nguyen Thai Hop, "The Complex Relationship between Catholics and Vietnamese Government," http://www.daminhvn.com/thuvien/tailieu/ghvn-nhanuoc.htm (original in Vietnamese).

5. Cf. La Croix International, "Catholics in Northern Vietnam Seek Help to End Persecution," https://international.la-croix.com/news/catholics-in-northern-vietnam-seek-help-to-end-persecution/3710.

6. MSN, "Vietnam War," http://encarta.msn.com/encyclopedia_761552642/vietnam_war.html.

7. Cf. Dang Thuy Tram, *Last Night I Dreamed of Peace: The Diary of Dang Thuy Tram*, trans. Andrew X. Pham (New York: Harmony, 2007).

8. Committee of Science and Society of Vietnam, *A Number of Questions of Catholic History in the History of Vietnamese People* (Ho Chi Minh City: Ho Chi Minh City Publication, 1988) (original in Vietnamese).

9. Phuong Nguyen and Tran Vu, "Angry Because of Environment Pollution," *Weekend Youth*, November 2, 2008): 14–16 (original in Vietnamese).

10. My Pham and Mai Nguyen, "Vietnam Says Recovery from Formosa Industrial Disaster Could Take a Decade," http://www.reuters.com/article/us-vietnam-environment-formosa-plastics-idUSKBN14C1F5.

11. Le Quoc Doanh, Ha Dinh Tuan (Vietnam Agricultural Science Institute), and Andre Chabanne, "Upland Agro-Ecology Research and Development in Vietnam," http://agroecologie.cirad.fr/pdf/1141426824.pdf (original in Vietnamese).

12. Tran My, "Protecting Forests as Protecting the Nation," http://tiengnoitu-dodanchu.org/vn/modules.php?name=News&file=article&sid=4981 (original in Vietnamese).

13. "Protective Forest Destroyed for Phu Yen Golf Course," http://english.vietnamnet.vn/fms/environment/177133/protective-forest-destroyed-for-phu-yen-golf-course.html.

14. Nguyen Cam, "Poison in Vegetables and Fruits: Being Controlled Superficially," *Women*, November 2, 2008, 6 (original in Vietnamese).

15. Tran Huu Quang, "Two Pathologies in Education," http://www.tuoitre.com.vn/Tianyon/Index.aspx?ArticleID=244234&ChannelID=118 (original in Vietnamese).

16. Thuong Hoang, "Education Has Become a Means of Exploiting Money," http://vietcatholic.net/News/Html/60503.htm (original in Vietnamese).

17. Peter Phan, "Ecclesia in Asia: Challenges for Asian Christianity," in *Christianity with an Asian Face* (Maryknoll, NY: Orbis Books, 2003), 171–83.

18. Peter Phan, *In Our Own Tongues, Perspectives from Asia on Mission and Incultura-tion* (Maryknoll, NY: Orbis Books, 2003), 6.

19. CBCV, "Pastoral Letter of the Year 1980," http://cbcvietnam.org/cbcv-s-messages/pastoral-letter-1980-of-cbcv.html, n.11.

20. Peter Phan, *In Our Own Tongues*, 6.

21. Cf. Jose Kavi, "Catholic Moral Theologians Scan Asian Reality," https://www.ncronline.org/news/global/catholic-moral-theologians-scan-asian-reality.

22. Ibid.

23. Cf. Fr. Tony Neelankavil, "The Charism of a Theologian in the Local Church," Paper presented in the 15th Colloquium of the Bishops and Theologians organized by the Doctrinal Commission of the Catholic Bishops Conference of India at NBCLC from July 8–10, 2010, on the theme Office and Charism within the Understanding of the Church as Participatory Communion.

24. Phan, "Ecclesia in Asia," 17.

25. Originally, this was "the king–subject" relationship, but today, it is more advisable to transfer it to "the homeland or nation–citizen."

26. Originally, this was "father–son" relationship; I would like to modify it as "parent–child" to adapt better to today's society.

27. Paul Lakeland, *The Liberation of the Laity: In Search of an Accountable Church* (New York: Continuum, 2003).

28. Christopher Vogt, "An Australian Perspective on the Role of the Moral Theologian in Church and Society," http://catholicmoraltheology.com/an-australian-perspective-on-the-role-of-the-moral-theologian-in-church-and-society/.

29. Binh Minh, "Rallies in Vietnam over Mysterious Mass Fish Deaths," http://viet-catholic.org/News/Html/183767.htm.

30. Halim Shebaya, "Pope Francis in Egypt: A Voice of Reason," http://www.aljazeera.com/indepth/opinion/2017/04/pope-francis-egypt-voice-reason-170429115853335.html.

31. Jesuits are considered to be the top of most intellectual congregations in Vietnam. So, if someone can teach in a Jesuit theologate, he/she will surely be qualified to teach in other theologates.

Catholic Ethics and the Construction of Social Reality in Contemporary Africa

Laurenti Magesa

Introduction

The varieties of ethical approaches, in terms of establishing norms and implementing them, are determined mainly by the concrete physical and social conditions in which people live, on the one hand, and, on the other, by their intellectual cognition and interpretation of these surroundings in favor of what is "good." Thus, while social norms are derived from human experience, they also deeply influence how individuals and societies live their lives. As Miguel A. De La Torre explains, "Ethics remains a reflection of the social location and . . . beliefs (or disbeliefs) of a given people,"[1] and also shapes them. What are the values or, in Emile Durkheim's words, the "collective or common conscience"[2] of the particular group or society, and how should these values be collectively sanctioned? None of the theoretical, academic, and methodological distinctions—autonomous, casuistic, situational, or virtue ethics[3]—affect in any fundamental way the question at the core of human morality and ethical enterprise, which consists essentially in searching for sustainable ways of social existence. This task is correctly described as the quest for the "good life," in terms of relationships between and among members of a human community and, further, between them and the surrounding environment.

The moral or ethical quest is almost always associated with, or related to, religious belief. Religion, as the expression of awareness of the existence of a transcendent power, whatever that may be, plays a vital role in the community's collective psyche in the development of moral and ethical principles and values. Religious belief guides the formation and application of ethical principles as required and acknowledged values in constructing social order. This is the link between morality and ideals associated with religious belief, regardless of how "religion" is determined and defined. From the Catholic moral perspective, the distinction between the theoretical and the practical dimensions of ethics, or what James F. Keenan has described as "fundamental moral theology, which concerns conscience, sin, love, virtue, authority, etc." and "applied ethics: social, sexual, medical, and corporate ethics,"[4] is the difference between reflection, theory or aspiration, and performance, as well as between norms and action. In the end, the

117

gap is hazy and ultimately unsustainable. Keenan appropriately explains that whatever may have been the case in the past about this question, "today we believe that fundamental moral theology needs to be applied and applied ethics needs fundamentals."[5] This close relationship between norms and their implementation is at the core of a new approach to African Catholic ethics.

Toward an African Catholic Fundamental Moral Theology

The inseparable connection between a community's quest for values and these values' impact on the existing environment demands a serious account of the latter, that is, the community's context. The methodological factors usually associated with the dynamics of human liberation in liberation theology are applicable here. They are appropriate to and for the development of an African Catholic fundamental moral theology. These aspects include the community's experience of current reality; the process of rational examination or "analysis" of the reasons for the existence of the situation in question, especially if it is inimical in any way to human dignity and the common good; and the application by the Catholic community of its belief in the God of Jesus to the existing experience for the purpose of transforming it in line with the community's belief in Christ's gospel.[6] As a result of this constant process of discernment, aided by attention to the goal of human liberty rooted in and inspired by the scriptures, in various African social contexts the Catholic community can formulate and develop fundamental guidelines for social transformation in accordance with the divine plan[7] and the Good News of Jesus for human liberation.[8]

To engage properly in the dynamics of developing an appropriate fundamental African ethics—that is, the search for *the most adequate formulation* for universal and permanent moral norms," to use the expression of Pope John Paul II[9]—it is not possible to avoid reevaluating the legacy of missionary Catholic ethics on the church in the continent. One important failure of this legacy is that it refused to take into consideration the positive moral ideals of prevailing African social philosophy and spirituality. Theologian Benezet Bujo has pointed this out. He notes how "the African version of Christianity is largely the consequence of the confrontation of African culture and religion with an absolutist Western form of the religion" that excluded positive contributions from the African worldview.[10] In terms of an African fundamental moral theology, this exclusion was a serious error on the part of the missionary evangelizers. Despite its shortcomings, the African culture is one foundation upon which Catholic moral norms should be built. All cultures are imperfect in one way or another, especially when confronted with the gospel of Jesus. Still, cultural imperfections "justify no attempt at their destruction, especially from external sources. While cultural transformation is desirable and often necessary, any attempt to eradicate any culture . . . is both reckless and foolish."[11] In Christian terms, it alienates the gospel from its culture and robs it of its roots.

This is what Pope Benedict XVI noted in his apostolic exhortation on Africa, *Africae munus*. The pope insisted that "In her concern for relevance and credibility, the Church needs to carry out a thorough discernment in order to identify those aspects of the [African] culture which represent an obstacle to the incarnation of gospel values, as well as those aspects which promote them."[12] Consequently, in the process of constructing principles of morality and ethics for Africa—an African fundamental moral theology—what is desirable pertains to the dynamics of incorporating the values of the gospel into the African culture at the same time as these values discover themselves already embedded, even if imperfectly, in the message of the gospel. In one word, this process is referred to as "inculturation."[13] In a profound way, the inculturation of the gospel should lead to personal and social transformation.

Pope Paul VI made this point forcefully to the bishops of Africa in 1969. Basing his claims on the "flourishing state of African studies," Pope Paul observed how "the ethnic history of the peoples of Africa, though lacking in written documents is . . . rich in individuality, spiritual and social experiences." As he specified, "*Many customs and rites, once considered to be strange, are seen today, in the light of ethnological science, as integral parts of various social systems, worthy of study and commanding respect.*"[14] Among the values of African culture he enumerated "the spiritual view of life," where "the presence of God permeates African life, as the presence of a higher being, personal and mysterious." He also mentioned the practical respect for human dignity in African customs and "the sense of family" and of community, "which in African tradition was family life writ large."[15]

Many years later, in 1995, Pope John Paul II substantially concurred with Pope Paul's observations and sentiments about the importance of African culture. Writing in his apostolic exhortation *Ecclesia in Africa* (The Church in Africa), he explained that, "In African culture and tradition the role of the family is everywhere held to be fundamental." He continued to note that, "Open to this sense of the family, of love and respect for life, the African loves children, who are joyfully welcomed as gifts of God . . . It is precisely this love for life," he observed, "that leads . . . [Africans] to give such great importance to the veneration of their ancestors. They believe intuitively that the dead continue to live and remain in communion with them."[16] Pope Benedict XVI explains this African sense of family and life:

> In the African worldview, life is perceived as something that embraces and includes ancestors, the living and those yet to be born, the whole of creation and all beings: those that speak and those that are mute, those that think and those lacking thought. The visible and invisible universe is regarded as a living-space for human beings, but also as a space of communion where past generations invisibly flank present generations, themselves the mothers of future generations. This great openness of heart and spirit in the African tradition predisposes you, dear brothers and

sisters, to hear and to receive Christ's message, to appreciate the mystery of the Church, and thus to value human life to the full, along with the conditions in which it is lived.[17]

The practical consequence of this notion of living is "solidarity," which Pope John Paul II observes and exemplifies. "African cultures have an acute sense of solidarity and community life," he remarks and notes as an example, "In Africa it is unthinkable to celebrate a feast without the participation of the whole village. Indeed, community life in African societies expresses the extended family." The pope expresses his "hope and prayer that Africa will always preserve this priceless cultural heritage and never succumb to the temptation to individualism, which is so alien to its best traditions."[18] For Pope John Paul II these values of African culture and religion represent "priceless human qualities which . . . [Africa] can offer to the Churches and to humanity as a whole."[19]

Accordingly, Bujo and many other African theologians ground African ethics and its practical dynamics totally in the African conception and reality of community and solidarity. In the African social structure, the community and the individual mirror each other as a "body." They have a shared identity, calling for "co-responsibility." What binds together the African community, and is therefore the foundation of African communitarian ethics, Bujo explains, is the centrality of life, to enhance, which requires participation and sharing. "The individual knows him or herself to be immersed in the community to such an extent that personality can develop only in it and through it."[20] Bujo further makes it clear that in African ethics this interdependence between the individual and the community is not "asymmetrical" but "mutual"; the individual and the community influence each other for good or evil. "Everybody's behavior and ethical action have consequences for the whole community: the good contributes to the increase of life, while evil destroys or at least reduces life."[21] Both the individual and the community are bound by similar moral rules whose goal is life. The crux of fundamental African morality is, therefore, its anthropocentric and holistic preference as well as its engaged or communitarian character.

Against Manichaean Dualism

Before the Second Vatican Council (1962–65), Catholic ethics was characterized by a predominant attitude, not of engagement, but of withdrawal or of retreat from worldly or "secular" concerns, in particular issues of a political and economic nature. There were, of course, a few notable theological exceptions to this stance, but the trend was universal. Underlying a certain interpretation of scripture was the notion of its "spiritual" emphasis. Some Catholic theologians and pastors sought to perceive in the Bible a contrast between the "secular" and the "spiritual" realms of human existence and experience, and they consequently emphasized the latter as the church's exclusive mission. Attention was often drawn, for instance, to the sayings of Jesus in the Gospel of John (17:13–19; 18:36), to the effect that Jesus's disciples should consider themselves to be "*in*" the world but not "*of*" the world. Little was said, on the contrary, of the opposite view, indicated most explicitly in the prophetic writings of the Old Testament, and seen in the attitude of Jesus himself toward the suffering presented in the New Testament, and later in the interpretations found in many of the writings of the postapostolic Fathers of the early Church.

Interpreting the scriptures, the Fathers present a consistent theological–pastoral view that concerns itself with the totality of the human person and the community, the "spiritual" and the "material" aspects of being. There is no antagonism in their ethical thinking between the two dimensions of the human existence. From the African conception of life and community, from the Bible, from the Fathers of the Church, and from other more recent authoritative church reflections, generically known as the social teaching of the church, the Catholic ethicist in Africa may not endorse a theology advocating strict dichotomy between body ("matter") and soul ("spirit"). Rather, a holistic approach to life will help steer the church away from unwarranted spiritualism and toward a more integrated engagement in the construction of a new social order. In line with these sources, it is apparent that attention to concrete reality, in which is to be found the active presence of God in the world, is more in keeping with authentic Christian faith about the responsibility of humankind in the world.

In the current circumstances of Africa, therefore, the efficacy of the Catholic ethicist's mission depends upon the appreciation of the holistic view of creation. The opposite stance, involving distrust of and flight from the physical world—characteristic of pre–Vatican II theology—evolved gradually. Before the Christian era, this latter stance manifested itself in different parts of the world, but in the history of Christian moral thought, it can be traced to the Persian gnostic philosopher Mani (c. 216–74). His teaching spread widely and influenced some sections of Christianity.

Manichaeism, as it eventually came to be known after its major advocate emphasized, as the primordial order of creation, the separation between knowledge and ignorance or light and darkness—corresponding to the "soul" and "matter."[22] At a certain moment in history, Mani maintained, these became mixed up. The ethical task at hand, according to Mani, was to restore this pristine separation when "light" or "knowledge" or spirit will rule the universe.

Of particular concern to Manichaean spirituality was the requirement of abstention from marriage and sexual contact. Because, according to Manichaeism, it was through marriage that human life—that is, matter in its most tangible form comes into the world through children—had to be avoided. For Mani, anything that was sensual and mundane, not leading to transcendence of the senses, was to be shunned. The mundane was seen as almost illusory and passing. Of lasting value and eternal were the invisible, spiritual things that freed the individual from material concerns. These were to be sought by everyone.

Blake Leyerle summarizes the Manichaean philosophy in a way that highlights its ethical influence on a certain perspective of Catholic theological ethics toward the world. He notes that according to Manichaeism, "Believers are to abstain from contact with matter. They renounce property, work, rest, war, hunting, business, and agriculture. They must show zeal in spreading knowledge of salvation."[23] As much as possible, whatever pertains to the physical material reality of humanity is to be avoided as corrupting: it is best for anyone not to engage in work or, if one has to do so, it is only to help the "elect" to avoid labor in favor of the occupations of the "light."[24] Accordingly, in Mani's prescription,

> The elect lived these precepts strictly. Travelling and preaching, they observed the three symbols: of the mouth, abstention from blasphemy, meat, and wine; of the hands, abstention from work and the destruction of plants and animals; and of the lap/breast, abstention from sexual contact. While practicing extensive fasting, they partook of ritual meals: in an atmosphere of prayer and hymnody, they liberated light particles through reverential eating of vine growing fruits, especially melons.[25]

The point is that much of this mentality was reflected in the encounter between Christianity and Africa since the fifteenth century. To a large extent, missionary evangelization ignored what we showed Keenan pointing out at the beginning of this reflection concerning the essential unity and necessary interaction between moral principles and empirical social action. Today, however, the African ethics of life in community should only be properly understood in terms of responding to concrete questions facing concrete people for the purpose of the advancement of the various dimensions of life—political, economic, environmental, and so on— toward the construction of an ever more desirable social order.

African Applied Ethics: Morality/Ethics in the Public Square

With reference to the crucial task of constructing social order, much of Catholic theology and pastoral practice in Africa had, as a consequence of their missionary legacy, a rather checkered history. On the one hand, some approaches exhibited deep concern for human welfare on earth through concrete social engagement. Others, on the other hand, displayed the tendency of withdrawing from practical commitment to social development, relegating it to what they described as the realm of "worldly authorities." Expressed in different words, the Catholic Church's theological and pastoral traditions have often presented an inconsistent, paradoxical picture.

While at some moments the church applied the saying, popularly attributed to St. Irenaeus (c. 125–202), that "The glory of God is man fully alive" ("*Gloria Dei est vivens homo*"),[26] at other times it displayed a Manichaean dualistic tendency of dividing up creation into two independent categories of the supernatural and natural. It ascribed all virtue to the former and all corruption to the latter. This theological dualism led to pastoral ambivalence. When the predisposition inspired by the holistic perception of humanity as equally body- and spirit-dominated, the church became fully involved in the advancement of human social order. When, on the contrary, the exclusive quest for the supernatural and metaphysical, often regarded as "life of the spirit," reigned as the ideal, the church became fundamentally suspicious of the material reality of the actual world. In this perception, "orthodoxy" outplayed "orthopraxis."

What liberation theology has brought to Christian (Catholic) theological–ethical discourse for almost half a century now is the insistence on orthodoxy and orthopraxis as equally important dimensions of Christian ethics. But liberation and political theologies are only transmitting and rendering current a long tradition of Christian belief in social action as an indispensable element of the gospel. The struggle for practical justice constitutes the gist of the social thought of the church, as it was summarized by the 1971 Ordinary Synod of Bishops in an oft-quoted paragraph. The synod stated quite unambiguously that "Action on behalf of justice and participation in the transformation of the world . . . [is] a constitutive dimension of the preaching of the Gospel." Consequently, "the Church's mission for the redemption of the human race" is incomplete without the liberation of humanity "from every oppressive situation."[27]

For Africa, the question at hand concerns how to achieve justice in the concrete political and economic reality of the continent. How must Christian mission be pursued in the contemporary social reality of Africa? Radical African ethicists like Emmanuel Katongole address this issue. First of all, they rightly question the wisdom of the prevailing Catholic socioethical paradigms that take the current structure of the African nation-state as the necessary context for the church's social engagement and action for transformation. Katongole argues that until now, "all the recommendations [for social action] assume that nation-state politics is the primary way to effect social change." This is the case "Whether Christian social responsibility is realized directly by influencing government policy (political paradigm), indirectly by motivating or infusing Christian action in the world through love (spiritual paradigm), or in partnership with the nation-state through relief services (the pastoral paradigm)."[28]

This approach is inadequate. In the present contexts of Africa, what is needed, as Katongole and other innovative African social ethicists are proposing, is a totally new social–ethical "imagination," one that will foster a new story, a new narrative for Africa. This continent, African ethicists now argue, needs a narrative that will lead to what Katongole, referring to St. Paul, describes as a "new creation" (2 Cor. 5:17)[29] or, in the portrait of the Book of Revelation, "a new heaven and a new earth" (Rev. 21:1). Jean-Marc Ela pictures it as "not a new world in the sense of a world beyond, but in the sense of a different world right here, a world being gestated in the deeds of the everyday."[30] Ethical paradigms that confine themselves to the structures of the nation-state, as we know the state in Africa, must be surpassed.

As is being proposed throughout this reflection, a new ethical paradigm for Africa must recall and base itself on the principle of life community as conceived in indigenous Africa. Here memory must play a role. The essence and goal of the new paradigm are the enhancement of life in all of its dimensions, and its dynamics are communion through participation and sharing. For this we need a novel social imagination. Perhaps this is the "reinvention" of Christianity, the grounding of social ethics in the contemporary African reality that Ela insists upon.

The new ethical paradigm proposed by Ela and other radical African ethicists is grounded in the fact that not only does the church have "a stake in the social-material activity of everyday life," as Katongole explains, "but that she can only be church to the extent she is the Kingdom of God 'gestated in the deeds of everyday life.'"[31] This is a dispensation that calls for a different approach in the formation of Catholic ethicists in and for Africa. A change of the ethical paradigm from a predominantly "spiritual" to a mainly "practical" orientation requires also profound modification in the training of professional ethicists. The emphasis that has traditionally been placed on doctrinal theology in seminaries, houses of formation, and Catholic institutes of higher learning must now be balanced by a similar accent on moral theology, concentrating on deep familiarity with the social sciences of politics, economics, anthropology, and sociology, including social analysis. History is also an area of great importance for a new social ethics. Knowledge of history helps to free the mind from a fundamentalist attitude toward biblical and doctrinal hermeneutics. Looking at the development of doctrine from a historical perspective is the only way to appreciate the relevance of a new ethical paradigm rooted in the African experience of life.

Conclusion

The new paradigm demanded for African ethics was already synthesized by Julius K. Nyerere in 1970, in a speech to Catholic women leaders titled "The Church and Society." There Nyerere insisted on the human person being the reason and goal of both the state and the church. True "development"—or liberation—which these institutions are there to promote, he said, involves "the creation of conditions, both material and spiritual," which facilitate human flourishing. As he analyzed it, the process involves "rebellion," the concrete rejection of any and all conditions that oppress the human person as an individual and as a society. To be "relevant," Nyerere insisted that the church must actively participate in this process of revolt. As he observed it then, this was unfortunately not the case. He noticed that

> representatives of the Church, and the Church's organizations, frequently act as if . . . development is a personal and 'internal' matter, which can be divorced from the society and the economy . . . They preach resignation; very often they appear to accept as immutable the social, economic, and political framework of the present-day world. They seek to ameliorate conditions through acts of love and of kindness where the beneficiary

of this love and kindness remains an 'object'. . . But when the victims of poverty and oppression begin to behave like . . . [human beings] and try to change those conditions, the representatives of the Church stand aside.[32]

The theological–ethical task, as Nyerere suggested, is to imagine and create models that facilitate active participation by the followers of Christ in the struggle "against those social structures and economic organizations which condemn . . . human beings to poverty, humiliation and degradation."[33] Only in this way will ethics be effectively transformative and therefore truly Christian.

Notes

1. Miguel A. De La Torre, *Doing Christian Ethics from the Margins* (Maryknoll, NY: Orbis Books, 2014), 6.

2. See Emile Durkheim, *The Division of Labor in Society* (New York: Collier Macmillan, 1933), 79–82.

3. These are quite complex ethical theories, but in simple terms "autonomous ethics" emphasizes the individual's competent decision in establishing the morality of an act; "casuistry" privileges attention to the particular instead of general rules for moral judgment rather than the other way around; "situation ethics" pays attention to the environment surrounding the act in assigning moral responsibility; and "virtue ethics" stresses the character disposition of the actor rather than the act itself or its consequences.

4. James F. Keenan, *A History of Catholic Moral Theology in the Twentieth Century: From Confessing Sins to Liberating Consciences* (London: Continuum, 2010), vii.

5. Ibid.

6. This process is often referred to as the pastoral or hermeneutic circle, and it is a fundamental method of liberation theology. See Joe Holland and Peter Henriot, *Social Analysis: Linking Faith and Justice* (Maryknoll, NY: Dove Communications and Orbis Books, 2000 ed.).

7. "I have indeed seen the misery of my people . . . I have heard them crying out because of their slave drivers, and I am concerned about their suffering. So I have come down to rescue them . . . and to bring them . . . into a good and spacious land, a land flowing with milk and honey" (Ex. 3:7–8).

8. "I have come that they may have life, and have it to the full" (John 10:10).

9. *Veritatis splendor*, no. 53.

10. Benezet Bujo, "Is There a Specific African Ethic? Towards a Discussion with Western Thought," in *African Ethics: An Anthology of Comparative and Applied Ethics*, ed. Munyaradzi Felix Murove (Scottsville, South Africa: University of KwaZulu-Natal Press, 2009), 113.

11. Laurenti Magesa, *What Is Not Sacred? African Spirituality* (Maryknoll, NY: Orbis Books, 2013), 11.

12. *Africae munus*, no. 36.

13. Some theologians today prefer the term *interculturation* or *intercultural living* to express this never-ending movement. For a very recent example of the discussion, see Anthony J. Gittins, *Living Mission Interculturally: Faith, Culture, and the Renewal of Praxis* (Collegeville, MN: Liturgical Press, 2015).

14. Paul VI, "*Africae Terrarum* (Land of Africa)—Message to the Countries of Africa," in *32 Articles Evaluating Inculturation of Christianity in Africa*, ed. Theresa Okure, Paul van Thiel, et al. (Eldoret, Kenya: AMECEA Gaba Publications—Spearhead Numbers 112–14, 1990), 16. Italics in original.

15. Ibid., 17–18. In *Ecclesia in Africa* (The Church in Africa), no. 42, Pope John Paul II elaborated the same thing by affirming: "Africans have a profound religious sense, a sense of the sacred, of the existence of God the Creator and of a spiritual world. The reality of sin in its individual and social forms is very much present in the consciousness of these peoples, as is also the need for rites of purification and expiation."

16. *Ecclesia in Africa*, no. 43.

17. Pope Benedict XVI notes in *Africae munus*, no. 69.

18. *Ecclesia in Africa,* no. 43.

19. *Ecclesia in Africa,* no. 42.

20. See Benezet Bujo, *The Ethical Dimension of Community: The African Model and the Dialogue between North and South* (Nairobi, Kenya: Paulines Publications Africa, 1998), 182.

21. Ibid. See also Benezet Bujo, *Foundations of an African Ethic: Beyond the Universal Claims of Western Morality* (Nairobi, Kenya: Paulines Publications Africa, 2003), 99–135.

22. On gnosticism, see http://www.newadvent.org/cathen/06592a.htm. See also Stephen A. Hoelle tau Stephanus, Gnostic Bishop, "The Gnostic World View: A Brief Summary of Gnosticism," http://gnosis.org/gnintro.html.

23. Blake Leyerle, "Manichaeism," in *The HarperCollins Encyclopedia of Catholicism*, ed. Richard P. McBrien et al. (New York: HarperCollins Publishers, 1966), 811.

24. Ibid.

25. Ibid.

26. Different interpretations are given to this saying. See, for example, Patrick Henry Reardon, "The Man Alive: Irenaeus Did Not Teach Self-Fulfillment," http://www.touchstonemag.com/archives/article.php?id=25-05-003-e. See also Philippe Delhaye, "Pope John Paul on the Contemporary Importance of St. Irenaeus," https://www.ewtn.com/library/Theology/IRENAEUS.HTM. However, it remains true that the dignity and well-being of humanity, when it is in accordance with the will of God, glorifies the Creator.

27. Synod of Bishops 1971, "Justice in the World," in David J. O'Brien and Thomas A. Shannon, eds., *Renewing the Earth: Catholic Documents on Peace, Justice and Liberation* (Garden City, NY: Image Books, 1977), 391.

28. Emmanuel Katongole, *The Sacrifice of Africa: A Political Theology for Africa* (Grand Rapids, MI: William B. Eerdmans, 2011), 58. Elsewhere, Katongole describes these as consisting in the "pious" and "pastoral" paradigms of theological ethics and distinguishes them from the "prophetic" paradigm appropriate for today. See Emmanuel M. Katongole, *A Future for Africa: Critical Essays in Christian Social Imagination* (Scranton, PA: University of Scranton Press, 2005), 153–55.

29. See Katongole, *The Sacrifice of Africa*, 59.

30. Quoted by Katongole, *A Future for Africa*, 153.

31. Ibid., 178.

32. Julius K. Nyerere, *Freedom and Development/ Uhuru na Maendeleo: A Selection from Writings and Speeches 1968–1973* (Dar es Salaam, Tanzania: Oxford University Press, 1973), 215.

33. Ibid.

The Church as a Family of God

The Role of Small Christian Communities in Evangelization in the Nigerian Context

Anthonia Bolanle Ojo

Introduction

Specifically speaking about mission in Africa, the model of church incorporated in contemporary small Christian communities (or SCCs) goes back to the early experience of the believers as described in the Acts of the Apostles (2:42): "They devoted themselves to the apostles' instruction and the communal life, to the breaking of bread and the prayers." This is the biblical foundation of the SCCs, which involves the gathering of the people who come together in the most basic and personal unit of the parish. This foundation reflects the model of the church as family of God emphasized by the Special Assembly for Africa of the Synod of Bishops. The church as a family of God model is an ecclesial option that focuses on building the church around the family. The concept of the family in Africa is based on the cherished value of community. This sense of community is a uniting force bringing together the whole society as a family. Through the African sense of community, each person within the community is recognized, assisted, encouraged, and promoted at various levels of social interactions. African communal mindedness and community-oriented values could be compared to the *koinonia* and *diakonia* of the early Christians.[1] Thus, the notion of the church as family of God is perhaps nowhere more visible than in the SCCs.

The SCC could be regarded as a "community of communities," small enough to create real community and personal relationships. It embodies some fundamental features of the ecclesiology of both the Second Vatican Council and the church as family of God, which encourage the dimension of community/communion and participation. Thus, SCCs are a significant new way of being church today, and they serve as a vehicle of parish and spiritual renewal. The SCC model of church helps to build up the parish community from within. Through it, more lay faithful participate in the work of evangelization. Hence, SCCs are a new way of being church in Africa.

The adoption of SCCs was promoted by the founding Fathers of Association of Member Episcopal Conferences in Eastern Africa (AMECEA) and the Catholic bishops of Eritrea, Ethiopia, Kenya, Malawi, Sudan, Tanzania, Uganda,

and Zambia. Such an approach implemented Vatican II's ecclesiology of communion in Eastern Africa. Moreover, the Catholic Church in this part of Africa has
recorded huge success in the work of evangelization, and it has been a viable model
for renewing the church-family from the grassroots level. However, despite the
significant benefits of the SCCs in promoting the work of evangelization and the
renewal of the church in Africa, this type of community is still not common in
the Nigerian church. Many Catholic churches in Nigeria are still parish-based. This
slows down the work of evangelization. It is believed that if properly employed in
Nigeria, SCCs will be a concrete expression of, and realization of, the church as
family model of church, which reflects the ecclesiology of Vatican II; and it will
also be an effective means of bringing the gospel message closer to the people at the
grassroots level. This is emphasized by Pope John Paul II in *Christifideles laici* (no.
23) when he writes, "So that all parishes of this kind may be truly communities of
Christians, local ecclesial authorities ought to foster . . . small, basic or so-called
'living' communities, where the faithful can communicate the word of God and
express it in service and love to one another; these communities are true expressions of ecclesial communion and centers of evangelization, in communion with
their pastors." Hence, this chapter discusses the SCCs as the reality of the model
of church as family of God, its roles in the work of evangelization, and the implications for the church in Nigeria.

Small Christian Community: Identity and Nature

The term *small Christian community* has been given various names in different
parts of Africa, such as living Christian communities (or LCCs), basic Christian
communities (or BCCs), etc. Though the names are different, the purpose remains,
that is, making the church in Africa more African and closer to the people. The
terminology used in official Catholic documents is "church of the home," "domestic
church," or "basic communities." Small Christian community can simply be defined
as a community of communities.[2] Small Christian communities make real the vision
of Vatican II that calls on the church to be (to shine forth as) "a people made one
with the unity (brought into unity) from the Father, the Son and the Holy Spirit."[3]
These communities are approved and encouraged by the universal church. They are
biblically based and historically proven to be a leaven for world evangelization and
church renewal.

Fundamentally, the small Christian community model of church is based on
the church as communion (*koinonia*). In terms of contemporary theology, this is
part of Trinitarian communion ecclesiology and a "communion of communities"
ecclesiology. The SCC members are called to a life of sharing modeled on the
Trinity. SCC therefore reflects the different segments of the church:

- an SCC is a communion of families;
- an outstation (also called an out-church, prayer-house, or chapel) is a
  communion of SCCs;

- a subparish is a communion of outstations;
- a parish is a communion of subparishes;
- a deanery is a communion of parishes;
- a diocese is a communion of deaneries;
- a country (for example, in the case of the national bishops' conference) is a communion of dioceses and archdioceses;
- the world church or global church is a communion of national and continental bishops' conferences.[4]

Thus, these communities decentralize and organize the parish community, to which they always remain united.[5] Life in a small Christian community is simply our baptismal brotherhood and sisterhood lived out practically with a few people, in conjunction with the universal church.

The SCCs are based on gospel-sharing, where Christians gather to celebrate the presence of the Lord in their lives and in their midst, through the celebration of the Eucharist, the reading of the Word of God, and witnessing to their faith in loving service to each other and their communities. Under the guidance of their pastors and catechists, they seek to deepen their faith and mature in Christian witness, as they live concrete experiences of fatherhood, motherhood, relationships, and open fellowship, where each takes care of the other. The SCCs are vibrant, spontaneous groups with little hierarchical structure. They are indispensable for the development of a well-grounded faith in the life of the Christian.[6] The small Christian communities can be said to be focal places of Christian life and vehicles for evangelization. The members of the small Christian communities are both hearers of the gospel and privileged beneficiaries of evangelization, as well as proclaimers of the gospel themselves; and they do this both in words and in actions. In and through them, the poor hear the Good News.[7]

It appears that, "Small Christian Communities take more root in the less privileged and rural areas and become a leaven of Christian life, of care for the poor and the neglected and of commitment to the transformation of the society. These communities thus become a means of evangelization and a source of new ministries."[8] In the renewed understanding of the church after Vatican II regarding her mission and ministry, the small Christian communities are a new way of being church. These communities are a sign of vitality within the church and an instrument of formation and evangelization.

An Ecclesiology of the Church as the Family of God in Africa

The Special Synod of the African Bishops (2009) emphasized the image of the church as the family of God. When the Synod used the image, it must have had the African family in mind. The African family is an extended one. It includes parents and their children, grandparents, uncles and aunts, nephews and nieces, and cousins; in short, people who are related by blood. The African bestows on every member of her extended family the same love, care, and concern that members of a nuclear family accord to one another. In the African family, each person's business is everybody's business; each person is his or her brothers' and sisters' keeper. In all these respects, the African family bears a striking resemblance to the biblical family of both the Old and New Testaments.[9]

Commenting on the position of the Synod, in *Ecclesia in Africa* (no. 63) Pope John Paul II writes,

> The Synod Fathers acknowledged it (i.e. the image of the Church as Family of God) as an expression of the Church's nature particularly appropriate for Africa. For this image emphasizes care for others, solidarity, warmth in human relationships, acceptance, dialogue, and trust.

In the same vein, John Mary Waliggo points out:

> The African Bishops could have chosen the Vatican II concept of Church as Communion or as People of God. They purposely chose Church as Family; they wanted to use the African family as the model for being and living Church. The family model includes everyone, baptized and non-baptized, involving every member. It serves well the emphasis on Small Christian Communities.[10]

One of the characteristics of family is the quality of relationships between family members. The church as a family cannot reach her full potential as church unless she is divided into communities small enough to foster human relationships. On the "Ecclesiology of the Church as the Family," the Final Message of the Bishops of Africa to the People of God, on "The Church as the Family and Small Christian Communities" (sec. 28), states, "The Church, the Family of God, implies the creation of small communities at the human level, living or basic ecclesial communities . . . These individual Churches-as-Families have the task of working to transform society." Hence John Paul II describes the characteristics of such communities as follows:

> Primarily they should be places engaged in evangelizing themselves, so that subsequently they can bring the Good News to others; they should moreover be communities which pray and listen to God's Word, encourage the members themselves to take on responsibility, learn to live an ecclesial life, and reflect on different human problems in the light of the Gospel. Above all, these communities are to be committed to living Christ's love for everybody, a love which transcends the limits of natural solidarity of clans, tribes, or other interest groups.[11]

The recent praxis of SCCs in Africa, according to Healey, can therefore be said to contribute to the development of the theology of the church-family of God. SCCs help to embody the values of inclusiveness, sharing, unity, and solidarity that form the contemporary family of God. Our models, therefore, are the first small community (the Trinity—Father, Son, and Holy Spirit) and the first small Christian community (the Holy Family—Jesus, Joseph, and Mary).[12] Kieran Flynn states, "It is in being transforming communities (of themselves and others) that SCCs realize their ecclesial identity in the Church as Family model. These individual (communities of) Church as Family have the task of working to transform society."[13] This is part of the social responsibility of SCCs as the family of God in Africa in the context of family ecclesiology. A key part of this transformation is a deeper evangelization that proclaims that the water of baptism is "thicker" than the blood of tribalism and promotes true communion between different ethnic groups. The SCCs actualize the African concept of family, based not on common blood but on common faith.[14] Thus, the African cultural relationships and the communal life are the foundation that provides a developing model of a church based on the African family and "Small Christian Communities are affirmed as the fundamental building blocks of the Church as Family of God in Africa."[15]

The Roles of Small Christian Communities in the Evangelization Mission of the Church

Evangelization was the task that Jesus entrusted to his disciples at the point of his departure from this world. He gave the mandate to his apostles to "Go, therefore, make disciples of all nations; baptize them in the name of the Father and of the Son and of the Holy Spirit, teach them to observe all the commands I gave you" (Matt 28:19–20; cf. Mark 16:15). Therefore, "the task of evangelizing all people constitutes the essential mission of the Church . . . Evangelization is in fact the grace and vocation proper to the Church, her deepest identity. She exists in order to evangelize."[16] It means bringing the Good News into all the strata of humanity and through its influence transforming humanity from within and making it new. Evangelization is an encounter; it happens when one person meets another. One of the rules of such an "encounter" is that both the one who proclaims and the one proclaimed to are changed. One cannot proclaim the Good News of God to another, nor encounter another in faith, without change happening to both of them.[17]

Hence, a significant agent of evangelization today is the concept of these "small Christian communities" or "base Christian communities" or "vital Christian communities." These communities are engaged in evangelizing themselves, so that subsequently they can bring the Good News to others.[18] In the small Christian communities, the lay faithful live the Christian faith by witnessing to it in their daily lives and also by proclaiming their faith to others. This commitment shows that in the church, the task of evangelization belongs to every baptized. As Vatican II affirms, "Every disciple of Christ has the obligation to do his part in spreading the faith."[19] The Council continues, "All sons and daughters of the Church should have a lively awareness of their responsibility to the world . . . They should spend their energies in the work of evangelization."[20]

The 1979 AMECEA Plenary Meeting points out that "Small Christian Communities are very instrumental in bringing the Gospel down to the lives of the people. They are an effective way of making people feel that they are fully part of the Church's evangelizing work."[21] Through the small Christian communities the lay faithful play a very relevant role in the whole process of evangelization. They can build up themselves into a community of faith and love. "Thus, the Small Christian Communities are means and occasion to proclaim the Gospel in a concrete manner and share God's love in an effective way."[22]

According to Pope Paul VI, in *On Evangelization in the Modern World* (no. 15), the church is an evangelizer, but it begins by evangelizing itself. The church has a constant need to be evangelized, if it wants to retain its freshness, vigor, and strength in order to proclaim the gospel. According to Barreiro, the small Christian communities, "with their evangelical poverty, simplicity, generosity, and courage, constitute a genuine *Kairos* and an authentic time of grace for this evangelization of the Church which Paul VI mentions."[23] The members of the small Christian communities are both hearers of the gospel and privileged beneficiaries of the process of evangelization, as well as proclaimers of the gospel themselves, and they do this both in words and in actions.[24] In other words, in the small Christian communities, the laity live the Christian faith by witnessing to it in their daily lives and also by proclaiming this faith to others. However, it must be said that the Holy Spirit is the principal agent of evangelization; it is the Holy Spirit who impels each individual to proclaim the gospel and, in the depth of consciences, causes the word of salvation to be accepted and understood (cf. *Evangelii nuntiandi*, no. 75).

Through the small Christian communities, many Catholics today have developed a new love for scripture and they give witness to God's word. They now explicitly discover the Word of God in the Bible as a source of nourishment for their religious life. The Word of God in scripture always serves as a source of inspiration and stimulation for their lives and actions.[25] Familiarity with the Bible is essential in the evangelization process and the small Christian communities become a supportive context to nourish the personal and communal relationship with God's Word. This familiarity is valuable in letting the members of SCCs see that faith and Christian life concern the totality of their lives. Familiarity with scripture and the resulting prayer life, which accompanies it, enable them to link faith and life by reducing or even eliminating a dichotomy that underlies the very existence of many Christians. In such a way, believers further integrate faith and life.[26]

In the small Christian communities, laypeople serve other laypeople in different matters, not depending on the priest's presence. In this model of church whose center is the laity, evangelization has produced numerous and significant conversions, especially by liberating human beings both individually and socially.[27] This is why Joseph Healey writes, "Small Christian Communities are one of the most successful pastoral approaches in terms of the laity's involvement in evangelization: The laity evangelizing the laity and sharing their lives in the spirit of charity with the Word of God at the center of their activity."[28] Looking at the relationship of the church as family of God with the involvement of the laity in evangelization, John Baur explains that the model of church as family of God requires that "all the faithful fulfil their vocation and mission in the Church . . . implying a change from the priest-based apostolate to a people-based apostolate which demands that the priest assumes the role of a community minded inspirational minister."[29] In this way, SCCs are reshaping the church's structure and self-definition.

Moreover, through their simple way of life, the small Christian communities incarnate the scriptures into the culture. This is referred to as inculturation. Today, inculturation is important both as a concept and a process. Its content is inherent in the words of John's Gospel: "And the word was made flesh and dwelt among us" (John 1:14). The Good News has to be made flesh in the lives and circumstances of those to whom it is proclaimed. This is a gradual and complex process, as the working paper for the 1994 First African Synod (no. 49) reminds us: "the process of the church's insertion into people's cultures is a lengthy one. It is not a matter of purely external adaptation, for inculturation means the intimate transformation of authentic cultural values through their integration in Christianity and the insertion of Christianity into the various human cultures."[30]

Thus, "the growth of SCCs helps Catholic evangelization in three ways. First, members of these groups receive a first-hand experience of discipleship. They grow in their own faith through reading and discussing Scripture, sharing in liturgies, doing works of service, and bonding in community. Second, members of these groups, convinced of their own positive experiences, develop fervor to invite others to this same richness. Finally, the Small Christian Community provides a ready place to nurture the faith of new members in the group."[31]

In connection with the work of evangelization, the SCCs are not only involved in proclaiming the gospel; they are also involved in promoting reconciliation, peace and justice, healing, and forgiveness among the people. Thus, "the Small Christian Communities can very well work as agents of promoting communion, the union of believers with God and among themselves, and thereby the believers can bear witness to Christ's love."[32]

The Implications for the Nigerian Church

Small Christian communities today are widely recognized as significant expressions of Christian life emerging in a variety of cultures and contexts throughout the world. During the 2009 African Synod, the strong feeling that the model of SCCs offers the best pattern for the renewal of ecclesiology in the African church needs to be addressed seriously in Nigeria. Since the mid-1960s, SCCs proved very successful in Latin America. In recent years, these communities have thrived in many local churches in Africa, most especially in Eastern Africa. There are few examples emerging here and there in Nigeria, but on the whole Nigerians are not very familiar with the SCCs. While some dioceses have active SCCs, in other dioceses they are nonexistent. Moreover, SCCs seem to regularly rise and fall. For example, SCCs started in the archdiocese of Lagos in 1977. However, by late 1980s the SCCs nosedived. In 1992, SCCs were rediscovered by the people. Now there are SCCs in many parishes of the archdiocese. As a second example, SCCs are vibrant in the old Oyo Diocese, now Oyo and Osogbo dioceses. In Ekiti diocese and Kaduna archdiocese, the SCCs are not widespread.

The benefits of small Christian communities cannot be overemphasized. As I indicated, the SCCs help in the renewal and growth of the local church. By belonging to SCCs, the members are called to live in communion with the Triune God, with one another, and with their pastors. They actively participate in Christ's prophetic mission by listening to the Word of God, proclaiming it, and giving witness to it. They are called to announce the message of total salvation, peace, and justice. Moreover, the SCCs empower people to denounce evil and all its manifestations in society—the idolatry of wealth and power, violence, injustices, and the culture of death.

Working within the contemporary context of parishes, dioceses, and the universal church, the SCCs enable the members to participate in the Christian and Catholic global faith community in the very manner the earliest Christians experienced, both on a personal and a communal level. Through the SCCs, the lay faithful in Nigeria will be enabled to exercise the common priesthood by actively participating in the liturgical celebrations, since they share in Christ's kingly mission. Moreover, by their loving service to others, especially the poor and the needy, their work for justice and peace for social transformation will be strengthened and enhanced. This is why in many parts of the world, SCCs are referred to as prophetic (evangelizing), priestly (worshipping), and kingly (serving) communities echoing Vatican II's vision of the church as people of God.[33]

It is well known that in the parish setting, it is actually not possible to develop personal relationships with all the faithful. Through the small Christian communities, both the pastors and the parishioners can entrust the care of the parish members spiritually and temporarily to the SCCs because, by belonging to these communities, the believers have close contacts with, at least, a limited number of parishioners; moreover, they feel the bond of community life, with a new sense of belonging and solidarity based on a common faith. Hence, SCCs help the members to pray together in communion with the universal church. While the majority of Christians find it quite difficult to pray individually in their ordinary lives, the small Christian communities help people grow together in their spiritual life by praying together regularly, following the liturgical calendar of the universal church. In small Christian communities the members are deeply influenced in their spiritual life by one another through the sharing of experiences lived in their daily life. These communities constitute the favoring milieu for both a personal and a communal spirituality.

The members of the small Christian communities try to put into practice the Word of God in their concrete daily lives. There are several methods for sharing the gospels. In practicing them, believers aim not only to meditate on the Word of God but also to live out in their daily life the knowledge they received from the gospel so that they could contribute to realize the Kingdom of God in this world. In Nigeria, the small Christian communities will challenge the unjust realities in our modern society so that believers could transform the world into the Kingdom of God as Jesus wished for us to accomplish.

The Nigerian church should embrace and promote small Christian communities for the purpose of effective evangelization, ministerial service, and pastoral care. The current parish structure and the available ministers cannot adequately cater to the ever growing population of Catholics. There is an urgent need to break up the parish set-up into small manageable units or cells, consisting of Christians who are able to know one another well; visit one another; and share in one another's joys and sorrows, anxieties and worries. Believers should not be lost in large parishes today. Small communities of faithful people who gather more regularly than once a week to pray together, to study the scriptures together, and to share the Eucharist as a true family could foster a greater sense of belonging and participation. To be truly family of God, the Nigerian church has the task of bringing the gospel to the people through SCCs. This will help the church to reach many of its members at the grass-roots. In Pope John Paul II's words, "Because the Church is communion, the new 'basic communities', if they truly live in unity with the Church, are a true expression of communion and a means of construction of a more profound communion. They are thus cause for great hope for the life of the Church."[34]

Inasmuch as SCCs are considered as a way of church renewal, they are not devoid of challenges. Some communities might become autonomous, seeing themselves as separate from the universal church. When they are not mentored, guided, and accompanied, the community leaders can also become powerful by assuming a role similar to that of the pastor. Instead of promoting the members' sense of belonging, some community members could become a source of division. Pope John Paul II therefore issued many cautionary remarks to these communities and to the priests who are charged with their pastoral care: "The dangers to which this new form of community structure is easily exposed are well known, but there emerges especially, and above all, the danger of considering itself a unique way of being Church, and, consequently, the tendency to detach itself from the institutional Church in the name of simplicity and of the authenticity of a life lived in the spirit of the Gospel."[35]

Conclusion

The church is exhorted to be salt and light in the world (cf. Matt. 5:13–16): in other words, an agent for fostering God's goodness. This chapter has proposed that small Christian communities are the most effective agents for responding to this exhortation in concrete ways in Africa. The small Christian communities embody some fundamental features of the ecclesiology of the family of God model, which encourages the dimension of community/communion and participation. Thus, the small Christian communities are a significant new way of being church today and serve as a vehicle of parish and spiritual renewal.

The church truly exists in communities in which everyday life and work take place, and among those basic manageable social groups where members can experience real interpersonal relationships and feel a sense of belonging. Hence, to be more effective in its work of evangelization, the church in Nigeria should promote SCCs. To reach its full potential as church and to be truly the family of God, the church in Nigeria should promote and strengthen small communities, laity based, in order to foster closer human relationships that will speed up the work of evangelization. Moreover, for SCCs to thrive and truly achieve their goals and objectives within the Nigerian church, the formation and training of the small communities' leaders should be considered as very important and urgent. This will help them to remain united with the universal church.

Notes

1. Elochukwu E. Uzukwu, *A Listening Church: Autonomy and Communion in African Churches* (Maryknoll, NY: Orbis Books, 1996), 113.
2. Joseph G. Healey and Jeanne Hinton, eds., *Small Christian Communities Today: Capturing the New Moment* (Nairobi, Kenya: Paulines Publications, 2006), 43.
4. Joseph G. Healey, *Building the Church as Family of God: Evaluation of Small Christian Communities in Eastern Africa* (Nairobi, Kenya: AMECEA Gaba Publications, CUEA Press, 2012), 10.
3. *Lumen Gentium (Dogmatic Constitution of the Church of the Church), Vatican Council II: The Conciliar and Post Conciliar Documents*, ed. Flannery Austin (Mumbai, India: St. Paul, 2001), 4.
5. *Redemptor missio*, no. 51.
6. Regina M. Bechtle and John J. Rathschmidt, eds., *Mission and Mysticism: Evangelization and the Experience of God* (Maryknoll, NY: Maryknoll School of Theology Press, 1987), 146.
7. Ander Barreiro, *Basic Ecclesial Communities: The Evangelization of the Poor* (Maryknoll, NY: Orbis Books, 1982), 105.
8. V. Samuel, *The Role of Laity in Evangelization through Small Christian Communities* (Asirbhavan: Eranakulam, 1999), 1, quoted in Genevieve Nneoma Ihenacho, SHCJ, "Small Christian Communities as a New Way of Evangelization in Africa," http://www.smallchristiancommunities.org/africa/africa-continent/240-small-christian-communities-as-a-new-way-of-evangelization-in-africa.html.
9. *Church in Nigeria: Family of God on Mission. Lineamenta for the First National Pastoral Congress* (Lagos: Catholic Secretariat of Nigeria, 1999), 85, no. 168.
10. John Mary Waliggo, "The Church-as-Family of God and Small Christian Communities," AMECEA Documentation Service, 429 (December 1, 1994), 1.
11. *Ecclesia in Africa*.
12. Healey, *Small Christian Communities Today: Capturing the New Moment*, 67.
13. Kieran Flynn, *Communities for the Kingdom: A Handbook for Small Christian Community Leaders* (Eldoret, Kenya: AMECEA Gaba Publications, 2007), 98.
14. Healey, *Small Christian Communities Today: Capturing the New Moment*, 86.
15. Flynn, *Communities for the Kingdom*, 98.

16. *Evangelii nuntiandi*, no. 14.

17. Frank DeSiano and Kevin Boyack, *Creating the Evangelizing Parish* (New York: Paulist Press, 1993), 9.

18. *Ecclesia in Africa*, no. 89.

19. *Ad gentes*, no. 23.

20. *Ad gentes*, no. 36.

21. Healey, *Building the Church as Family of God*, 115.

22. Samuel, *The Role of Laity in Evangelization through Small Christian Communities*, 2.

23. Barreiro, *Basic Ecclesial Communities*, 68.

24. Ibid., 1.

25. DeSiano and Boyack, *Creating the Evangelizing Parish*, 13.

26. Milton Azevedo, *Basic Ecclesial Communities in Brazil: The Challenge of a New Way of Being Church* (Washington, DC: Georgetown University Press, 1987), 129.

27. Antonio Butkiewicz, "Pastoral Commitment to BCCs in Bolivia," in Healey and Hinton, *Small Christian Communities Today*, 9–17.

28. Healey, *Building the Church as Family of God*, 115.

29. John Baur, *2000 Years of Christianity in Africa: An African Church History*, 2nd ed. (Nairobi, Kenya: Pauline Publication, 2009), 16.

30. First Synod of Bishops of Africa (1994), no. 49, https://ecclesiainafrica.wordpress.com/2010/02/.../the-1994-synod-a-kairos-for-africa/

31. Ihenacho, "Small Christian Communities as a New Way of Evangelization in Africa."

32. Samuel, *The Role of Laity in Evangelization through Small Christian Communities*, 2. Quoted in Ihenacho, "Small Christian Communities as a New Way of Evangelization in Africa."

33. *Apostolicam actuositatem*, no. 10, http://www.vatican.va/archive/hist_councils/ii_vatican_council/documents/vat-ii_decree_19651118_apostolicam-actuositatem_en.html.

34. *Redemptor missio*, no. 51.

35. John Paul II, "Address to Members of the Sacred Congregation for the Clergy," October 20, 1984 [translated into English from the original Italian].

Toward a Prophetic and Hope-Bearing Ethic for Cuba

Aldo Marcelo Cáceres

Introduction

Why a prophetic and hope-bearing ethic for Cuba? Because, as I stated in an interview in Madrid: "Cuba is living a crucial moment in its history; it is in a subtle dynamic of reforms and changes. And, the same people, from their creativity and their possibilities, benefit from this for their own growth." That is, the population is looking for alternatives for personal and familiar development. Moreover, I believe that Cuba faces a great challenge: to define and debate its own path. In order to generate a more prosperous and sustainable society, it must appeal to the principle of responsibility that conforms to a commitment to the common good, with greater openness to popular participation in decision making. At this moment Cuba is poised to witness to the world how to build something in common, using the best resources of the people and the nation, without external impositions. I share the observations of a Norwegian international relations expert who, at a conference in Cuba, argued that the best alternative for the global community is to accompany the adjustment processes of the economic, social, and political models in Cuba.[1] I would add, those processes that are considered necessary, good, and just, for a better present and future, are the ones that take into account "all the people, every Cuban, and all Cubans": the ones that ensure that ultimately the human person is valued, and her or his dignity is respected.

Therefore, taking into account the current Cuban scenario, before a society "framed in its contradictory realities and uncertainties about its possible courses,"[2] it is urgent to offer a lucid ethical orientation that helps to overcome the "ethics of resignation," one strictly shaped by work and endurance.[3] Such an ethic opens new horizons to achieve a life worth living, that is, a full life. That is why, despite the fact that "some changes are being made for the better," it is urgent to discern the way forward from civic coresponsibility in an environment of freedom and sincere dialogue. Together we search for strategies that little by little address the social, economic, legal, and political problems. As we perfect or transform these strategies, our common project unfolds, opening new paths of development for society.

This common project will be viable if it takes into account the human being in all of her or his dimensions, allowing itself to be projected in society with autonomy and with due guarantees. In addition, not only must it allow for a better quality of life and social welfare, but at the same time it must strengthen the moral and spiritual

138

dimensions. Reestablishing the bond between all Cubans is only possible from this place of renewal. Cubans living on the island—regular citizens, those belonging to the political sphere, and those outside Cuba for various reasons—have the task of creating spaces for dialogue and reconciliation, making a wager on a homeland of brethren, which they are called to be. Theirs alone is the establishment of this common project, from the birth of a new social conscience, a new fraternal mentality, so that overcoming all fear, indifference, enmity, and rancor, they might be able to build a common house, a more humane and humanizing people and society. This mentality must be "cordial," giving rise to love, so that this common task of building fraternal bonds, reconciliation, communion, solidarity, truth, and justice may be incarnated. As the Cuban bishops say,

> love is the column that holds firm the development of family and society. A more just, more humane, more prosperous society is not built only by moving mountains or evenly by the more equitable distribution of material goods [. . .] but lack of fraternal love, and all the more selfishness and hatred, are graver threats, and, ultimately, the cause of all the other problems.[4]

In short, it takes love "to turn the happiness of others into one's own happiness."[5] In Aristotelian terms, we must seek and work toward a love that allows each child of the Cuban people to achieve *eudaimonia* or happiness, in the sense of achieving a "more objective and stable personal and social state,"[6] true "human flourishing."

Who Can Offer This Prophetic and Hope-Bearing Ethic?

The exercise of sowing hope today, without hiding or turning away from the truth, without renouncing a prophetic stance, is done by the Cuban Catholic Church. In its own way, as an institution in the midst of the Cuban people, it has accompanied the many changes that have transpired. It has also evaluated these changes while making its voice heard, always trusting God's time and teaching. Taking this into account, the church (bishops, religious, priests, and a large number of Catholic laity) is able to deploy critical, constructive, and hope-filled thought in light of the gospel of human experience and its social teaching. As an expert on the person, as mother of all Cubans and teacher from the heart of the gospel, the church not only enlightens, guides, and accompanies its people, but also motivates and favors the creation of small participatory spaces for discernment, where listening, dialogue, and reconciliation are practiced, as a sign of fruitfulness and commitment to the common good.

These are small spheres where a culture of encounter is practiced implicitly and explicitly. One of its greatest gifts is the inclusive attitude of these groups, since believers, nonbelievers, and Cubans of different political thought and religious confession participate. This confirms "the existing pluralism in Cuban society." The principal motivation in these arenas is to seek collectively possible ways for Cuba to be a more just, free, prosperous, and fraternal society. And the church, without renouncing its Christian specificity, lets the Cuban people know that all who open themselves to God and allow themselves to be guided by Him are never lost. The presence and role of the church is discreet and prudent, performing the hard task of creating bridges in the midst of this society.

What Do Cuban Bishops Tell Us?

The Cuban bishops are one of the most significant voices. They have collegially developed a *social morality* by means of documents and public addresses that offer us a faithful reading of reality and a rich magisterium of a prophetic and hopeful character.[7] In the magisterium of the Cuban bishops we find reflected, to a great extent, the feelings of the Cuban people and the actual situation of the country. This is largely due to the presence of all the "Cuban actors" who, in the key of the incarnation, know and understand the joys and hopes, the sorrows and anguishes of men, especially of the poor and those who suffer (cf. *Gaudium et spes*, no. 1). This Cuban church has accompanied its communities of faith, the people of God, never feeling alienated or separated from the people. Additionally, it is helping to forge a *social conscience*, urging Cubans, as brethren and citizens, not to disregard reality, but to commit themselves decisively to the present and the future of the country they yearn for.

What Changes Do We Recognize and Value?

In the *economic* sphere, the following are growing phenomena: self-sufficiency within the nonstate sector (personal or family business), cooperatives (agricultural and nonagricultural), timid opening of wholesale markets, reopening of some sugar centers, a new foreign investment law (enacted in April 2014) that promotes mixed enterprises, and a deep wager on tourism as one of the main sources of income, among others. In the *social* sphere, this growth is reflected in Cubans' free access to beaches and hotels, permission for the purchase and sale of homes and cars, the explosive growth of cell phones, improvements in Internet access, high levels of security in the city and the countryside, the return of high schools and preparatory institutes to the cities, and welfare and social assistance programs for the most vulnerable groups.

In the *political* sphere, the process of normalization of relations between the United States and Cuba will have to be weighed against the stance taken by Donald Trump. Other changes include the strengthening of relations with the European Union and other countries, participation in international forums, Cuba's role in the Colombian peace process, and the release of several political prisoners. The *religious* sphere shows changes that include a better relationship with the Catholic

Church and a new dialogue after the visit of Pope Francis, the facilitation of a meeting between Francis and the Russian patriarch Kirill, the cooperation of both the Catholic Church and other confessions in social projects, and the opening of complementary education centers. Permits are granted to carry out processions and other public manifestations of faith. Finally, in the *cultural* sphere, Cubans are a people of great artistic flourishing, offering diverse fields, events, and institutions with international extension and recognition.

What Other Changes Are Necessary and Urgent?

Before specifying the urgent changes needed for this society, the bishops tell us:

Trusting in the Lord, we hope that these reforms, as well as other actions that we consider necessary, will be attained, for we experience anguish in the citizenry with respect to these aspirations, since many of our fellow citizens have their hopes set on it . . . The urgency of these changes is grounded on lives lived under limitations, scarcity, lack of personal or family progress of most Cubans, who feel that life ends as years go by without being able to realize the aspirations proper of every human being and family. Among the young there are many who do not yet see the conditions to carry out their life project, who see the possibility of achieving this in other countries as an attractive prospect.[8]

The bishops believe that in order to concretize hope, it is necessary to overcome the different forms of poverty that affect the most vulnerable and disadvantaged, to exert great effort toward stopping the flight of human capital (a wealth of the Cuban nation, the loss of which presents deep costs to the country).[9]

These necessary changes and actions are an increase in salaries that allows for a life of dignity and family security; greater opportunities for initiative and creativity in production; distribution and consumption of goods and services; the creation of new areas of work and opportunities for all those men and women who are waiting to develop their skills and to put their incalculable potential at the service of society; improvement of the public transportation system, education, and health; solving the problems of clothing, food, housing, and social security pensions; establishing a participatory state that favors the autonomy of the legislative and judicial powers; and the development of a strong and responsible social autonomy that allows the development of viable projects for the common good such as encouraging and supporting the social and political projects of intermediate institutions and associations. There is also a need for greater autonomy for trade unions and broadening freedoms for the mass media.

The bishops argue that hope for a better future also implies a new political order: "in our Cuban reality we believe it essential to update national legislation about the political sphere. For some time incipient spaces of debate and discussion in different instances and environments emerge, sometimes created by the citizens themselves: intellectuals, youth and others, who, from the bottom, have expressed in different ways their vision of necessary changes in Cuba, with serious and diverse opinions and proposals. This indicates that Cuba is called to be a pluralist society."[10]

Spaces for Discernment and Formation

These spaces promote the voices of *creative minorities illuminated by the Word of God, which seek the formation of a civic conscience, and the diffusion of and witness to the principles of the social doctrine of the church*. This reality imposes the need for dialogue as "the only way to achieve and sustain the social transformations taking place in Cuba."[11]

Those spaces, or spheres, committed to the common good and the destiny of the country, are as follows:

- The *Centro de Convivencia pensando Cuba* (*Center for Coexistence for Thinking Cuba*) was established in 2008 in the Diocese of Pinar del Río. Its aim is to create pluralist thought and generate peaceful proposals to promote inclusion, freedom of expression, citizen participation, and social justice and democracy for the present and future of Cuba. It publishes the now well-known journal *Vitral*.
- The Archdiocese of Havana supports the *Institute for Humanities and Ecclesiastical Studies for the Laity* in the Cultural Center P. Félix Varela. This is cutting-edge work since almost 80 percent of the students are non-Catholics who are seeking the degree in humanities and a license in social sciences. This project promotes a solid formation for social conscience, envisioning new horizons and openness to the larger world. It is worth noting two key journals that reach many homes in our parishes: *Espacio Laical (Space of the Laity)* and *Nueva Palabra* (*New Word*). Intellectuals from Cuba and foreigners inculturated in Cuba participate and freely express various topics about the Cuban reality as well as everything that can contribute to the project for the nation they so long for.
- There are other groups that open the doors to believers and nonbelievers, as well as people of diverse political thought, including *Cuba-emprende* (project of the Archdiocese of Havana with several sponsors), *communion and liberation, economy of communion,* and *Cuba-possible*. There are also small spaces that promote religious life in Cuba along with the laity-involved projects of social development, values education, and integral development.[12]

From these spaces, the church and the people demand the establishment of healthy social and economic prosperity supported by solid moral and spiritual foundations. The voice of the church in Cuba puts it this way: "Our people long to live in a country that harmonizes justice and freedom, prosperity and solidarity, well-being and moral and spiritual values."[13] Therefore, a social project that gives rise to spaces for the promotion of worthy projects of personal and family life is urgently needed. This will make possible the eradication of the lies and corruption, fear and hopelessness, which continue to be a hallmark of Cuban society. Today's proposal for a *prosperous and sustainable socialism* will depend on all Cubans, seeking strategies by means of consensus to ensure that creativity, talent, and skills are not frustrated, avoiding the loss of human capital out of the country. The idea is to create real conditions for the development of the capabilities of each Cuban so that, motivated by commitment to the common good, they see that there are guarantees for the defense and promotion of the responsible freedom of the person. In addition it is necessary to embody the principles of solidarity and subsidiarity, such as the universal destination of created goods.

Toward a Prophetic and Hope-Bearing Ethic

The Christian worldview and its incarnation in contemporary Cuban society have the ongoing challenge of reaching the heart and conscience of every Cuban. It has the beautiful mission of rekindling the prophetic spirit of Jesus in the communities of faith in order to reach the "peripheries that need the light of the Gospel"[14] to establish the Kingdom of God and his righteousness (cf. Matt. 6:33). The option of a *prophetic ethic* must be accompanied by a praxis of encounter, accompaniment, and a preferential option for the weakest, the poor, the disinherited, and those who suffer because of so many injustices.[15] The option for a *prophetic ethic* invites men and women to let God reign in their lives and in the midst of the people, so that all are dedicated to weave projects of social welfare and be participants in the project of salvation of God the Father through his Son Jesus Christ. Therefore the church of and in Cuba must continue assessing "especially everything that belongs to the social order and to the attainment of the common good,"[16] without "remaining on the margins in the struggle for justice,"[17] planting seeds of hope in every direction, seeds of the Kingdom of God, that sprout from the "loving heart of Jesus Christ."[18] As a mother concerned and committed to her children, the church is engaged in the construction of a decent society, a new people, the fraternity dreamed of by God.

The Christian message in Cuba is expanding and shifting little by little. Hence we need to continue to offer *an ethical orientation that is both prophetic and a sower of hope*. In this concrete scenario, the prophetic attitude and mission needs to have not only a "public" face but a "more visible body" that emphasizes social duties, justice, and law. In the face of fear, silence, and the blindness of many, we must be the voice of those who have no voice. We must provide alternatives for a healthier society and its institutions, freely giving opinions guided by grace on every dimension that impacts citizens.[19] Each one, individually and as people, must be deeply conscientious of personal, social, and structural sin, as well as all failures as a country. The church must not govern this society, but it does offer the proclamation of God's love and guidance accompanied by their respective criteria, adding to the common discernment that seeks that which humanizes and dignifies every child of this homeland. From the strength of the Word of God and the person of Jesus Christ, we must continue to question everything that goes against the Kingdom of God, through prudent denunciation, while at the same time announcing the newness of God, making a strong call to sincere conversion, accompanied by a call to hope.

The freshness and beauty of the gospel must help the people experience the presence of God, merciful Father in their midst. This is a God of the people, who has never forgotten God's children and who acts mysteriously as a source of freedom and new life. Thus, the ethical voice revives in Cubans the "memory of the people," awakens in them a "critical and affective memory," that values the bonds of a shared destiny that unites them, appreciating the gifts received in order to channel them toward building a better society.

Sowing Christian hope is urgent and necessary for the Cuban people to continue walking toward the realization of that future good, trusting in God's faithfulness and what God can do in their lives. For this reason, the Cuban church cries out that "hope does not disappoint" (Rom. 5:5), that conversion to Jesus Christ is *that* hope which gives life abundant to the many dry bones that need new life (cf. Ezek. 37:1–14). We sow hope so that the revitalizing spirit of God helps us to stand, to create communion, and to walk together (cf. Ezek. 37:10). It also aids conversion and the eradication of all those sins that lead to ruin, to open the possibility to have a "new heart and a new spirit" (cf. Ezek. 18:30–31). Like the disciples at Emmaus, there is a movement from disenchantment to the newness of God (cf. Luke 24:1–50), so that from encountering Jesus we might be converted to a deeper hope, going out to the existential paths to meet so many people locked in their wounds. We go out to encounter the wounded in the flesh and listen to them calmly, offering comfort and directing them toward that new creation and salvation that Jesus Christ promises us. Thus, the task of sowing hope seeks to include everyone, so that from *discernment, without cowardice or coercion*, we might expand horizons based on an ethical and spiritual basis that allows Cubans to seek what is good, what they want, and where they want to go. Hence everyone commits to "prophesy," to proclaim good and to fight against evil, so that the Kingdom of God and God's justice can be realized here and now. This commitment requires the following proposals:

We are called to change some structures and to transform society as we journey toward justice.

Justice is present when people's lives are organized according to God's plan, and everything is how God wants it to be. Social structures must contribute to the *affirmation of the inalienable worth of the human person and her or his dignity*. Thus, the responsibility of developing greater flourishing of individual and collective autonomy surfaces from the affirmation of the human as subject. This implies the defense and promotion of a greater degree of *the responsible freedom of the person*, a precious gift that God has given us in order to be fruitful and obtain for ourselves and our families the fruits of decent work. This freedom also allows for participation in those decisions that affect the personal, family, and social future. With this in mind, I echo the thinking of Pope Benedict XVI:

> Integral human development presupposes the responsible freedom of persons and peoples; no structure can guarantee such development from outside nor above human responsibility. The promising but illusioned messianisms always base their own proposals on the negation of the transcendent dimension of development, sure to have everything at their disposal. This false security becomes a weakness, because it involves the subjugation of the person, reduced to a means for development, while the humility of one who receives a vocation becomes true autonomy, because it makes the person free.[20]

At the same time, there is the guarantee and defense of human rights as a real commitment to human dignity.

Moreover, care for the life and destiny of each of the Cubans involves the reconstruction of a social model with institutional and legal changes that guarantee and foster a greater role for popular participation in the decision making and strengthening of a culture of solidarity for achieving a prosperous and sustainable society. Hence, it behooves the government to seek the good of all citizens, managing in the best way possible the fair interests of each group and region of society. At the same time it is called to promote a participatory state that will definitely replace the paternalistic state. The government is called to create all the possible conditions and instruments that allow for the impact and functioning of intermediate associations oriented toward the common good.

We are called to change relationships and renew the community as we journey together in solidarity.

The principle of solidarity must be engaged with greater maturity and coresponsibility, in order to strengthen the social fabric, preferentially opting for the most vulnerable, needy, and poor of society. This is a renewed solidarity, exercised by everyone with justice and equity, especially by those involved in the political and economic spheres. This culture of solidarity must be accompanied by the principle of subsidiarity that enables true integral human development. Recall that this "subsidiarity is primarily an aid to a person, through the autonomy of intermediate bodies. Such aid is offered when the person and the social subjects are not able to fend for themselves, always implying an emancipatory purpose, because it favors freedom and participation in assuming responsibilities. Subsidiarity always respects the dignity of the person in whom it finds a subject always capable of giving something to others."[21] Thus, uniting these two principles, we generate projects of greater socialization/social humanization and review all social policies so that they are enjoyed fully by all citizens. This dynamic includes the challenge of continuing to improve the educational system toward an integral formation of the human being, enhancing both spiritual and moral dimensions. And, it is extremely important to be partial to the incarnation of the "use of the goods of the earth," given by God to each and all, that through their work they may dignify themselves and cooperate for the social good. There are other forms of property that have to be extended to the greatest possible number of people (knowledge, technique, technology, etc.) to ensure the basic conditions for participation in development.

We are called to change our ways of thinking and to reimagine conscience as we journey on the path of spirituality.

Christian humanism, which is open to transcendence in dialogue with other visions about the person in society, has the challenge of inviting the cultivation of a spirituality of self-donation and gratuitousness, which springs from love, so that we become incarnate in love of others and social love. From this inner experience of love can be sown hope, balance, well-being, life, peace, and compassion. This spirituality sheds light on the personal conscience in order to strengthen the social conscience needed to rebuild the community, either by uplifting moral criteria or by generating social dialogue and establishing social friendship from a spirit of reconciliation. Moreover, Cuban society has the mission of deploying creativity by opening up new spaces of fraternity and commitment for the common good from its cultural and religious riches. In short, Cuban identity with its wisdom is called to take the opportunity to progress with maturity, to rebuild everything that is needed to make the common home fraternal, dignified, and free, always open to a hope that never disappoints.

Notes

1. See V. Bye, "How Should the World Accompany the Process of Adjustment of the Cuban Social Model?" *Espacio Laical* 2 (2014): 18.

2. Ovidio D'Angelo Hernández, "Cuba: Inevitable Individualisms or Possible Inclusive Solidary Society? Experiences and Questions," *Espacio Laical* 1 (2017): 22.

3. Cf. Teresa Díaz Canals, "The Promise Island: A Vision of Social Morality in the Cuban Present," *Espacio Laical* 4 (2014): 13–17.

4. Cf. Conference of Catholic Bishops of Cuba (COCC), *Message, Love Awaits All*, nos. 9–11, Havana, September 8, 1993.

5. Ibid., no. 17.

6. Alberto de Mingo Kaminouchi, *Introduction to Christian Ethics* (Salamanca, Spain: Sígueme, 2015), 72.

7. Cf. COCC, *The Voice of the Church in Cuba: 100 Episcopal Documents* (Mexico: National Work of the Good Press, A.C., 1995); COCC, *National Cuban Ecclesial Encounter: Final Document and Pastoral Instruction of the Bishops of Cuba* (Mexico: National Work of the Good Press, A.C., 2005); COCC, *Together We Build the Morning*, Pastoral Global Plan 2006–2010, *Message to Jesus by Mary, Charity Unites Us*, Havana, September 8, 2008; COCC, *On the Way to Emmaus*, Pastoral Plan of the Catholic Church in Cuba, 2014–2020; COCC, Pastoral Letter, *Hope Does Not Disappoint (Rom. 5:5)*, Havana, September 8, 2013.

8. COCC, Pastoral Letter, *Hope Does Not Disappoint (Rom. 5:5)*, Havana, September 8, 2013, nos. 22–23.

9. Cf. ibid., nos. 25–28; COCC, *Pastoral Plan of the Catholic Church in Cuba ,2014–2020*, nos. 18–40.

10. COCC, Pastoral Letter, *Hope Does Not Disappoint (Rom. 5:5)*, nos. 31–32.

11. Ibid., no. 33.

12. Cf. CONCUR, Congress of the Consecrated Life in Cuba, Memoirs, El Cobre, Santiago de Cuba, November 16–20, 2015.

13. *Pastoral Plan of the Catholic Church in Cuba, 2014–2020*, no. 30.

14. *Evangelii gaudium (EG)*, no. 20.

15. Cf. Enrique Colom-Ángel Rodríguez Luño, *Elected in Christ to Be Saints: Fundamental Moral Theology Course* (Madrid: Palabra, 2000), 338–39.

16. Cf. *EG*, no. 182.

17. *EG*, no. 183.

18. Ibid.

19. Cf. Ibid.

20. *Caritas in Veritate (CV)*, no. 17.

21. *CV*, no. 57.

BIG CHALLENGES REQUIRE MAJOR TRANSFORMATIONS

Suggestions from Bolivia

Claudia Montes de Oca Ayala

This essay reflects on the current Bolivian historical process, which is immersed in a regional and global process—and with which we share challenges, hopes, frustrations, and pain—with theological elements referring to ecclesial identity and mission. The ethical–prophetic criteria that inspire this reflection are renewed by the Second Vatican Council, generated, and developed in Latin America to identify alternatives that offer hope to our lives and history.

The essay is articulated in three parts. The first part, "Signs of the Times?" identifies the current reality and its challenges. It invites us to reflect on a church that is still not convinced of the seriousness of the ongoing crisis and the need for prophetic radicalism. The second part, "Generating Hope," provides theological tools to discern those signs of the times and to feed new processes, or renew others, motivated by the values of the gospel and expressed in actions. Finally, some of these actions are suggested in the third part: "Forging New Horizons for Life."

Signs of the Times?

We are living realities that surpass understanding and tolerance. Among other challenges, we are facing a probable third world war,[1] poverty, trafficking of human beings, violence toward girls, boys, and women, and terrorism, along with climate change and its consequences that negatively affect impoverished sectors and aggravate migratory flows.

All these challenges hardly motivate the feelings and life projects of the majority of the population; on the contrary, they provoke discouragement and distrust. There is a relative consensus that we are in a crisis of civilization. Many voices affirm that we are undergoing a process of paradigm changes, deep searches for meaning, and a crisis of the criteria established since modernity that has shaped humanity and, particularly, Western societies.[2]

In the last two decades, as a result of complex processes and from a critical–ethical perspective,[3] profound historical changes occurred in the Latin American region. They strengthened both hope and optimism. Changes to social sectors—which were historically invisible and impoverished socially, culturally, economically, and politically—generated challenging expectations and promoted the participation of social groups in the construction of joint projects based on the promotion of the common good.

The achievements that were made possible are important and in some cases transcend history. Among them is the new Political Constitution of the Bolivian Plurinational State.[4] However, especially during the present decade, there were serious signs of corruption in the processes and attrition to the proposals that fed them. Currently, a clear example of this crisis is Venezuela.

Bolivia's Process of Change

In the 1990s, Bolivia strengthened processes that generated alliances in favor of transformations in the social, cultural, economic, and political dynamics of the country. The indigenous and peasant people positioned their claims in the public debate, thus stressing the need to make profound and real changes[5] regarding their group identity and cultural diversity within the framework of an ethical criteria of justice.

The process that led to the election of Evo Morales as president of Bolivia—with almost 54 percent of the vote—expresses the search for recognition, inclusion, participation, and transformation desired by the majority of the Bolivian population. This is a population made up of economically disadvantaged sectors and a middle class that sought the recognition of a decolonized identity, the realization of a common social and just project, and the affirmation of national sovereignty.

The socialist political–ideological proposal, articulated with the demands mentioned above, provided an interesting alternative, more due to the lack of proposals than for its own ideological project. Faced with the political crisis of traditional parties, in the 1990s the political alternative Movimiento al Socialismo (MAS) gathered together different national social sectors and presented Evo Morales as a presidential candidate with a political agenda that included the indigenous people's issues and the recovery of national sovereignty.

Eleven years have passed since President Morales assumed the country's leadership. The results are not as convincing as his first promises were, due to inconsistencies, public policies that are contrary to the interests of the process of structural transformation, and to public corruption.

Regarding the demands of the indigenous peoples, several changes were politically approved and implemented—for example, the active recognition of the diversity of indigenous peoples as nations, which generated a significant change in the formal denomination of the Bolivian state (now called Plurinational State of Bolivia, formerly known as National State of Bolivia). Moreover, government entities were created to attend to the demands of these nations, and many laws also underwent modifications in line with the new Political Constitution of the state.

Likewise, the process of diversity and intercultural dialogue has been formally established, but it is taking a long time to be fully implemented and the achievements are insufficient—even more so with respect to the daily relations between the inhabitants of a country that is still characterized by discrimination.

The process of political affirmation of cultural dignity and diversity implies decolonization. In Bolivia, this category is essential to understanding its current historical process. It refers, on the one hand, to the indigenous peoples' fight to be, think, feel, and act autonomously, confronting the hegemonic power that denies the dignity of the other.

On the other hand, it is crucial to continue the processes of affirmation and promotion of life in all its different languages, transforming and liberating the subordinate realities that depend on current neocolonial structures of power.

The ancestral knowledge offers significant contributions to generate alternatives to the current planetary crisis. In Bolivia, among the indigenous peoples, there is an ethical category regarding the meaning of life that has been translated as "living well," and means to live in harmony and balance with all forms of life.

Living well today is a widely shared ethical point of reference since the experience of indigenous peoples has spread to other areas of society. However, it is used more discursively than transformationally. The most obvious and critical example is the inconsistency between the environmental issues that affect the nation and the economic policies of the Bolivian state that deny the possibility of promoting life and that violate Mother Earth.

On the other hand, the Bolivian cultural reality is similar to postmodern Western culture: anthropocentrism, hedonism, overestimation of human subjectivity, consumerism, and relativism are among the most outstanding cultural traits influencing current structures and colonizing our lives and projects. As in much of the planet, technological advances have generated important changes in our lives and our human relations. The rapid pace of the flow of information demands immediacy and makes it difficult to form a critical conscience. The media do not manifest an appropriate ethical maturity that matches the demands of its informative and educational role. On the contrary, the media prefer to encourage distraction; they choose events of a tragic and violent nature, broadcasting them in a yellowish and even morbid tone. In addition, they lack political objectivity and disseminate biased messages for or against the current government.

In this identification of the structural causes affecting the Bolivian reality, we must mention the forms of patriarchies/patriarchalism that have constituted the social, economic, political, religious, and cultural systems. The different types of violence currently being experienced are also the product of this unjust structure of subordination of women and other vulnerable groups. The actual process of decolonization requires, for its true realization, a process of "de-patriarchalization," understood as the process of affirming the dignity of women with a practical realization of their rights within the framework of gender equity.

The Church in Bolivia

In the regional context, the contribution of the Catholic Church has been significant: through the actions of evangelization keyed toward human promotion, and during the historical processes that eradicated military dictatorships and recovered and strengthened democracy. The church, after the Second Vatican Council and until the 1990s, has clearly identified itself with the preferential option for the poor, providing and developing processes of integral formation so that the poor are subjects of their own liberation: "it is impossible to understand the forces that have reached the indigenous peoples' claims, and the political movements linked to them, without the contribution made, in a sustained way, by groups of Christians who were driven by the General Conferences of the Latin American episcopate."[6]

The Bolivian Bishops' Conference, during this historical process, has provided several elements of analysis, particularly through pastoral letters:[7]

- *Earth, Fertile Mother for All* (2000) addresses the serious problems related to land tenure and access to it by the poor.
- *Water—Source of Life* (2002) deepens the issue of access to water for all.
- *Building a Bolivia for All: Towards the Constituent Assembly* (2006) offers inputs to assess and contribute to the process of emitting a new Political Constitution for Bolivia.
- *Catholics in Today's Bolivia: Presence of Hope and Commitment* (2011) is aimed at the Catholics and to the whole society to motivate the participation of all citizens in the process of the country's transformation.
- *The Universe—Life's Gift of God* (2012) considers environment and human development in Bolivia.
- *Today I Put before You Life or Death* (2016) is a pastoral letter on drug trafficking and drug addiction.

These documents represent important tools for interpreting and reinforcing the Bolivian historical process. However, in the last decades—and this is not a local phenomenon[8]—the ecclesial hierarchy has strengthened actions that are characterized by a kind of conservative orthodoxy and apology of the faith framed in a weak doctrinal interpretation among its lay members. The effects are manifested in a laity indifferent to realities that demand lights of hope.[9] Moreover, the greater support for lay members' movements, such as the Neocatechumenate or Opus Dei, obstructs Latin American ecclesial processes such as the ecclesial base communities or spaces of theological and biblical popular reflection, among others.[10]

In 2015, Pope Francis's visit to Bolivia inspired a period of ecclesial and social mobilization. The people's response to his visit exceeded ecclesial expectations, and the church received an important message from Pope Francis. Nevertheless, for the Bolivian church and its society, the subsequent pastoral efforts were insufficient to give continuity to the meaning of this particular event.

Generating Hope

The previously presented reality may generate hope but only if there are positive changes in Bolivia. During his visit, Pope Francis recognized the inclusion of broad sectors in economic, social, and political life; emphasized the protective character of the new Constitution with regard to minorities and the environment; and invited participation and dialogue. He also stressed that these processes require education in the values of citizenship, because "if growth is only material, there is always the risk of creating new differences."[11]

Addressing the Bolivian church, Pope Francis identified her as a mother, by encouraging her to communicate the joy of the gospel, to be salt of the earth and light of the world. He emphasized that her mission has as its perspective the preferential option for the poor, the persons who are discarded and excluded by the system. In that understanding, the bishops speak to society in the name of the mother church, and their voice must have a prophetic character.[12]

According to *Evangelii gaudium*, the message of Pope Francis in Bolivia shows the need to experience a church that reaches out of itself to meet the poor, overcoming the dangers of any attitude inspired by paternalism and assistentialism, and affirming the need of horizontal and sincere dialogue in the realization of equal dignity, diversity, and promotion of the person.

A Renewed Ecclesiology: The Church as People of God—A Church That Reaches Out of Herself

The Second Vatican Council represents a historic milestone for the church. However, more than fifty years after the event, many of its challenges have yet to be accomplished and the changes achieved are still insufficient. Pope Francis is offering important tools to reactivate the motivations that fed Vatican II, among them, those related to the ecclesiological identity. The way in which the church understands and places herself existentially and historically defines how she carries out her mission. In this sense, the category *church–people of God* represents a fundamental contribution of the Council.

Church–people of God affirms that the ecclesiological identity is a main aspect of the divine project. The church as a community of people of God recovers the original identity offered by God to its original community and accepted by Christianity in the figures of our predecessors in the faith, during the first centuries. This category strengthens the communal relations between the members of the church, reaffirms the equal dignity of its different ministries, highlights the coresponsibility in the mission, and opens itself to self-criticism and humble learning in community. The church–people of God that has no borders and welcomes diversity and that, in particular, approaches the outcasts of systems and structures, is the community where Jesus himself lived.[13]

The category people of God, pilgrims in history, expresses the attitude of movement, of permanent search, of knowing oneself in a process of ongoing maturity and liberation, surpassing the human temptation of comfort and settling down that immobilizes and causes blindness to the pain and signs of death of the contemporary world. The church–people of God, motivated by the spirit of Jesus Christ, does not remain static, but, like a pilgrim, walks endlessly, meeting those in need of hope.

The history of salvation expresses an attitude of God that goes out to meet God's people, the whole of humanity. God takes the initiative to love us, to call us, and to walk with us. This is how *EG*[14] reminds us that the church develops, through a theologically coherent journey, in light of Vatican II and its ecclesiological criterion, to meet the contemporary human beings, to welcome the joys and sorrows of today's societies, and to strengthen the openness to sincere dialogue in the accomplishment of the evangelizing mission.

The Option for the Poor

The renewal that the Second Vatican Council inspired in Latin America generated a fruitful analysis of the reality and history of the region. The Bishops' Conferences of the continent (CELAM) reflected the historical processes of our countries by expressing an evangelical ecclesiological understanding articulated with the doctrine, the tradition, and a renewed biblical exegesis. The documents of Medellín, Puebla, and Santo Domingo show a clear ethical and even political perspective of the Christian message that reaffirms solidarity as an expression of justice and a manifestation of love,[15] from the viewpoint of the preferential option for the poor.

The history of salvation makes manifest an option for the poor (with regard to troubling human conditions) to welcome the divine promise of life in abundance. The preferential option for the poor, as an ecclesiological attitude in the fulfillment of the Christian mission, corresponds to the church's very identity defined by the experience of Jesus.[16] *EG* reaffirms this truth: "Today and always, 'the poor are the privileged recipients of the Gospel.'"[17] This is one of the fundamental criteria of Pope Francis's message and proposal for a structural ecclesiological reform in the mission of the church.

The preferential option for the poor is an ethical criterion that, at present, can be understood as a compulsory condition for every Christian. In particular, it means

- Liberation from the condition of absolute disability of the poor and, in the words of Pope Francis, of those who are *discarded* by the system;[18]
- Just reaffirmation of the principle of the social doctrine of the church that affirms the *universal destiny of goods*;[19]
- Criticism of the idolatrous monetary system, the market economy, and the consumerism that degrade the freedom of human beings and their dignity; and[20]
- An alternative approach to building a new world, by affirming the life and dignity of all, especially of those who are "discarded."

In Latin America, the poor have specific faces: children, women, and indigenous people. In coherence with the Christian virtue of justice, to assume their stories means to overcome the welfare attitude that limits the role of the people as agents and protagonists in their liberation process. Pope Francis, regarding the participation and contribution of the poor in these historical transformations, affirms, "You, the most humble, exploited, poor, and excluded, can and do much. I dare to say that the future of humankind is largely in your hands, in your ability to organize . . . in your participation as protagonists in the great national process of transformation. Do not fall short!"[21]

Intercultural Dialogue—Living Well [22]

The epochal change we are living demands that Christianity offers its message of hope by understanding, in a prophetic and critical way, the current reality and by proposing transforming alternatives that affirm the dignity of life, justice, peace, and love. This epochal change highlights the need to identify and present other alternative historical and transforming criteria of modernity, because the modern paradigms of civilization evidenced their unsustainability and denied legitimate alternatives to other ways of living and to understanding of the meanings and horizons of life.

One of the main factors of current historical deconstruction is the overcoming of the empowerment of a privileged human rationality as a tool for understanding the current reality. To address the complexity of the human condition, rationality is considered the privileged approach. However, rationality is not the only referent of ethical discernment. The human condition is shaped by a complex fabric of dimensions and different ways of perceiving and receiving, of understanding and positioning ourselves in the realities that we live.[23] Knowledge is a human construct. It is the result of a process in which rationality participates alongside other possibilities of knowing the different realities, including, of course, values and the realities that transcend the historical context, like utopias.

Questioning the privilege that modernity gave to human rationality offers the opportunity to recognize other criteria of discernment of senses of life. Today, postmodernity affirms human subjectivity. Hence, subjectivity has a privilege granted to it as a legitimate space in the processes of discernment of senses and understanding of reality. Yet, subjectivity is still framed in an anthropocentrism that relativizes and objectifies diversity, hindering an intercultural relationship that affirms the dignity of life in all its meanings and manifestations.[24]

The Bolivian ancestral knowledge offers millenary knowledge, fruits of experience, and discernments articulated with a sacred referent. The worldviews of the peoples of the region produced a knowledge that implies the integrality of the human being and of the human relation with the environment from a perspective of reciprocity, opposed to the anthropocentric and androcentric approaches of

Western modern knowledge. Hence, the Bolivian ancestral knowledge represents a valuable contribution in this time of searching for horizons of meaning of life that surpasses the serious shortcomings of modernity.

The Bolivian indigenous peoples have developed their stories according to a horizon translated into Spanish as "vivir bien,"[25] living well, although in its translation this expression does not adequately explain the original meaning that can be understood as to live life in its fullness, to know how to live in balance "in harmony with the cycles of Mother Earth, of the cosmos, of life and of history, and in balance with all forms of existence."[26] Living well refers to a way of living that has as its center life in harmony with the community and nature, understanding that this relationship has a sacred character. Breaking balance and provoking disharmony means altering the cycles that life guarantees in all its forms and puts at risk its promotion. Hence, the lives of human beings are in interdependence with the other expressions of life.

Living well reveals a different understanding of the Western conception of living characterized by development, accumulation, and the commodification of nature. In the indigenous worldview, a fundamental element is the affirmation of the religious referent as opposed to its underestimation or indifference in the modern Western culture. This underestimation questions the possibility of understanding life and other living realities apart from this founding criterion. "For the original Indian spirituality, the universe is a living being, a sacred space dynamic and polyphonic. A reality that speaks from the divine . . . The utopia of harmony and permanent concern to maintain or recover it when it is lost is the basis of the original ethics. In this view, sin . . . refers to the non-fulfillment of a rite of care of networks of reciprocity."[27] In this spirituality, accumulation breaks the balance and harmony between communal relations and nature. Because this is a break with the sacred, it is not compatible with living well.

In the daily life, rituality articulates the sacred dimension with everything that implies life; that is, there are no antagonistic dualisms as defined by modernity: body and spirit, good and evil, sacred and profane, and so on. These dualisms would segment the subjectivity of the person and could explain the inconsistencies of Christian identity and a corresponding ethics that causes a divorce between faith and life.

The phenomenology of Christian rituals implies an anthropology that articulates the dimensions of the human condition and that is different from the modern anthropology that segmented the integrality of the human being. The integral apprehension of life contributes to the transformation of the current world system that puts at risk the promotion of life in all its manifestations.

Christian ethics can enter into dialogue with indigenous spiritualities and indigenous ethics to cooperate today with real alternatives that not only remained for millennia but are the result of a praxis that manifests respect for life and the sacred, recognizing the articulation of both realities and enabling the continuity of history within the framework of a horizon of true meaning for it.

Forging New Horizons for Life

The challenges of the Bolivian reality, in general terms, are the same as those of a large part of humanity: the realization of justice, the practical affirmation of the common good as a reference for economic policies, the critical ethical discernment in politics, the intercultural and interreligious dialogue, the respect for nature and all forms of life, and the strengthening of processes that offer alternative models of development. To address these challenges we need to develop and/or motivate other processes: the decolonization of the religious, the overcoming of anthropocentric and androcentric ideologies, and the ethical–critical deconstruction of the modern world system in the West. These processes are broad and complex; hence, it is not possible to develop them in this essay. However, identifying them is essential to integrating them in the analysis and argumentation of Catholic theological ethics.

The ecclesiology promoted by Pope Francis is linked to the proposals of the Second Vatican Council and to the demands of local and regional realities that contextualize these guidelines and demand renewed interpretations. By focusing on Vatican II and on the local reality, we can propose the following actions toward ethical realization of the ecclesial mission by promoting what some call an "ethical code":[28]

- It is necessary for us to seek the permanent renewal of our ecclesiological self-understanding, by reaffirming our identity as the people of God who are pilgrims in history with a clear lay eschatological sense of the work of salvation here and now. This should happen by opting for the poor and the excluded, by working for transformation with them and from their point of view. Liberation implies the liberation from the sinful situations mentioned above. Moreover, it is urgent to construct alternatives of life with a horizon of meaning motivated by the love of life. In ecclesial contexts, this means the promotion of analysis and reflection by laypeople to examine what they live daily and to promote a creative and transformative participation.
- Dialogue does not necessarily mean reaching agreements. The church needs to promote this type of dialogue even in the ecclesial context. The ecclesial dialogue with feminist theologies[29] can initially be a meeting space that feeds utopian processes, complementing each other in the same horizon of God's project.
- The renewal of Christian anthropology is also needed, by overcoming the antagonistic dualist categories that privilege certain dimensions at the detriment of others with respect to their participation in the processes of knowledge construction, moral discernment, definition of decisions, and actions. Likewise, Christian ethics and morality require the development of their reflections and theoretical constructions based on the articulation

between the individual and her/his context, which demands a process of decolonization of the categories and myths of modernity in relation to the processes of knowledge construction.

- The involvement in the social processes of poor sectors (e.g., social movements) that are fighting for the visibility of their denunciations and proposals is also required. This involvement also demands to articulate with them what is needed to promote real alternatives for society.

- It is important to radically assume the analysis and reflection of the encyclical letter *Laudato si'* to promote a critical discernment of the social, economic, political, and cultural reality of humanity and to foster an activist pastoral approach that articulates doctrinal formation with social and political participation. Pope Francis states: "The common house of us all is being plundered, devastated, and vexed with impunity. Cowardice in their defense is a grave sin . . . There is a clear, definitive, and ethical imperative to act that is not being fulfilled . . . I ask you, in the name of God, to defend Mother Earth."[30]

- Finally, the articulation of Christian ethics and its theoretical construction (in theological discourse) should be done in dialogue with the ethics of indigenous peoples, as a sign of affirmation of the dignity of these peoples while searching to realize the Christian values and the ethical criteria of living well.

Christianity has a true message to offer to humankind. At present, the death and pain that people suffer are the cry of God's creatures, and they join the ecological crisis with its violence exerted on Mother Earth and on the whole divine creation. We cannot remain indifferent. Catholic ethics is the prophetic dimension of the ecclesial mission. Affirming and realizing the vision that is constitutive of Catholic ethics is essential to making the ecclesial message credible and coherent with the church's identity.

Notes

1. Pope Francis, in his address to the participants of the Second World Meeting of Popular Movements, affirmed that we are experiencing a "third world war in quotas." Conferencia Episcopal Boliviana, *Francisco en Bolivia. Discursos y Homilías. Viaje Apostólico del Santo Padre Francisco a Ecuador, Bolivia y Paraguay* (La Paz: Presencia, 2015), 59. Personal translation.

2. *Evangelii gaudium (EG)* identifies the present time as a "epochal change" (no. 52).

3. The critical–ethical analysis of Latin American processes identifies as a milestone the "celebration, in 1992, of the 500 years of discovery" of the American continent. On this occasion, the reasons for the celebration were questioned, transforming a modern and superficial historical perspective (from the conquerors' viewpoint) and positioning a critical and ethical historical proposal framed in justice and the affirmation of dignity: making poverty visible at the expenses of the native peoples. Then, the categories of colonialism and

decolonization regained sense and meaning . . . 1992 forced us to think about our problem from beyond the not only modern matrix, which is 500 years old, but also Latin American, which is 200 years old. Juan José Bautista, *Hacia una crítica-ética de la racionalidad moderna* (Bolivia: El Grito del Sujeto, 2007), 149. Personal translation.

4. The new Political Constitution of Bolivia is the result of a construction process that had its most important formal moment in the Constituent Assembly held between August 2006 and December 2007. Almost ten years after its conclusion, the challenges of the Assembly reemerged. See Moira Zuazo and Cecilia Quiroga San Martín, eds., *Lo que unos no quieren recordar es lo que otros no pueden olvidar. Asamblea Constituyente, descoloni-zación e interculturalidad*, 3rd ed. (La Paz: Fundación Friedrich Ebert, 2012).

5. The Bolivian history has different foundational moments: the precolonial period; the colonial period or the subordination of the local population to the Spanish crown (traumatic process); and, after a long period of revolutions promoted by indigenous and mestizos, in the year 1825 the republic was born. Later, the Revolution of April 1952 generated important changes for the recognition of the citizenship of the indigenous population and women and their right to vote. A guiding thread of this historical fabric is the political recognition and participation of indigenous and rural populations. This participation was usually mediated by third parties (i.e., middle class, army, traditional politicians, etc.) without the possibility of a meaningful direct representation.

6. Armando Raffo, "De Rio de Janeiro a Aparecida. Aportes del Episcopado Latino-americano y Caribeño al dinamismo de sus pueblos y a la Iglesia universal," *Sal Terrae* 95, no. 4 (2007): 293. Personal translation.

7. These documents constitute the magisterium of the Bolivian church, in http://www.iglesia.org.bo/ Personal translation.

8. Several voices affirm that the Latin American church has changed radically; those who participate and know the ecclesial dynamics within its different contexts can corroborate it. For example, Pedro Trigo criticizes these changes and describes a pietistic and corporatist church. See Pedro Trigo, *Echar la suerte con los pobres de la Tierra: Propuesta para un tratamiento sistemático y situado* (Venezuela: Centro Gumilla, 2015).

9. According to a study carried out by the Ecumenical Network of Theologians of La Paz, within the church, many women have a superficial knowledge of the problem of violence against women in society; idealize community ecclesial experience; do not identify any situation of violence in their ecclesial communities; do not know the concept of symbolic violence; and affirm that the power relations (e.g., machista and clerical) established in the churches are divine will. Cf. Diagnostico, *Relaciones de género en comunidades religiosas desde la perspectiva de mujeres Católicas y Evangélicas de las ciudades de La Paz, El Alto, Cochabamba y Santa Cruz* (La Paz: Red Ecuménica de Teólogas de La Paz, 2016). See also Red Ecuménica de Teólogas de La Paz, *El Roi: el Dios que me ve. Visibilización de la violencia a las mujeres en espacios eclesiales* (La Paz: Pachamama, 2016).

10. Victor Codina points out that in the 1970s and 1980s, the Latin American church was a prophetic church that opted for the poor. However, in the later decades, the church entered into a "social and ecclesial night." Victor Codina, "Dios ha pasado por América Latina," *Sal Terrae* 95, no. 4 (2007): 320.

11. Conferencia Episcopal Boliviana, *Francisco en Bolivia*, 10. Personal translation.

12. Ibid.

13. Victor Codina calls the ecclesial characteristic of permanent movement a continuous Abrahamic nomadism, to describe the essential attitude of seeking and finding God

in daily life and in life itself. See Equipo Ilamis, *Urbes, un acercamiento teológico-misional* (Cochabamba, Bolivia: Itinerarios, 2013), 7–10.

14. *EG*, no. 20, explains this foundation, by traversing the history of salvation from Abraham to Jesus Christ, and by motivating an ecclesiological understanding of "departure."

15. The Christian proposal regarding the understanding and realization of justice is related to human projects of affirmation of human dignity and freedom. In this sense, as far as the social condition of human beings is concerned, justice is a human political aspiration. This desire, in the experience of God, finds a radical motivation as a manifestation of love.

16. The option for the poor is a theological category rather than a cultural, sociological, political, or philosophical category. See Irene Tokarski, *Para trabajar con ética* (La Paz: Fundación Jubileo, 2015), 20–29.

17. *EG*, no. 48. Pope Francis quotes: Benedict XVI, "Address to the Brazilian Bishops in the Cathedral of São Paulo, Brazil" (May 11, 2007), 3.

18. The Latin American theology, which inherited and is motivated by liberation theology, has as its fundamental category in its theological architecture the preferential option for the poor, precisely as an affirmation of the gospel and its priority attention to these groups; to opt for them means to reaffirm its identity and mission. Pedro Trigo, in his book *Echar la suerte con los pobres de la Tierra*, offers a proposal for a systematic theology that is physically placed in this category from within the reality and Latin American processes of transformation. See Pedro Trigo, *Echar la suerte con los pobres de la Tierra* (Venezuela: Centro Gumilla, 2015).

19. In this regard, Pope Francis, in his address to the popular movements of the world held in Bolivia in 2015, proposes three tasks to assist in solving the most urgent needs of humanity: "The first task is to put the economy to the service of peoples . . . the just distribution of the fruits of the earth and human labor . . . is a moral duty. For Christians . . . it is a commandment. It is a question of giving back to the poor and to the peoples what belongs to them. The universal destiny of goods . . . is a reality prior to private property." Conferencia Episcopal Boliviana, *Francisco en Bolivia* (La Paz: Presencia, 2015), 55–56. Personal translation.

20. In various messages and documents, Pope Francis clearly denounces the present idolatrous role that people and societies have assigned to money. In his visit to Bolivia, he affirmed that, "when capital becomes an idol and directs the choices of human beings, when greed for money protects the whole socioeconomic system, it ruins society, condemns man, and makes him a slave." Ibid., 52. Personal translation. With a theoretical construction that dismantles modern epistemological architecture, Franz Hinkelammert proposes the necessary elements to understand the crisis of modernity, the present situation of the Western civilization and, particularly, Latin America, to suggest patterns that contribute to the processes of transformation of historical contexts framed by ethical criteria such as dignity, justice, and the common good. See the works of Franz Hinkelammert, Hugo Assmann, Enrique Dussel, Juan José Bautista, and Rafael Bautista, among others.

21. Conferencia Episcopal Boliviana, *Francisco en Bolivia*, 52. Personal translation.

22. This section refers to an article published by the Foreign Ministry of Bolivia. See Claudia Montes de Oca, *Cambio de época, oportunidad para el diálogo interreligioso* (La Paz: Cancillería del Estado Plurinacional de Bolivia, 2015).

23. "This anthropological understanding, moreover, has been generated in a context in which human rationality is prioritized to the detriment of other dimensions of the constitution of the subject and particularly of the transcendental or divine reality. This characteristic

of modernism challenges, for example, the possibility of understanding life from criteria of faith." Centro de Promoción del Laicado Ricardo Bacherer, CEPROLAI, *Medio Ambiente, Creación Divina. Nuevos estilos de vida, vida en abundacia* (La Paz: CEPROLAI, 2013), 26. Personal translation.

24. The ideal of modern Western culture, which is centered on the self-sufficient, autonomous, and independent individual, leads to individualism and it is currently in crisis. In the 1980s, Robert Bellah conducted research in the United States and verified negative psychosocial effects of individualism as alienation, loneliness, unhappiness, and inability to maintain relationships, among others. Later, other theorists continued this research and analysis, concluding that the "great Western ideal of self-realization . . . leads to egocentricity and narcissism, which on the other hand are also the cause of mental disorders both neurotic and psychopathic. The self-centered individual loses contact with reality." Albert Nolan, *Jesus hoje. Uma espiritualidade de liberdade radical* (Sao Paulo: Paulinas, 2008), 41–46. Personal translation.

25. Living well, or good life, are translations of the *aymara suma qamaña, quechua sumak kausay, guaraní teko kavi, mapuche kyme mogen*: terms that indigenous peoples use to express the meaning of life. See Fernando Huanacuni Mamani, *Vivir Bien/Buen Vivir. Filosofía, políticas, estrategias y experiencias regionales* (La Paz: Convenio Andrés Bello, 2010), 37–49.

26. Ibid., 46.

27. Simon Pedro Arnold, "El Buen Vivir, una interpelación teológica," *Diálogos* 8 (2015): 28–34.

28. The expression "ethical code" is used to refer specifically to the ethical dimension of evangelization, by considering that the Christian mission of salvation is an action offered to humanity, either as a collective horizon and as a system of ethical criteria for life in society, more than as an individual horizon, that is, as a proposal for a personal life project.

29. The contributions of feminist theology are irreversible. The church cannot ignore them. On the contrary, it could accompany them by promoting a new world order based on new social relations of gender. See Olga Consuelo Vélez, "Movimientos feministas y Cristianismo," in Darío García et al., *Reflexiones en torno al feminismo y al género* (Bogotá: Digiprint, 2004), 49.

30. Conferencia Episcopal Boliviana, *Francisco en Bolivia*, 80.

THEOLOGIANS AND
PUBLIC ETHICAL DISCOURSE IN SLOVENIA

Roman Globokar

Every ethical reflection is determined by its context. Ethics is never an abstract discipline but always exists within a specific historical and cultural environment. Christian ethicists must always pay attention to the context they live in and do their best to live the gospel in their personal and social life. As Vatican II stressed, we—the ecclesial community—are on a pilgrimage and are called "to work with all men in the building of a more human world" (*Gaudium et spes*, no. 57). In a pluralistic and democratic society, the most appropriate way to achieve this is through dialogue where everyone has the right to present their views on certain common challenges and where everyone is invited to take part in the joint effort of looking for solutions to those challenges. In this essay, I would like to reflect on the current social context and on my experience of being a theological ethicist in Slovenia.

Social Context of Secularization in Slovenia

Slovenia is a young democracy. The country has taken slow steps toward a pluralistic and open society. After forty-five years of Yugoslav communism, Slovenia proclaimed its independence in 1991 and introduced democratic changes. On December 23, 1990, the 88.5 percent of electors (94.8 percent of those participating) voted in favor of independence. It was a clear rejection of the totalitarian state of Yugoslavia and the fulfillment of an old dream of a Slovenian state. Democratic pluralism was introduced, and a rapid economic and political development took place. Slovenia was the most developed of the former communist countries in Europe. In 2004, Slovenia joined the European Union, and in 2007, it became a member of the Eurozone and the Schengen Area—the first of the new members. However, this smooth and rapid progress can hinder the critical view of the process of democratization in the country. The mentality cannot change in an instant. There are still efforts to truly learn to engage in dialogue and to establish a pluralistic way of solving common issues.

Religion in the Public Sphere in Communist Yugoslavia

Since 1991, from a legal point of view, the democratic Constitution of the Republic of Slovenia has stipulated a strict separation of church and state (articles

7 and 41). This separation was first drafted into the communist Constitution in 1946 and subsequently interpreted in the sense of limiting the public expression of religious freedom. The objective of the communist Constitution was to remove religion from the public realm and, ultimately, to end its influence. Religion was defined as an exclusively private affair. Moreover, it was next to impossible for the people of faith to reach the higher ranks of society. These were reserved for members of the Communist Party, the membership of which was not compatible with being a believer. However, as Slavica Jakelić observes, the churches in Yugoslavia provided for the survival of Catholicism: "The churches, in effect, created a parallel public realm in what otherwise would have been a private sphere of life. It is there that church representatives became the institutional voice in defending basic human rights, including religious freedom."[1] As such, the Catholic Church attracted not only believers but secular humanists as well. Jakelić points out the paradox of exclusion of religion from the public sphere in Yugoslavia: "Inadvertently, however, this approach established collectivism at the centre of believers' private religiosity. Contrary to the modern Western European religious experience, with the individual as its main agent, the 'private' Catholicism of Bosnian, Croatian, and Slovenian societies became connected with strong institutions and specific communities."[2] The parallel realm of the Catholic community was established, but it was prohibited to enter into the public sphere. "Public articulation—by the clergy, theologians or the lay public—of opinions that were unacceptable from the perspective of the socialist authorities led, in a number of instances, to surveillance by the security service and imprisonment on the basis of anti-state activities."[3]

The Catholic Church in Slovenia was very active in the independence movement and entered the democratic period with large moral capital and credibility. For a long time, the church was the only organized force of opposition in Slovenia. In the mid-1980s, when the democratic process started, the Catholic Church actively participated in and supported the emerging political opposition. Many theologians took part in the fight for human rights and sovereignty of our country. The Justice and Peace Commission of the Slovenian Bishops' Conference published several statements to support democratic development, human rights, and political pluralism. However, very soon the positive image of the church faded away in the public eye. There are many different reasons for this decline; some stem from the church itself and others from post-communist social development.[4]

Religion in the Public Sphere after the Slovenian Independence

After the period of religious oppression in the totalitarian system, some representatives of the church hierarchy expected a revival of religious life in the sense of a re-Catholicization of Slovenia. Their idea was a "Catholic Slovenia." The real Slovenian should be a Catholic or at least of Catholic culture. They wanted continuity with Slovenia before the Second World War, when the 1921 and 1931 censuses both determined a strong Catholic majority (97 percent) in Slovenia. The majority of Slovenians rejected these expectations. The number of people who declared themselves Catholic declined drastically immediately after the switch to democracy. During communist times, the first census that included the question of religion was carried out in 1953; on that census, 82.8 percent of Slovenians declared themselves Catholic. In 1991, the year of independence, the percentage dropped to 71.6 percent; in the most recent census, in 2002, only 57.8 percent of citizens declared themselves Catholic. Other research shows a similar picture. The younger generations, people living in urban areas, and more highly educated people increasingly declare themselves unaffiliated with any religion. In the World Values Survey Wave Six (2010–2014), religion was considered very important in life by 11.2 percent of the respondents from Slovenia and rather important by 21.7 percent. For the majority of citizens, religion is not important. Almost the same results are evidenced in Eurobarometer 2010: 32 percent of Slovenians declared a belief in God, while 36 percent affirmed their belief in something spiritual or in a life force. The Slovenian Catholic Church, which was the first religious institution to enter the public realm in the former Yugoslavia in the mid-1980s, was very soon marginalized in public life.

In the last decade, a significant decrease in church practices is clearly illustrated in the 2016 annual report of the Slovenian Bishops' Conference. The number of church weddings fell from 3,495 in 2005 to 2,420 in 2015, a decline of more than 30 percent. In relation to civil weddings, in 2015, church weddings comprised only 38 percent. A similar declining trend is observed in the proportion of baptized children. Despite an increase in childbirth in Slovenia between 2005 and 2010, the number of baptisms decreased. Ten years ago, almost 73 percent of children in Slovenia were baptized in the Catholic Church, while only 55 percent were baptized last year. Until the 1980s, less than 10 percent of children were born outside of marriage, but then the numbers rose sharply. In 1990, the proportion was 25 percent; in 2000, 38 percent; in 2010, 55 percent; and in 2014, 58 percent of children were born outside of marriage. The percentage of practicing Catholics going to church every Sunday is under 15 percent. In my opinion, the main problem of the Catholic Church in Slovenia is its inability to sincerely face this situation and to critically reflect on the last twenty-five years.

Difficulties of the Catholic Church in Democracy

After the restoration of political pluralism and democratic government, the Catholic Church, like numerous other civilian institutions, reclaimed its possessions, which had been nationalized by the Yugoslav communist government. The democratic government decided for full restitution of the church properties confiscated by the previous regime, and this decision was sharply criticized by the main mass media in Slovenia. In my opinion, no real mass media pluralism was established after the democratic changes, and, in the case of the majority of mass media, this area of civil society has remained in continuity with the former system. The idea of a rich and greedy church was widely spread in society and intensified in the mass media. The financial scandal surrounding the economic collapse of the Archdiocese of Maribor in 2011 affected the entire Catholic Church; in the eyes of Slovenians, any trust in the moral authority of the church was lost. In the following years, the Vatican deposed four Slovenian bishops for failing to act against the economic scandal and for improperly reacting to the situation. This brought additional trouble for the Catholic Church.[5] The church authorities mainly accused the media for biased and sensationalist reporting about the financial collapse of the Archdiocese of Maribor, but the reaction of the leaders of the Slovenian church was not always appropriate, and a thorough examination of their troubling decisions has not yet taken place.

As I indicated above, the lack of plurality in the mass media has decelerated the democratic process in Slovenia. The majority of the information about the church and religion is biased and creates prejudice. Religion as such has been seen as an obstacle to democratization and a possible source of new totalitarianism. There was a fear that the Catholic Church, as the biggest religious institution, would impose its moral convictions into law and onto all citizens regardless of their religious affiliation. Since the first moment of democratic change, there was propaganda in the mass media against clericalism and the influence of the church in political life. Every mention of Christianity or Christian values in public discourse was interpreted as an interference of the church into politics. Although the Christian Democratic Party won the first democratic elections in 1990, its role became marginal in political life after 1992. Liberal democratic and left-wing parties have mostly governed during the past twenty-five years. Our society is based on liberal values, such as individual and social rights, freedom of choice, equality, tolerance, and neutrality of state in matters of religion. As a consequence, the level of inequality remains among the lowest in Europe.[6]

Slovenia is a country based on secular values. However, in the recent referendums addressing ethical questions, the majority of Slovenians voted to promote traditional values. In public referendums, the liberal laws voted by the government were abolished through direct vote. In 2001, 72.36 percent of voters voted against the possibility that single women could access in vitro fertilization (IVF). In 2003, 57.53 percent of participants agreed that stores should be closed on Sundays. In 2012, 54.55 percent of participants voted against the possibility of marriage among same-sex persons. In 2015, 63.51 percent of voters did not confirm the new Family Act that would provide the same rights to both homosexual and heterosexual couples.[7] These results highlight a paradox: the supporters of liberal and left-wing parties agreed with the traditional values of life and family. The Catholic Church was actively involved in the referendums' campaigns. A clear statement of the Catholic bishops was read in all churches a week before each referendum; priests and laypeople were engaged in the public debate before each referendum; and, before the last two referendums on the Family Act, a group of citizens was formed to oppose it.[8]

On the other hand, after the democratic changes, the Catholic Church has been unable to introduce religious instruction into public schools. There is no mandatory course on religious education in public schools in Slovenia. At the beginning of the democratic changes, the main goal of the liberal democratic school reform was to prevent any influence of the Catholic Church in the educational process. During the process of the so-called de-ideologization of the Slovenian schools, the Marxist ideology was to be removed and the basis for the neutrality of school constructed. The White Book on Education published in 1995 declared, "State schools are lay and shall not be under the monopolistic influence of individual churches, parties, or groups supporting a specific worldview."[9] Any education focusing on values has been prohibited in the public school system. In the opinion of Slavko Gaber, the former minister of education, the task of the school system is just to instruct and not to educate. The schools' neutrality should be guaranteed by excluding any religious and ethical issues from the curriculum. The Organization and Financing of Education Act from 1996 states, "At public kindergartens and schools, confessional activity may not be allowed. The confessional activity referred to in the previous paragraph of this Article shall encompass: catechesis or the confessional teaching of religion with the goal of inculcating this religion; courses where a religious community decides on the content, textbooks, teacher education, and adequacy of individual teachers for teaching; organised religious ceremonies."[10] In 2011, wide public reflection on the school system in Slovenia detected a lack of religious and ethical themes in public schools. The final document affirms, "In the field of ethics and religion, the primary school should ensure that all pupils get some basic knowledge."[11] However, there is no suggestion for how to carry out such an education, meaning that in the Slovenian public schools there is still no systematic religious and ethical education.

Divisions within the Slovenian Nation and the Need for Reconciliation

In the public sphere in Slovenia, another unsolved pressing question concerns the assessment of the events that occurred in Slovenia during and immediately after the end of the Second World War. In the first two months after the war, the communist regime executed about 15,000 "adversaries of the nation," many of whom were civilians. The great majority of these executions were perpetrated without any legal proceedings. During the communist period, this crime was never admitted.[12] Moreover, many opponents to communism were forced to migrate to the West, including almost the entire prewar political, cultural, and clerical elite. Following a violent takeover, the communists not only controlled the entire political power, they also seized all the material goods through confiscation or nationalization. After the fall of the totalitarian system, many affected families sought moral acknowledgment of what had been done to their deceased relatives and the revision of the history of a nation. The national reconciliation, however, has not yet occurred. The Slovenian nation is still deeply divided between, on the one hand, those who supported the communist armed resistance to the German, Italian, and Hungarian occupation during the Second World War and carried out the communist revolution, and, on the other hand, those who supported the anti-communist resistance of the Slovenian Home Guard, which protected people from the revolutionary terror but tactically collaborated with the Italian and German occupying authorities. During the Second World War, the Catholic Church supported the anti-communist groups and was, therefore, described as "a traitor to the country" during the communist period. This label is still used in the public discourse.

In 1990, in Kočevski Rog, the main place where the executions took place, there was a commemoration for all the victims of the postwar terror. In that occasion, the Archbishop of Ljubljana, Alojzij Šuštar, the last president of the Slovenian Communist Party, and the first elected president of Slovenia, Milan Kučan, shook hands as a symbolic gesture of reconciliation and a new beginning. But later, the process of reconciliation advanced very slowly. There were no legal proceedings against the perpetrators of these executions. Only in 2016 were the first victims excavated from the mass graves and buried in common graveyards near Maribor. In 2017, a monument to all victims of war and afterwar terror was erected in the center of Ljubljana. Many people, from the left and the right, were against this monument, but it could be considered a step forward toward national reconciliation.

Unfortunately, intolerant statements in the media and on social platforms confirm the presence of divisions and hostile attitudes within the younger generations. The unsolved past and the lack of national reconciliation underlie the current political manipulation of what occurred during and after the Second World War. There is an urgent need for a joint statement on national reconciliation.

Theological Contributions: A Personal Perspective

Beyond Prejudices

Slovenia is a secular society filled with many prejudices against Christianity and the Catholic Church. The prejudices are an inheritance of the communist system, and are strengthened by the lack of religious education in public schools and the inability of the Catholic Church to use appropriate language to express its positions. In addition, personal negative experiences while interacting with the church and its representatives have also contributed to this negative image. It is often the case that what is related to religion and the church is seen as old-fashioned, not connected to real life, and nonscientific. In this sense, theology itself is often understood as a nonscientific and socially irrelevant science. A statement of the Slovenian philosopher Friderik Klampfer, one criticizing that in a lay country a moral theologian is a member of the national commission for medical ethics,[13] is an illustrative example of this attitude. According to many, a theologian is a representative of the institutional church and as such, not suitable to be a member of expert committees within a democratic and pluralistic society. However, my personal experience proves the exact opposite. As a theologian, I have been an equal member of various ethical and educational commissions for many years and enjoy respect from colleagues from other disciplines. It is true that at the beginning, other members often looked at me with skepticism. They could not imagine how a theologian could participate in common debates on ethical and social questions. What they expected was an apologetic advocacy of Catholic positions rather than an open and dialogical approach to finding common solutions.

A Dialogical Approach

A dialogical approach is not only a pragmatic choice but also one that originates from the methodology of theological ethics. Theological ethics in itself is a dialogical discipline that always looks to interact with the concrete social reality. Even the process of secularization, which in many ways determines the social climate in Slovenia and Europe, presents a challenge and an opportunity for theological ethics to enrich its statements and encourages it to critically articulate its views in the public sphere.[14] The process of secularization has denounced the religious primacy in the field of ethics and has claimed the primacy of reason over against any reasoning informed by religious discourse. Secularization, as such, does not exclude the role of religious communities in the ethical discourse. Theological ethicists, however, should present their arguments at the court of reason. A theologian can no longer assume the Christian foundations of the majority of the population. Nothing is taken for granted; it is necessary to justify any position. However, as I learned from my teacher Klaus Demmer, there is no pure, self-evident moral reason, but rather every statement is rooted in its own metaphysical, cultural, historical, and anthropological preconditions.[15] There is no neutral, rational position, but every statement is marked by its cultural and anthropological backgrounds. It is important to be aware of these preconditions in one's own positions but also in the positions of the other participants in public discourse. The task of theological ethicists is to examine critically the different statements and their metaphysical and anthropological basis. Moreover, it is very important to have courage and pursue alternative ways of being engaged in today's society. For Demmer, "A theologian has the courage to address roughness, the lack of understanding and contrast. He can be perceived as a nuisance but not as someone who refuses the dialogue . . . For many sceptical contemporaries, a theologian looks for answers to questions which nobody else asks."[16] Demmer noticed that today, for many people, the contribution of a theologian is at best a luxury that could be easily discarded. However, even these cases could become a new opportunity for theologians. They should address others from positions of power, claiming that they teach the ultimate truth, but they should also invite all citizens to reflect about fundamental questions in life.

This approach requires four steps: first, it demands a deep understanding of the topic that needs to be examined and studied (e.g., facts, scientific data, research, etc.). Second, it is necessary to situate the topic in its own context and examine it through the prism of Christian anthropology (i.e., by taking into account the four sources of Christian ethics: scripture, tradition, experience, and reason). Third, dialogue with other participants in the discussion (i.e., hearing their arguments and understanding their points of view) is essential. Fourth, in the public discourse, there is the need to define and articulate one's statements in clear and convincing manners (after having examined the anthropological background of these statements). One of the biggest challenges for theological ethicists is the manner of presenting our views to the public. Our contemporaries do not easily understand the nuances and richness of theological language and reasoning. Furthermore, theological discourse rejects any model of heteronomous morality where the individual is subordinated to mere obedience to authority. Even believers expect from theologians arguable positions that are credible and persuasive, based on facts, and that promote the full realization of personal and social life. Moreover, most of our contemporaries are not interested in considering the theological relevance of statements of the magisterium of the church and rightly stress how moral demands should be presented in an understandable and convincing way.

Areas of Ethical Engagement

After reflecting on the challenges of theological reflection in the Slovenian context, and on the privileged methodological approach, in this section I discuss possible areas of ethical engagement in light of my own experience by focusing on academic life, bioethics, and education.

As a theologian, I teach at the University of Ljubljana, which is a state university. The theological faculty has been an equal partner in academic life since 1992. In society, there are some voices arguing against the public funding of theological studies because it is perceived as contradicting the constitutional separation between church and the state. In the academic sphere, sometimes a question about the status of theology as a science surfaces. But formally, during the last twenty-five years, theology has had the same privileges as other faculties. There is also an ongoing initiative to establish a Catholic university that the faculty of theology could join. In my opinion, there are many reasons in favor of remaining a part of the state university. Mainly, in such a way, theology is an equal partner in interdisciplinary dialogue between different sciences; moreover, the members of the theological faculty serve on various expert committees at the national level, and the theological students can combine theological studies with other courses from other disciplines; and last but not least, the theological work is fully financed by the state. The main challenge is a rapid decline of students in the last decade, because of the limited perspectives for employment for lay students. In other European countries, theology students can apply for the positions of religion teachers. Since in Slovenia there is no religion education in public schools and the church does not show interest in hiring theologians, young people avoid enrolling in theological studies. There are some additional challenges in the process of teaching seminarians and lay students. Four of these challenges follow: to develop an adequate terminology of theological ethics in the Slovenian language, to choose suitable foreign theological literature for students, to motivate them to reflect on their own moral experience, and to equip them with substantial knowledge to empower them in participating in ethical discourse within the church and also in the public sphere.

In Slovenia, there are only three theological ethicists. In addition to being professors at the faculty, we also have administrative responsibilities. Two of us are directors of Catholic school centers, and the third one is a secretary of the Slovenian Bishops' Conference. In terms of theological expertise, each one of us covers the entire field of theological ethics ranging from fundamental moral theology to bioethics, sexual ethics, and social ethics. Because of the need to be familiar with a wide range of topics, there is no real opportunity to conduct more in-depth research of certain theological areas. Since Slovenia is a small country and the Slovenian language is not widely spoken, we interact with ethicists from abroad. Traditionally, we have been well connected with Central Europe, but recently we have joined several international committees of theological ethicists.

The National Bioethics Committee

At the beginning of my academic career, I was invited to join the National Bioethics Committee. This has been a very positive experience of interdisciplinary dialogue in which as a theologian I can contribute to finding ethical solutions to medical and pharmaceutical dilemmas. I often ask medical experts to explain the issues we are addressing. My role is to ask questions about whether one particular act or way of proceeding violates human dignity. The rich tradition of moral theology allows me to illuminate specific areas with some basic questions. Sometimes, I have a chance to provoke discussion about specific dilemmas by pointing at the implicit anthropology present in different ethical options. As I mentioned above, each moral judgment is grounded in a particular anthropology. Hence, I try to explicitly address the anthropological and metaphysical horizon of the different positions.

As a theological ethicist, I am committed to promote the dignity of every human person and to prevent any form of discrimination. Each person has equal dignity, irrespective of nationality, sex, state of health, or economic conditions. Above all, I feel committed to giving voice to "the weak" or "the poor" in society, to those who have no voice or whose voice is not heard. As a theological ethicist, there are many chances to be interviewed by the media or to engage in debates on the Internet in order to draw attention to injustices in society and to various violations of human dignity.

Education

The third area I have been involved in for more than sixteen years is education. I have been teaching a module on ethics as part of the course "Religion and Culture" in a high school. Moreover, as an administrator, I am heading the biggest Catholic school in Slovenia. These roles also give me the opportunity to be involved in the educational policy of our country. As a member of the National Board of Experts for Education, I participate in elaborating the strategy of education at the national level. Methodologically, moral theology helps me build the bridge between Christian anthropology and the challenges of education today. Together with others engaged in Catholic education, we constantly strive to make Catholic schools equal partners within the common Slovenian education system instead of being a parallel school system. The equal participation of Catholic schoolteachers in various expert state bodies facilitates this process. Cooperation allows the overcoming of prejudices that are still present against any form of private education in Slovenia.

After the period of "de-ideologization" that excluded any type of education focusing on values in schools, we are currently striving for some kind of ethical education in public schools. The total exclusion of religion from schools promotes and strengthens the process of radical secularism that aims at excluding the church from the public arena. While we are developing the curricula and course books for religious education at Catholic schools, we are aware that, in the future, these or similar teaching materials could also be used in public schools. Our approach is, therefore, dialogical and interconfessional. We try to show that such a form of religious education is also possible within our secular and pluralistic society.[17]

Conclusion

Theological ethics is a bridge between the rich moral tradition of the church and the contemporary secular society. As all citizens, we are inevitably influenced by the society in which we live. Bearing this in mind, theological ethicists are trying to contribute to public discourse. Theologians should neither try to situate themselves outside of the social realm nor condemn the contemporary society as morally decadent. We are part of our secular society. Hence, our theological reasoning and our social engagement are always conditioned by our concrete historical and cultural contexts. However, our mission as theologians is to elaborate, from our rich moral tradition, methodologies and criteria for the critical appraisal of our social and ecclesial community. We need to be both humble and conscious of our social determinism, but also courageous to propose some alternative solutions in collaborating with other social agents for the common good in society. Christian anthropology is an inexhaustible source of inspiration for building a better world for everyone.

Finally, as a theological ethicist, I occasionally feel uncomfortable. Within the secular society, it happens that I am under suspicion. As a representative of the Catholic Church, I am identified as someone who wants to impose an authoritative and dogmatic moral teaching. Moreover, some conservative circles in the church are uncomfortable with a theological approach that does not limit itself to repeating the teachings of the magisterium of the church but also aims at promoting reasoning on specific issues and tries to foster dialogue and convincing rational arguments while addressing diverse positions. As I explained above, there is no contradiction between reason and faith. In order to understand human life and its actions more deeply, dialogue between various sciences and the contributions of theological ethical reflection should be encouraged. Such a dialogue is a dynamic process in which theologians critically examine specific social contexts, dynamics, and situations by considering the four sources of theological ethics: Scripture, tradition, reason, and experience. This methodological approach allows theology to remain connected to real life, and concrete human experience becomes the starting point of theological thinking and action.

Notes

1. Slavica Jakelić, *Collectivistic Religions: Religion, Choice, and Identity in Late Modernity* (Farnham, UK: Routledge, 2010), 48.

2. Ibid., 49.

3. Aleš Črnič et al., "Religious Pluralisation in Slovenia, " *Teorija in Praksa* 50, no. 1 (2013): 205–32, at 216.

4. Egon Pelikan, "The Catholic Church and Politics in Slovenia," in *Religion and Politics in Post-Socialist Central and Southeastern Europe: Challenges since 1989*, ed. Sabrina P. Ramet (Basingstoke, UK: Palgrave Macmillan, 2014), 115–30.

5. In 2015, only 5 percent of the respondents to the survey on Slovenian public opinion expressed full trust in the church. http://www.adp.fdv.uni-lj.si/opisi/sjm15/.

6. OECD, *Understanding the Socio-Economic Divide in Europe*, January 26, 2017, 8, https://www.oecd.org/els/soc/cope-divide-europe-2017-background-report.pdf.

7. All the results can be found at http://www.dvk-rs.si/index.php/si/referendumi.

8. Tadej Strehovec, "Vloga katoliške civilne družbe v zavzemanju za družbeno pravičnost," *Bogoslovni Vestnik* 72 (2012): 373–82.

9. Janez Krek, ed., *Bela knjiga o vzgoji in izobraževanju v Republiki Sloveniji* (Ljubljana: Ministrstvo za Šolstvo in Šport, 1995), 27.

10. Ministry of Education, Science and Sport of the Republic of Slovenia, *Organisation and Financing of Education Act*, Ljubljana 2014 (article 72), http://www.mizs.gov.si.

11. Janez Krek, ed., *Bela knjiga o vzgoji in izobraževanju v Republiki Sloveniji 2011* (Ljubljana: Ministrstvo za Šolstvo in Šport, 2011), 43.

12. Igor Bahovec, "Odnos do preteklosti in slovenska razdeljenost: medvojno in povojno obdobje kot torišče delitev in naloga za prihodnost," *Bogoslovni vestnik* 74 (2014): 41–53.

13. Friderik Klampfer, *Cena življenja: razprave iz bioetike* (Ljubljana: Krtina, 2010), 12.

14. Ivan Janez Štuhec, "Sekularizacija kot priložnost za novo religioznost," *Bogoslovni vestnik* 72 (2012): 609–18.

15. Klaus Demmer, *Selbstaufklärung theologischer Ethik: Themen—Thesen—Perspektiven* (Paderborn, Germany: Ferdinand Schöningh, 2014), 27–28.

16. Ibid., 27.

17. Roman Globokar, ed., *Religious Education in Slovene Schools: Evaluation and Perspectives* (Ljubljana: Zavod sv. Stanislava, 2010); Drago Čepar and Roman Globokar,

eds., *Religious Education in the World Today* (Ljubljana: Zavod sv. Stanislava 2013); Roman Globokar, Tadej Rifel, and Marko Weilguny, eds., *The Mission of Catholic Schools: An Answer to the Challenges of Today and Tomorrow* (Ljubljana: Institute for Education Research and Development, 2015).

SPLENDORS AND SHADOWS OF THE ECCLESIAL CHARACTER OF MORAL THEOLOGY BY POLISH MORAL THEOLOGIANS

Konrad Glombik

There is no famous Polish moral theologian that has undergone a doctrinal investigation by the Congregation for the Doctrine of the Faith. The encyclical letter *Veritatis splendor (VS)* by John Paul II was received critically by many moral theologians in different countries, while Polish moral theologians received this document uncritically and wrote many commentaries on it. Those facts are connected with the understanding of the ecclesial character of moral theology and the place of theologians in the church as well as the church's mission of transmitting the Christian moral message. A lot of studies and contributions by Polish moral theologians are dedicated to the documents of the Catholic Church, especially those written by John Paul II, and are commentaries on them. This kind of understanding of moral theology has its splendors and shadows and shows the self-understanding of moral theologians, their place and mission in the church, the character of moral theology, and the understanding of ecclesiology. The present essay critically analyzes the foundations and causes of the strict connection between moral theology and ecclesiology from the point of view of Polish moral theology. In particular, it analyzes the nature of the connection between moral theology and ecclesiology, the reasons for it, the kind of moral theological studies to which this leads, and which understanding of ecclesiology is the basis for it.

Moral Theology in the Church and for the Church

For Polish moral theologians, the assumption concerning the ecclesial roots of moral theology is unquestionable. According to the most popular handbook of moral theology, published by Stanisław Olenid (1919–2005), the Christian moral message as a topic of Catholic moral theology is a dynamic effort of reflection and teaching concerning the deeper understanding of the faith and for the service of the church. This effort is not undertaken in isolation from the reality that persists and lives in the church. Moreover, it is situated in the specific historic period, with its intellectual and cultural climate and with respect to the self-understanding of the church, and it depends on the knowledge that is possible to achieve, particularly in light of the contribution of human sciences.[1]

In this framework and historical space, moral theology fulfills its task of reflection on the faith. Hence, it should be rooted in the faith and it should be faithful to the Word of God. Moral theology cannot be a simple transmission of the revealed truth but a deeper systematic reflection on it and always should be an indicator of the faith of the church without which it misses its sense and justification.[2]

Moral theology as a reflection on morals takes place in the church. It is a theological science that analyzes, estimates, and explains human conduct, that finds the source of life in God, in Jesus Christ the way to the goal of Christian life, and in the Holy Spirit the inspiration to love. Moral theology benefits from faith and reason in explaining biological, psychical, and spiritual conditions of the life of Christians in the ecclesial community.[3]

The ecclesial character of moral theology is connected with the fact that it is developed in the church and serves the community of believers. For moral theology, the church is not a strange instance but the basis of its existence, and the church determines it. The ecclesially oriented moral theology is an answer to the Word of God, and it is a form of wisdom of faith in the context of the communal character of the Christian vocation. Hence, moral theology also has an ecclesial character. The church is for Christians a place of moral knowledge, which comes from Jesus and the Holy Spirit. The church is a spiritual space in which Christians recognize the will of God.[4]

The ecclesial character of moral theology is connected with the participation of theologians in the life of the church. For theologians the church is the space in which they receive access to specific knowledge related to the faith of the Christian community and have the possibility to participate and experience Christian life, which is the subject of their reflections. The engaged character of participation of theologians in the life of faith of the church does not disturb the objectivity of their theological analyses and narrations; on the contrary, the faith makes it possible to be moral theologians and makes them witnesses of the transmitted truth. In the church, theologians discover truth, which they have not created by themselves, and serve this truth. The discovery of moral truth requires from moral theologians both radicalism and perfection in order to respond to the moral message of meeting Christ present in the church.[5]

This ecclesial character of moral theology is connected with the communal reorientation of moral theology during and after the Second Vatican Council. The reality of the church depends on the unity with God made possible in Christ and, at the same time, on the concrete elements that shape this life. Hence, there is interdependence between the development of human beings and the progress of the ecclesial community.[6] In this context, moral theology is a scientific analysis and presentation of morality according to the teaching of the Catholic Church.[7]

The constitutive aspect of the identity of moral theology is the deep connection with the church. In light of Pope John Paul II's encyclical letter *Veritatis splendor*, it follows that moral theologians have obligations connected to their relation to the church. They instruct believers about precepts and practical norms that the church with its authority promulgates; search for deeper rational justification of the ecclesial teaching; argue in order to convince about the importance of magisterial teaching and the need to follow it by stressing its connection and reference to the final human goal; and highlight the biblical base, ethical meaning, and anthropological motivation, which are the foundation of the moral doctrine of the church and of the Christian vision of the person (*VS*, no. 110). In fulfilling their mission of teaching the moral doctrine of the church, moral theologians should educate believers so that they are able to achieve moral discernment, to pursue truth, and to search for help with fidelity in God's grace (*VS*, no. 113).[8]

The Magisterium and Moral Theologians

According to Polish theologians, the ecclesial character of moral theology is strictly connected with the magisterium of the Catholic Church. The church received the Word of God from the apostles and transmits it to God's people through the magisterium. The magisterium explains the revelation, interprets it authentically, and teaches it authoritatively. The teaching of theologians is the result of human reflection on the Word of God, and it is based on faith. The magisterium and the reflection of theologians serve the Word of God, and between them there should be harmony. The magisterium is above theological reflection because it has received from Christ the commission to watch over the transmission of the faith being faithful to the revelation. In fulfilling this task, the magisterium can benefit from the contributions of theologians.[9]

Theology is the expression of the conscious faith of the church as the community of believers, and it is a cognitive instrument that makes it possible to hold the magisterium thanks to the systematization of the faith, the elaboration of theological ideas, and the compact argumentation that theologians articulate. Theologians benefit from the authoritative teaching of the church and receive the statements and theological formulations accepted and approved by the magisterium.[10]

Moral theology serves the people of God and its faith and participates in transmitting the Christian moral message. The task of transmitting the faith concerns every believer, including the moral theologians and bishops (magisterium). The place of moral theologians is between the faith of all believers and the magisterium of the church. The moral theologians should be attentive to protect their faith from public opinions on moral themes. Moral theologians are invited to faithfully embrace the teaching of the magisterium, and the magisterium should promote the moral theologians' search for the truth in the complex ethical questions of believers in today's society. The teaching of the magisterium is neither limited to parenetic and pastoral, nor more to inviting normative statements. Moreover, the task of moral theologians is not only to offer a running commentary of the documents of the magisterium. The task of moral theologians is also to elaborate arguments, and to examine the social, even biological and psychical consequences of the duty to follow the moral norms formulated by the church's magisterium.[11]

Polish moral theologians stress the final character of decisions of the magisterium. In the field of morality, the task of the magisterium is "discerning, by means of judgments normative for the consciences of believers, those acts which in themselves conform to the demands of faith and foster their expression in life and those which, on the contrary, because intrinsically evil, are incompatible with such demands."[12] Such decisions, for example those concerning the specific conclusions of the commandments of the decalogue or particular regulations based on the natural law, should have the final word and end possible discussions of moral theologians. In these cases, the magisterium is not simply presenting its own positions, but it is teaching on behalf of the church, and believers have the right to authoritative magisterial teaching that follows the law of God. From this point of view, when they occur, polemics or contestation of statements of the magisterium in regards to moral questions by theologians are contradictory with the ecclesial communion and with the correct vision of the hierarchical structure of the church as the people of God. According to Ireneusz Mroczkowski such contestation cannot be recognized as a correct expression of the Christian freedom.[13]

The connection between moral theology and the magisterium should neither entail captivity by the latter of the former nor compromise their scientific autonomy. Moral theologians have a right to search for the right ways to maintain the autonomy of scientific thinking and to search for the right space for theological disputes. Of course this autonomy can neither mean disassociation from revelation nor disregard of the ecclesial context of the faith to which they belong. The freedom of moral theologians is for the good of church and for the quality of theological reflection. Moral theologians should not forget that they teach in the name of the church and have the task and responsibility to make present the church. The magisterium should recognize the scientific character of moral theology, its methodology and rational argumentation, but moral theologists should be aware of their own limitations and should not believe that they could or should replace the magisterium.[14]

Moral theology as an ecclesial science feeds off the tradition of the church and draws off the actual magisterium. Moral theologians' responsibility is not only to make comments on pontifical documents and statements of the Vatican congregation, but to develop the theological thinking on the basis of the principles marked out by the Bible and by the tradition. The task of moral theologians is to search how to explain, address, and, if it is possible, resolve actual theological questions and problems that exist in today's church. Moral theologians rely on the way of the experience of past generations and on their reactions to the changing times. Hence, it is important for moral theologians to be faithful to the truth that is guarded by the church.[15]

The strict connection between the magisterium of the church and moral theology is stressed by *VS*, no. 110. According to Polish moral theologians, *VS* clarifies that the authority of the magisterium of the church in the teaching and explaining of moral principles is unquestionable. In this encyclical letter, the competence and authority of the magisterium is so strongly accentuated that the value of the existential experience of believers in the moral message of the church is reduced.[16] The range of theological competence of the magisterium cannot be limited to general constant principles; it also concerns the concrete situational and conditioned conclusions. The documents promulgated by the magisterium concerning concrete moral questions should delineate the borders outside which theory and practice do not correspond with the requirements of moral law and Christian message. Moral theologians situate within these borders their broad field of freedom for research, reflections, and comparisons with the results of their research, as well as observations nourished by their pastoral experience. In cases of theological controversies, the magisterium has the last word. If the magisterium intervenes in problematic cases, its intervention should not concern theologians as persons, but rather the contents of their publications. There is no possibility of creating a counter-magisterium or a parallel "theological" magisterium that would depend on the arguments of the majority of opposing theologians and that would offer believers alternative norms of behavior. Such a hypothetical counter-magisterium would confuse the believers. Theologians should be obedient to the magisterium. Divergent theological opinions of moral theologians expressed as contestation and a public polemic to statements of the magisterium are creating contradiction and division within the ecclesial community, and they are challenging both the importance and the role of the ecclesial hierarchical structure within the people of God.[17]

Theologians should not forget that they are not called primarily to transmit the results of their own personal theological research but that they are called to teach in the name of the church. Because they teach not in their own name but in the name of the church as faithful teaching subjects, the task of moral theologians is to present what the church teaches in moral theology. If moral theology is a way to serve the church, then the authority of the magisterium cannot be seen only as an external force.[18]

Some Problematic Questions

According to Polish moral theologians, the ecclesial character of moral theology is inseparable from theological investigation and research, and it is its constitutive element. The strict correlation of moral theology with the magisterium of the Catholic Church has positive and negative aspects, splendors, and shadows. The following discussion concerns some problematic questions that are connected to the ecclesial character of moral theology.

Contributions and Studies

Generally speaking, one problem with theology in Poland is the choice to limit the sources of theology to the magisterial documents, particularly the teaching of

Pope John Paul II. This limitation depends on the fascination of Polish theologians for the Polish pope and the need to study his great heritage. For some theologians, their emotional connection with John Paul II blinds them from considering critically some aspects of his teaching. Their interests mostly focus on national issues and debates instead of considering what might concern all people and nations. In studying the teaching of John Paul II, insufficient attention is given to highlight themes concerning the role of laypeople in the church, the place of women in Christianity, the problems concerning the missionary endeavors and evangelization, and the understanding of the church as communion.[19]

On the one hand, moral theology in Poland shows its ecclesial character and unity with the Holy See by focusing on the teaching of the magisterium, by stressing the magisterial role to guarantee the orthodoxy of theological thinking, and by the positive magisterial educational contributions. On the other hand, this way of proceeding slows down the development of theology and weakens its dynamics and openness to the problems and challenges of the context of the modern world. The Polish moral theology is doctrinally correct, but, to ordinary believers, it is neither interesting nor credible. Moral theology becomes more and more theoretical and traditional but less and less existential in character and is not able to address new questions of the current social, cultural, and religious processes in Europe and in the world.

A further problem related with the strong ecclesial character of Polish moral theology is the lack of serious theological disputes and the limited number of schools of theological thinking. On the one hand, there is a Polish moral theology that is institutionally strong, with many theologians conducting their research at faculties of theology. On the other hand, some studies and publications are more like reports than examples of creative thinking, or they avoid addressing present and pressing historic questions, or they prefer to translate and repeat the ideas of leading Western theologians.[20]

The postconciliar Polish moral theology can be characterized as faithful to the tradition. Its renovation and development after the Second Vatican Council took place in a quieter atmosphere than in Western countries, free from disputes and polemics. The Polish moral theologians are profoundly respectful of the magisterium. In particular, they were faithful in adhering to the statements of the magisterium during the renovation of the church in the years of the Second Vatican Council and after the Council. Later, there were no critical voices of Polish moral theologians to *Humanae vitae*. In the publications of Polish moral theologians, the abundant references to the documents of the Second Vatican Council and to the pontifical documents indicate their respect of the tradition and of the magisterium. Their approach expresses their understanding of the ecclesial character of moral theology.[21]

The ecclesial character of moral theology causes Polish moral theology to be more about interpreting, explaining, commenting, and reporting than creating anew and developing original theological thinking, and proposing new points of view and solutions to challenging questions and issues. Polish moral theologians do not have the courage to present their own opinions. Moreover, the Polish moral theology aims at being doctrinally right. In the past century there were not any doctrinal mistakes. Polish moral theology cherishes faithfulness.[22]

One of the contemporary challenges for moral theologians is how to articulate their argumentations in moral theology. Assertions such as "this is the teaching of the church" or "I believe God wills it" are insufficient. Moral theology is a normative science and it is at the service of the church. To elaborate modern, logical, and rational argumentations in addressing moral questions to live faithful Christian lives serves both the magisterium and all believers.[23]

Teaching on Conscience

One of the important questions of moral theology, which relates to its ecclesial character and the importance of the magisterium, concerns conscience and, particularly, its normative character and the process of its formation. There is no doubt that conscience is obliged to do what is objectively morally good, which is formulated in norms and is protected by them. The decisions of an individual's conscience cannot be reduced to the simple application of general norms, although the role of binding objective criteria and the ability to make judgments of conscience, in dealing with what has been recognized as objectively right by moral teaching, is indisputable for moral theologians. The problem arises in understanding the erroneous conscience in cases where error is invincible and in discussing the normative character of the judgments of conscience in these cases. For many moral theologians, in such cases, the decision of this invincible, erroneous conscience should be respected because in making this decision, the conscience does not lose its dignity as the ultimate instance in formulating concrete judgments. Within the church, the magisterium helps Christians to form their conscience, but both the magisterium and conscience are subjected to the moral truth.[24] According to Eberhard Schockenhoff, it is possible for Catholics to responsibly live their lives by following the ecclesial moral teaching, but their conscience is not subsidiary to the magisterium of the church.[25]

According to Polish moral theologians the understanding of conscience as the superior instance relativizes the statements of the magisterium. If conscience is recognized as the highest authority in guiding moral behavior, the role of the magisterium is weakened. The ecclesial moral norms are not the last word to address concrete situations and hence the final word belongs to one's conscience. However, a fake concept of conscience should be avoided where conscience is not obligated to follow the true knowledge of the objective moral order, and the role of norms is limited. Polish moral theologians stress the need of a positive cooperation between what the magisterium teaches and conscience. The magisterium helps people to shape their conscience, and Christians should abide the holy and certain teachings of the church. The magisterium does not lead conscience to alien truths but reveals truths that the conscience should follow and develop. The magisterium also serves one's conscience.[26]

In the twentieth century, the study of conscience conducted by Polish theologians did not explain the dignity of the erroneous conscience, but it is limited only to discussing what *Gaudium et spes*, no. 16, writes on this matter. Conscience does not judge infallibly, and it can be mistaken. Hence, conscience should be formed. In any case, truth is the source of dignity of conscience: in the case of right conscience, the source is objective truth, and in the case of wrong conscience, it is what human beings subjectively recognize wrongly as truth. If conscience is wrong because of one's fault, then conscience betrays its own dignity.[27]

In an age where one's freedom seems to lead to a generalized absolution from assuming one's responsibilities, the important moral task is to stress the teaching of the church on conscience. The church aims at promoting people's education, and it is on the people's side. The church should show to the current and next generations how the ecclesial moral teaching does not deprive people of their freedom, but it leads people to true freedom.[28] It is important to recognize the positive role that the magisterium can have in educating the consciences of believers. Statements of the magisterium that address moral issues should never be perceived as disturbing the freedom of consciences of Christians because freedom should never be understood as separate from the truth but always and only as inseparable from the truth.[29]

The teaching on conscience of Polish moral theologians is strictly connected with the authority of the church and the magisterium. There are no voices that exhort following one's conscience in instances where this could lead to choices that appear to be opposite to the teachings of the church. The magisterium plays an important role in forming the consciences of believers, and the believers should be obedient to the final decisions of the church.

The Ultimate Value of Ecclesial Documents

According to Polish moral theologians the magisterial statements have an ultimate value. When the Holy See in its documents has made decisions regarding the sphere of morals, no discussions should follow. The magisterial statements should be respected with no distinctions, in all cases and in the same way. According to *Veritatis splendor*,

> In proclaiming the commandments of God and the charity of Christ, the Church's Magisterium also teaches the faithful specific particular precepts and requires that they consider them in conscience as morally binding. In addition, the Magisterium carries out an important work of vigilance, warning the faithful of the presence of possible errors, even merely implicit ones, when their consciences fail to acknowledge the correctness and the truth of the moral norms which the Magisterium teaches.[30]

Hence, the role of the magisterium is not limited to present general aspects of Christian morals, but it concerns specific situations, and it formulates norms that should guide the believers.[31]

In light of this approach, the skepticism of Polish moral theologians toward Pope Francis's apostolic exhortation *Amoris laetitia* can be understood. In particular, the following statement concerning the interventions of the magisterium is considered problematic:

> Since 'time is greater than space,' I would make it clear that not all discussions of doctrinal, moral or pastoral issues need to be settled by interventions of the magisterium. Unity of teaching and practice is certainly necessary in the Church, but this does not preclude various ways of interpreting some aspects of that teaching or drawing certain consequences from it. This will always be the case as the Spirit guides us towards the entire truth (cf. Jn 16:13), until he leads us fully into the mystery of Christ and enables us to see all things as he does. Each country or region, moreover, can seek solutions better suited to its culture and sensitive to its traditions and local needs.[32]

After *Amoris laetitia*, with Pope Francis's assertion on the limited necessity of interventions of the magisterium in moral issues and the possibility of various interpretations of some aspects of magisterial teaching, one can observe a strange situation in Polish moral theology. Polish moral theologians who defended the teaching of the magisterium, particularly the documents promulgated by John Paul II criticized by moral theologians from Western European countries, took a distanced or critical position toward the teachings of Pope Francis. According to Paweł Bortkiewicz, the problem is the discrepancy between *Amoris laetitia* and *Veritatis splendor*. If we accept, affirms Bortkiewicz, that *Amoris laetitia* admits the primacy of the discernment of conscience about the objective reality, we head toward the classical question, what is more important, freedom or truth? If we accept such interpretation of *Amoris laetitia*, he claims, we reject truth and stand on the ground of the absolution of freedom. This position, he insists, is against the teaching of Jesus, who clearly says, "You will know truth and the truth will make you free" (John 8:32). Moreover, it is also against the teachings of John Paul II's encyclical letter *Veritatis splendor*.[33]

Diverse Ecclesiological Understandings

Undoubtedly there are differences between Polish and Western European moral theologians in the understanding and reception of *Amoris laetitia*, in addressing the issue of the place of the magisterium in moral theology, and in discussing various themes in moral theology. In these pages, there is not enough space to show all these differences, but at least the difference in the understanding of ecclesiology can be mentioned here. Polish moral theologians generally understand the church as the people of God and the body of Christ. They relate this ecclesiological approach to their understanding of moral theology as teaching morals to the people of God. This teaching is manifested in the ecclesial community, and it helps the believers to realize the vocation. Hence, there is an intimate connection between the church as a people of God and Christian morality. The ecclesial membership influences the existence of Christians. Moreover, it empowers them in performing their ordinary activities and new goals that specify their tasks and that have consequences for their Christian identity.[34]

In their contributions, Polish moral theologians generally pledge for the conciliar ecclesiology stressing the community of people of God, and they highlight the hierarchical understanding of the church in presenting specific issues. In explaining moral problems the deciding voice has neither given to the moral agent nor to well-justified and articulated statements of moral theologians, but to the statements of the magisterium. In doing this, they highlight their exclusively hierarchical approach. The postsynodal apostolic exhortation *Amoris laetitia* follows and integrates the reflections and debates of two synods. The synodal contribution shows how the task of the bishops is not only to illuminate and educate the conscience of the believers but also to be attentive to how the Holy Spirit is illuminating the consciences of the believers. The formation of personal conscience is a task of the whole community of believers and not only of the hierarchical church because the individual believers are integral to the whole ecclesial community.[35]

Conclusion

Undoubtedly moral theology is an ecclesial reflection on morals and should be developed within the church; for the community of believers; and, at the same time, for the world. In the most recent pontifical documents of Pope Francis, *Evangelii gaudium* and *Amoris laetitia*, new ecclesiological dimensions are stressed, particularly on the church as people of God "on the way," and the importance of synodality. Moreover, Pope Francis invites us to consider that not all moral answers to the multiple moral questions should be decided exclusively by the magisterium.[36] Hence, the contemporary moral theology and their representatives face new challenges. The experience of believers should be addressed and integrated more carefully in the theological discourse, and the magisterium should be understood more at the service of people in accompanying them to address their moral problems. This approach invites Polish moral theologians to examine their consciences. The renovation of the church and of moral theology as an ecclesial reflection on morals will take place by listening to the voice of the Holy Spirit,[37] "until he leads us fully into the mystery of Christ and enables us to see all things as he does."[38] The ecclesiological vision articulated in the pontifical documents of Pope Francis should lead moral theologians to reconsider the ecclesial dimension of moral theology and the reciprocal relations between the magisterium and moral theologians. It is an important contemporary challenge for moral theologians everywhere today, not only in Poland.

Notes

1. Stanisław Olejnik, *Dar. Wezwanie. Odpowiedź. Teologia moralna*, vol. 1: *Wprowadzenie i idea wiodąca* (Warsaw: Akademia Teologii Katolickiej, 1988), 12–13.

2. Ibid.

3. Ireneusz Mroczkowski, *Teologia moralna. Definicja. Przedmiot. Metoda* (Płock: Płocki Instytut Wydawniczy, 2011), 22.

4. Janusz Nagórny, "Natura teologii moralnej," in *Polska teologia moralna czterdzieści lat po Soborze Watykańskim II*, ed. Janusz Nagórny and Jerzy Gocko (Lublin, Poland: Wydawnictwo Archidiecezji Lubelskiej "Gaudium," 2006), 116; Janusz Nagórny, "Teologia moralna jako eklezjalna nauka wiary w świetle Veritatis splendour," in *Jan Paweł II. Veritatis splendor. Tekst i komentarze*, ed. Andrzej Szostek (Lublin, Poland: Redakcja Wydawnictw Katolickiego Uniwersytetu Lubelskiego, 1995), 289–91.

5. Andrzej Derdziuk, "Eklezjalny charakter teologii moralnej," *Roczniki Teologiczne* 44, no. 3 (2007): 8.

6. Franciszek Greniuk, *Katolicka teologia moralna w poszukiwaniu własnej tożsamości* (Lublin, Poland: Redakcja Wydawnictw Katolickiego Uniwersytetu Lubelskiego, 1993), 178–79.

7. Władysław Wicher, *Podstawy teologii moralnej* (Poznań, Poland: Księgarnia Św. Wojciecha, 1969), 64.

8. Sławomir Nowosad, "Rola Magisterium Kościoła w teologii moralnej," in *Veritatis splendor. Przesłanie moralne Kościoła. Materiały z sympozjum KUL, 6–7 grudnia 1993*, ed. Bernard Jurczyk (Lublin, Poland: Redakcja Wydawnictw Katolickiego Uniwersytetu Lubelskiego, 1994), 145–46.

9. Olejnik, *Dar. Wezwanie. Odpowiedź*, 11–12.

10. Bogusław Inlender, Stanisław Smoleński, and Stanisław Podgórski, *Powołanie chrześcijańskie. Zarys teologii moralnej*, vol. 1, *Istota powołania chrześcijańskiego* (Opole, Poland: Wydawnictwo Św. Krzyża, 1978), 20–21.

11. Mroczkowski, *Teologia moralna*, 31–34; Nagórny, "Natura teologii moralnej," 118.

12. Congregation for the Doctrine of the Faith, *Instruction "Donum veritatis" on the Ecclesial Vocation of the Theologian* (Rome, 1990), 16.

13. Mroczkowski, *Teologia moralna*, 34.

14. Nagórny, "Natura teologii moralnej," 118–19.

15. Derdziuk, "Eklezjalny charakter teologii moralnej," 9; Janusz Nagórny, "Teologia moralna," in *Jan Paweł II. Encyklopedia nauczania moralnego*, ed. Janusz Nagórny and Krzysztof Jeżyna (Radom, Poland: Polskie Wydawnictwo Encyklopedyczne, 2005), 541.

16. Piotr Morciniec, "Kompetencje Urzędu Nauczycielskiego Kościoła w kwestiach moralnych. Analiza współczesnego nauczania Kościoła," in *Vivere in Christo. Chrześcijański horyzont moralności. Księga Pamiątkowa ku czci Księdza Profesora Seweryna Rosika w 65. rocznicę urodzin*, ed. Janusz Nagórny and Andrzej Derdziuk (Lublin, Poland: Redakcja Wydawnictw Katolickiego Uniwersytetu Lubelskiego, 1996), 215.

17. Morciniec, "Kompetencje Urzędu Nauczycielskiego Kościoła w kwestiach moralnych," 218–21; Nowosad, "Rola Magisterium Kościoła w teologii moralnej," 147–48; Nagórny, "Teologia moralna jako eklezjalna nauka wiary w świetle Veritatis splendor," 292–93.

18. Nagórny, "Teologia moralna jako eklezjalna nauka wiary w świetle Veritatis splendor," 293.

19. Andrzej A. Napiórkowski, "Teologia polska wobec wyzwań współczesności," in *Kościół w życiu publicznym*. *Teologia polska i europejska wobec nowych wyzwań*, ed. Rada Naukowa Konferencji Episkopatu Polski (Lublin, Poland: Wydawnictwo Katolickiego Uniwersytetu Lubelskiego, 2004), 41–42.

20. Napiórkowski, "Teologia polska wobec wyzwań współczesności," 43–44.

21. Józef Kopciński, *Polska teologia moralna XX wieku* (Cracóv, Poland: Wydawnictwo Naukowe Papieskiej Akademii Teologicznej, 2004), 266–77.

22. Franciszek Greniuk, "W poszukiwaniu tożsamości polskiej teologii moralnej," in *Szkice o teologii polskiej*, ed. Stanisław C. Napiórkowski (Poznań, Poland: Księgarnia św. Wojciecha, 1988), 36–37; Kopciński, *Polska teologia moralna XX wieku*, 273–74.

23. Tadeusz Zadykowicz, "Problem argumentacji w teologii moralnej—istota i potrzeba uwspółcześniania," *Roczniki Teologiczne* 62, no. 3 (2015): 17–18.

24. Martin M. Lintner, "Dignity of the Human Person and Primacy of Conscience," in *Theological Ethics in a Changing World. Contemporary Challenges—Reorientation of Values—Change of Moral Norms?*, ed. Konrad Glombik (Opole, Poland: Redakcja Wydawnictw Wydziału Teologicznego Uniwersytetu Opolskiego, 2015), 66–68; Karl Golser, "Gewissen," in *Neues Lexikon der Christlichen Moral*, ed. Hans Rotter and Günter Virt (Innsbruck-Wien, Austria: Tyrolia, 1990), 285.

25. Eberhard Schockenhoff, *Wie gewiss ist das Gewissen? Eine ethische Orientierung* (Freiburg i.Br., Germany: Herder, 2003), 234.

26. Morciniec, "Kompetencje Urzędu Nauczycielskiego Kościoła w kwestiach moralnych," 217.

27. Zbigniew Wanat, *Sumienie w blasku prawdy. Polska teologia sumienia XX wieku* (Toruń, Poland: Wydawnictwo Naukowe Uniwersytetu Mikołaja Kopernika, 2012), 262.

28. Wanat, *Sumienie w blasku prawdy*, 286.

29. Ibid., 288–89.

30. *VS*, no. 110.

31. Nagórny, "Teologia moralna jako eklezjalna nauka wiary w świetle Veritatis splendor," 292.

32. *Amoris laetitia*, no. 3.

33. https//ekai.pl/wydarzenia/polska/x105254/ks-prof-bortkiewicz-o-liscie-kardynalow-do-papieza-w sprawie-amoris-laetitia.

34. Wojciech Bołoz, *Eklezjalne aspekty moralności chrześcijańskiej* (Cracóv, Poland: Instytut Teologiczny Księży Misjonarzy, 1992), 9–11.

35. Antonio Autiero, "Amoris laetitia und das sittliche Gewissen. Eine Frage der Perspektive," in *Amoris laetitia—Wendepunkt für die Moraltheologie*, ed. Stephan Goertz and Caroline Witting (Freiburg i.Br., Germany: Herder, 2016), 108–9.

36. Hans J. Pottmeyer, "Das Kirchenverständnis von Papst Franziskus als Schlüssel zu Amoris laetitia," in *Amoris laetitia—Wendepunkt für die Moraltheologie*, ed. Stephan Goertz and Caroline Witting (Freiburg i.Br., Germany: Herder, 2016), 326–31.

37. Wojciech Giertych, *Rachunek sumienia teologii moralnej* (Cracóv, Poland: Wydawnictwo M, 2004), 9.

38. *Amoris laetitia*, no. 3.

Giving the Floor to the Poor

New Challenges for Catholic Ethicists in France

Grégoire Catta

May 28–29, 2017, Tours (France), a middle-sized city 130 miles from Paris. One hundred twenty people are gathered for a weekend of theology in the diocesan center. Among them are a dozen "professional theologians" (i.e., scholars, professors, and students). But for once they are not the ones doing most of the talking. Rather, they are here to listen. Those who are really "doing theology" are, or have been, homeless, jobless, broke, and marginalized. They know how insecure life can be. They are those whom society at large—including the mainstream church—prefers not to see.

In France, there are various faith groups all over the country for people on the margins: the *Fraternité Saint Martin,* the *Diaconie du Var,* the *Famille Bartimée,* and others. These groups are linked through a network, the *Saint Laurent* network, whose charter explains, "The Saint Laurent network connects various Christian groups who journey within the Church on a path of faith and fellowship with people enduring severe poverty and social exclusion, and taking their lived reality as its starting point. Its heartfelt desire is that this path becomes the path of the whole Church."[1]

Over this May weekend, the participants spent two days considering the reality of work. They shared experiences; they reacted to texts written beforehand by some of the participants; they reflected on passages from the Bible or the pope or theologians. They expressed and shared the insights they had as people of faith, experiencing God in various ways and articulating something of God's saving mystery of love. In short, they did theology together: *theo-logy,* the endeavor of speaking about God. On Sunday, they took part in the Eucharist in the cathedral, with the bishop presiding. They read the readings; they contributed to the prayers of the faithful; at the end, they processed out with the bishop, as a sign that *they* were the church. It was as though they were living out the saying attributed to Saint Lawrence, the third-century deacon and martyr. Asked to produce the church's treasures, Lawrence allegedly said, "Behold in these poor persons the treasure which I promised to show you . . . the Church's crown."[2]

The May 2017 event in Tours is part of a broader process that is taking place in the church in France. A major manifestation of this process was *Diaconia 2013,* a large gathering in the sanctuary of Lourdes in May 2013. This essay begins by presenting this process and some of its main features. Then, I will link the movement to the traditional principle of the option for the poor that has been newly highlighted for us by Pope Francis. "The peripheries," paradoxically, should be the heart from which the church can breathe. The poor "have much to teach us . . . we need to let ourselves be evangelized by them."[3] At the end, I will reflect on the implications of this movement for "professional theologians" in the conventional sense. We need to take more seriously the genuinely theological authority of the poor and how it helps us encounter the God revealed in Jesus Christ.

The *Saint Laurent* Network and the *Diaconia* Project

The *Saint Laurent* network was born in 2005, during the celebration of the fiftieth anniversary of the *Cité Saint-Pierre* in Lourdes, a large compound founded in 1955 by *Secours Catholique–Caritas France* to provide shelter and food for families in need, according to a wish of Saint Bernadette. The *Cité Saint-Pierre* has become an international gathering place to pray, meet, and think about the thematic of poverty and charity, welcoming people in need for care and hope, whatever their resources are. At the *Cité Saint-Pierre* there is no fee, and each pilgrim gives according to his or her means. To celebrate its jubilee, the *Cité Saint-Pierre* gathered pilgrims from all over France. Various groups and communities decided to strengthen their ties. Some were connected with *Secours Catholique*; others were living out the intuitions of Father Joseph Wresinski, the founder of ATD Fourth World;[4] others had other specific histories. They all shared a desire to give the poorest their proper place in the church. The network is constituted around a few key events: a large and festive gathering in Lourdes every other year, an annual theological meeting dedicated to the experience of faith of the poor, and members visiting each other in order to learn from each other and "to announce and receive the Good News of the Gospel."[5]

The *Saint Laurent* network has been a driving force behind the wider *Diaconia* project within the French church at large.[6] In November 2009, the Conference of French Bishops wrote, "The forms poverty takes today are not particularly new, but they are severe . . . We appeal to all Catholics in France to put forward specific proposals initiating new ways of living."[7] In response to this appeal, the project *Diaconia: servons la fraternité* was launched by the National Council for Solidarity in 2011. This three-year process, involving all the dioceses, sought to promote greater solidarity with people experiencing fragility, and thus to increase hope. It was inspired by Benedict XVI's teaching that service of brothers and sisters is a means of following Jesus Christ and living the Christian faith.[8] As we know, the church has a triple mission: not only the preaching of the Word of God (*martyria*) and the celebration of the sacraments (*leitourgia*) but also the service of charity (*diakonia*).

During the first year, Catholics were invited to focus on the situations of fragility and precariousness around them, noting both the deep-seated problems and the signs of hope. They were also asked to reflect on what it actually means for us to serve one another. Testimonies were gathered and compiled in hundreds of "books of miracles" and "books of wounds." In the second year, Catholics were invited to reach out to people far away from the church, to learn what these people had to say about service, and to reflect on the connections between celebration (*leitourgia*) and service (*diakonia*).

The climax of the *Diaconia* project was a large gathering in Lourdes in May 2013. Twelve thousand delegates came together for three days from all the French dioceses. They celebrated joyfully and pooled their experiences over the previous two years of the project. They returned home with renewed inspiration to live out fruitfully the diaconal dimension of the church. Of those 12,000 people, 3,000 (one-fourth) were "wounded persons": persons living in poverty, homeless people, people with disabilities, and so on. They came from networks like *Secours catholique* or the *Saint Laurent* network, but also from *L'Arche,* the community founded by Jean Vanier centered on people with mental disabilities. Their presence in such significant numbers informed the whole process of the gathering. The French theologian Alain Thomasset commented:

> In their encounters with people in extreme fragility, the delegates had a quite unexpected experience of joy. As the process continues in the dioceses, people committed to acts of solidarity are discovering that the service of the poor is not only an ethical implication of their faith but a source of renewal for their faith. The poor themselves are increasingly becoming the main actors in the struggle against poverty and injustice.[9]

The large gathering energized existing local communities and projects, and brought new ones to life. In a generally well-off suburb of Toulouse, a large city in the south of France, the *Famille Bartimée* (Bartimaeus Family) was founded in 2011 by parishioners newly aware of the presence near them of people in extreme poverty. Every month a group including twenty to thirty people experiencing poverty and exclusion, along with parishioners in more stable financial circumstances, gathers for a Sunday of "friendship and sharing."[10] They share a meal and then spend a whole afternoon together. They reflect in groups on the gospel; they pray; they exchange news; they engage themselves in theater performances or drawing. Most have attended the parish Mass in the morning, sitting in the front rows and maybe reading or taking part in the offertory procession. In the *Famille Bartimée*, people who would otherwise be marginalized find support and recognition. They become part of the whole parish community and contribute to it. Another initiative of the same kind began in Tours after the Lourdes gathering, with the name *Fraternité Saint Martin* (Saint Martin Fraternity), after the patron saint of the diocese, a Roman solider famous for having shared his coat with a beggar.

Moreover, a parish near Paris has developed what it calls *Réseau de proximité* (network of closeness).[11] The idea is to promote solidarity by building contacts between people who need help and people who have help to offer. Of course some people fall within both categories. No money changes hands, but time, labor, and skills are shared. People are helped with transportation to a medical appointment, when they are moving, or when they need to fill out forms. The network involves parishioners, and under the responsibility of the pastor, the parish manages it. But the network's membership extends far beyond churchgoing Catholics. Operational for more than a decade, the network has stimulated other expressions of solidarity: potluck meals, especially during the summer, when those who cannot afford vacations can feel lonely; a gospel choir; liturgical innovations. What matters is that the social or diaconal dimension of the church's life is now something more than a niche interest for people who like that sort of thing.

Many other initiatives could be pointed out, and of course, the impact of *Diaconia 2013* has been different from one diocese to another.[12] Two key points should be stressed. First, *Diaconia* represents a decisive rediscovery of the diaconal dimension of the church. In some countries like the United States, churches were from the beginning, and now still remain, very much involved in social work, health care, emergency relief, and care for those in need. By contrast, the political and ideological history of France since the French Revolution has resulted in the state taking full responsibility in these areas and developing civil institutions for this purpose. Catholics thus were tempted to reduce the mission of the church to liturgy and catechism. Even after the transformations initiated by Vatican II, the service of charity could too easily be seen as the mission of a few specialists, the "social justice" people, engaged in organizations like *Secours catholique*. *Diaconia* rehabilitates a vision of charity and justice as essential to the church. Solidarity, social concern, and care for those most fragile and in need are organically linked both to witnessing the faith (*martyria*) and to celebrating the sacraments (*leitourgia*). The connections are constitutive, reciprocal, and mutually enriching.

Second, *Diaconia 2013* has highlighted the need for the church to listen to the poor, the excluded, and the fragile because they have a central role to play in the life of the church. They are not, or not primarily, objects of compassion; they contribute to the very reality of the church. As a group of them put it powerfully during the Lourdes gathering:

> Together we're going to set up another way, a different kind of experience—one of real listening and sharing when we talk . . . This might be the beginning of something else—we might open the Church's eyes to another dimension, to a way of following Christ in his way of being with the poorest. He travelled the same path as the poor.[13]

Option for the Poor

These two features of the *Diaconia* project and the Lourdes gathering highlight a fundamental principle in the life and teaching of the church: the option for the poor.

Concern for the poor has been present in the life and teaching of the church since its origin, but the idea of "a preferential option for the poor" has its roots in the twentieth-century Latin American church. It is not surprising, then, that in 2013 the election of Francis, the first pope from this continent, has given the idea renewed impetus. The pope declares that he wants "a poor Church for the poor,"[14] and makes powerful gestures such as paying homage to the migrants dying in the Mediterranean Sea, visiting a shanty town inhabited by Roma, or welcoming a meeting of popular movements at the Vatican. But he goes further. He has *developed* the church's teaching on this topic,[15] along lines close to what we have seen lived out in the *Réseau Saint Laurent* and in *Diaconia*. Opting for the poor is not merely an ethical *consequence* of Christian faith, but something *constitutive* of that faith, and indeed a *source* on which that faith draws. Opting for the poor has a theological foundation, a theological orientation, and theological outcomes.

This point comes through strongly in some recent papal teaching documents. In *Evangelii gaudium* (*EG*), Francis dedicates a whole chapter to the social dimension of evangelization. He reaffirms that concern for the poor, for the marginalized, and for those who are excluded, is central to the Christian faith. In his letter to the Galatians, Paul's insistence that we should not forget the poor still stands as a criterion of action for Christian communities today. In Pope Francis's words, "We may not always be able to reflect adequately the beauty of the gospel, but there is one sign which we should never lack: the option for those who are least, those whom the society discards" (*EG*, no. 195). In *Laudato si'* (*LS*), Francis repeats his call "to hear both the cry of the earth and the cry of the poor" (*LS*, no. 49). Christians are invited to be instruments of God "for the promotion and liberation of the poor" (*EG*, no. 187), and "instruments of God our Father, so that our planet might be what God desired when he created it" (*LS*, no. 53). They are called to work "to eliminate the structural causes of poverty and to promote the integral development of the poor" (*EG*, no. 188).

But Francis here is merely restating in his own striking words what Benedict XVI had already been saying in *Deus caritas est* (*DCE*), in a passage that influenced deeply the theological reflection grounding the *Diaconia* project. The German pope insisted that "the Church cannot neglect the service of charity any more than she can neglect the Sacraments and the Word." Indeed, as exemplified by the history of the early church, "love for widows and orphans, prisoners, and the sick and needy of every kind, is as essential to her as the ministry of the sacraments and preaching of the Gospel" (*DCE*, no. 22). *Diaconia,* defined by Benedict as "the ministry of charity exercised in a communitarian, orderly way" (*DCE*, no. 21), is constitutive of the faith, not a mere consequence of it.

Francis is thus following Benedict XVI, and indeed John Paul II, in saying that "the option for the poor is primarily a theological category rather than a cultural, sociological, political, or philosophical one" (*EG*, no. 198). The option has a strong Christological grounding. "Our faith in Christ, who became poor and was always close to the poor and the outcast, is the basis of our concern for the integral development of society's most neglected members" (*EG*, no. 186). It is a matter of adopting "this mind . . . which was in Jesus Christ" (Phil. 2:5, cited by *EG*, no. 198). Jesus himself "identified with the little ones (cf. Mt 25:40)" (*EG*, no. 209).

Nevertheless, Francis does add distinctive touches of his own. It was John Paul II's encyclical *Sollicitudo rei socialis* (*SRS*) that marked the official incorporation of the option for the poor in the universal magisterium: "[The option] affects the life of each Christian inasmuch as he or she seeks to imitate the life of Christ, but it applies equally to our social responsibilities and hence our manner of living, and to the logical decisions to be made concerning the ownership and use of goods" (*SRS*, no. 42).

For John Paul, the preferential option for the poor is a key ethical principle, and concern for the poor and their needs is a primary and fundamental criterion for judging economic systems and political decisions. It also motivates actions for the common good.

Francis in no way denies such arguments. However, he also insists that the poor "have much to teach us." In *EG* he explains:

> Not only do they share in the *sensus fidei*, but in their difficulties, they know the suffering of Christ. We need to let ourselves be evangelized by them . . . We are called to find Christ in them, to lend our voice to their causes, but also to be their friends, to listen to them, to speak for them and to embrace the mysterious wisdom which God wishes to share with us through them. (*EG*, no. 198)

In *LS* he highlights that this option "demands before all else an appreciation of the immense dignity of the poor in the light of our deepest convictions as believers" (*LS*, no. 158). For Francis, the poor and the marginalized are our teachers. We need to learn from them. They contribute to the revelation of God's wisdom.

This affirmation is strong and challenging. We are called not only to be truly attentive to the poor and to seek their good but also, and more specifically, to appreciate them "in their goodness, in their experience of life, in their culture, and in their ways of living the faith." The poor are not merely the object of our concern. They are to be listened to, admired, and loved. In this way, "the authentic option for the poor differ[s] from any ideology, from any attempt to exploit the poor for one's own personal or political interest" (*EG*, no. 199).

That God "wishes to share with us through them . . . a mysterious wisdom" is powerfully illustrated by what was shared at the end of the *Diaconia* gathering in Lourdes by the group *Place et parole des pauvres* (The Role and the Word of the Poor), constituted of men and women experiencing poverty and exclusion. One person wrote,

> What we have learned in our group . . . is that 'God is true!'[16] I have encountered people who were experiencing suffering, abandonment, and the Cross, and also living a resurrection. It is the entirety of the Gospel

that is true. True, not because I force myself to believe. No! My brothers and sisters are those who tell me that 'God is true.' The words of confidence and hope become something meaningful. These words come to life within me because they are true and real in the lives of others. I need my brothers and sisters in order to discover that the Gospel is true—and I need particularly those whose paths are more painful.[17]

Étienne Grieu explains that something crucial is touched here. "The journey travelled with those who live, in their particular life story, something of Christ's paschal mystery (his Cross, his suffering, his being abandoned, his resurrection) reveals the power of the Gospel—of the *entirety* of the Gospel as the person says. Faith thus becomes something more than a set of beliefs imposed from outside; it becomes life." Those who are poor, suffering, and abandoned are always "bringing the Church back to the faith."[18]

Theological Work

What do these developments imply about the work of theology? Alain Thomasset, speaking on moral theology at a CTEWC conference in Kraków in 2014, put the question this way:

Are we listening to the voice of the poor? As moral theologians, whose vocation is to help people in their struggles to live and act well, are we really informed about the sufferings of marginalized people in our societies? Are we able to be the heralds of their voice? Are we ready to learn from them, recognizing that their experience is unique, and that this experience gives them a wisdom inaccessible to us?[19]

As theologians, each one of us has to face such questions. In this last part of the essay, first I will look at some of the publications that have emerged from the *Diaconia* project. Second, I will focus on the testimony of two theologians involved in the project who have already been mentioned: Étienne Grieu and Alain Thomasset.[20]

Publications

From the beginning, *Diaconia* had not only a steering committee but also a theological team. The latter produced eleven short theological papers aimed at helping people understand the notion of *diaconia* more deeply. The titles speak for themselves: "Diaconia: Service in Fraternity and Following Christ," "Diaconia and the Word of God," "Diaconia and Liturgy," "Diaconia and Politics," "Pastoral Challenges for Diaconia 2013," etc.[21] Some religious journals and magazines devoted dedicated issues to *diaconia*.[22] Moreover, books and edited collections reflecting theologically on the whole process were published.[23] Strikingly, these publications focused on *diaconia*, and the emphasis shifted to "fraternity."[24] *Diaconia* suggested action but remained obscure: to live a life shaped by *diaconia* means to serve, to reach out to those who are most in need, to fight for justice, etc. But what became clear was that such action depended on living the type of relationships Jesus Christ had inaugurated by revealing that we are adoptive sons and daughters of God, brothers and sisters. The Kingdom of God, announced by Jesus, the building up of which is the church's mission and *raison d'être*, is a kingdom of "fraternity."[25]

This move from service to "fraternity" provides the context for understanding why the "word of the poor" is so important. The group *Place et parole des pauvres*, cited previously, started to reflect on *diaconia* in 2010, a long time before the gathering in Lourdes. They met twenty-seven times, each time for a full day of reflection, following methods that have been developed for several decades in the ATD Fourth World movement to help the voiceless contribute in a public discussion. Their work is an important theological outcome of *Diaconia*.[26] They presented it at the beginning and the end of the 2013 gathering in plenary sessions, with 12,000 people present, including 100 bishops. This enabled all those who were present to feel comfortable about speaking out, especially those whose sufferings tend to render them invisible and who thus do not dare to speak. Their contributions were strongly felt during the various forums organized the following day on specific topics, and in the small mixed sharing groups.

"Fraternity" implies reciprocity and inclusiveness: no one is excluded; everyone gives and receives; all contribute and all benefit. As the opening statement of *Place et parole des pauvres* explained, "One of the ways in which Jesus Christ dedicates himself to the service of others is by giving them the floor . . . The Holy Spirit has given every one of us a mission . . . Everyone is on earth to do something."[27]

Some "professional" theologians have taken notice. The group of theologians engaged in *Diaconia* knew that *Place et parole des pauvres* existed, but did not really interact with them before the gathering in Lourdes. In the theology group's final document, produced after the Lourdes assembly, they wrote powerfully what they had learned:

> We discovered that their way, sometimes a very surprising way, of receiving the Gospel was opening up new perspectives. The Good News, when given again to us by these people, becomes much stronger. Notions of salvation, hope, memory, and forgiveness resonate differently in the heart of those who live on the precipice. Yes, the poor evangelize us. This is not a mere slogan.[28]

Two French Theologians

One member of the *Diaconia* theology group, Étienne Grieu, has pioneered ways of doing theology on the basis of how people narrate their experience. His doctoral thesis approached a classical question in fundamental theology: how it is that people can make an act of faith. But he approached this old question in a new way, by analyzing how thirty different Catholics, most of them social activists, told their life stories. He has also long been engaged among people living in extreme poverty and who place the option for the poor at the heart of their engagement. Nonetheless, when I interviewed him, he shared that until recently he had been reluctant to work directly with sayings and personal stories of marginalized or poor people, for fear that he would fall into instrumentalization and ideology. *Diaconia 2013* and other experiences with the *Réseau Saint Laurent* helped him make a breakthrough. As he explains it now, to work with the words of people living in precariousness is rather different from working with narratives of activists. The latter are constructed and organized. The former are very often scattered and lacking coherence. At first, you do not know how to work with them. The process requires time. One needs to listen very carefully in order not to miss something important. But it is possible. And good things can come.

Over the last three years, Grieu has led a theological research seminar, involving also grassroots activists, on the theme of hope. The seminar reflected on a precious resource: more than sixty hours of interviews broadcast on a Catholic radio station in the south of France by an investigator really interested in what the poor had to say on various topics. The outcome was a book whose title speaks for itself: *What Makes Us Live When It All Falls Apart: Theology in the School of the Poorest.*[29] One of Grieu's doctoral students has done more detailed work on this material,[30] and another is working on how the poorest live out the reality of forgiveness.[31]

For his part, Alain Thomasset, who was also in *Diaconia*'s theology group, is a moral theologian. He had already been sensitized to the importance of giving the floor to the poor through his experiences of "people's universities" sponsored by ATD Fourth World, and through retreats given to people in extreme poverty. Nevertheless, the *Diaconia* gathering in Lourdes provided him with a new and decisive stimulus, reflected in the quotations from his work given above. For him, there is still much to do if the poor are to be recognized in the way they should as a theological source for moral theology.[32] But, at least as a gesture, he often starts his workshops and talks on *Amoris laetitia* with a direct recording of the voice of Martine, a woman on the margins. Martine's input can often help a group move beyond the standard polarizations regarding sexuality and marriage, and to recognize the important social dimensions of the issue. In the leading journal of French-speaking moral theology, where he is the chief editor, some authors are now referring explicitly to the voices of the poor. They may well, for example, cite documents elaborated by the *Réseau Saint Laurent*.[33]

Conclusion

Of course, these examples are modest, and challenges remain. How can we give the floor to the poor in our theological endeavors? How can the experience of life on the margins really nourish theology? What has happened in France in recent years with *Diaconia* is very much in line with what Pope Francis has been tirelessly putting forward in his actions and in his teachings. The poor, the excluded, those who for various reasons are at the margins of society have much to teach us. Mysteriously, they even can be said to be a preferential channel of God's wisdom. This cannot but make a difference in how we do theology.

Notes

1. Charter of the *Réseau Saint Laurent,* http://reseau-saint-laurent.org/IMG/pdf/st-laurent-a5-bat.pdf.

2. Cf. *Butler's Lives of the Saints and Other Sources by John Gilmary Shea* (New York: Benziger Brothers, 1894), http://sanctoral.com/en/saints/saint_lawrence.html.

3. *Evangelii gaudium,* no. 198.

4. *ATD Quart Monde* (ATD Fourth World) is an international movement of solidarity and collaboration with families in extreme marginalization. Joseph Wresinski, a diocesan priest, founded it in France in 1957. Today it is an international nongovernmental organization with no religious or political affiliation: www.atd-fourthworld.org.

5. Charter of the *Réseau Saint Laurent,* http://reseau-saint-laurent.org/IMG/pdf/st-laurent-a5-bat.pdf.

6. I use "*Diaconia*" or "*Diaconia* project" to refer to the three-year process involving the whole church of France; "*Diaconia 2013*" refers to the gathering that occurred in Lourdes on May 9–11, 2013.

7. Conférence des Évêques de France, *La charité du Christ nous presse,* November 8, 2013, http://diaconia2013.fr/diaconia-cest-quoi/.

8. Cf. Benedict XVI, *Porta Fidei: Apostolic Letter,* 2011, 14.

9. Alain Thomasset, "Contemporary Challenges and Opportunities: The Western European Perspective," *Colloquia Theologica* 20 (2015): 20.

10. This community is described in Étienne Grieu and Vincent Lascève, *Vers des paroisses plus fraternelles. Les plus fragiles au cœur de la communauté chrétienne* (Paris: Éditions Franciscaines, 2016), 37–78.

11. Ibid., 15–36.

12. Particularly noteworthy are the initiatives now going back for three decades, led by Gilles Rebêche, a permanent deacon, in the diocese of Toulon under the label *Diaconie du Var.* The *Diaconia* project and the Lourdes gathering gave these initiatives significant publicity. See http://www.diocese-frejus-toulon.com/-Diaconie-Servir-.html.

13. Quoted by Thomasset, "Contemporary Challenges and Opportunities," 20.

14. Francis, *Address to Representatives of the Communications Media,* March 16, 2013.

15. I have developed this argument further in Grégoire Catta, "Learning from the Poor: Francis's Deepening of the Preferential Option," in *Public Theology and the Global Common Good,* ed. K. Ahern, M. Clark, K. Heyer, L. Johnston (Maryknoll, NY: Orbis Books, 2016), 3–13.

16. The French phrase—*Dieu, c'est vrai*—is almost impossible to translate. The idea is that God is truly real, not a mere idea, not the object of any doubt.

17. Quoted in Étienne Grieu, *J'ai besoin de toi pour découvrir que Dieu c'est vrai* (Paris: Salvator, 2013), 7–8. My translation.

18. Ibid., 8.

19. Thomasset, "Contemporary Challenges and Opportunities," 20.

20. I interviewed both of them in June 2017.

21. All the papers are published together in "Diaconia: Servons la fraternité," *Documents Épiscopat* no. 4, 2013, http://diaconia2013.fr/category/documents/documentationstheologiques/notestheologiques/.

22. For example, *La diaconie dans le dialogue entre charité et justice, Cahiers de l'Atelier,* Hors-Série no. 1 (2012); *Célébrer la diaconie, Cahiers de l'Atelier,* no. 534 (July–September 2012); *Diakonia. Le service dans la Bible, Cahiers Évangile,* no. 159 (March 2012); *La mystique du service. Un autre regard sur la diaconie, Christus,* no. 237 (January 2013); *Frères et sœurs. De la fratrie à la fraternité, Christus,* no. 240 (October 2013); Mathias Nebel, "La notion néo-testamentaire de *diakonia*: Une difficile reconnaissance," *Revue d'Ethique et de Théologie Morale,* no. 268 (May 2012): 79–102.

23. Cf. Patrice Sauvage, *Servons la fraternité: Quand l'Église se fait fraternité* (Paris: Éditions Franciscaines, 2014); Gwenola Rimbault and Odile Pontier, eds., *La force de la fraternité: Des récits pour penser la diaconie* (Paris: Éditions Franciscaines, 2013); Grieu, *J'ai besoin de toi pour découvrir que Dieu, c'est vrai.*

24. Though its referent is thoroughly biblical and Christian, the word "fraternity" is now often felt to be awkward in English: it seems to exclude women, and it can also denote groupings among college students that could be ethically problematic. These difficulties are far less marked in French, in which the term is widely understood and accepted. Note, too, its presence in the French national motto, originating with the Revolution—*Liberté* (liberty), *Égalité* (equality), *Fraternité* (fraternity)—a convergence that suggests interesting paths of dialogue with nonbelievers.

25. Sauvage, *Servons la fraternité,* 66–89.

26. Two main texts from the group, presented at the beginning and at the end of the gathering, respectively, are available: http://diaconia2013.fr/wp-content/uploads/Message-Place-et-Parole-des-Pauvres-9-mai.pdf; http://diaconia2013.fr/wp-content/uploads/gpePPPinterventionfinale.pdf.

27. Groupe Place et Parole des Pauvres, *Message d'ouverture.* My translation.

28. *Note théologique 11. Après le rassemblement Diaconia 2013 allons de l'avant en Église avec les pauvres,* 3, http://diaconia2013.fr/wp-content/uploads/Note-theologique-11-V5.pdf.

29. Étienne Grieu, Gwennola Rimbaut, and Laure Blanchon, *Qu'est-ce qui fait vivre encore quand tout s'écroule? Une théologie à l'école des plus pauvres* (Namur, Belgium: Lumen Vitae, 2017).

30. Laure Blanchon, *Voici les noces de l'Agneau: Quand l'incarnation passe par les pauvres* (Namur, Belgium: Lessius, 2017).

31. A noticeable production of theological works trying to give a theological echo to the contributions of people living in great precariousness is appearing. Gwennola Rimbaut, *Les pauvres interdits de spiritualité? La foi des chrétiens du Quart-Monde* (Paris: L'Harmattan, 2009); Gwennola Rimabaut, ed., *Partager la parole de Dieu avec les pauvres* (Paris: Desclée de Brouwer, 2013); Dominique Fontaine, *L'Évangile entre toutes mains* (Ivry-sur-Seine, France: Les éditions de l'Atelier, 2016).

32. "Moral theologians should be attentive to the Word of God, . . . to Tradition and the magisterium in charge of interpreting it, . . . to women and men of their time, . . . but also to the poor (the little ones, those who are always affected by the organization of the society

and who indicate where human beings are hurt in their dignity).” Alain Thomasset, *Interpréter et agir: Jalons pour une éthique chrétienne* (Paris: Cerf, 2011), 26.

33.   For example, on the topic of work, see Luc Dubrulle, “Grâce sans visage et grâce du travail: Critique du revenue universel,” *Revue d'Ethique et de Théologie Morale* no. 295 (September 2017): 39–48.

Part III

Fields of Conflicts

RECONSIDERING SELECTION OF LIFE IN THE CULTURAL CONTEXT OF JAPAN

Challenge of the Japanese Catholic Church

Haruko K. Okano

Where the Problem Is

In the late 1960s to the 1970s, there were heated global arguments both for and against contraception and abortion. In Germany, the United States, France, and other countries, people claimed that the decision about abortion was a matter related to the individual's right to reproduction and that it should be detached from the control of nations or churches, and that claim was ultimately affirmed. In Japan, in contrast to other countries, the concept of an individual's right had no chance of coming to the surface. The Eugenic Protection Act was enacted in Japan in 1948, well before Western countries legalized abortion and sterilization for eugenic reasons. In other words, abortion was promoted within the framework of national population-control policy at an early stage in Japan, compared to the rest of the world.[1]

The movement to acquire women's reproductive rights as a part of the women's liberation movement occurred in Japan at almost the same time as in Western countries, but it did not take the form of protest against the view of life or family promoted by the state or churches as it did in Western countries. Therefore, neither women nor men had the opportunity to deliberate subjectively about their own estate and to become conscious of the issue and its significance for reproduction, abortion, and the family. In Japan, sterilization and abortion have been promoted as a political part of national population control policy, and especially as part of the policy of maintenance of the traditional family. The purpose of the Eugenic Protection Act was to prevent the birth of poorly developed children, in order to contribute to the construction of a civilized country. In 1966, for the first time, a revision to the act led to the deletion of inappropriate terms, and the revised act was called the Mother's Body Protection Act. In the fifty years preceding the revision, 845,000 cases of sterilization were formally recorded.[2] In recent years, the number of abortions has become much smaller compared to the peak years of the 1950s and 1960s, but still, at the beginning of the 2000s, 300,000 cases a year have been reported.[3] In 2014, according to the statistics of the Ministry of Health, Labor and

Welfare, the number decreased to 181,905.[4] This is an official number, though it is certain that quite a few illegal cases have gone unreported.

Thanks to the rapid progress of genetic engineering and reproductive technology, the system for diagnosing serious diseases not only at the fetal stage but as early as the zygote stage now exists in modern society. Particularly since 2013, the latest prenatal diagnoses leading to births that do not damage the baby have also spread rapidly in Japan. Needless to say, such diagnoses do not necessarily lead to abortions. It is known that this technology is useful for fetal therapy, which is often conducted in Japan, helping caregivers and parents to be prepared for their future situations.

It is now an appropriate time to fully consider the following fact: In line with the report[5] of 2016, more than 30,000 persons had a prenatal diagnosis, and in cases where there are positive indications of medical problems with the fetus, 97 percent of the mothers have opted for abortion. When, however, the diagnosis leads to a selective abortion, a new ethical problem—different from conventional ones in which such diagnoses are unknown—occurs. When this kind of selective abortion is carried out and popularized, one can choose the so-called desired life from the "undesired life." We again have the problem of eugenic thinking, which encourages the selection of the kind of people we want to admit into our society, for our own convenience. The people who control and judge these matters today, with some exceptions, are basically not representing nations or political powers, as it used to be, but rather are ourselves, the ordinary members of society. As a result, the eugenic way of thinking becomes a problem in our minds. We are further tempted to enhance certain characteristics or prevent defects in our children by manipulating their genes.

This is not something denounced as "bad" by nations or any other powers, but it gives rise to a new ethical question: Is it possible for a person to clearly separate in his or her mind the difference between having an abortion because of a fetal defect coupled with a wish to have a healthy baby later from discriminating against handicapped people in society? When many individuals decide independently to have an abortion, the answer to this question brings us to the horns of a dilemma: the dilemma that the birth rate of handicapped children will decrease, and existing handicapped children will come to be labeled "failures to have abortions" or "children unwanted by society." Abortion of a defective fetus is an individual decision, but it does not remain within the realm of the individual. Such a value judgment takes root widely as a part of the general social consciousness. The thought that handicapped people are unhappy is a product of such a consciousness structure in society.

In Western countries, Christian churches have, for better or worse, played the role of serving as a brake to stop industrial capitalism from one-sidedly using lives as their tools and scientists from misusing people as their materials, but in Japan there are no such religious institutions or thoughts serving as an ideal basis to prevent abortions or to care for the people concerned. Furthermore, even healthy fetuses are aborted comparatively easily in Japan, as I stated earlier. If the reason of having a genetic defect is added to the justifications given for abortion, I am afraid that there will be a rush of abortions that can hardly be stopped. The Western discussion is not easily applied in Japan.

First, I would like to report the message of the Catholic Bishops' Conference of Japan, introduce the controversy in Japan over prenatal diagnosis, and examine the merits and demerits of the right to self-determination concerning selective abortion. Then I will reconsider this issue from the viewpoint of theological ethics and feminism in order to tentatively draw an alternative social design and try to show what an ideal society should be like.

Message of the Catholic Bishops' Conference of Japan

Traditionally in Japan, the foreign religions of Buddhism, Confucianism, and Christianity have coexisted along with the indigenous religion of Shinto. In the face of such multireligiousness, the Catholic Bishops' Conference of Japan, which has historically taken a special position in the mind of Japanese people, has sent messages based on the encyclical *Redemptoris missio* in order to promote interreligious dialogue in cases of ceremonial occasions and participation in the liturgies and worship in temples and shrines, following the principle of respect for others.[6]

The bishops' remarkable and epoch-making message, which was first sent as a reflection upon the nuclear power station accident in Fukushima, is, in my view, a courageous statement leading to a way of getting away from our civilization's dependence on nuclear power. It has, for the first time, caused actual dialogues and solidarity among many influential religious organizations that today are establishing the ethical foundations for dealing with social problems in their global dimensions. Thus, Japanese religions are at last facing the practical problems of social ethics.

Within the frame of our reconsideration, the "Guideline for Problems Concerned with Life" (*Inochi eno manazashi*), which was just published by the Catholic Bishops' Conference of Japan (2017 in Tokyo), is particularly significant. Based on the encyclical *Laudato si'* of Pope Francis, there is actual talk about integral ecology, which includes all the problems of bioethics and environmental ethics. As its "basso continuo," the theme resounds with the message: "all work to protect life and to bring it into bloom is in cooperation with God's Creation."[7] From this perspective, this guideline expresses reservations about cases in which a prenatal diagnosis results in abortion, for the Catholic Church takes the view that the human rights of handicapped people must also be respected. The Japanese church is apprehensive about the fact that Japanese society is not properly friendly toward handicapped people. In this situation, some people think that prenatal diagnosis is desirable for their happiness.[8] The Catholic Church in Japan is thus involved in the ethical dilemma between the Christian bioethical demands and the traditional Japanese view of health and society.

The Bishops' Conference of Japan, based on the *Instruction on Respect for Human Life in Its Origin and on the Dignity of Procreation—Replies to Certain Questions of the Day*,[9] insists explicitly that a possible prenatal diagnosis for having a child with an abnormality or an inherited disease should not constitute grounds for a death sentence for a fetus. The Catholic Church of Japan is especially apprehensive about discrimination against handicapped people following the ongoing doctrine of economy for economy's sake and the popularization of eugenics. The human life as fetus would be an object for selection depending on whether it is handicapped or not handicapped, or whether it is useful or a burden to the society.[10] In light of such apprehension the Catholic Church makes its position clear: individual and sincere "informed consent" is indispensable, meaning it is essential to fully understand the prenatal diagnosis and subsequent options.[11]

The *Inochi eno manazashi* vision for a "barrier-free society" is remarkable. It is based on the March 23, 1981, Document of the Holy See for the International Year of Disabled Persons. It makes the following declaration: "The quality of a society, the quality of a civilization is decided on by the extent to which the most powerless in the society have respect." According to the thinking of the Vatican, the Japanese Guideline describes the vision: "We don't hold on to the understanding of a medical model that somebody is handicapped; rather, we ought to call our attention to the social model, realizing that a society itself is more handicapped, if its handicapped people don't live easily and happily."[12]

It seems to me that the innovative message of the Bishops' Conference of Japan suggests a certain antithesis to the conservative view of life in the homogenous society of the island country of Japan. I would like to reflect in detail on the controversy over prenatal diagnosis in Japan.

The Present Controversy over Prenatal and Preimplantation Diagnosis

The Merits and Demerits of Eugenics

In England, eugenics developed at the beginning of the twentieth century, involving cultural figures and highly educated people. It took the form of persuading physically "inferior" people (including alcoholics and the mentally disordered) to cooperate with voluntary sterilization. Later, in the United States, compulsory sterilization was carried out on people who were assumed to be "the inferiors" based upon data results of a large-scale statistical investigation of genealogies. Nazi eugenics eventually resulted in the Holocaust. The Nazis forcefully conducted euthanasia on the handicapped and "the inferiors," and massacred Jewish people in an unprecedented manner.

In Japan, as I mentioned previously, the Eugenic Protection Act was enacted after World War II, in 1948, legalizing the compulsory sterilization of the handicapped and the "inferior." It continued in effect until 1996. When the 1970s began, the old ideas of eugenics were reconsidered all over the world, because they had violated human rights and discriminated among racial groups. Meanwhile, new ideas of eugenics became influential. Today it has become possible, indeed without the unsafe technology of amniotic fluid examination, to diagnose disorders in the fetal stage, and this has led to selective abortions. The old eugenics was accompanied by compulsory sterilization and abortion, whereas the new eugenics has been accompanied by an individual's voluntary abortion. It has been a method for eliminating fetuses with certain qualities.

What does such a new eugenics mean to us? We cannot say that it is a safe and harmless gospel for life merely because it is not conducted compulsorily by a nation as it was before. An individual's voluntary selection is only one step removed from selection that is controlled or compelled by a nation, society, or community. The scientific examination of the history of eugenic thinking has proven that this is true.

A way of thinking, which was affected by the new eugenics, has given rise to the worst case of mass murder in a home for the mentally and physically handicapped, and this has shaken all Japan. In July 2016, after midnight, a former caregiver killed nineteen handicapped persons and wounded twenty-six seriously. According to the press, the young culprit had been admitted to the hospital because of his abnormal speech and behavior.

I believe his actions implied the following line of thinking: "The lives of the handicapped cost a huge sum of money. The nation does not approve of euthanasia, so I will execute these handicapped people instead of the nation, because the handicapped merely cause misery, sorrow, and unhappiness." Judging from this mass murder case, not a few people have gotten the impression that eugenics is still a deeply rooted state of mind in Japan, for in this country the thought that life in itself is of great value is not yet a matter of course.

The Present Condition of the Debate over Prenatal/Preimplantation Diagnosis and the Right to Individual Decisions

Both prenatal diagnosis and preimplantation diagnosis create the possibility of carrying out a certain kind of treatment or operation at an early stage more effectively. The Roman Catholic Church has consistently declared, "From the time that the ovum is fertilized, a life is begun which is neither that of the father nor of the mother; it is rather the life of a new human being with his own growth."[13] Still, they permit these diagnoses. It is in the following cases that such diagnoses become ethical problems:

1. The case in which people try to improve the health and abilities of babies by engineering a fetus or a fertilized egg. This requires the manipulation of the fetal life. There is a new eugenics in the background.
2. The case in which people do not want to view themselves as making a defective fetus or embryo. This rejects the existence or emergence of a defective fetus or embryo because the parent or couple does not accept the existence or emergence of a defective fetus or embryo. There is the core thought of the old eugenics in the background.

3. The case in which people abort or discard a defective fetus or fertilized egg. This deletes the existence of a fetus itself. There is also the core thought of the old eugenics in the background.[14]

The message that "a handicap is a kind of character defect" is widespread in modern developed countries, but we are not sure how deeply it is rooted in social psychology. More than a few doctors and researchers think, even now, that prenatal diagnosis is a means for preventing congenital disease, believing that they have to recommend that people get an abortion if their fetus has a defect. Cyprus, for example, has introduced prenatal diagnosis as a preventive technology in order to decrease the incidence of a form of recessive hereditary anemia called beta-zero thalassemia. They have recommended that people get a diagnosis and, if positive, an abortion; consequently, the incidence of this kind of anemia has been zero in Cyprus since 1988.

Based on this reality, it has been pointed out that the gap between developed countries and the developing countries in advanced life science technologies is getting wider.[15] Genetic manipulation conducted for improvement is, as a matter of course, limited to prosperous societies or people of affluence.

It is also becoming clear that there are double standards when prenatal diagnosis is viewed on a global scale. The freedom of abortion was achieved in the United States in the 1970s from the standpoint of giving women the right to choose, but it ignited a controversy, and ever since then abortion has been a political issue, with those who are pro and con sharply opposing each other. When prenatal diagnosis was developed, women were allowed to voluntarily select the abortion of embryos that had severe congenital defects. Prenatal diagnosis functions, so to speak, as a measure for preventing the birth of a congenitally defective child.

On the other hand, in Japan in those days, social assistance for severely handicapped people was far behind that of other countries, and the families of those people were burdened. Society recognized this, and local governments started movements to prevent the birth of "unhappy children." As a result, handicapped children were labeled "unhappy children."

In a surge of such movements, a group of people who were handicapped by brain paralysis, calling themselves the Aoi Shiba no Kai (Green Lawn Association), took a radical position against prenatal diagnosis, stating that it would lead to the killing or the elimination of handicapped people, as it shares the same fundamental way of eugenic thinking as that of the Nazis. Prenatal diagnosis was considered, so to speak, to be a litmus test for eugenic thought. Influenced by this radical criticism, the Mother's Body Protection Act enacted in Japan in 1996 ultimately did not adopt the Fetus Article proposed in 1976, which would have allowed selective abortion for congenital disorders of a fetus.

For the Japanese people, prenatal diagnosis has become a sensitive issue that makes people nervous because it is related in our minds to eugenic thinking. Incidentally, the Aoi Shiba Association, which revealed the underlying eugenic thinking in prenatal diagnosis, took the standpoint of not seeking a definitive answer of yes or no, allowing the possibility of selective abortion if the parents make that decision.

This Japanese criticism was considered strange by people in English-speaking countries, because they thought it was illogical to oppose selective abortion in the case of a defective fetus when abortion was allowed for other reasons. However in Germany, also a developed country where people are sensitive to eugenic thinking, opposition to selective abortion was proposed, just as in Japan, in the 1980s. Because they rejected abortion based on eugenic thinking, selective abortion has been conducted legally in Germany in accordance with the Medical Article (Criminal Law, Article 218) only for reasons of the mother's emotional and physical welfare; and in Japan, abortion is allowed for financial reasons in accordance with the Mother's Body Protection Act.

Dilemma Regarding the Right to Individual Decision

Almost all modern societies have a dual structure of health and welfare policies—both in preventing the birth of defective children in the form of respecting the mother's decision and in protecting the handicapped if they are born. However, it is possible to criticize the concept of disease, both mental and physical, as always being an unhappy phenomenon. That concept may be seen as only a product of the quest for "happiness above all" held by a modern society that created the formula that health equals happiness. The conditions of "disease" and "health" are both teleological in nature, named superficially by humans based only upon human thought. Behind the wish to have a healthy child, there may also be a psychological attitude that sick children are unhappy. We have to ask who decides what is happiness and unhappiness. Not a few congenitally handicapped people themselves, or their families, deny this formula. A clinical psychologist, Mariko Tamai, who has a son with Down syndrome, clearly explains it in this way: "I have learned through my taciturn son that people are unhappy not because they have a handicap but because they are not considered other than unhappy when they have a handicap."[16]

We can understand that the structural form of placing "disease/handicap" and "health" as polar opposites aggravates the problem of "unhappiness."

If we look back in history, nations have justified eugenic thinking ever since the age of Plato. The reproductive rights that women finally obtained under the rule of patriarchy, which have lasted nearly two thousand years, are important rights that have distinguished the twentieth century. This concept of the individual's right to self-determination, applied to women, served to overcome the old eugenic way of thinking. However, it is still difficult today to assess what kind of power the reality of self-determination is motivated by or what it is set forth in opposition to. In either case, it is difficult to find a legitimate basis to prohibit selective abortion based upon this right of self-determination, but ethically we must at least make an effort to establish a society that would not deny the existence of the handicapped or deprive them of their right to life.

I would like to review the German debate about preimplantation diagnosis, because I clearly see the dilemma of the role of self-determination in this dispute. A clinical application of preimplantation diagnosis, which unites in vitro fertilization with gene analysis technology, is already being advanced in some countries, including England and the United States. The Japan Society of Obstetrics and Gynecology also authorized this diagnosis with some conditions in 1998 after a long national discussion in Japan.

Preimplantation diagnosis is considered to have the following two advantages:

1. It enables a mother to avoid a selective abortion, which could be a problem if genetic defects were diagnosed later on by prenatal diagnosis.
2. It might be a blessing for people who have given up trying to have a baby because they were worried about the possibility of giving birth to a genetically defective one.[17]

However, clinical application of this technology is not permitted in German-speaking countries, including Germany, Austria, and Switzerland. Germany in particular has instituted the Embryo Protection Law, after cautious discussion with representatives of the Catholic Church, the handicapped, and the network of those who are against prenatal diagnosis. Prenatal diagnosis is permitted for the purpose of treatment, but it is opposed for the following reasons:

1. From the perspective of human dignity, creating an embryo for the purpose of diagnosis is viewed as treating the embryo as a tool.
2. From the perspective of the right to life, selecting only certain embryos to survive is a problem.
3. Using the image of bursting the bank of a river, even with strict conditions, once preimplantation diagnosis is permitted, the human desire to want a healthy child will be enlarged even to the extent of asking for a made-to-order person or a clone, and it will be impossible to put the brakes on this trend.
4. Discrimination against the handicapped and their families will become more extreme. As a result, social cohesion will be damaged.[18]

What we Japanese need to focus on is the discussion of this matter based on human dignity and the right to life. The German people do not believe that the influence wielded by the results of diagnostic technology is the only problem. They criticize the use of preimplantation diagnosis itself. The declaration that the embryo, which has the potential to become a person, has dignity really means that the embryo is not a tool to be used for something but that it is an entity that should be respected as the aim itself, a purpose that is beyond the reach of any calculable computation. Preimplantation diagnosis is criticized because it is conducted not to give treatment to the subject to sustain its life but to deny its existence.

Japanese people talk repeatedly about human dignity in their discussions, but they often receive criticism that the meaning of their words is practically void because Christian messages have not infiltrated the Japanese culture. In the traditional world of Japanese thought, neither the concept that human dignity really exists nor the concept that human beings are created in *imago Dei* is conceivable. These ideas are two sides of the same coin.

I am not sure to what extent the right-to-life viewpoint is well established in Japanese society, yet it is important nevertheless. The right-to-life viewpoint is a barometer with which we can recognize the absurdity of the idea of selecting irreplaceable life as either worthy or unworthy to live.

This is only an example, but when we look at the debates on preimplantation diagnosis in Germany, we can see that the matter of self-determination is deeply related to the worldview, the human view, and the sense of values of the society we belong to. It is a problem if we leave it to the politico-economic welfare policy of the state to decide on the selection of human life based on its calculations, but it would not be a substantial solution to the problem, either, if we leave the decisions to individuals or to lonely couples to decide for themselves.

Reconsidering the Selection of Life from the Viewpoint of Feminism and Theology

A Woman's Right to Self-Determination Is Not an Issue of Individual Privacy

In the patriarchal Roman Empire, a fetus was treated legally as one of its mother's organs.[19] In the eighteenth century, according to their medical records, German women thought that their fetuses were the transformations of their own organs.[20] Therefore, in those days, there was no conflict between the rights of mothers and those of their fetuses. The Judeo–Christian tradition, which provided and modernized reproductive standards, was interested in the fetus itself, denounced abortion as murder, and at an early stage upgraded the position of a fetus to their neighbor, according to Philon of Alexandria in the first century B.C. and in the Christian Church in the second century A.D.

In this way, there were two different understandings side by side, on the civil level and on the religious level, concerning the status of the fetus. Based on these views, the controversy over abortion in the modern Western world is engaged in by those who call themselves pro-life (those who respect the life of a fetus) and those who describe themselves as pro-choice (those who try to protect women's right to have an abortion). The dichotomy in the conflict between the rights of women and the rights of fetuses is based on the assertion of those with the pro-life view.

Those with the pro-choice view have basically tried to liberate women's reproductive rights from the patriarchal nation or society, the church's dicta, or the misconducts that should have been morally denounced. If some women believe that conception is their own physical change and the delivery of a child is their own conduct, the fetus is not considered a "person" within their body, so they are free to decide whether to give birth to the fetus or not.

However, today a lot of people, including many Christians, recognize a fetus as a person, or, if not a person, at least some entity different from the mother. But when a woman decides to get an abortion, the question is raised again as to whether the decision is truly the woman's autonomous self-determination.[21] For example, the World Health Organization declared in 1997 that selective abortion based on self-determination is not an act of eugenics.[22]

"Autonomous consent" is also mentioned in discussions about informed consent. The concept of autonomy is employed as though it were an acquittal (a so-called indulgence) of eugenics. It incidentally causes new problems, however. For instance,

1. It might violate the rights of women, such as those who are underage, mentally deficient, or victims of violence, who cannot adequately exercise autonomous consent.
2. The burden of personal responsibility for one's choices might be too heavy after making this decision.
3. Self-determination, with individualism as an underlying belief, might exclude others such as the woman's partner and other surrounding people.
4. Self-determination that depends on medical technology might objectify women's bodies through medical treatment and use them as tools. Women thus might lose their independence.

Similarly, with respect to making the decision about selective abortion, we should ask to what extent concerned women and men (we should not forget the concern of men and their real involvement) are substantially involved, because self-determination is exercised, for better or worse, in relationship with other people.

On the other hand, in the past in Japan, institutions such as the church (which puts forth reproductive standards) were not established. In Japan, each clan, each local government in modern society, or immediately the patriarchally structured family system gave its reproductive standards to the individuals within its purview. Therefore, there was hardly an opportunity for people to claim the right to life or the human dignity of fetuses based on religious authority in Japan.

Instead, the rituals for the aborted or miscarried ("water baby" or Mizuko in Japanese) held at temples of Buddhism or some new religions have functioned and prevailed as a method of caring for the spirits of deceased fetuses and the minds of the women and men concerned. I would like to mention here only the fact that this ritual has been accepted informally as one of the Japanese Catholic Church's ceremonies and that it has spread quietly further into other Asian countries.

The ritual is often carried out anonymously. It has been a way that the parents who have lost their babies by miscarriage or abortion have consoled themselves. Many Japanese women (and men) who had to secretly kill these small lives by abortion have tried to heal their loneliness and the pain in their mind, and lighten the burden of their responsibility in this way. Through this, we see various complex problems that exist within the issue of self-determination.

A Proposal from the Perspective of Feminism and Theology

There is no unified opinion in Western feminist theology or feminist ethics with respect to the stance toward reproductive medicine. Still, there is a broad area of agreement. I would like to describe alternative ideas on the theme of "selection of life" from this viewpoint.

First, both feminist theology and feminist ethics believe that spirituality is important. Both bring forth discussions such as, "Who is the ultimate owner of life?" This is the core understanding of Judeo–Christian theology, which is commonly agreed on by both feminist theologians and ecofeminists. The Bible states, "With you is the fountain of life" (Ps. 36:9). "In his hand is the life of every living thing and the breath of every human being" (Job 12:10). "I am the vine; you are the branches. Those who abide in me and I in them bear much fruit" (John 15:5). There are many messages in the Bible that state that our life is given by God. The main concepts of ethics, such as human rights, human dignity, and sacred life, are derived from our understanding of the Bible. In this context, the role of parents is to cooperate with the work of the creator, God.

Second, there is the recognition that autonomy and self-determination are possible only in relationship. When human beings are understood with relation to God, they have autonomy as *imago Dei*. There is no doubt that reproductive autonomy, or the right of women to self-determination, is a very important step for women's liberation in moving away from the control of the patriarchal nation and the paternalism of the modern medical system. However, true individual autonomy (self-determination) becomes possible only in the network of complex relationship with others. We are fundamentally bound to and deeply embedded in our surrounding context.[23] In many cultures, for example, there are still various rites of passage, such as a celebration on the seventh day after the birth of a child, visiting a shrine for the 7-5-3 festival in Japan, the coming-of-age ceremony, baptism, the order of confirmation, and so on, which serve to unify or bond the relationship of families to ancestors, relatives, and members of communities or institutions, even though some of these rites have become only semblances. This fact tells us that relationship is the essential foundation for human coexistence, even in a society that does not assume the existence of God. This relationship is the source and the basis of human existence for feminists. The characteristic of a relationship in which divine power seems to emerge is understood to be one of mutuality.[24]

Then what should be done in order for women to decide independently in this complex web of relationships? First of all, doctors should communicate well enough with patients to keep the relationship of interdependence or complementarity. Second, doctors and other health care professionals should become conscious of the vulnerability associated with autonomy, and should actively stimulate autonomy in their patients and encourage them to decide what is right for themselves. For that reason the perspective of "care" becomes important in order for the principle of self-determination to function together with that of social responsibility.

Third, "care" has been defined as "to take on responsibility to make efforts for the betterment of other people," according to French philosopher Paul Ricoeur.[25] The word "care" has been criticized by feminists because it often has been used in establishing paternalistic relationships. However, once this new meaning of "taking care of others for their betterment" is included, this word today can become an essential component for offsetting the danger that a limited sense of self-determination can pose in the area of reproductive technology.

Fourth, the viewpoint of biblical justice has been applied in order to verify the relationship of power. Biblical justice can sometimes become a rather hackneyed concept, but the message in the Bible concerning justice is still fresh for feminists. Justice in the Bible means elevating those who live at the bottom of society. Justice obligates people in power to direct society so that socially disadvantaged people can acquire rights and respect as human beings and decide things independently.

Justice in the medical field means that the following viewpoints take root in society. Women should be cared for so that their bodies are not controlled by others or utilized as a means to someone else's purpose. Nations or social systems and structures should be monitored so that they do not manipulate women's autonomy with their power of standardization. A power should be criticized if it stigmatizes a particular group of people as inferior through limiting socially acceptable characteristics of genes or unilaterally defining the normal or the abnormal with the logic of those who are strong. I am thinking even about the kind of political power that enacts a law that forces the admission into a clinic of a mentally handicapped person who is in danger of committing a criminal act. As mentioned above, the case of the mass murder of handicapped people in the year 2016 has given rise to such legal action by the Japanese government. But this is too hasty a solution for such a complex problem of life.

I would like to describe a blueprint for an alternative society based on the viewpoints of feminist theology, ethics, and also the intentions of the Catholic Church of Japan: one that offers an innovative view of society. In this society, women are not forced to abort a defective fetus. Mothers (and fathers) are the ones who make the decisions about whether to give birth to a child. This society creates a system that supports mothers if they have handicapped babies. The handicapped are not discriminated against or subjected to prejudice. With or without handicaps, every person must be treated as a precious being. There is enough information available for raising handicapped children with various social support systems. This will be a society where every person feels fundamental peace of mind in developing human relationships, because she or he is unconditionally accepted as a member.

Notes

1. This essay is a supplement to my Japanese article "Inochi no Senbetsu," in *Spirituarity to Inochi no Mirai*, ed. Susumu Shimazono and Yu Nagami (Kyoto: Jinbun-shoin, 2007), 76–90 (translated: "Reconsidering Selection of Life from the Viewpoint of Feminist

Theology," *The Meaning of Life in the 21st Century*, ed. Don Hanlon Johnson [Tokyo: Yoko Civilization Research Institute, 2008]).

2. Sweden has given compensation to the victims of compulsory sterilization since 1999. In Japan, the actual condition has not yet been investigated sufficiently. See Shohei Yonemoto et al., *Yuseigaku to Ningen-shakai* (Tokyo: Kodansha, 2000), 172.

3. See the statistical chart of *Ippan Shadan-hojin.Nihonkazoku-keikaku* No. 742, 2016, http://www.ifpa.or.jp/paper/main/ooo559.html.

4. See http://www.mhlw.go.jp/toukei/saikin/hw/eisei_houkoku/13/dl/gaikyo.

5. Newspaper report in *Asahi-Shinbun*, September 28, 2016.

6. Catholic Bishops' Conference of Japan, *Katorikku-kyokaino Shoshukyo Taiwa no Tebiki (Guideline for the Interreligious Dialogue with the Other Religions)* (Tokyo, 2009).

7. Catholic Bishops' Conference, *Inochi eno Manazashi* (Tokyo: Katorikku Chuou-kyogikai, 2017), 81.

8. Ibid., 83.

9. Congregation for the Doctrine of the Faith, *Instruction on Respect for Human Life in Its Origin and on the Dignity of Procreation—Replies to Certain Questions of the Day* (Rome, 1987).

10. *Inochi eno Manazashi*, 85.

11. Ibid., 86–87.

12. Ibid., 88–89.

13. Congregation for the Doctrine of the Faith, *Declaration on Procured Abortion*, no. 12 (1974), http://www.vatican.va/roman_curia/congregations/cfaith/documents/rc_con_cfaith_doc_19741118_declaration-abortion_en.html.

14. This classification of eugenic thoughts is based on Masahiro Morioka, *Seimeigaku ni Naniga dekiruka* (Tokyo: Keiso Shobo, 2001), 336.

15. Yonemoto et al., *Yuseigaku to Ningen-shakai*, 271ff.

16. Mariko Tamai, "Tenohira no-nakano Inochi," in *Zenkoku Kirisutokyo Shogaisha-dantai Kyogikai*, ed. Yorokobi no Inochi (Tokyo: Shinkyo Shuppansha, 2000), 31.

17. Shinichiro Morinaga, "Chakusho-shindan ni taisuru Rinriteki Shiza," in *Seishoku Igaku to Seimeirinri*, ed. Takashi Nagashima et al. (Tokyo: Taiyo Shuppan, 2001), 71.

18. Ibid., 84.

19. Haruko Okano, "Inochi no Hajimari," in *Seimei: Shoroh-byoshi no Uchu (Iwanami Koza)* (Tokyo: Iwanami-shoten, 2004).

20. Barbara Duden, *The Woman beneath the Skin: A Doctor's Patients in Eighteenth-Century Germany* (Cambridge, MA: Harvard University Press, 1998).

21. Azumi Tsuge, "Seishoku niokeru Josei no Jikoketteiken Shiron," in *Kenko to Gender*, ed. Naomi Nemura and Hiroko Hara (Tokyo: Akashi, 2000), 103.

22. Ibid., 107.

23. Susan Shah Wynn Benhabib and Ann Don Chin are representatives of such a view. See also A. Pieper and Hille Haker.

24. Feminist theologians, such as Carter Heyward, Rosemary R. Ruether, and Dorothee Sölle, represent the thinking on mutual theology. See Carter Heyward, *Und sie rührte sein Kleid an. Eine feministische Theologie der Beziehung* (Stuttgart, Germany: Kreuzverlag, 1986).

25. Paul Ricoeur, *Oneself as Another* (Chicago: University of Chicago Press, 1995).

Justice as Healing

Reflections on the Understanding of Justice, Based on an Indian Experience of Criminal Justice Delivery in a Rural Non-Christian Community

George Kodithottam

Introduction

Justice is usually understood as giving every person his or her rights. It is a duty toward others, measured by the rights of others. One does justice when one fulfills one's duties toward others by giving to every person what is due to that person. However, God's justice goes far beyond giving others their rights. It refers to God's righteousness (Matt. 5:45; Rom. 4:5), which justifies the sinners and gives them that for which they have no right at all. It focuses not on the rights but on the well-being of all, including those who have forfeited their rights. This essay is born out of my reflection upon an experience of the criminal justice system in a rural non-Christian community in North Gujarat (India) that focused on the well-being of all concerned by putting stress on healing the victim, the offender, and the community as well.

The Experience

My experience took place in a rural agricultural–pastoral (cattle-keeping) community of "Rabari"[1] people in the Mehsana district of North Gujarat, India. The Rabaries practice Hindu religion and have a social organization characterized by the clan system. There are different clans, and the clan councils function at the village, area, and whole-clan levels. These councils play a very important role in the lives of Rabaries, as they have great authority over all matters of the community. The community has its own concept of justice and a well-established and functional justice delivery system managed by the clan councils. All major disputes are settled by the councils, keeping in mind the overall welfare of the community.

In one of the villages, a Rabari man was killed in a land dispute by another Rabari man from a different village. The offender was arrested and put in jail by the state police. After the completion of the necessary police investigations, the case was committed to the appropriate court of law under the relevant provisions of the

Indian Penal Code. If proved guilty by the court, the offender could be given up to the death penalty. In the state criminal justice system, the central concern was to prove the guilt of the offender and give him the maximum punishment possible under the law.

While the state's legal process was going on, the community also initiated its own process of delivering justice. Their central concern was to repair the harm suffered by the community. In the community's perspective, the harm was not only the death of a member and its consequences for his family. It also included the possible long incarceration of, or even the death penalty for, the offender by the state criminal justice system and the consequent deprivation and sufferings of the family of the offender and its consequence for the village and for the entire community. The clan councils of the two villages involved in the incident met, and the initial discussions began at that level. The offense was viewed primarily as harm experienced by the community as a whole. Punishment to the offender was not conceived in terms of making him suffer harm in proportion to the harm he caused, but rather in accepting the responsibility of causing the harm and of repairing it to the extent humanly and practically possible. The extent of the damages was assessed and possible ways of repairing the damages were proposed. Claims and counterclaims were made with regard to the concrete ways to repair the harm, which would necessarily include material compensation to the family of the victim. The material compensation is calculated on the basis of what the victim's immediate family would need to lead their lives reasonably well. If the offender or his family is not capable of giving what is agreed upon, the entire community in his village must take on the responsibility. Apart from the material compensation, certain time-bound social sanctions or restrictions on the offender, his family, and sometimes even on his entire village are imposed. In the given case, the claims and counterclaims could not be reconciled at the level of the village councils. Therefore, the matter was taken up in the area council. The area council, which had about seventy members, had five prolonged nightly meetings, lasting five to six hours each and spreading over five fortnights. It was the responsibility of the village of the offender to feed the members of the council on the days of the meetings. Finally, an agreement was reached on the quantum of material compensation and on the mode and extent of the sanctions.

Though the state officially does not recognize the authority of the community's justice system, the judge in the state court (who was well aware of the community's justice process) continued to postpone the court proceedings until the community came to an agreement. The unofficial arrangement in the community is that once the agreement is finalized in the community, the witnesses for the prosecution would see to it that the case is not proved in the state court and the accused is set free. The judge is aware of this understanding between the parties within the community and facilitates this arrangement by postponing the legal procedure in the court. In the present case, in furtherance of the decisions reached in the community council, the witnesses for the prosecution turned hostile in the court and, finally, the criminal case of murder was not proved in the state court and the offender was set free. However, the offender and his village together fulfilled the restorative and retributive measures decided by the community to repair the harm caused, and they also accepted certain time-bound social sanctions/restrictions imposed upon them so that the matter was brought to a close.

In this entire process, justice meant healing at three levels: at the level of the victim's family, the offender and his family, and the community as a whole. Though anger and desire for revenge were initially very much present, and the early deliberations in the village-level council meetings were dominated by such emotions, the area council managed to make the process reason based. In the final decisions and agreements, anger and revenge had no role at all. Justice, which aims at the well-being of all, including the offender, is thus brought about through community solidarity.

Conventional Views on Criminal Justice

In the traditional Christian teaching, justice is explained as rendering to each person or human community what is their own and what is due to them by right. This means giving to others what they have a right to get and also not taking away from others what belongs to them. When we fail on either of these counts, justice is violated. Such violation has to be remedied. Remedy implies that the injured person is indemnified and active punishment is given to the culpable offender. Violated justice is restored by means of restitution to the extent possible and punishment to the offender in proportion to the guilt. Punishment is seen from two different perspectives: punishment aimed at bringing better consequences through reforming the offender and discouraging other potential offenders, and punishment in order to restore the moral system. To restore the moral system, criminals should be punished in proportion to their crime. Here, punishment is understood as the best and the most morally acceptable response to crime. Imposing punishment is considered a virtue of the authority when given with common welfare and the correction of the guilty in mind, and a virtue of the guilty when accepted in a spirit of repentance.

Retributive Justice

When punishment is given as a means for restoring the moral system, the retributive aspect of justice is stressed. Retributive justice is founded on the idea that an offender should be made to suffer for his or her offense. It focuses on the punishment of the offender as opposed to his or her rehabilitation. Punishment means some deprivation, something unpleasant that is administered by the society and imposed by a legal authority. The law of retaliation (Code of Hammurabi, *Lex talionis*), "an eye for an eye and a tooth for a tooth," seems to be the justification for punishment. The underlying assumption is that a guilty person should suffer pain.[2] In retributive justice, crimes are seen as offenses against the state, which is the custodian of the moral system, and not as conflict between individuals and against the integrity of the community.[3] The final goal of retributive justice is not rehabilitation, reparation, restoration, or the prevention of future offenses, but giving punishment to the offender in proportion to the gravity of the crime. The justice delivery system focuses on establishing the guilt of the offender based on past behavior and on imposing pain on the offender for the offense committed. Any deterrent effect of punishment is only consequential and hoped for. The state's responsibility is limited to awarding punishment to the offender, and the offender's accountability is reduced to only undergoing the punishment. Appropriate punishment is seen also as a response to society's cry for justice and as reflecting the public abhorrence of the offense. The quantum of punishment is decided based upon the depravity of the offense and the demands of the "collective conscience of society." Not awarding punishment is seen as unfair to the victim and also to the society.

Limits of Retributive Justice

The justification of punishment given to the offender with the correction of the guilty and common welfare through establishment of the rule of law in mind is generally accepted. However, as Michelle Maiese[4] points out, in the practice of retributive justice, there is often a tendency to move from just retribution to revenge. Urge for revenge comes from anger, hurt, bitterness, and hatred, and leads to retaliation. In retaliatory punishment, the victim seeks to make the offender suffer in return, and the punishment is likely to be many times more severe than reparation. Here punishment is given more for the satisfaction of victims and those sympathetic to them, and not for establishing justice. Human passion for retaliation necessarily results in violence, an exchange of evil for evil. Retaliation always creates further antagonism and injustice. The closer we get to evil in responding to evil, the more the everyday reality of our individual and collective life becomes embroiled in the dialectic of victims and executioners. A vengeful victim is a potential executioner who focuses only on the harm he or she suffered and not on any healing or restoration. We should realize that a new cycle of violence is not the necessary outcome of past sufferings. Revenge does not bring the relief that the victims require, but rather creates new victims and victimizers. We need to get away from the dialectic of victims and executioners and take an attitude of empathy. Empathy for the offender helps the victim to become free from the urge for revenge and retaliation. The capacity for empathy allows one to struggle against one's capacity for violence.

Giving punishment based on the depravity of the offense and the demands of the "collective conscience of society" (the public anger and desire for revenge) is also problematic. The public sentiment for revenge can often pervert the idea of justice. In such cases, "justice" is typically defined emotionally rather than with intent for fairness or prevention. Justice demands a certain level of seclusion, and a genuine desire for justice permits sorrow at the crime rather than anger.[5] Those moved by sorrow at the pain of the victims are less likely to view the perpetrators as "subhuman," despite the horrors they have perpetrated, and will be able to conceive of the idea that we need to respond in a more constructive way to violent crimes. But those moved by the sentiment of anger very quickly end up viewing the perpetrators as "less than human." In retributive justice, since crime is defined primarily as a violation of the state, the interpersonal and intracommunity nature of crime is obscured; conflict is seen as individual versus the state, and the link between the victim and the accused is ignored. The offense is defined in purely legal terms, devoid of its moral and social dimensions. Consequently, retributive justice is oriented mainly toward punishing the offender and not making the victim whole again. For punishment, retributive justice relies heavily upon incarceration, and experience all over the world shows that increasing the harshness of punishments does not necessarily reduce crime.

Restorative Justice

Restorative justice focuses primarily on restoring what is broken by catering to the needs of all parties affected and involved. Therefore, the emphasis is put on rehabilitating the victim, the offender, and the community. In restorative justice, punishment of the offender is only a secondary goal and that, too, as part of restitution. The process of restorative justice, which is necessarily inclusive, involves all stakeholders in an effort to address the harm and seeks to find out what needs to be done to make things as right as possible for all concerned, and then tries to take all steps to achieve that goal. The victim, the offender, and the community participate together in this process. It views crime as being much deeper than simply breaking a law and instead tries to reach the root of crime. Crimes break relationships and shatter the lives of human beings and of the entire community. Justice therefore requires that those relationships be restored and that those lives be healed. Restorative justice is founded on the sense of solidarity and therefore its processes are inclusive and involve all stakeholders in the effort to repair the harm. Solidarity, as both Pope John Paul II and Benedict XVI explained, is "a sense of responsibility on the part of everyone with regard to everyone."[6] Restorative justice focuses on the needs of the victims and the offenders, as well as the involved community, instead of just punishing the offender. What is operational here is an ethic of responsibility and accountability. Accountability comes naturally with community and interdependent relationships. When people are connected and interdependent, maintaining relationships becomes more important than escaping blame or avoiding pain, and people will become more ready to be accountable. Therefore, the process of restorative justice takes a community-based approach to dealing with crime, the effects of crime, and the prevention of crime. Restorative justice operates from a belief that the path to justice lies in problem solving and healing rather than in punitive isolation. Primacy for relationship, respect for all involved, accepting responsibility for any harm caused, commitment to repair the harm to the fullest extent possible, and reintegration into the community of all persons who may have felt alienated are the five ingredients in restorative justice.[7]

Principles of Restorative Justice

The important principles on which restorative justice is based, as enunciated by the Conflict Solutions Center in Santa Barbara, follow:[8]

1. A crime is, first and foremost, an act against people and relationships; second, an act against the community; and third, an act against the law.
2. By committing the crime, the person creates an obligation to the victim, the community, and the state.
3. When the offending persons meet that obligation, they are taking responsibility for their actions, and begin to understand and value their relationship with other people, the community, and the law.

The justice process becomes restorative when:

1. It shows equal concern for victims, offenders, and the community.
2. It encourages offender accountability to repair the harm caused to victim, family, and community, and focuses on the repair rather than on punishment.
3. It provides opportunities for direct and/or indirect dialogue between the stakeholders.
4. It encourages collaboration and reintegration rather than isolation.

In the restorative approach to justice, crime is seen as an act against another person and the community and as creating both individual and social responsibility. Response to the crime is focused on the harmful consequences of the offender's wrong action and on finding ways and means to remedy the harm. Without remedying the harm, punishment alone is not effective in changing behavior but is disruptive to community harmony and good relationships. Therefore, the processes of restorative justice focus on the problem solving, on liabilities/obligations, and on the future. It put emphasis on dialogue and negotiation, and sees restitution as a means of restoring both parties. In restorative justice, victims are central to the process of resolving a crime and its after effects, and all parties are directly involved in the process.[9]

Justice as Healing

Our criminal justice systems (the Anglo-Saxon version) put stress on retributive justice as a means of establishing justice in society where punishment to the offender is motivated more by desire for retaliation than common welfare and the correction of the guilty. In the traditional Christian teaching on justice, retributive justice is also given an important role. It is explained as a necessary means to restore violated justice through denunciation of the crime. Here punishment is seen primarily as the emphatic denunciation by the community of a crime, and therefore, all crimes must be punished.

God's Justice

We began with citing Matthew 5:45 and Romans 4:5 on God's justice and God's righteousness, which also justifies the sinner. God's justice is that God always acts in accordance with Godself's character. Saving and bringing creation to wholeness is the will of God, and God acts in accordance with that will. All the biblical words for justice relate to the fairness, judgment, love, and healing of God. The Hebrew word *shalom*, one of the most holistic words for justice in the Bible, means both "justice" and "peace." Shalom includes "wholeness," or everything that makes for people's well-being, security, and, in particular, the restoration of relationships that have been broken. Justice, therefore, is about repairing broken relationships among people according to God's will. Justice, in this sense, is also about restoring our broken relationship with God to what God intends for us, which includes our role in God's purposes for all of Godself's creatures and for the world that God has made.[10]

The understanding of justice as repairing broken relationships points to the communitarian nature of justice. We have seen that a criminal justice system based on retribution cannot accomplish satisfactorily the repairing of brokenness at various levels. But restorative justice is more apt for such a purpose. What we have seen in the Rabari case is an instance of the application of the principles of restorative justice where the whole focus was on repairing of brokenness, and it was achieved to a satisfactory level.

Rabaries are practitioners of the Hindu religion. The Hindu ethic is based on the concept of *dharma*. *Dharma* is understood as the innermost nature, the essence, the implicit truth of all things. The word *dharma* comes from the Sanskrit root *dhr*. It stands for "upholding the interrelatedness of all that is." *Dharma* literally means "that which one lays hold of and which holds things together." It is the essential foundation of all that lives and moves.[11] All of us are held together by that same foundation. We are able to outgrow individualism and espouse the cause of our fellow humans because we and our fellow humans are the expression of the same reality. Therefore, oneness of all is the normative content of *dharma*. In this sense, fundamentally, we live in a moral universe or an eternal moral order. In the Hindu ethical thought, there is a firm conviction that the universe is pervaded by the moral order. This moral order is understood not as a fixed eternal order but as "orderliness." When this moral order is internalized, it becomes the "individual *dharma*" (*svadharma*), and the moral law becomes an innate law in every person. This *svadharma* is understood as an inborn moral sense in every person. As

Somen Das explains, "*Svadharma* is the categorical imperative from within. This is the subjective counterpart of the objective moral reality. There is no subject–object dichotomy in Hindu ethics and morality. It is the inbuilt directedness—an unwritten moral tendency or constancy."[12] One's duties and obligations within this order have to be discovered in each situation with discernment and love. *Dharma* as the innate moral law is the fundamental law of our nature, which leads us to ethical behavior by moving us from self-consciousness to coconsciousness. Moral law is central to the conception of reality in India. Mahatma Gandhi was an ardent advocate of *dharma* as the moral law. He considered *dharma* as the ontological basis of morality and ethics. God has ordered the universe, and we are called to live an ordered life according to the plan of God. St. Paul conveys a similar understanding when he says, "God is a God of order and not of disorder" (1 Cor. 14:33). Gandhi understood *dharma* as truth and explained truth as that which God is, and that which God made things as, and that which God wills them to be. Truth is the law of our being, and to know the moral law is to know our true nature. Therefore, truth is the substance of morality.[13]

Dharma emphasizes the oneness of all and affirms unity in diversity. It understands diversity in the context of primordial unity and therefore sees no basic opposition. One only needs to work through the tensions and polarities. In this sense, *dharma* is the principle of unity and of relationship. As Somen Das points out, "*Dharma* espouses dialectic, not a dichotomy."[14] An ethics based on *dharma* focuses on avoiding dualism, which results in fragmentation and chaos; it tries to avoid/heal division and conflict among people.

In the process of establishing justice, the Rabari community was following the ethic of *dharma*. Their justice process was focused on repairing the brokenness and reestablishing the interrelatedness of the persons and the wholeness of the community. In this process, all the stakeholders, the family of the murdered person and their village, the offender, his family and his village, and the whole Rabari community of the area were active participants. They functioned on the assumption that the concrete content of justice in a specific situation can be determined only by the involved parties through dialogue. The murder caused much anger in the family and the village of the victim, and demand for revenge did come up from them. However, the community leaders managed to assuage all such feelings and demands. They stressed the aspects of loss and pain, both at the individual and community levels. During the process, anger and desire for revenge were transformed to a sense of sadness and empathy. This sadness and empathy had embraced both the victim's family as well as that of the offender—the offender's family because of the punishment the offender would surely get from the state court. This collective sense of pain and empathy led the families involved to look for solutions that would remedy the harm that already had happened and prevent further harm from happening. The victim's family also came to accept the reality that causing harm to the victim and his family was in no way going to make their situation any better. The community leaders were led not only by their concern for the family of the victim but also by their commitment for the well-being of the whole community. Therefore, they together searched for and found solutions that will ultimately heal personal wounds and repair the brokenness in the community.

It is important to note that in the entire process an application of principles of restorative justice was at play, yet the aspect of punishment also was included. The punishment imposed had a wider meaning than understood in retributive justice, where a meaningful relationship is created between the offense and the ways that the offender can make amends to the victim.[15] The offender and his entire village were given a certain punishment in the form of time-bound sanctions that were more symbolic than debilitative. The punishment imposed was not retaliatory, but reformative and deterrent. It stressed not only the personal responsibility for the offense but also the collective responsibility. Therefore, punishment was given to the offender, his family, and also his village in varying/graded degrees. Such punishment has greater reformatory and deterrent possibilities as the whole community is made to be responsible. The efforts to reform and deter are finally grounded in the sense of solidarity in the community.

Another noteworthy aspect of the justice process was that punishment was not seen as part of justice for the victim as is happening increasingly in our societies. The assumption that a guilty person should suffer pain and the idea that the violated order of justice is restored through punishment leads to the notion that punishment of the guilty is part of the justice deserved by the victim. Punishment of the offender is taken as part of the rights of the victim. In the Rabari justice system, punishment of the offender was totally delinked from justice for the victim. Therefore, a sense of revenge or retaliation had no role in deciding the nature or quantum of punishment. The sole consideration was reformation of the offender and a deterrent for potential offenders. Justice for the victim was conceived only in terms of repairing the harm to the fullest extent possible. Care was taken to minimize the damaging effect of punishment on the relationship within the community. The entire process was future oriented and focused on solving a problem affecting the entire community, through fulfilling obligations and responsibilities. Elements of both retributive justice and of restorative justice were incorporated in the ultimate determination. It was a process of justice that primarily aimed at the well-being of all through repairing and restoring relationships at the personal and community levels. Restitution and punishment were part of it to the extent that they were needed for the well-being of all.

Conclusion

In a multireligious and multicultural world, it is important that Christian ethics gleans insights from the ethics practices and experiences in various communities, Christian as well as non-Christian. In doing so, the Catholic ethicist fulfills the duty of scrutinizing the signs of the times and of interpreting them in the light of the gospel as enjoined by the Second Vatican Council.[16] Such multicultural and multireligious experiences would contribute significantly to understanding Christian revelation more comprehensively and adequately in concrete situations in a pluralistic world. The religions of the world can help in developing a world ethic with their experience of transcendence and with their commitment to righteousness and objectivity. It is an opportunity to deepen our understanding of the nature and the role of religions and to renew our resolve to articulate a world ethic that is truly interreligious, and based on the richness and the plurality of religious experiences without denying our Christian conviction and commitment.

Notes

1. "Rabaries" are an originally nomadic people, today found settled on the outskirts of cities, towns, and villages in the states of Madhya Pradesh, Haryana, Rajasthan, and Gujarat in the northwestern part of India. They have a population of around one million people, according to the 2011 census of India.

2. Abhishek Mohanty, *WBNUJS, Retributive Theory of Punishment: A Critical Analysis*, 1, https://www.lawctopus.com.

3. The major paradigm shift from understanding of crime as a victim–offender conflict within the context of community to conflict between the state and the offender took place with the decree of Henry I, securing royal jurisdiction over certain offenses in twelfth-century England. Cf. Mark Umbreit, "Restorative Justice through Victim-Offender Mediation: A Multi-Site Assessment," *Western Criminology Review* 1, no. 1 (1998): 1–28, http://wcr.sonoma.edu/v1n1/umbreit.html.

4. Michelle Maiese, "Retributive Justice" (2004), http://beyondintractability.org/essay/retributive-justice.

5. There is a beautiful recent example of this in Etienne Cardiles, the companion of Xavier Jugele, a French policeman who was shot and killed on April 20, 2017, by a jihadist in Paris and, who said at a remembrance ceremony led by President Francois Hollande that he felt no hatred, only deep pain. Reported by Agence France-Presse, Paris, *Hindu, Kochi*, April 26, 2017.

6. *Sollicitudo rei socialis*, no. 38; *Caritas in veritate*, no. 38.

7. http://rjusticesbc.pbworks.com.

8. http://www.cscsb.org/index.html.

9. A table illustrating the differences in the approach to justice between retributive justice and restorative justice is available at http://www.cscsb.org/restorative_justice/retribution_vs_restoration.html.

10. Cf. Jim Wallis, "How the Bible Understands Justice," https://www.onfaith.com.

11. Cf. Somen Das, *Christian Ethics and Indian Ethos*, 2nd ed. rev. (Delhi: ISPCK, 1994), 159.

12. Ibid., 163.

13. Cf. ibid., 160.

14. Ibid., 163.

15. Kathleen Daly gives a more comprehensive understanding of punishment in "Revisiting the Relationship between Retributive and Restorative Justice," in *Restorative Justice: From Philosophy to Practice*, ed. Heather Strang and John Braithwaite (Aldershot, UK: Dartmouth, 2000), 8–11, www98.griffith.edu.au/dspace/bitstream/handle/10072/1051/?sequence=1.

16. *Gaudium et spes*, no. 4.

Transforming Electoral Violence in Africa

Anne Celestine Achieng Oyier-Ondigo

Introduction

Over the past two decades, Africa has seen dozens of conflicts over a variety of issues. One of the contemporary concerns that generate violence is elections. While elections are used in many conflicted regions to end violence, in Africa they have become a source of internal civil strife and a death trap. Electoral violence is defined by Fischer as "acts or threats of coercion, intimidation, or physical harm perpetrated to affect the outcome of an electoral process."[1]

According to this definition, the violence is clearly intended to skew the outcome of the results. The process of voting, therefore, may be very peaceful; however, the outcome is often manipulated. According to Machika, manipulation is achieved by threats, intimidation, and arbitrary deaths.[2] The violence may take place in the preelection, election, or postelection period; however, in Africa it often occurs during the tallying of results, prompting postelection violence (PEV). Many African countries brace themselves for electoral violence each election year. In Kenya, electoral violence has been occurring since the inception of multiparty politics in 1992. Other countries that have manifested recurrent electoral violence include Nigeria, Burundi, Ethiopia, Zimbabwe, Lesotho, the Democratic Republic of the Congo (DRC), Congo, Togo, Gabon, Guinea, Gambia, Ivory Coast, and Uganda.[3] During the electoral period, ethnic cleansing and genocidal tendencies erupt. The most recent violence in Kenya, in August 2017, involved ethnic profiling of the Luo group and killed over one hundred people.[4] Electoral violence has consequences on the future of a society and its development.[5] This trend of violence is killing democratic prospects and its establishment. This essay explores the causes of this violence as well as transformative approaches in mitigating the phenomenon, taken from the church's social teachings on the use of conscience in voting for credible leaders. A transformative model is advanced, which aims at behavioral change that works toward the common good and respects human dignity and the rights of each individual.

The Causes of Electoral Violence

The undercurrents and the root causes of electoral violence include structural factors, unethical practices, human rights violations, and socioeconomic factors.[6]

Structural Factors

Government structures are basic institutions that govern a society. Political institutions such as the judiciary, the executive branch, the legislature, and the electoral management body (EMB) are mechanisms that are utilized to execute essential government functions in order to serve its citizenry. The institutions reflect a nation's culture, values, policies, history, and aspirations. According to Oyier-Ondigo, governments have structures that create laws and policies, implement them, and deliver resources to the public.[7] Though these structures often reflect how a society is run, they can either be violent or peaceable.[8] Objective structures that serve equitably are known to generate peace, while unjust, exclusive ones generate violence. Johan Galtung, the peace guru, posits that institutional structures are termed violent when they produce oppression, discrimination, and exploitation, and deny citizens certain rights.[9] According to Galtung, structural violence is systemic, embedded within institutions of power, and is abusive to the citizens' economic, social, and political rights. Such structures have weak institutions that sustain, engender, and reinforce unabated corruption. This subsequently leads to impunity and immunity even in violent actions such as electoral violence.

Electoral violence is recurrent in Africa as one of the approaches citizens use to vent their anger toward the unsatisfactory election process. The demonstrations that lead to violence are an indictment of the lethargy of unjust structures or a clinging presidency, and express the need for change. However, the demonstrators are often suppressed or killed by incumbent regimes, shattering their voices. Electoral violence perpetrators are hardly ever charged in courts of law, and there are no international courts for rigged elections. As a result, the perpetrators maintain cycles of violence each election year with impunity and immunity.

Corruption

Corruption in manipulating election outcomes is a pressing issue undermining democratic gains in Africa.[10] Lindberg explains that corruption involves unethical and fraudulent conduct.[11] Rannenberger, the US ambassador to Kenya, claimed in the 2008 elections that there was compelling evidence of corrupt practices in the tallying of votes, causing sporadic electoral violence.[12] In Kenya, President Uhuru Kenyatta was quoted as stating that though corruption was a reality, he was unable to counter it.[13] His expression indicates how entrenched corruption is within Kenya's government. Transparency International (TI) noted that there is a connection between the prevalence of corruption and electoral violence.[14]

According to TI, Kenya is ranked as the most corrupt state in the East African region. In a study by Oyier-Ondigo, countries with a lower corruption index, such as Tanzania and Rwanda, experience less electoral violence, while Kenya, Burundi, and Uganda, which are more corrupt, experience the phenomenon each election year.[15]

Weak Democratic Institutions

Democracy is a form of government characterized by institutions, rights, and functions designed to serve the citizens.[16] According to Miller, democratic institutions can be weak or strong, depending on the political terrain and functioning.[17] Weak institutions play a major part in encouraging electoral violence. The weakest institutions that are prone to political manipulation in Africa include the EMB, the police, the judiciary, and the executive branch. Not only are they seen by the public as having the least authority to make independent decisions but they are also unrepresentative of the citizens, merely serving the interests of political elites. Fossungu argues that in weak institutions, major decision making is centralized in the presidency and the executive branch.[18] He further argues that this encourages overreliance on the executive for crucial decisions, rendering them swayable.[19] The EMB, which is responsible for running elections, has been documented for having failed the Kenyan citizens severely. The chairman of the Kenyan EMB stated that he did not know the winner of the 2007 presidential election. However, he went ahead and announced the incumbent as the winner, "quoting duress" from political elites, sparking sporadic violence. According to Adolfo, EMBs should be made independent by the laws of the country.[20] Simply making institutions autonomous is not enough. In fact, Kenyan institutions are now independent, but they still generated violence in the 2017 election.

Unethical and Unjust Practices

A democratic culture that has ethical standards begins with a legitimately elected leadership through a credible process.[21] Girard contends that the most important element for state survival is legitimacy as accorded by its citizens.[22] On the other hand, rigged elections produce illegitimate power. Illegitimate power exhibits unethical behavior working to accomplish self-interest and those of their cronies circumventing public interest. Such a leadership is prone to abuse of human rights. In turn, the citizens may resort to violence.[23] The violence, as can be inferred, operates as a catharsis. In this respect, Girard claims that violence becomes a cleansing force that frees the citizens from feelings of despair, inferiority, and inaction.[24] In the same breath, Kalisa claims that the choice of violence by citizens in authoritarian regimes makes them fearless and restores their self-respect in an otherwise autocratic environment.[25] Moreover, Kalisa asserts, "To rid themselves of powerlessness, the citizens in unjust violent structures must resort to violence as a direct consequence of the violent nature of autocratic domination." He argues that "violence in such situations becomes a means for dismantling the autocracies and replacing them with self-determinism."[26]

Use of violence as advocated by Kalisa contrasts with Gandhi's nonviolent strategies in similar contexts.[27] According to Parel, Gandhi argues that unethical economic or political structures must be dismantled by ordinary citizens' actions, albeit nonviolently.[28] Fanon, in a related concept, envisions a continuation of violence in unethical autocratic states until a national consciousness of good morals is transformed to produce peace.[29] To this end, electoral violence will continue until ethical structures that generate peace are in place.

Human Rights Issues

Human rights violations are particularly experienced in states that are illiberal. Illiberal states abuse the human rights of its citizens. The abuse of one of these human rights may imply abuse of several others since the rights are intertwined and pivot on one another. Demonstrations by the citizens to protest shambolic elections have been met by severe human rights abuse by the police, government militia, and the army.[30] According to Human Rights Watch, the governments of Gabon and Uganda used militia groups to scatter perceived opposition groups, raping women and girls.[31]

Other rights that are violated during election violence include the right to freedom of assembly, right to open association, right to information, right to suffrage, right to life, right to peaceful demonstrations, right to free speech, and right to free movement. The media in Kenya in 2008, in Uganda in 2014, and in Burundi in 2016 were banned from airing any election issues.[32] In these same states, freedom of movement was also truncated, and curfews were put in place in opposition strongholds.[33] Peaceful demonstrations were banned, and youths were arbitrarily arrested, detained without trial, and many lost their lives as a result of police extrajudicial killings.[34] As Philip Alston reports, hundreds of brutal summary executions had been carried out with impunity by the Kenyan police in 2008.[35] There was also a lack of equal protection for all by the law, and cases of rape, torture, arbitrary killings, and forced displacements were rampant.[36]

Socioeconomic Factors

Economically based factors, such as poverty, inequality, unemployment, poor health care, inadequate education facilities, poor infrastructure, and lack of basic human needs have contributed to electoral violence.

Violence during elections has been linked to poverty. Those who demonstrate and protest are the proletariats. The role of poverty as a cause of violence is an outcome of social processes within government structures. Conflict, in this sense, is context related, arising from situations in the environment such as unjust socioeconomic conditions that breed social inequalities.[37] Scholars Snodgrass, Ochieng, and Oyier-Ondigo argue that one of the key causes of conflict is poverty induced by scarce resources and unmet basic human needs (BHNs).[38] Unmet BHNs, such as employment, food, shelter, clothing, education, and health care, are known to trigger violence.[39] The BHNs are vital and a precondition for survival, so much so that their scarcity may profoundly elicit hostility.[40] In a study of electoral violence in Kenya, it was found that there was more violence among the poor regions than among the wealthy.[41] This was attributed to the high rate of unemployment, which stands at 65 percent.[42]

There is evidence of the relationship between socioeconomic differentials in poverty levels, unemployment, resource allocation, and violence.[43] The current analysis corroborates the view of Ubomba-Jaswa that failure to meet BHNs triggers conflict and violence. This evidence is comparable to the findings on causes of electoral violence in 2008 in Zimbabwe. Research showed that, among other causes, poverty and the unemployment level (which was at 54 percent) were major causes of the violence in Zimbabwe.[44] This was also true of the electoral violence in Ivory Coast in 2010 and Nigeria in 2010, where the unemployment of youth escalated violence after perceived election-rigging claims.[45]

The relationship between citizens' poverty levels and electoral violence may be rooted in the populace's hopes that elections would bring a change in the regime with better developmental prospects in terms of employment. Calderon points out that societies with higher levels of institutional support for their less-fortunate citizens are less likely to degenerate into violence.[46]

Transformative Approaches in Mitigating Electoral Violence

To mitigate and transform electoral violence in Africa, there is a need to change violence-generating structures into ethical, peaceable ones. This is because ethical elections require a new moral vision. *Gaudium et spes* clearly articulates this ethical task for the salvation of the world by interpreting the teachings of Christ. This task facilitates the freedom of, and respect for, our lives as civil voters and the well-being of our neighbors. The ethical task aims at voting with a moral conscience—voting for those who respect human dignity and rights and seek to advance the common good.

The Ethical Conscience

Gaudium et spes reminds us of the fundamental Christian teaching of our origin: that we are made in the image and likeness of God.[47] In this way, human beings, created in the image of God, are endowed with the gifts of intellect, self-awareness, and free will.[48] Free will empowers us to discern, impelled by our conscience, the law written in our hearts.[49] According to Keenan, "Conscience is the voice of God within us, urging us to love our God, ourselves, and our neighbors and . . . determine . . . a course of action."[50] Conscience gives three essential responsibilities to self, neighbor, and God.[51] As a consequence, we should tolerate and respect others' conscientious decisions. The use of our conscience for decisions inspires us to live ethically. It is imperative that for African elections to be ethical, its people must vigilantly act according to the dictates of the conscience against the dark forces of corruption and other unethical inhumane practices that bedevil our African continent today. To act according to the dictates of the conscience enables all to contribute toward the establishment of a civic order. The rights of conscience in civic duties are also recognized by the church.[52] Hence, all persons have the right and obligation to follow the authentic prompting of their conscience when voting, a civic duty of all eligible citizens. Government has at the same time a responsibility to protect the free choices of the people.

Performance of civic duties following the dictates of the conscience is always a challenge, particularly during elections. Most people in Africa brace themselves for tough, mendacious environments in such times. Their conscience is always put to the test in the performance of their civic duties as public servants of the electorate. In demanding justice in elections, many have been threatened, injured, and killed by their own decadent governments. This includes those who have paid a great price by not supporting corruption during elections. Many have been killed or ran to exile for safety. Some have been threatened or banished by their governments, and have lost their citizenship, friends, and the cultural environment they were brought up in. Among those who allegedly tolerated corruption are the EMB of Kenya in 2007, the EMB of Zimbabwe in 2008, and the EMB of Nigeria in 2010. As such, the citizens of these states lost their lives in electoral violence.

A few brave public servants working with the EMBs had to resign or migrate. These included the EMB vice president, Spes Caritas Ndironkeye, and Illuminata Ndabahagamye of Burundi, who jetted out, leaving behind resignation letters, after Nkurunziza insisted on running for an illegal third term in 2015.[53] Another recent example is that of the EMB technology manager Christopher Msando of Kenya who was tortured and brutally killed for refusing to comply with election malpractices three days before the election.[54] In Nigeria, official presidential results in some rural areas recorded over 100 percent voter turnout in the 2010 election.[55] This means that either choice for any public servant has consequences. Those who knowingly assisted in manipulating the outcome of the elections plunged their countries into violence. Those who rejected manipulation were either killed or are in exile. Violence for power has claimed more civilian lives in countries like Zimbabwe, Nigeria, and Kenya than any civil wars.

The Nigerian electoral violence of 2010 turned into religious violence between Christians and Muslims.[56] A power struggle with secondary religious motives in the early 2000s turned into a full-blown, Muslim-against-Christian conflict in the Central African Republic. "Seleka," the Muslim group, and the Christian "anti-balaka" militia have killed more than three thousand civilians.[57] The Kenyan electoral violence of 2008 turned into an interethnic crisis where the Kikuyu tribe targeted the Luo ethnic group while the Kalenjin ethnic group killed Kikuyus and the Kisii tribes.[58] The electoral violence experienced in South Africa in 2016 turned racial, pitting the blacks against the white minority, while in Somalia it turned into clan violence in the 2002 power struggle.[59]

From the various illustrations in Africa, the conscience is therefore an important weapon in the fight against unethical power struggles in Africa. The church has to continue training and socializing the conscience for sane politics and civil order that sustain peace. There are signs that all is not lost. There are hopeful signs of trained consciences standing up against evil for the sake of the people. However, more has to be done to sustain the war against evil.

The Common Good

Gaudium et spes, having assured us of our conscience as a weapon against evil, calls us to live by the moral principle of the common good. The common good calls us to love others and commit to social justice for all without discrimination. This morality makes sense in our African political environment, where extreme poverty escalates as the gap between the rich and the poor increases. It also makes sense in an environment where politicians polarize their citizens along ethnic, racial, and religious lines. The call for the common good is a just call for equal distribution of state resources, just institutions, integrity in the electoral process respecting the choices of the people, and building of trust between and among citizens, constantly emphasizing the interdependence of the individual and the social environment. The common good also calls for the organization of all institutions in the civil service to meet the needs of the people, both individual and societal. This fosters strong institutions and better government services. Strong ethical institutions serve their citizens equally. They ensure that their conscientious decisions and policies work toward better services for the common good. Rigged and manipulated election outcomes and violations of people's right of choice become obsolete. Credible elections give a deserving voice to the citizens. The voice of the people leads to a social order permitting equal political representation, conversely making better the lives of individuals. *Gaudium et spes* insists that all institutions must be organized to meet the needs of the people.[60] Where institutions focus on the common good, fraudulent elections are loathed.

Human Dignity—Human Rights

The church calls on all citizens, not just political leaders, to respect the human dignity of each person.[61] The dignity of the human person flows out of the fact that we are all created by the same God in Godself's semblance. According to Transparency International, most socioeconomic blunders in Africa are caused by corrupt, inhumane practices.[62] In their view, Africa is still plagued with a variety of socioeconomic issues that dehumanize the dignity of its people.[63] These dehumanizing concerns include poverty, unjust distribution of scarce resources, unemployment, and inequality that continue to increase the gap between the wealthy and the poor. Correspondingly, *Gaudium et spes* draws our attention to socioeconomic injustices that dehumanize, and asserts that "a great number of people are still tormented by hunger and misery [such as unemployment], and entire multitudes do not know how to read or write."[64] Unemployment is among the many practices that dehumanize people. This is illustrated in Table 1.

Table 1: Youth Employment by Identity

Country	Youth Unemployment	Ethnic Imbalance	Frequency of Electoral Violence
Kenya	63%	By ethnic marginalization	1992, 1997, 2002, 2007, 2013, and 2017
Ethiopia	59%	By ethnic marginalization	2005, 2010, and 2015
DRC Congo	33%	Does not marginalize	2001, 2015 and ongoing
South Africa	21%	Does not marginalize	2016
Nigeria	66%	Religiously marginalizing	2000, 2005, 2010, and 2015
Rwanda	9%	No marginalizaton	None

Source: Transparency International report 2015.

As seen in Table 1, most African states that marginalize on the basis of ethnic identity not only experience increased levels of youth unemployment but also have frequent recurrent electoral violence. In Kenya, 63 percent of the youth are unemployed. Employment is ethnically based, and there have been six recurrent instances of violence related to elections. Employment in Nigeria discriminates on a religious basis and shows four recurrent instances of violence related to power struggle. The reformed Rwanda after the 1994 genocide employed Rwandese based on academic merit and hardly has electoral violence. South Africa employs based on academic weight and racial balance, with a 21 percent unemployment level. Unemployment breeds absurd inequalities and extreme poverty because many African governments prohibit subsidies to unemployed persons, leading to a dehumanizing life. Discrimination on any basis lowers the human dignity of any person and must be rejected.

Human rights begin with the most fundamental of rights, including the right to life and to those things necessary for basic human survival. Underlying the principle of the common good is respect for the human person who is endowed with basic and inalienable rights ordered to his or her integral development. In Catholic teaching, human rights include not only civil but also economic rights; this means that when people are without a chance to earn a living, they are being denied basic rights.[65] Society must ensure that these rights are protected.[66] Violation of human rights occurs worldwide, and Africa is not an exception. African leaders and their citizens are called to respect the human rights of each person. The right to life is particularly violated during violence related to elections. The church proclaims that human life is sacred and that the dignity of the human person is the foundation of a moral vision for society.[67] This belief is the foundation of all the principles of the social teaching.

Hence, the loss of life during election violence violates the right to life. Irrational examples include President Jammeh of Gambia, who, during his 2017 campaign, threatened to behead opposition supporters, journalists, and all gay people, and to hunt and kill sorcerers.[68] The recent 2017 electoral violence in Kenya saw a gross abuse of human life. Extrajudicial killing by state forces did not spare women and children. Among the dead were six children, including a six-month-old baby.[69] Some of those killed were forced out of their houses and shot dead. The inalienable right to life of every innocent human individual is a constitutive element of a civil society and its legislation.[70] Therefore, public authority is obliged to respect the fundamental rights of each person and the conditions for the exercise of his or her freedom.[71] Government exists to prevent gross abuses that harm persons and society and eliminate sinful inequalities.[72]

Gaudium et spes tells us that all have a duty to respect the universal and inviolable rights of everyone, welling from a virtuous moral conscience and focusing on the human dignity of each person, and upholding the common good of the community. The Catholic Catechism clarifies:

> Political authorities are obliged to respect the fundamental rights of the human person. They will dispense justice humanely by respecting the rights of everyone, especially of . . . the disadvantaged. The political rights attached to citizenship can and should be granted according to the requirements of the common good. They cannot be suspended by public authorities without legitimate and proportionate reasons.[73]

Besides, Pope Benedict enlightens us that the promotion of human rights remains the most effective strategy for eliminating inequalities.[74]

Political authorities who manipulate the outcome of an election violate the people's right of civic choice. That vice must be countered by ethical virtuous behavior. The rights of each individual and the people's choices must be safeguarded by all mandated institutions. This is only possible if all people work ethically, utilize their conscience, respect the human rights and dignity of each person, and work hard toward the just common good.[75]

Conclusion

Electoral violence in Africa perpetuated by the political elites is an ethical issue. The church's social teaching is a rich treasure of wisdom about building a just society and living lives of holiness amidst the challenges of contemporary society, which include electoral violence. Though the causes of electoral violence are multifaceted, the church offers a multitiered approach to managing the phenomenon. Listening to one's conscience, people can discern and transform the societal ills that bedevil humanity. The church's call to promote the common good includes minding the welfare of vulnerable members of society. It also demands that each person contributes generously to the establishment of a civic order in which rights and duties are more sincerely and effectively acknowledged and fulfilled.[76] A well-ordered human society requires that people recognize and observe the mutual rights and duties of each individual because "individual human beings are the foundation, the cause and the end of every social institution."[77]

Notes

1. Jeff Fischer, *Electoral Conflict and Violence: A Strategy for Study and Prevention* (Washington, DC: International Foundation for Electoral Systems, 2013), 22.

2. Machika Sule Usman, *Causes and Consequences of Youth Involvement in Electoral Violence* (Kano, Nigeria: NVS Press, 2009), 4.

3. Anne Achieng Oyier-Ondigo, "The Role of Transformative Mediation in Electoral Violence: The Case of Kenya 2007–2008" (PhD diss., Nelson Mandela University, Port Elizabeth, South Africa, 2016), 3; and Dimpho Motsamai, "When Elections become a Curse: Redressing Electoral Violence in Africa," *EISA Policy Brief Series*, 1 (Johannesburg: EISA Publishers, 2010).

4. Tuko News, "Ethnic Profiling of Luos: Police under Direction of Government Are Killing Luos," http://www.tuko.co.ke/136755.

5. Machika Sule, *Causes and Consequences of Youth Involvement in Electoral Violence* (Kano, Nigeria: CIGI Printers, 2009), 6.

6. Oyier-Ondigo, "The Role of Transformative Mediation in Electoral Violence," 183.

7. Ibid.

8. Ibid.

9. Johan Galtung, "Violence, Peace and Peace Research," *Journal of Peace Research* 6, no. 3 (1961): 171.

10. Staffan Lindberg, "Are African Voters Really Ethnic or Clientelistic? Survey Evidence from Ghana," *Political Science Quarterly* 123, no. 1 (2008): 95–122.

11. Ibid.

12. Karuti Kanyinga and Duncan Okello, *Tensions and Reversal in Democratic Transitions: The Kenya 2007 General Elections* (Nairobi: Society for International Development, 2010), 11.

13. Huffington Post, "Corruption in Kenya," http://www.huffingtonpost.com/washington-osiro/corruption-in-kenya.

14. Transparency International, *Country Profile and Facts Report* 44 (2013), https://www.transparency.org/country.

15. Oyier-Ondigo, "The Role of Transformative Mediation in Electoral Violence," 186.

16. Richard F. Miller, *States at War: A Reference Guide to Delaware, Maryland and New Jersey in the Civil War* (London: University Press of England, 2015), 87.

17. Ibid.

18. Peter Fossungu, *Democracy and Human Rights in Africa: The Politics of Collective Participation and Governance in Cameroon* (Bamenda, Cameroon: Langaa RPCIG, 2013), 190.

19. The term *government branches* has been used in this study interchangeably with *arms of government*, *branches of government*, or *organs of government* to mean the same thing. Jerome Lafargue explains that these institutions of government have different powers and functions to perform. The executive branch supervises the general administration of the state and implements policies. The legislature debates and makes laws necessary to regulate the society. The judiciary's function is to determine and administer justice to the citizens. And

yet the EMB runs all that pertains to elections. Jerome Lafargue, *The General Elections in Kenya, 2007* (Nairobi: African Books Collection, 2009), 14.

20. Eldridge Adolfo, "Electoral Violence in Africa," *The Nordic Institute Africa-Uppsala*, Policy Notes 3 (2012): 4.

21. René Girard, *Violence and the Sacred* (London: Bloomsberg Publishing, 2013), 58.

22. Ibid.

23. Ibid.

24. Girard, *Violence and the Sacred*, 58.

25. Chantal Kalisa, *Violence in Francophone African and Caribbean Women's Literature* (Lincoln: University of Nebraska Press, 2009), 10.

26. Ibid.

27. Anthony Parel, *Gandhi's Philosophy and the Quest for Harmony* (Cambridge: Cambridge University Press, 2006), 132.

28. Ibid.

29. Frantz Fanon, *The Wretched of the Earth: The Handbook for the Black Revolution That Is Changing the Shape of the World* (New York: Grove Weidenfeld, 1961), 18.

30. Tuko News, "Ethnic Profiling of Luos."

31. Human Rights Watch, *Policy Paralysis: A Call for Action on HIV/AIDS-Related Human Rights Abuses against Women and Girls in Africa* (Nairobi: HRW Publications, 2003), 13.

32. Ibid *Abused Rights and Election Malpractices in Africa*, 5 (2016).

33. Ibid.

34. Philip Alston, *Report of the Special Rapporteur on Extrajudicial, Summary or Arbitrary Executions: Election-Related Violence and Killings* (Geneva: UN Publications, 2010), 7.

35. Ibid.

36. United Nations Human Rights Council, *Report of the Special Rapporteur on Extrajudicial, Summary or Arbitrary Executions—Mission to Kenya* (A/HRC/11/2/Add.6) 10 (2008).

37. Jacob Bercovitch, "Problems and Approaches in the Study of Bargaining and Negotiation," *Political Science* 36, no. 22 (1984): 125–44.

38. Lyn Snodgrass, *A Comparative Case Study of the Emerging Role of Conflict Resolution in Education Transformation in Two South African Schools* (unpublished PhD diss., Nelson Mandela University, 2005); Martin Ochieng, *Africa: Politics and Democratization* (New York: Routledge, 2012); and Oyier-Ondigo, "The Role of Transformative Mediation in Electoral Violence."

39. Dennis Baker and Richard McMahon, *Human Needs and Scarce Resources* (Manila, Philippines: Plontyne, 2015), 20.

40. Tarja Varynen, *Culture and International Conflict Resolution: A Critical Analysis of the Work of John Burton* (Manchester, UK: Manchester University Press, 2001), 33.

41. Oyier-Ondigo, "The Role of Transformative Mediation in Electoral Violence," 206.

42. Edward Shizha, *Remapping Africa in the Global Space: Propositions for Change* (Brantford, Canada: Springer, 2014), 58.

43. Peter Ubomba-Jaswa, *Ethnic Causal Differentials in Early Childhood Mortality in Kenya* (Madison: University of Wisconsin Press, 1989), 323.

44. Thabang Tlalajoe, *Evaluation of the 2012 Lesotho National Assembly Elections* (Maseru, Lesotho: UNDP, 2012), 12.

45. Sarah Sakina, *Electoral Violence in Africa* (Lagos, Nigeria: Mynner Publications, 2012), 92.

46. Farley Calderon, *Electoral Violence: The Dynamics of Conflict* (Colombia: Nexas Press, 2013), 23.

47. Gen. 1: 26.

48. *Gaudium et spes*, no. 12.

49. Ibid.

50. James F. Keenan, *Virtues for Ordinary Christians* (New York: Rowman and Little-field, 1996), 26.

51. Osamu Takeuchi, "Three Modes of the Embodiment of Conscience," in *Conscience and Catholicism: Rights, Responsibilities, and Institutional Responses,* ed. David DeCosse, and Kristin Heyer (Maryknoll, NY: Orbis Books, 2015), 27–38.

52. See *Pacem in terris*.

53. Aljazeera News, "Election Official Flees Crisis-Hit Burundi," May 30, 2015, http://www.aljazeera.com/news/2015/05/election-official-flees-crisis-hit-burundi-150530124830312.html.

54. *New York Times*, "Kenya Election Murder" August 6, 2017, http://www.nytimes.com/2017/08/06/opinion/kenya-election-murder.

55. Standard Newspaper, "The Tallying of Votes Exceeded the Total Number of Voters: There Was More than 100% Turn-Out," August 28, 2013; Nigeria Press, "In Lagos, the Votes Exceed Voters" May 6, 2010.

56. https://www.hrw.org/news/2011/05/16/nigeria-post-election-violence-killed-800.

57. https://www.cfr.org/global/global-conflict-tracker/conflict/violence-in-the-central-african-republic.

58. Simon Mann, *A Political Mugging in God's Own Country* (2008).

59. RefWorld Somali Country Report, *Country Information & Policy Unit Immigration and Nationality Directorate* (London: RefWorld Publication, 2004), http://www.refworld.org/pdfid/40a887840.pdf.

60. *Gaudium et spes*, no. 25.

61. *Gaudium et spes*, no. 14.

62. Transparency International, *Good Governance and Strong Institutions* (Nairobi: TI Publications, 2013), 45.

63. Ibid.

64. *Gaudium et spes*, no. 4.

65. US Catholic Bishops, *Economic Justice for All* (1986), http://www.usccb.org/upload/economic_justice_for_all.pdf.

66. Ibid.

67. US Catholic Bishops, "Seven Themes of Catholic Social Teachings" (2005), http://www.usccb.org/beliefs-and-teachings/what-we-believe/catholic-social-teaching/seven-themes-of-catholic-social-teaching.cfm.

68. See Jamie Yaya Barry and Dionne Searcey, "Gambia's President, in Power 22 Years, Loses Election," *New York Times,* December 2, 2016, https://www.nytimes.com/2016/12/02/world/africa/gambia-election.html.

69. Tuko News, "Ethnic Profiling of Luo" (2017).

70. *Catholic Catechism*, para. 2273.

71. *Catholic Catechism*, para. 2254.

72. *Catholic Catechism*, para. 2237.

73. Ibid.

74. Pope Benedict XVI, Address to the United Nations, Catechism of the Catholic Church on Common Good (April 2008).

75. *Gaudium et spes*, no. 9.

76. *Pacem in terris*, no. 31.

77. *Mater et magistra*, no. 219.

The Moral Question of Terrorism in Divided Societies

Perspectives from Africa

Elias Omondi Opongo

Introduction

Terrorism in Africa has emerged as a major menace that seems to bring forward variant representations of societal challenges that ought to be evaluated from religious, economic, social, political, and cultural perspectives. The phenomenon has yielded unsettling results, from the rise of extremism (especially along religious lines) to mass deaths and humanitarian crises. Terrorism is not a new issue in the continent, but its manifestations have morphed over the years to represent a variety of activities. The Organization for Economic Cooperation and Development (OECD) marked on its Global Terrorism Index 2016[1] a 650 percent rise in deaths caused by terrorism, with Nigeria alone accounting for nearly 72 percent of the attacks that took place in Africa in 2015. The Tunisian beach of Sousse, in June 2015, was the site of one of the most gruesome bloodbaths in the history of the country, where a man carried out a fouled-up attack that wounded more than thirty people, among them Tunisians, French, Britons, Germans, Belgians, and at least one Irish citizen. The attack, which was later claimed by the Islamic State of Iraq and Syria (ISIS), was one of the grimmest ever seen by the government of Tunisia.

According to IHS Jane's Terrorism and Insurgency Centre, across Africa, in 2015, "there were 738 attacks, which resulted in 4,600 fatalities. Attacks have increased over 200 percent and fatalities by more than 750 percent."[2] In other words, terrorism has become commonplace in a number of African countries and has largely been manifested by extreme acts of violence, intimidation, and a show of military power. There have been several attacks carried out by Al-Qaeda in the Islamic Maghreb. Their first major attack was executed in November 2015 on the Radisson Blu Hotel in Bamako, Mali. It was later followed by an attack on the Cappuccino Café and Splendid Hotel in Ouagadougou, Burkina Faso, in January 2016. In March 2016, the group claimed responsibility for an attack that killed nineteen people in Grand Bassam, a popular seaside town in Côte d'Ivoire, on the outskirts of Abidjan. Similarly, Nigeria, Cameroon, and Chad have known the menace of Boko Haram, while Kenya, Uganda, and Somalia have experienced numerous attacks from Al-Shabaab, a terrorist group from Somalia. In 2015, Al-Shabaab killed 147 students at the Garissa University in northern Kenya. Several other attacks have been carried out in different places in the country by the same group.

This essay analyzes the nexus between morality and extremism in terrorism. The analysis is an extraction of the countless ongoing contemporary issues around terrorism in Africa, the recent terror attacks, their significance against a backdrop of global phenomenon of terrorism, radicalism and recruitment of youth and children from impoverished backgrounds, and the rise in the use of women and young girls in terror activities.

The discourse in this essay is divided into three parts. The first looks at the nominal definitions of terrorism, the discrepancies that arise out of such definitions, and implications of these diverse understandings. The second analysis focuses on religion and terrorism in Africa and its various manifestations. The third undertakes a moral analysis of the terrorism phenomenon, arguments for justification of acts of terrorism, and the moral dilemmas for persons often engaged in acts of terrorism. Subjecting terrorism to a moral discourse risks engendering misunderstandings, misinterpretations, and misrepresentations. However, given the extent of the harm caused by terrorism; the vulnerability of the populations, both as victims and perpetrators; and potential social–political instability that comes because of terrorist acts, it is vital to conduct this moral analysis.

Conceptualizing Terrorism

Conceptualizing terrorism solely within the framework of violence blurs the attempts to understand the broader aspects of the phenomenon. As such, any moral conceptualization of terrorism ought to consider the evaluation of acts of terrorism themselves, the social–economic and political context, and the religious implications of such acts. Drawing from such a broad evaluation, there are two main pillars of moral analysis: the radical ideologies that justify the violent actions and the social contexts under which the terrorist acts take place.

Martha Crenshaw, in her book *Terrorism in Africa*,[3] sheds light on how terrorism—commonly used to mean a tactic that uses violence or the threat of violence as a coercive strategy to cause fear and political intimidation—was the main feature and highlight within resistance movements, military coups, political assassinations, and various intra- and interstate wars that have affected most African states at some point during the continent's transition to independence and subsequent postcolonial period. She further mentions that terrorism was not "an isolated phenomenon" for African states or the region. In fact, it has been noted to have been an issue of concern for years but was later brought to the fore by the 9/11 terrorist attacks on the United States of America.[4]

To a great extent, terrorism is a highly disputed concept. Some academics contend that the term is malleable and open to many different definitions and interpretations.[5] Schmid compiles a list of definitions of terrorism, noting that the tactic has been employed by a diverse group of people in several areas in pursuit of a broad range of issues.[6] He identifies some variables that make it difficult to define terrorism, including divergent sociopolitical and legal notions that compete with popular notions, the endorsement and criminalization of certain groups that might not necessarily be involved in terrorist attacks, and variant manifestations of terrorism over the years that make it difficult to identify a unified representation of the phenomenon.

In 2004, the United Nations came up with a definition of terrorism as

> criminal acts including against civilians, committed with the intent to cause death or serious bodily injury, or taking of hostages with the purpose to provoke a state of terror in the general public or in a group of persons, or intimidate a population or compel a government or an international organization to do or to abstain from doing any act.[7]

This definition examines terrorism as "an act of terror" for its own sake or with the intention of achieving an objective or making a public statement over an issue of concern. In this sense, terrorism is seen as organized acts of violence that use human lives as a means of achieving political, social, or economic goals. However, terrorism has developed further into the online facilities, hence the term *cyberterrorism*. The US Federal Bureau of Investigation defines cyberterrorism as any "premeditated, politically motivated attack against information, computer systems, computer programs, and data which results in violence against noncombatant targets by sub-national groups or clandestine agents." Cyberterrorism, also known as electronic terrorism, is gradually becoming a matter of concern given the vulnerability of many institutions with sensitive information online.

The above discussion demonstrates that there are as many typological classifications and categorizations of terrorism as there are definitions. Typological models have several advantages, as they are used as a basis for alternative definitions.[8] First, the broader scope of a problem can be analyzed and presented. Given that terrorism is multifaceted, it can represent a diverse range of issues, such as religion, beliefs, theological interpretations, historical injustices, and social, cultural, economic, and political differences, none of which is singled out. Second, it highlights the scope of the problem, which can either take a global or national perspective. Third, it narrows down the response mechanism once the scope of the problem has been identified. Focusing on the type and root cause of violence, then, douses the tension over the definition of terrorism. As such, experts and scholars[9] in security issues have defined and described terrorism in different systematic typological classifications.

Political terrorism refers to the use of violence or threats by one political faction to threaten, intimidate, or suppress the other. Often, civilians fall victim to violent attacks meant to express grievances against a respective government.[10] Quiggin[11] emphasizes that "terrorism, like war, is the continuation of politics by other means. Indeed, terrorism has been an integral and normal part of politics on the spectrum of 'political' activity for almost as long as organized polities have existed." Gaynor[12] proposes the revision of the term terrorism to mean "the intentional use of, or threat to use violence against civilians or against civilian targets, in order to attain political aims."[13]

Revolutionary terrorism is a textbook phrase that has been used to refer to those whom we now praise as "freedom fighters" involved in armed struggle against their colonial masters. This was the case for many African leaders and chiefs during anticolonial wars such as the Mau-Mau in Kenya, Chimurenga in Zimbabwe, and African National Congress in South Africa, where legends like Nelson Mandela of South Africa, and Jomo Kenyatta of Kenya, and their followers were referred to as terrorists by the British colonial regime. Revolutionary terrorism is thus founded on contrasting motives for revolution such as social transformation, claim of denied rights, assertion of ethnic and racial identity, and progressive ideology.

State terrorism, on the other hand, is a type of terrorism carried out by governments against perceived enemies of the state. It can either be directed internally toward native adversaries or externally against adversaries in the international domain.[14] This has been a common characteristic especially of dictatorial states that are against opposing ideas. As such, the African continent has had a number of situations that could qualify to be state terror acts, such as the brutal crackdown against opposition leaders in Zimbabwe and Uganda, the Eritrean and Cameroonian governments' suppression of dissident voices, and Ethiopia's oppression against the opposition parties. Uganda has taken an equally militant approach to dealing with opposition leaders, particularly during the electioneering period. The government, for example, has disrupted political rallies, beaten up politicians, and imprisoned them in some cases. These acts of intimidation and harassment have gone against the basic rights of the opposition leaders and their supporters. President Omar al-Bashir of Sudan is the first sitting head of state to be indicted by the International Criminal Court for crimes against humanity, while in the newly independent South Sudan, the people are calling for a war crimes investigation given the brutal nature of the current conflict between the government and opposing forces.

Religion and Terrorism in Africa

Even though there seems to be a shift in the diverse terrorist groups, mostly associated with radicalized Muslims, Christians have historically known many extremist groups that have attacked and persecuted people of other faiths such as Muslims and Jews. Hoffman[15] records that even though terrorism and religion share a rich history, their manifestation tend to be overshadowed by the ethnonationalist/ ideological and separatist ideas of the time. To a great extent, religion has been used to justify terrorist acts. Scott Appleby[16] in his book *Ambivalence of the Sacred* asserts that religion has played an ambiguous role both for peace and violence. Examples from South Africa, Israel, Central African Republic, Somalia, and Nigeria have shown that religion can be used for extreme acts of violence.[17]

The new era of religious extremism can be traced to the Iranian Muslim Revolution,[18] while in Africa the Lord's Resistance Army (LRA) from Uganda—which dates back to the 1980s—is one of the pioneer groups that justified violence by use of religion. The LRA stood for a new state under the rule of the Ten Commandments and until now has not shown any clear motivation for a political agenda. Since its inception, the group has not only been notorious for using child soldiers and committing heinous crimes but has also evaded Ugandan military forces and operated in different parts of Africa, including South Sudan, Uganda (its place of origin), the Central African Republic, and the Democratic Republic of the Congo. There have also been various outbursts of religious extremist groups across the continent like Al-Shabaab, which evolved from the Islamic Union Courts in 2006 and later established itself as a jihadist terror organization and has kept to its area of operation, which is largely the Horn of Africa. Just like Boko Haram, Al-Shabaab campaigns for the strict observance and spread of Sharia law while shunning Western culture. On the other hand, the Central African Republic poses a unique case where religious extremism is not limited to Muslims, but rather both Muslims and Christians. The anti-balaka, which is predominantly Christian, and the Selèka, which is comprised of Muslim militia, have been terrorizing the country for nearly a decade.

To a great extent religious extremism tends to manifest itself in countries or regions where the normal systems of governance are weak and social relations are breaking down. The problem lies not only in the unprecedented nature of the attacks but also in the indiscriminate and lethal nature of them. Heidi Schultz, a reporter for National Geographic News, in a brief analysis of the nature and character of the Boko Haram, states that "the main aim of Boko Haram was to make northern Nigeria an Islamic state. Although it has ties to other African terrorist groups, it has few jihadist ambitions beyond Nigeria. Western interests are rarely targets of its attacks."[19]

While it is notable that religion plays a fundamental role in the perception of faith and society, misinterpretations of scriptural and theological tenets often form the bases and justifications for global terrorism through what is termed as radicalization. Radicalization refers to the process by which an individual or group holds extremist views over certain social, religious, or political views and could go to the extent of pursuit or enforcement of these views through the use of advocacy, campaigns, coercive actions, or violence. In relation to terrorism, radicalization is associated with justification of extreme acts of violence.

There are a number of variables that explain recruitment into extremist groups. These include levels of education, economic status, religious identity, political and religious convictions, and search for a deeper meaning in life, social identity, or share of economic resources. In an argument over the appeal of religious extremism, Avalos,[20] in his book *Fighting Words: The Origin of Religious Extremism,* argues that most religious conflicts are a result of competition for scarce resources. The fight to control the oil-rich zones in Iraq by ISIS is an indication that terrorist groups seek to finance their activities through lucrative economic activities like the sale of oil or minerals, but also through remittances from their supporters and sympathizers.

A number of scholars[21] have asserted that extremist Islamic groups tend to recruit those who are from poor families, unemployed, and less educated. In fact, economic incentive among the unemployed could be a factor in the recruitment of the youth. Many disenfranchised youth feel left out in society and consider joining radical extremist groups as a means of gaining new identities, recognition, and a social group that help propel them toward new aspirations in life. There is little evidence that Boko Haram, Al-Shabaab, or Ansar Dine[22] pay a salary to their members like other radical Islamist groups. However, some residents of Nigeria who were interviewed stated that Boko Haram fighters would be paid about 40,000 Naira (US$200) per month, almost double the average wage in Nigeria. In Kenya, a youth returning from Somalia after fighting alongside Al-Shabaab stated that he "was enticed with salary payments of between US$150–200 (Sh15,000 to Sh20,000) a month [and] was also told [he] will get a senior position after attaining an Islamic law certificate."[23] In such cases, financial rather than ideological motives explain the attraction to joining terrorist groups. A study by Shuaibu and Salleh[24] revealed that Boko Haram insurgency has been able to recruit a large number of youth simply because of the high rate of poverty in the region, which is subsequently marked by illiteracy and unemployment.

The assertion that terrorist groups often recruit among socioeconomically deprived populations is to some extent true but does not sufficiently explain the complexities around recruitment, radicalization, and self-sacrifice undertaken as a noble cause. Examples around the world have shown that terrorist groups recruit from all social groups in society, whether poor or rich. For example, ISIS, Al-Shabaab, Al-Qaeda, and Boko Haram have all recruited their members from poor, rich, and educated sectors of the society, harvesting their diverse talents. Those who join these radical groups join them for different reasons that tend to justify their terrorist acts. Hence, a moral evaluation needs to weigh out these diverse factors.

Moral Evaluation of Terrorism

Can terrorism ever be morally justified? The moral evaluation of terrorist acts has to be grounded on issues of contention around justice, equity, preservation of human dignity, and national and regional stability. In other words, the ends have to be balanced with the means employed. According to Scheffler,[25] "Terrorism may sometimes be a response to great wrongs, and great wrongs may be committed in opposing it." This is in line with Thomas Aquinas's *principle of double effect*, which states that an action tends to have two effects: the intended and unintended. This means that the evaluation of the intentions, means used, and impact are crucial in any assessment of human action. Bica[26] holds the opinion that "by focusing upon the moral significance of intention and its relevance to moral agency and responsibility, it morally distinguishes 'accidental' killing from murder, claiming that only the latter is prohibited." As such, terrorism is intrinsically evil, but its evaluation ought to be juxtaposed with the grievances brought forward by the terrorists and the ultimate intention. For example, terrorist activities by the Irish Republican Army in Northern Ireland needed to be examined in light of the oppressive British systems on the majority of the population. This by no means justifies terrorist acts, but rather brings to light the complex layers of arguments, concerns, fears, claims to justice, and independence in the course of an armed struggle.

Identification of certain acts as "terrorist" should not only be limited to nonstate actors. As explained above, state terrorism has often led to armed resistance leading to more violence and loss of life. As such, terrorism, whether by nonstate actor or government agents, is not justified. The challenge lies in the qualification of specific acts as "terror" and determination of who qualifies these actors as terrorists. In other words, moral evaluation is often conducted with a bias against nonstate actors, while being more lenient to state terrorism. For example, massive bombings conducted by the US government in both Iraq and Afghanistan could be termed "terrorist acts" by the victims of these attacks.

Many violent extremist groups as well as organized state terror use the just war theory to justify their actions. Just war stipulates that while going to war may seem bad, it is perhaps not always the worst option there is and conceivably a necessary evil to society for the greater good. Rooted in Catholicism, just war doctrine provides a set of guidelines that should govern war by ensuring that there is just cause, right intention, legitimate authority, and reasonable hope of success. Just war tradition also propagates noncombatant immunity in the cause of war or conflict.

However, in many cases both terrorist groups and governments limit themselves to "just cause" as a justification for violent engagement. The media plays an important role in justifying violent acts by governments. The US-led war on terror is cast by American and Western media as defensive and necessary to promote democracy, while at the same time the immediate victims of these wars are simply defined as "collateral damage," justified under the principle of double effect as unintended effect. This tends to water down the strict moral evaluation of such acts. In other words, a full moral evaluation of such violent acts within the just war framework would have to take into account reasons justifying the war, the conduct of war, and impact of the war on the population in the immediate and long term. Whenever any group feels that their rights have been violated, they are likely to retaliate within the moral scale interpretation of civil rights. Unfortunately, such retaliations tend to affect people who are innocent and have nothing to do with the infringement of other people's rights, hence, the argument from a number of philosophers and scholars that retaliatory attacks should normally be aimed at those directly responsible for acts of injustice and not the innocent populations.[27]

For one to understand the moral dilemma behind the killing of noncombatants by terrorists, one needs to ask whether terrorism is part of or another type of war. In the theories and practice of war there is a very distinct moral division between targeting noncombatants directly and harming them as part of collateral damage. Acts of terror in this case are said to be "the killing or injuring of a random collection of people who happen to be in a certain place at a certain time."[28] This is obviously based on the assumption that these individuals carry with them no liability. As a justification for the 9/11 attack, Osama bin Laden said that

The American people should remember that they pay taxes to their government and that they voted for their president. Their government makes weapons and provides them to Israel, which they use to kill Palestinian Muslims. Given that the American Congress is a committee that represents the people, the fact that it agrees with the actions of the American government proves that America in its entirety is responsible for the atrocities that it is committing against Muslims.[29]

Bin Laden thus placed a sense of responsibility and liability on the American people, claiming that Americans are in one way or another taking part in the vices of their elected leaders. Al-Qaeda is one of the forerunners of the recent radical Islamist movement that has often been referred to as a terrorist group. In a declaration from the World Islamic Front for Jihad against the Jews and Crusaders, written in 1998, the group announced their ambitious intention to "kill the Americans and their allies—civilians and military." This declaration, which is now considered one of the most important public messages from Al-Qaeda, began by quoting *Sura At-Taubah* of the Quran, urging Muslims to recognize their duty to "slay the idolaters" all over the world. However, the verse, as it was written in the declaration, only quoted half of the verse and left out the second half where it is stated, "but if they repent and fulfil their devotional obligations and pay the *zakat*, then let them go their way, for God is forgiving and kind." The interpretations or misinterpretations of religious writings are a strong weapon for radical Islamist groups, making uneducated people vulnerable to their principles. They only pick the parts of the verses that fit their message and fail to put them in context.[30]

Although Al-Qaeda made it clear that their target is non-Muslims, Boko Haram and Al-Shabaab victims have mainly been Muslims. The use of religion has been manipulated to encourage self-sacrifice through suicide missions. The year 2016 saw a steep rise in the use of suicide terrorism globally, with 469 suicide bombings executed by 800 perpetrators in twenty-eight countries, causing the deaths of about 5,650 people.[31] A report by the Institute for National Security Studies indicates that Boko Haram in Nigeria was responsible for half of the suicide attacks that took place in Africa, with fifty-three attacks in 2016, while Al-Shabaab in the Horn of Africa was a close second with twenty-five attacks, Al-Qaeda in the Islamic Maghreb carried out three attacks, and the rest were carried out by other militia and nonreligious-affiliated militia. The numbers are anticipated to rise as terrorist groups continue to campaign for the use of this technique as a means to an end.

In an effort to explain the use of females and children in suicide missions, Sawicki[32] notes that "If the security forces identify a female or child bomber, the act of stopping them by killing them is a public relations coup for the terrorists. The video of that act can be used in propaganda efforts ceaselessly." It is easier for women to maneuver to areas that would otherwise be inaccessible to men. There is a debate in Africa over the use of women and children as suicide bombers. Globally, in 2016 there were forty-four suicide attacks carried out by seventy-seven women and resulting in more than four hundred fatalities.[33]

It should be noted that a large part of these attacks took place in Africa.[34] Split opinions exist as to whether this new move is a show of bravery on the part of the extreme groups or rather a last resort and desperate move aimed at manipulating vulnerable populations to be used in conducting such heinous acts.

As noted above, nonconsequentially, terrorism is intrinsically considered to be wrong on its own, and many times it may not be because of the harm done, but rather because of the imbalance it brings to society, its moral reasons notwith-standing.[35] As such, the issue with terrorism is that it infringes on other universal rights, the right to life particularly. Counterterrorism actions by governments have equally led to implementation of policies that tend to infringe on people's rights. These policies have to a great extent interfered with civil rights, such as the rights to privacy, migration, and freedom of association. For example, after the Westgate attacks in Kenya, the government tightened its migration and refugee policies. Not only did the government officially close the Somalia border, citing the impending security concerns due to spillover of Al-Shabaab terrorists, it also underscored that a majority of those radicalized to join the terrorist group took refuge in urban centers within the country, and this might be another way in which terrorism spread in the region. There are also humanitarian crises as people seek safe havens away from terrorist-affected zones, creating large numbers of internally displaced persons and refugees with subsequent environmental degradation and proliferation of small arms and light weapons. This has been the case in Somalia, Nigeria, and Iraq, where populations have fled from Al-Shabaab, Boko Haram, and ISIS–controlled areas, respectively. Similarly, there is psychological trauma related to experiences of violence, particularly among survivors.

Terrorism creates negative space for business transactions and hinders poten-tial investors from coming into the country. It however nurtures negative business activities such as corruption, which do not benefit the country in any way. Global Peace Index estimated that terrorism cost the world a total of US$89.6 billion as of 2015, which was a drop from the previous years. Most countries affected attribute the loss of nearly 5 percent of their respective gross domestic product to terrorism activities. Libya ranks highest in Africa with 5.7 percent, while South Sudan is next with 4.8 percent, Nigeria with 4.5 percent, Niger with 2.1 percent, and the Central African Republic with 2.1 percent.[36] Kenya's tourism industry has been hard hit by terrorism, losing close to US$500 million. The number of tourists dropped from 800,000 in 2014 to a low of nearly 700,000 in 2016.[37] The industry has had an increase in the number of cancellations of hotel bookings and tour plans, subse-quently resulting in job losses.

Conclusion

Moral assessment of terrorism can take different perspectives, depending on the analysis of the intention, means used, and impact on the populations. Evidently, terrorism is intrinsically evil and ought to be evaluated from that perspective prima facie. However, in the same stream of analysis, it is important to analyze the injustices brought forward by the terrorist groups in order to address and measure justice on both sides. In most cases the grievances brought forward by the terrorist groups are annulled on the ground of the means used to express the grievances, which in most cases entails the targeting of innocent civilians who bear no direct responsibility in said grievances. While Thomas Aquinas's principle of double effect would be relevant in analyzing the intended and unintended effects of the act of terrorism, it remains limited in morally evaluating terrorist acts given the intrinsic evil nature of the terrorist acts. The focus today should be on finding diverse peaceful means of addressing global injustices and dissuading powerful nations from militarization of conflicts.

Notes

1. Institute of Economic Studies, *Global Terrorism Index* (College Park: University of Maryland, 2016).

2. IHS Intelligence, "Numbers Show Dramatic Rise of Terrorist Attacks in Africa Over Past Six Years, IHS Says," 2015, http://news.ihsmarkit.com.

3. Martha Crenshaw, *Terrorism in Africa* (New York: G. K. Hall, 1994).

4. United Nations, "Agreed Definition of Term 'Terrorism' Said to Be Needed for Consensus on Completing Comprehensive Convention against It," 2005, https://www.un.org/.

5. Louis Jacobson, "What's the Definition of 'Terrorism'?" *Politifact*, July 9, 2013, http://www.politifact.com/truth-o-meter/article/2013/jul/09/whats-definition-terrorism/; United Nations, 2005, "Agreed Definition of Term 'Terrorism' Said to Be Needed for Consensus on Completing Comprehensive Convention against It," https://www.un.org/; Leonard Weinberg, Ami Pedahzur, and Sivan Hirsch-Hoefler, "The Challenges of Conceptualizing Terrorism," *Terrorism and Political Violence* 16, no. 4 (2004): 777–94.

6. Alex P. Schmid, *The Routledge Handbook of Terrorism Research* (London: Routledge, Taylor & Francis Group, 2013).

7. United Nations, Resolution 1566, adopted by the Security Council at Its 5053rd Meeting, October 8, 2004, http://www.cfr.org.

8. Mark Moyar, "Typologies of Terrorism," 2016, https://www.hoover.org/research/typologies-terrorism.

9. Steven Barkan and Lynne L Snowdenm, *Collective Violence* (New York: Sloan, 2008); James P. Sterba, *Terrorism and International Justice* (New York: Oxford University Press, 2003).

10. Alex P. Schmid and Albert J. Jongman, *Political Terrorism: A New Guide to Actors, Authors, Concepts, Data Bases, Theories, & Literature* (New Brunswick, NJ: Transaction Publishers, 2008).

11. Tom Quiggin, "Terrorism as Politics by Other Means: Global Brief," 2010, http://Globalbrief.Ca.

12. Boaz Gaynor, "Defining Terrorism: Is One Man's Terrorist Another Man's Freedom Fighter?," *Policy Practice and Research* 3, no. 4 (2010): 287–304.

13. Ibid.

14. Gus Martin, *Understanding Terrorism* (Thousand Oaks, CA: Sage Publications, 2003); Bruce Hoffman, *Inside Terrorism* (New York: Columbia University Press, 2006).

15. Bruce Hoffman, "The Confluence of International and Domestic Trends in Terrorism," *Terrorism and Political Violence* 9, no. 2 (1997): 1–15.

16. R. Scott Appleby, *The Ambivalence of the Sacred: Religion, Violence, and Reconciliation* (Lanham, MD: Rowman & Littlefield Publishers, 2000).

17. Bruce Hoffman, *Inside Terrorism* (New York: Columbia University Press, 2006).

18. Dorothy Parvaz, "Iran 1979: The Islamic Revolution That Shook the World," 2014, http://www.aljazeera.com.

19. Heidi Schultz, "Nigeria's Boko Haram: Who Are They and What Do They Want?" 2014, http://news.nationalgeographic.com.

20. Hector Avalos, *Fighting Words: The Origins of Religious Violence* (Amherst, NY: Prometheus Books, 2005).

21. Barry M. Rubin, *Guide to Islamist Movements* (Armonk, NY: M. E. Sharpe, 2010), 574; Salman Akhtar, *The Crescent and the Couch: Cross-Currents between Islam and Psychoanalysis* (Lanham, MD: Jason Aronson, 2008), 114.

22. Ansar Dine is a paramilitary terrorist group of insurgents based in Northern Mali but operating throughout the country to impose Sharia law (https://www.trackingterrorism.org/).

23. Calvin Onsarigo and Charles Mghenyi, "Al Shabaab Defectors Tell Their Stories," *The Star*, November 18, 2015, http://www.the-star.co.ke/.

24. Salisu Salisu Shuaibu, Mohd Afandi Salleh, and Abdullahi Yusuf Shehu, "The Impact of Boko Haram Insurgency on Nigerian National Security," *International Journal of Academic Research in Business and Social Sciences* 5, no. 6 (2015): 254–66.

25. Samuel Scheffler, *Equality and Tradition: Questions of Moral Value in Moral and Political Theory* (New York: Oxford University Press, 2012).

26. Camillo C. Bica, "Another Perspective on the Doctrine of Double Effect," *Public Affairs Quarterly* 13, no. 2 (1999): 131–39.

27. Igor Primoratz, "Terrorism," *Stanford Encyclopedia of Philosophy*, 2015, https://plato.stanford.edu/entries/terrorism/#MorIss.

28. Ibid.

29. Usāma Ibn-Lādin, Bruce B. Lawrence, and James Howarth, *Messages to the World: The Statements of Osama Bin Laden* (London: Versa, 2005), 140.

30. Donald Holbrook, "Using the Qur'an to Justify Terrorist Violence: Analysing Selective Application of the Qur'an in English-Language Militant Islamist Discourse," *Perspectives on Terrorism, North America* 4, no. 3 (2010).

31. Illana Kricheli, Yotam Rosner, Aviad Mendelboim, and Yoram Schweitzer, *Suicide Bombings in 2016: The Highest Number of Fatalities* (Tel Aviv: Institute for National Security Studies, 2017).

32. John Sawicki, "Why Terrorists Use Female and Child Suicide Bombers," *Health Progress* 97, no. 4 (2016): 38–42.

33. Avi Issacharoff, "2016 Was Deadliest Year Ever for Suicide Bombings Worldwide," *Times of Israel*, January 6, 2017, http://www.timesofisrael.com/2016-was-deadliest-year-ever-for-suicide-bombings-worldwide/.

34. Ibid.

35. Camilio C. Bica, "Terrorism and Response: A Moral Inquiry into the Killing of Non-Combatants," 2017, http://isme.tamu.edu/JSCOPE04/Bica04.html.

36. Institute for Economics and Peace, "The Launch of the IGAD Capacity Building Programme against Terrorism and the Opening of the ISS Office in Addis Ababa," 2006, https://www.issafrica.org/.

37. *Kenya Vision 2030, A Globally Competitive and Prosperous Kenya*, 2007, https://www.researchictafrica.net.

Counting the Uncounted

A Theo-Ethical Imperative for the Theological Ethicist in Raising a Challenge to Widespread and Unrecognized Practices of Exclusion

Mary Jo Iozzio

When Jesus heard this, he withdrew from there in a boat to a deserted place by himself. But when the crowds heard it, they followed him on foot from the towns. When he went ashore, he saw a great crowd; and he had compassion for them and cured their sick. When it was evening, the disciples came to him and said, "This is a deserted place, and the hour is now late; send the crowds away so that they may go into the villages and buy food for themselves." Jesus said to them, "They need not go away; you give them something to eat." They replied, "We have nothing here but five loaves and two fish." And he said, "Bring them here to me." Then he ordered the crowds to sit down on the grass. Taking the five loaves and the two fish, he looked up to heaven, and blessed and broke the loaves, and gave them to the disciples, and the disciples gave them to the crowds. And all ate and were filled; and they took up what was left over of the broken pieces, twelve baskets full. And those who ate were about five thousand men, besides women and children.

Immediately he made the disciples get into the boat and go on ahead to the other side, while he dismissed the crowds. And after he had dismissed the crowds, he went up the mountain by himself to pray. (Matt. 14:13–23)

This miracle of the loaves and fishes reports a command—"you give them something to eat" (Matt. 14:16)—and its fulfillment—"those who ate were about five thousand men, not counting women and children" (Matt. 14:21). The narrative sets a precedent for the care of a people hungry for hope: Jesus pitied the crowd, healed their sick, and fed them. Worldwide today people still hunger for hope, attention, and welcome; many of the uncounted and often unaccounted for are people with disabilities—the deaf, mute, blind, lame, and possessed—as well as women, children, and other disadvantaged people of Jesus's attention.

247

Jesus's miracle of the loaves and fishes is instructive for Christians on a number of accounts. For example, the resemblance to the Eucharist and its life-sustaining grace is unmistakable. Many people were able to eat and have their fill, their hunger satisfied; God provides. The five loaves hold a metaphorical link between Jesus and Moses—Moses relied on God's providence to feed the Israelites with manna from heaven in their desert sojourn (Exod. 16), and it was Moses who gave the five books of the Pentateuch/Torah to the people—establishing Jesus in the line of teachers and on a par with, if not greater than, Moses. Similarly, the loaves connect Jesus to Elijah and Elisha, both of whom relied on God's providence to feed others. Elijah fed himself and later fed the Widow at Zarephath and her household (1 Kings 17), and Elisha fed 100 men with twenty barley loaves (2 Kings 4; cf. John 6:9)—establishing Jesus in the line of prophets and also greater than these. Finally, the twelve remaining baskets of food allude to the twelve tribes of Israel, confirming Jesus as Messiah and Lord.[1] Most of those present and certainly the learned among them would recognize these connections. The compilers of the New Testament canon were somewhat conversant with the Jewish genesis of Jesus's ministry and were mindful of the Gentiles who came to believe in Jesus as God's promises fulfilled; a consensus of New Testament scholars accepts that this gospel was written by a Jewish Christian for a Jewish Christian community among and including Gentiles after the 70 CE destruction of the Second Temple.[2] Not as readily instructive is the reference to the women and children, its add-on the linchpin I want to explore in this essay.

I offer this summary of the precedent set by Jesus to offer an agenda of inclusion for those presented as what seems an afterthought by the gospel author. I argue that the add-on of women and children is a deliberate "catch-all" for the invisible people who ought to be counted and accounted for in the communal ecclesial life; further, the passage may be concerned with them in particular.[3] In what follows I unpack this narrative, illustrate its accounting practices, and, using Catholic social teaching (on human dignity, subsidiarity/participation, and solidarity/preferential option for and with those who are poor or otherwise marginalized), examine the force and reception of Matthew's example in light of the hopes and experiences of Catholics and others with disabilities.

The church teaches that people with disabilities (PWD) and the nondisabled are equal. To follow this teaching, the church must be more proactive than at present in promoting justice for PWD and in providing effective measures to ensure that PWD have full access to and accommodations for participation in the communal and sacramental activities of Catholic life. Unfortunately, like women and children, the many faithful who are disabled typify a mostly invisible, silent, and closeted reality: PWD have been uncounted, their presence and voices ignored, and they continue to be denied among other activities access to both certain sacraments and parish/community life, not to mention access to education, recreation, and social, political, and commercial life. This injustice requires exposure and repair, and Catholic social teaching has the foundations upon which the church can reverse the patterns of degradation, exclusion, and discrimination PWD have faced. These foundations supply the imperatives on (1) what is right for those who lack a voice on account of their having been marginalized and otherwise oppressed, and (2) the options for the church's address of its failures to account for its sins against individuals and PWD near and far.

Unpacking the Narrative

Note that although the passage opens with Jesus having learned of the beheading of John the Baptist and his being troubled by the news, the gospels are not bound by contemporary standards of the passage of time. (The story of John's beheading precedes this passage, but its placement does not necessarily mean that the events were so chronologically close. Matthew uses the literary device for what follows, in particular, to compare the rule of an arrogant tetrarch with the rule of Jesus the Messiah.[4]) John was his cousin after all, a charismatic and fearless prophet, accusatory of the adulterous Herod Antipas and of the religious leaders (Scribes, Sadducees, and Pharisees), murdered at the whim and fear of those with power. Jesus must have been both aggrieved and a bit frightened at the likelihood of a similar fate.[5] He had been teaching and proclaiming God's love in the towns, healing folks in body–mind–spirit, and, like John, charging with woes those who fail themselves and the people who may be in their charge. Many people had gone out to hear Jesus, perchance to be comforted by his care, his words, and his deeds; whether in the towns or in Matthew's juxtaposition of these events in this presentation of brutal news, the crowds followed him. He needed the distance of time and space to grieve and pray: What would be next? Disembarking, he saw the crowd, was moved by compassion, and healed those in need (cf. Matt. 14:14).

The crowds are anxious. They had heard about John, and, knowing of his fate, now turn to Jesus; intrigued by and interested in his teaching, they may be curious as well about Jesus's reaction to the news. They seek him for the consolations he offers in their hopes that the Kingdom is surely near: confirmed to John by the works Isaiah foretold of the Messiah, Jesus admits "the blind see, the lame walk, lepers are cleansed, the deaf hear, the dead are raised, and the poor have good news proclaimed to them" (Matt. 11:5; cf. Isa. 29:18 and 35:3, 5–6). As Zechariah spoke of his and Elizabeth's child, John would announce Jesus as the dawn that broke upon the people then and now, "to shine on those who dwell in darkness and the shadow of death, and to guide our feet into the way of peace."[6] The crowds would have remembered, too, the promises for a time free of oppression when there will be peace, justice, and righteousness.[7] The crowds of men and women and children are hungry not so much for bread and fish as they are hungry for assurances in those tumultuous times: "for Jesus the Son of Man in the events of the future dawn [i.e., the Kingdom of God] and of his teaching as the authoritative guide for life in the present."[8] This crowd will be challenged, as were members of the early Christian ecclesiae and as the church remains today, by Jesus's compassion and the requirements of discipleship. An "encounter with God's mercy mandates a life which expresses mercy; . . . the presentation of Jesus' compassionate ministry to the crowds provides the audience with examples of the discipleship required from them."[9] Extend mercy to those in need: welcome them, heal them, teach them, feed them, befriend them.

The juxtaposition of the banquet narratives points to two different orders and two different ways of being with others: the banquet of Herod Antipas (Matt. 14:6–11) reflects an order of despotic albeit oligarchic control where "pride and arrogance, scheming, and even murder . . . take place at a royal court." It is an exclusive affair. Conversely, the banquet of Jesus offers an order of unrestricted inclusion and compassionate service where "there is healing, trust, and sharing . . . in a 'deserted place.'"[10] The townsfolk must have been encouraged by Jesus's allure. Given the evangelizing intent of the gospel, Matthew's cast of thousands informs the life of discipleship. (Consider the placement of this passage: out of twenty-eight chapters in this gospel, at chapter 14, the welcome–healing–feeding of the 5,000+ is midpoint.) In the broader context of the Matthean text, although scholars do not concur on a five-part division of chapter and verse or on a strict chiastic structural organization,[11] Matthew 14 (part three) serves as a hinge between two major discourses: the Beatitudes (Matt. 5:3–13; in part one) and the hearers' success or failure in following them in the judgment (Matt. 25:31–46; in part five). The Beatitudes present the core dispositions, virtues, and communal spirit—humility, solidarity, meekness, social justice, mercy, integrity, peacemaking, and bearing persecution for the sake of righteousness—required of those who would be disciples.[12] The judgment presents the measure of discipleship in the exercise of compassion and mercy toward all those awaiting the fulfillment of promises.[13] The banquet Jesus hosts thus functions as a hermeneutic for the disciples, the crowds, and for Christians today: first course, work the Beatitudes; second, organize the men, women, and children and have them recline; third, bless the offering; fourth, serve the meal such that none leave hungry and others are still welcome (as twelve baskets remain); fifth, only after their bodies–minds–spirits have been satisfied, dismiss them; and, insofar as Matthew inserts what appears to be the activities of the next day in another round of healing (Matt. 14:34–36), . . . repeat tomorrow.

Accounting Practices

While there were about five thousand men who gathered, interpreters recognize that this number is likely exaggerated; even if hyperbole, it implies a sizeable figure. Add to the five thousand at least one woman and one child to each of these men, and the number increases threefold to fifteen thousand. And yet, drawing on current world demographic data reports of a fertility rate from two to six children per family in agrarian subsistence economies,[14] this gathering of men could add at least three (mother plus two children) to seven (mother plus six children) or an average of five more people to the group (mother plus four children), increasing the number gathered by as many as twenty-five thousand for a total crowd of thirty thousand people. Then again, this larger number may not include women who were not mothers, so let's add one more woman to each of the numbered original five thousand men, bringing the total fairly reliably to thirty-five thousand! As Harrington notes, "By adding this phrase [not counting women and children] to Mark 6:44, Matthew enlarges the numbers of people affected by the multiplication, thus making it even more spectacular."[15]

Now about Matthew's thirty thousand uncounted women and children: who are they and why has the author added them? On one level such an accounting raises the stakes of the New Way to recognize God's in-breaking Kingdom: all are welcome. On another level such accounting may accuse those who fail the discipleship Beatitude.

As the Matthean author relies on Mark's Gospel and the Q source, and offers the narrative of Jesus's ministry in ways particular to a Jewish Christian diaspora with increasing Gentile members (perhaps in Antioch), this gospel alone adds the reference to women and children. Each of the gospels includes a similar miraculous and abundant feeding of a multitude. Moreover, it is the only miracle recounted in all of them, with only minor variations as to number of persons, how many and what kind of loaves and fishes, and location (cf. Mark 6:30–44; Luke 9:10–17; John 6:1–15). Evidently, for Matthew's author, recognizing that women and children were present is important; no doubt, they were part of the emerging ecclesia. Further, including them not only adds to the size of the gathering, it amplifies the impact of the proclamation that God in Jesus cares for everyone: men, women, children, and the sick among them (in spite of persecution, Roman occupation, and political intrigue). Decisively, the addition reinforces the operative hermeneutic function that reveals Jesus as the Incarnate God in the midst of a people hungry to receive Good News![16]

Another possibility is potentially overlooked in the crowd of some fifteen to thirty-five thousand men, women, and children. I cannot help but look to those among them, perhaps many of them in the crowd that day as "the sick" whom Jesus healed. I wonder, who are these "uncounted" persons? Matthew uses the term *sick* sometimes as a general category, as in this passage, and at other times with more precision. When precise, among the general notion of those who were sick or ill, "those afflicted with various diseases and pains, demoniacs, epileptics, and paralytics" would be included (Matt. 4:24). These particular uncounted would today be recognized as PWD. Of course, the narrative does not offer any hints about their number; hence, another form of extrapolation is needed. I assume that the occurrence of disability from the ancient world to the present has remained steady. Thus, if as many as 20 percent of the world's populations are people with one or more disabilities today,[17] comparative reckoning of PWD would include one thousand men (20%/5,000) among those counted, and between three thousand (20%/15,000) and seven thousand (20%/35,000) of the full crowd—these numbers of likely PWD are no small crowd. Note moreover that living with disability is not equal to being sick or ill or in need of medical intervention to relieve the condition(s) of their lives (PWD will "get sick" with about the same or perhaps a little more frequency as nondisabled folks). That caveat aside, in terms of the historical period in which the gospels and most of the Hebrew and Christian scriptures were written, sickness and disability were very likely conflated.[18] Nevertheless, and insofar as many PWD of physical and/or behavioral, developmental, or mental kinds have been relegated to the nondisabled's categorization of them as permanent children,[19] even if not children by age in fact, PWD would surely be included in the anonymous mass of the often overlooked uncounted in this passage.

The Force and Reception of the Uncounted PWD through a Catholic Social Teaching Lens

From most historical accounts of ancient civilizations—in their religious and philosophical texts, legal documents, medical practices, literature, and other cultural artifacts—PWD have been identified as part of the societies in which they lived, at times with positive and at other times (most?) with less than ideal experiences. For example, uncovering the history requires creative and linguistic legerdemain as "ancient writers applied the shifting and fluid category of disability in biographies, physiognomics, political invective, philosophical and medical treatises on disability. Disability was used ad hoc by the ancient writers whenever it seemed appropriate to the literary or rhetorical context."[20] Clearly, the now "catch-all" term, people with disabilities, will not be found in ancient or modern texts; it is a term fraught with generalization and oversimplification, yet its now-broad use and acceptance by many, including PWD themselves, compels its usage across disciplines. Thus, without recourse to a singularly identifying term, scholars have retrieved these histories by looking for clues in the texts by references to infirmity (sickness), disfiguring marks (blemishes, scabies, leprosy), physiological/anatomical difference (dwarfism, palsy, lame), sensory limits of sight or hearing, mute (and other speech impediments), and idiot-mad-fool-demoniac (possessed).[21]

Since antiquity PWD have not fared well. However, improvement has been forthcoming, especially with the advent of the mid–twentieth-century initiatives for civil rights in societies organized around a population divided by dominant and subservient minoritized social, political, and ecclesial groups.[22] Consider, in the world of dualistic segregations, superficially identifiable differences have been used to categorize and, invariably, establish hierarchies that ranked individuals and communities on the basis of their conformity to a norm. For PWD these categorizations have resulted most frequently in their oppression,[23] from exposure at or near birth to neglect, to violent abuse: a state of affairs contrary to the inherent dignity belonging to every person by virtue of the *imago Dei* each embodies, experiences that can be tolerated no longer.

The church of late has awakened to PWD. While Catholicism has a long history of reaching out to people with one or another disabling condition that compromise their positions in their communities—from monastic traditions of hospitality and the development of hospital apostolates—today vocal advocates from the Vatican to Catholic policy makers are both noteworthy and admirable. The church holds witness to the graces of sacramental life, theological reflection, and social advocacy with preference for those who are poor and/or otherwise vulnerable.[24]

Catholic social teaching has the potential to contribute prophetically to increasing the active, as opposed to symbolic or perfunctory, presence of PWD in the ecclesia. The teaching on the *imago Dei* serves as the foundation to understanding the church's position toward every person and the defense of her/his human rights to life, freedom, and truth; on this foundation the subsequent development of Catholic social teaching principles rests. Working through the lens of human dignity to encourage active presence in every Catholic community, I focus on the principles of subsidiarity/participation and solidarity/preferential option for and with PWD. This moment in time offers an opportunity for the church, through its traditions of theological ethics, to address its unrecognized practices of exclusion. The imperative is clear: PWD belong in and to the church.

Imago Dei

Among other trajectories that the teaching on inherent human dignity takes, of special interest here is the theological anthropology that establishes definitively the relational characteristic of God in Godself and therefrom to God's creation of humankind in God's own image. Insofar as whatever is contemplated about God reflects a self-referential appreciation of the *imago Dei* human being, debates from the early church concerning the "who–what–why" of God at the start of creation to the Incarnation resulted in confirmation of the Trinity and of God's own *kenosis* into corporeal nature. When the Christian tradition holds that the Trinity is perfect independent relationality in the tri-personal *perichoresis* of unity in diversity, God *in se* is inclusive of God Incarnate.[25] The *imago Dei* must then reflect God, albeit imperfectly, as an interdependent if not dependent relationality between, among, and for one another. This theological anthropology challenges any insult one person or group may harbor over and against another as well as failures to open wide the doors of mercy.

The Incarnation changed the course of revelation by its definitive identification of God with creation, forestalling any subsequent dismissal of earth matter and God's dwelling therein. Moreover, since the Incarnation, the scandalizing reality (beyond God become human) of Jesus's ignoble death—crucifixion by nails, ropes, and lance—was annulled in the Resurrection of the now Disabled God and in the liberation of all those who had been and/or remain oppressed.[26] A Disabled God theological anthropology must account for this feature of Trinitarian *kenosis*. A theological anthropology of the radical dependent relationality of God Incarnate must reckon with embodied vulnerability. And radical dependent relationality moves theologizing about the *imago Dei* to the concrete realities that the Incarnate

God and human and other beings experience. As an operative hermeneutic, this symbol of God functions to acknowledge vulnerability to scandal and violence, as well as to celebrate the relationships that sustain us.[27] This theologizing exposes the successes and failures of inclusion that discipleship requires.

Subsidiarity/Participation

Participation is the concrete expression and cornerstone of the principle of subsidiarity, which individuals bring to bear in association with others.[28] Regrettably, on account of its hierarchic structures, the church relegates subsidiarity to the domain of secular governing and political affairs in matters of personal decision making and free association; however, subsidiarity needs to be engaged in ecclesial affairs as well. Consider, if "subsidiarity respects personal dignity by recognizing in the person a subject who is always capable of giving something to others,"[29] where is this subject in the ecclesia? Moreover, if "it becomes absolutely necessary to encourage participation above all of the most disadvantaged, as well as the occasional rotation of political leaders in order to forestall the establishment of hidden privileges,"[30] where then are PWD? The radically dependent relational nature of all humankind commends subsidiarity/participation in every sphere.

And yet, PWD have been denied opportunities to participate in and contribute to ecclesial life. For example, Canon Law excludes some from priestly candidacy (Canons 1029 and 1041) and restricts the Eucharist to those with a particular mental capacity, denying thereby many with developmental disabilities (Canons 912–14) on the basis of an ableist medical judgment regarding their capacity to fulfill the ministry or to understand the mystery.[31] Alongside these canonical obstacles, architecturally many churches are straightforwardly inaccessible to people with mobility impairments and others who are deaf: ecclesial life that remains inaccessible effectively excludes PWD from exercising their "principled" right to participate and to share in the Good News.

Solidarity/Preferential Option for and with the Poor

> From the moment of his conception to his death, Jesus stood so near (and in solidarity with) those who are vulnerable that he identified himself with the poverty of Nazareth as well as with those who could be subjected to death by stoning or crucifixion, to the gossip surrounding a bastard child or of cavorting with sinners and lepers, and to the vagaries of a colonial power over a people in occupied territory.[32]

The *kenosis*—from incarnation to crucifixion—confirms God's posture before and with humankind; it is God's singular solidarity in–with–for those who are poor and/or otherwise marginalized. In *kenosis* there is no dire reality to which God would not stoop.

As cautioned on sickness, living with disability(ies) does not necessarily signal a dire life. However, as the oppressions and stigmatizations PWD experience continue, they are marginalized thereby and likely impoverished as well.[33] Both their marginalization and impoverishment are relievable by a reversal of the attitudinal barriers among the nondisabled that exclude. Such relief will be found with an increase in access to the ecclesia and all of the ministries and services offered there to PWD as participants and recipients. Such presence raises awareness in the ecclesia of friends, neighbors, coworkers, children in parks and schools that PWD will be where the nondisabled can be; and where they are not, a welcome–healing–feeding approach must be made.

People Still Hunger

The number of PWD in both secular and religious settings remains small and nearly absent from the main, in spite of the fact that they are 20+ percent of the global population. If they are absent, they cannot be counted, nor can they exercise their vocations as *imago Dei* of subsidiarity/participation or of solidarity/preferential option. And yet, their absence from the assemblies of human commerce goes largely unrecognized. If they have been excluded by architectural and/or attitudinal barriers, the nondisabled people who gather in those places simply don't think of them! The Americans with Disabilities Act (ADA) offers one remedy to their absences: public institutions must provide accommodations for PWD.[34] Unfortunately, religious institutions are exempt from a significant number of ADA provisions. The failure to accommodate PWD excludes them from the assemblies of the faithful, effectively keeping PWD both out of sight and out of mind.

The church has been slow to respond with wholesale remedies for this hurtful state of affairs. While the US National Catholic Partnership on Disability "works collaboratively to ensure meaningful participation of [PWD] in all aspects of the life of the Church and society,"[35] the faithful take their cues from a charity model to patronize PWD, use them as spectacles of long-suffering, or earn good deeds' credits . . . then closeted until another occasion. Popes John Paul II, Benedict XVI, and Francis have embraced PWD, but their loving outreach, captured in photographic spreads, reinforces the barriers to actualized participation of and solidarity with PWD. "The disabled need more, in terms of both access to the Church and inclusion in it."[36] PWD deserve more than they currently receive but not more than the nondisabled already enjoy. Their radical dependence on others—from a family's loving care to teachers, friends, community infrastructures, and the church—is justly proportionate to the radical dependent relationality of the nondisabled: let every person with disabilities be counted!

Contrary to the welcome–healing–feeding of Jesus's banquet, such failures indict the nondisabled of unexamined privilege and the sins of their unrecognized practices of exclusion.

Notes

1. See Raymond E. Brown, *An Introduction to the New Testament* (New York: Doubleday, 1997), 135–36, 171–74, 187; Richard Thomas France, *The Gospel of Matthew, The New International Commentary on the New Testament* (Grand Rapids, MI: Wm. B. Eerdmans, 2007), 10–13, 556–57; Daniel J. Harrington, SJ, *The Gospel of Matthew, Sacra Pagina Series* (Collegeville, MN: A Michael Glazier Book, Liturgical Press, 2007), 1–25, 218–23 hereafter *Matthew*); John Nolland, *The Gospel of Matthew, The New International Greek Testament Commentary* (Grand Rapids, MI: Wm. B. Eerdmans, 2005), 19–64, 585–94; and Manlio Simonetti, ed., *Matthew 14—28* (Downers Grove, IL: InterVarsity Press, 2002), 6–10.

2. The author writes in Greek that is good, is familiar with the Jewish scriptures and the law, and who "could use Jewish rhetoric and themes without explanation . . . [this evangelist] is particularly concerned with determining the proper relationship between Jesus and the Torah." Harrington, *Matthew*, 1, 8.

3. See Megan McKenna, *Not Counting Women and Children: Neglected Stories from the Bible* (Maryknoll, NY: Orbis Books, 1994), 8.

4. See Harrington, *Matthew*, 220–21.

5. See McKenna, *Not Counting Women and Children*, 7–32.

6. International Commission on English in the Liturgy, "Canticle of Zechariah," in *Liturgy of the Hours, Morning Prayer* (Totowa, NJ: Catholic Book Publishing, 1976); cf. Luke 1:76–79.

7. See Isa. 29:19–21 and 61:1–3.

8. Harrington, *Matthew*, 19.

9. Warren Carter, "The Crowds in Matthew's Gospel," *Catholic Biblical Quarterly* 55, no. 1 (1993): 65.

10. Harrington, *Matthew*, 221.

11. See David R. Bauer, *The Structure of Matthew's Gospel: A Study in Literary Design* (Sheffield, UK: Almond Press, 1988).

12. See Yiu Sing Lúcás Chan, *The Ten Commandments and the Beatitudes: Biblical Studies and Ethics for Real Life* (Lanham, MD: Rowman & Littlefield, 2012), 141–226.

13. See James F. Keenan, SJ, *The Works of Mercy: The Heart of Catholicism*, 3rd ed. (Lanham, MD: Rowman & Littlefield, 2017).

14. See Central Intelligence Agency, "Total Fertility Rate," *The World Fact Book 2013–14* (Washington, DC: Central Intelligence Agency, 2013), https://www.cia.gov. The average rates are based on a sample from geographically like ancient Palestine: Afghanistan 5.22, Burundi 6.04, Egypt 3.53, Gaza Strip 4.3, Jordan 3.18, Nigeria 5.13, Pakistan 2.68, Turkey 2.03, West Bank 3.33. The CIA reports an average global fertility rate of 2.42.

15. Harrington, *Matthew*, 220. See also McKenna, *Not Counting Women and Children*, 8.

16. See Paul Ricoeur, "Toward a Hermeneutic of the Idea of Revelation," *Harvard Theological Review* 70, no. 1/2 (1977): 1–37.

17. See World Health Organization, "Chapter 2: Disability—A Global Picture," in *World Report on Disability* (Geneva: WHO Press, 2011), 19–53.

18. See Heidi Marx-Wolf and Kristi Upson-Saia, "The State of the Question: Religion, Medicine, Disability, and Health in Late Antiquity," *Journal of Late Antiquity* 8, no. 2 (2015): 257–72.

19. See James J. Liesener and Judith Mills, "An Experimental Study of Disability Spread: Talking to an Adult in a Wheelchair Like a Child," *Journal of Applied Social Psychology* 29, no. 4 (1999): 2083–92; Kenneth L. Robey, Linda Beckley, and Matthew Kirschner, "Implicit Infantilizing Attitudes about Disability," *Journal of Developmental and Physical Disabilities* 18, no. 4 (2006): 441–53; also Lydia X. Z. Brown, "Not a Child; Don't Treat Me Like One," *Autistic Hoya* (December 2, 2012), http://www.autistichoya.com.

20. Christian Laes, "Introduction: Disabilities in the Ancient World—Past, Present and Future," in *Disability in Antiquity*, ed. Christian Laes (London: Routledge, 2017), 8.

21. See Lae, *Disability in Antiquity*, for essays on the ancient Near East, including India and China, the Greek world, the Roman world, the late ancient world including the Christian east and west, rabbinic Judaism, and Islam; also Chomba Wa Munyi, "Past and Present Perceptions toward Disability: A Historical Perspective," *Disability Studies Quarterly* 32, no. 2 (2012), http://dsq-sds.org/article/view/3197/3068.

22. See Mary Jo Iozzio, "God Bends Over Backwards to Accommodate Humankind . . . While the Civil Rights Acts and the Americans with Disabilities Act Require [Only] Minimum Effort," *Journal of Moral Theology* 6, no. 2, special issue 2 (2017): 10-31.

23. See Henri Jacques Stiker, *A History of Disability* (Ann Arbor: University of Michigan Press, 2002); Bruce G. Link and Jo C. Phelan, "Conceptualizing Stigma," *Annual Review of Sociology* 27 (2001): 363–85; Erving Goffman, *Stigma: Notes on the Management of Spoiled Identity* (Englewood Cliffs, NJ: Prentice Hall, 1963); and Nora J. Baladerian, Thomas F. Coleman, and Jim Stream, *Abuse of People with Disabilities: Victims and Their Families Speak Out* (Los Angeles: Spectrum Institute, 2013), http://disability-abuse.com/survey/survey-report.pdf.

24. See Mary Jo Iozzio, "Catholicism and Disability," in *Disability and World Religions: An Introduction*, ed. Darla Y. Schumm and Michael Stoltzfus (Waco, TX: Baylor University Press, 2016), 115–35.

25. See Catherine Mowry LaCugna, *God for Us: The Trinity and Christian Life* (New York: Harper Collins, 1991), 22–24 and 270–78.

26. See Nancy L. Eiesland, *The Disabled God: Toward a Liberatory Theology of Disability* (Nashville: Abingdon Press, 1994), 89–105.

27. See Mary Jo Iozzio, "The Writing on the Wall . . . Alzheimer's Disease: A Daughter's Look at Mom's Faithful Care of Dad," *Journal of Religion, Disability, & Health* 9, no. 2 (2005): 49–74.

28. Pontifical Council for Justice and Peace, *The Compendium of the Social Doctrine of the Church* (Vatican City: Libreria Editrice Vaticana, 2004), §189 (hereafter, *Compendium*).

29. *Caritas in veritate*, no. 57.

30. *Compendium*, §189.

31. Catholic Church, *Code of Canon Law* (Vatican City: Libreria Editrice Vaticana, 1983).

32. Mary Jo Iozzio, "Solidarity: Restoring Communion with Those Who Are Disabled," *Journal of Religion, Disability & Health* 15, no. 2 (2011): 141.

33. See Nora Groce, Gayatri Kembhavi, Sheila Wirz, Raymond Lang, Jean-Francois Trani, and Maria Kett, *Poverty and Disability: A Critical Review of the Literature in Low- and Middle-Income Countries* (London: Leonard Cheshire Disability and Inclusive Development Centre, 2011).

34. The Americans with Disabilities Act of 1990 and ADA Amendments Act (2008), Public Law 110-325, https://www.ada.gov.

35. National Catholic Partnership on Disability, "Our Mission" (n.d.), http://www. ncpd.org.

36. David M. Perry, "Pope Francis Needs to Do More than Kiss the Disabled," *Crux, Taking the Catholic Pulse*, June 14, 2016, https://cruxnow.com.

Moral Deafness and Social Sin

Feminist Theologians and the
Bishops from a US Perspective

Barbara Hilkert Andolsen

The 1960s was a time of major changes in the lives of Catholics across the globe and in the lives of American women. Despite the openness shown by the Second Vatican Council, Catholic bishops in the United States had very little contact with emerging scholars of feminist theology. This missed opportunity to learn about women's oppression and to offer the support due in justice to a new movement for full human rights for women is another sad sign of the social sin of sexism in the life of the American Catholic Church.

The Social and Historical Setting

In 1960, the US Federal Drug Administration approved the first hormonal birth control pill. As a new form of technology, the birth control pill intensified debate among Catholic ethicists concerning the moral permissibility of using so-called artificial methods of birth control.[1] In the same decade, a social movement to promote Women's Liberation emerged in the United States. In 1963, Betty Friedan published a best-selling book, *The Feminine Mystique*,[2] which analyzed the discontents of college-educated women who found themselves trapped in the rather vacuous role of suburban homemaker. By the end of the 1960s, public demonstrations and marches on behalf of Women's Liberation were receiving widespread media coverage. The Women's Movement, as portrayed by mass media in the United States, originated as a secular movement.

From 1962 to 1965, Vatican II brought together the first truly global assembly of bishops. The mandate of the Council was to reconsider church life and the position of the church in the world post–World War II. Of course, there were no women among the assembled bishops. While theological advisors and ecumenical observers were invited, all of these were male, until the final two sessions of the Council, when fifteen Catholic women were appointed as auditors. These female auditors were invited to join, as nonvoting participants, in meetings of committees that were preparing draft conciliar documents. A story is told that, at a drafting session for *Gaudium et spes*, one bishop read a florid passage about feminine

259

contributions to the church. Noticing that the few women present looked unimpressed, this bishop insisted that Rosemary Goldie, a laywoman from Australia, tell him what she thought. Goldie replied, "You can omit all those gratuitous flowery adjectives, the pedestals and incense, from your sentence. All women ask for is that they be recognized as the full human persons they are, and treated accordingly."[3]

In the United States, Catholic women, partly inspired by Vatican II, began to pursue advanced degrees in Catholic theology. Prior to the 1960s, advanced preparation in theology in most of the US Catholic universities was the exclusive province of ordained priests. Since the 1950s, a nationwide Sister Formation Conference had pressed successfully for better education for women religious. The movement provided a foundation for women religious to pursue advanced degrees in the professions, in the arts and sciences, and, by the 1970s, even in theology. A surprising number of Catholic laywomen, single and married, began studying for the doctorate in theology as well—at Catholic universities as these institutions began accepting women as doctoral students and in historically Protestant doctoral programs in religion. In 1968, Mary Daly published the first book in Catholic feminist theology, *The Church and the Second Sex*.[4] Daly documented a heritage of misogynist statements by the great [male] thinkers in the Catholic tradition. She heavily criticized the church's propensity for putting women "on a pedestal" while denying women cultural, economic, political, and theological influence. In 1973, Daly published *Beyond God the Father*,[5] pursuing theological changes that would be necessary for Catholic theology to become consonant with Women's Liberation.

Throughout the 1980s and 1990s, other theologically trained Roman Catholic women contributed to an explicitly feminist theology.[6] By feminist here I mean a theology that takes women's experiences seriously as material for theological reflection and a theology premised on the equal human dignity of women and men—a dignity rooted in the Creator's love, not in personal achievements or cultural traditions. Throughout the early development of US feminist theology, there was little contact between most of the American Catholic bishops and this new group of women theologians. However, there was a vibrant theological discussion among Catholic, Protestant, and Jewish feminist theologians. Feminist scholars studying other world religions were also included in feminist theological dialogues.

Catholic bishops, even as individual leaders of dioceses, displayed limited awareness of the Women's Liberation Movement, nor was there any serious public consideration of the movement's ethical and theological significance at first. That is, until 1973, when the US Supreme Court ruled on *Roe v. Wade*.[7] The court held that abortion was a personal and medical matter to be decided by a pregnant woman and her doctor without interference from the government. A state government could, but was not required to, restrict or ban access to abortion after the fetus reached viability. The secular feminist movement had been pressing strongly for the end of government involvement in determining whether a woman would have access to a safe and noncriminal abortion. The American Catholic bishops had been pressing for the government to legally ban all elective abortions. The Supreme

Court decision giving wide latitude for a woman's right to choose an abortion—coming as it did so early in the Women's Liberation Movement—alienated some of the goodwill toward the Women's Movement that might otherwise have been forthcoming from some of the bishops. It froze the American Catholic bishops in an overwhelmingly adversarial posture against a major social movement on behalf of women's full human rights. In order to understand the failure of the American bishops to respond more supportively to a movement for full human rights for women, it is helpful to consider the theological concept of "social sin."

Social Sin

The idea of social sin is derived in part from an increased emphasis on understanding the church as a community of believers, who, as pilgrims, are on a journey toward the Kingdom of God. As *Lumen gentium* says, in one sense the church is "the initial budding forth of that kingdom."[8] But, at the same time, the church at any moment in history is *not yet* the fullness of Kingdom of God. The church sometimes stumbles along its pilgrimage route. *Lumen gentium* also emphasized collegiality throughout the church. The idea that Catholics should work together for the good of the church was applied to all levels of the church—parish councils, diocesan councils, regional groups of bishops, and the synod of bishops.

Most scholars connect new language about social sin with the documents from the regional meeting of the bishops from Latin and Central America in Medellín, Colombia, in 1968. The most momentous decision to come from the Medellín meeting was a decision that the church throughout Latin and Central America was called by God to be a church of the poor. The preferential option for the poor prodded theologians and social scientists to identify social institutions that oppress the poor. Theologians were prompted to recognize sins that were not solely individual sins. Theologians from the region insisted that it was also necessary to analyze those intersecting social arrangements that perpetuated the privileged lives of the upper class at grave costs to the poor. If Catholics were to be held morally accountable for the devastation wrought by widespread poverty, then Catholics would have to take responsibility—collectively as well as individually—for dismantling the institutional and social arrangements that blighted the lives of the poor. Catholic theologians across the globe found the development of an explicit notion of social sin useful to urge Catholics in their nations to take responsibility for evil social patterns and unjust interlocking institutional systems that oppressed more vulnerable persons.

I contend that the church as a pilgrim people on a journey toward the Kingdom of God can manifest various social sins. Patriarchy, that is, the distribution of inordinate power and privileges to men and the maintenance of social systems permitting and encouraging male dominance over women, is one powerful example of a social attitude that blights the holiness of church and the success of its witness to the Kingdom of God. The fact that sexism has been maintained and perpetuated within the Roman Catholic Church throughout virtually all of its existence highlights the depths of its evil.[9]

One sexist practice to which the many American bishops, a number of curial officials, and recent popes are tempted is a failure to listen patiently, nondefensively, and deeply to the experiences and the wisdom of women. Women theologians have been proposing important ideas, but men—especially the American bishops appointed by John Paul II and Benedict XVI—seemed then and seem now to ignore what women theologians are saying. They tacitly reject feminist scholars' investigation of sexism as a social sin. In particular, the bishops propose no new courses of action or changes in church thinking and practice, which would be more consonant with women's full human dignity.

The Futile Attempt to Draft a Pastoral Letter on Women's Concerns

Rejection of the Original Dialogical Method

A disheartening example of the American bishops' failure to hear women's assertions of equal human dignity with men and the bishops' failure to advocate ecclesiastical change to make the church a sign of the Kingdom of God as a discipleship of equals can be seen in the failure of the National Conference of Catholic Bishops (NCCB) to produce a pastoral letter on women's concerns despite nine years of trying. This failure to hear what Catholic feminists were saying and to respond with moral empathy and wisdom is ironic because the initial method of gathering material for the pastoral letter included unusually widespread consultations with Catholic women. The US bishops' drafting committee called for meetings in each diocese where Catholic women would address broad discussion questions. The local bishop frequently attended and listened to the opinions expressed by Catholic women in his diocese. It has been estimated that over 75,000 Catholic women participated in these meetings or submitted written comments to be considered by the bishops' committee. The first draft of the bishops' pastoral letter on women's concern, "Partners in the Mystery of Redemption," made ample use of the thoughts women expressed during this grassroots listening process.

Indeed, one aspect of the first draft that was praised by a number of theological commentators was the way that the first draft was structured as if it were a dialogue between Catholic women and the bishops' committee. In each of four topic areas, there was (1) a report on diverse women's thoughts on the topic, including with ample use of women's own words; (2) a review of elements in the heritage of the church that were related to the topic under discussion; and (3) a response by the bishops to their female dialogue partners in light of the Catholic heritage. In this first draft, the bishops even suggested that certain church practices or attitudes should be reexamined and, perhaps, changed. For example, the bishops recommended inclusive language in church prayers; they were receptive to women as altar servers, as lectors, and, perhaps, as deacons; they even suggested further theological reflection on the ordination of women.

The way in which the topic of women's exclusion from ordained ministry was handled from draft one to draft two is an excellent example of abandoning the dialogical style. In the first draft, the writers accurately report the criticisms feminists made about the exclusion of women from ordination. In the second version, the only perspective is that of bishops who are pastorally concerned by the lack of "peaceful" reception of the Vatican's restatements of the traditional teaching that only males can be ordained. The bishops present the Vatican's prohibition of female ordination as unchangeable. Concisely the bishops declare that the church's enduring practice of a male-only priesthood "constitutes a tradition which witnesses to the mind of Christ and is normative."[10] Therefore, the church in the twentieth century was bound to maintain the male-only priesthood. There was no room for dialogue on this point.

Some American Catholic bishops and some clergy at the Vatican found the format of "Partners in the Mystery of Redemption" unacceptable. It was precisely the appearance of a dialogue between Catholic women and the bishops that was disturbing. The implied listening posture of the bishops on the committee was unsettling. These critics contended that in the church the bishops and the pope have roles as teachers, understood as those who proclaim knowledge to be accepted and pondered by less knowledgeable laypeople. The bishop should teach. The laywoman should listen and bring her thoughts and behavior into conformity with the bishops' teachings. Insisting on firm reaffirmation of the hierarchical magisterium's positions on controversial points, the traditionalist bishops and the Vatican persuaded the drafting committee to reframe the organizational structure for the second, third, and fourth drafts. The pastoral letter became a one-way communication from church authorities (the bishops) to religious and lay Catholics. Between the first and the second draft, the quantity of quotations from American Catholic women was substantially cut back. There were still quotations from women, some of them critical of the church's teachings, practices, and institutions, but such quotes were less frequent and more dispersed throughout the text.

Selected Changes in Content

In this short essay, I can discuss only a few important changes in the content of the pastoral letter over the drafting process. First, how did each draft treat sexism in both society and the church? At first, the committee defined sexism as prejudice "which makes judgments about people based exclusively on their sex rather than on knowledge of their character, ability or achievement."[11] Sexism imposes the greater hardships on women. The drafters say, "The sin of sexism depersonalizes women. It makes them objects to be possessed and used. It degrades dignity. It dismisses women as unimportant, as mere subordinates or appendages."[12] In the bishops' response to women in the final section of "Partners in Redemption," the bishops discuss partnership with women in the church. Without using the term "social sin," the writers seem to acknowledge the serious way in which sexism has compromised the moral witness of the church throughout the centuries.

> Fidelity to the foundational principles and canons of our Christian heritage requires a careful examination of religious and social systems, structures and styles that have marred the mutual respect which ought to exist between the sexes. Women have suffered from profound as well as petty discrimination because of an attitude of male dominance which, in any form, is alien to the Christian understanding of the function of authority. Regrettably this attitude has often influenced family and church structures and distorted the way in which we understand the truth of our heritage.[13]

Drafters explained another aspect of sexism in the second draft: "In the past, church and society have erred in considering women almost exclusively in relation to men and in regarding only men as fundamentally autonomous."[14] The second draft offers a fuller description of sexism: "Sexism [is] the conscious or unconscious acceptance of the subservience of one sex to the other; the exploitation of one sex for the satisfaction of the other; the treatment of one sex as an object to be possessed more than as a peer or a full person."[15] The third draft gives more attention to sexism as a sinful attitude. "Sexism is rooted in the erroneous conviction, whether subtle or overt, 'that one sex, male or female, is superior to the other in the very order of creation or by the very nature of things.'"[16] This error and the sinful attitudes it generates lead to evil in the world. However, in the fourth version the bishops warn that "to identify sexism as the principal evil at work in this distortion of relationships between women and men would be to analyze the underlying problem too superficially."[17] The drafting committee for version four discusses a loss of faith in Catholic sexual teachings, the consequences of the sexual revolution, an uncritical adoption of a birth control mentality, and, importantly, a failure to value the fundamental sexual differences established by the Creator as problems separate from sexism, but quite harmful to the interests of women.[18]

There is, however, not a clear appeal to the theological concept of social sin in any of the drafts, although a similar idea is suggested. The writers of the first draft judged sexism to be a "social and moral evil."[19] Thus, the writers indicate that sexism creates and maintains social structures consistently detrimental to women. Still, their language pointing to both social evil and moral evil does not seem to me to communicate directly that social patterns that persistently disadvantage women are a moral evil, that is, a sin. Nevertheless speaking for the bishops, the text indicates that all Catholics have a responsibility individually and collectively to reject social patterns that undermine the full dignity of women as human persons.[20]

The second draft is also unclear or ambivalent about social sin. For example, the writers say that if sexism is knowingly and willingly accepted and acted upon, it is sinful, which would indicate individual sins. However, the bishops also describe an unconscious sexism. While this unconscious attitude may predispose human beings toward unjust patterns of domination and subjugation, it seems not to rise to the level of intentionality necessary for personal sin.[21] Nonetheless, the drafters specifically indicate that where sexism is embedded in the institutions of society, even invisibly, it perpetuates oppressive structures and unjust conditions.

In draft three, the bishops seem to put even more emphasis on the personal dimension of sexism as a sin. Their definition of sexism includes specific mention of attitudes, and they advocate conversion (which involves a moral and spiritual reorientation of an individual's attitudes) as a critical dimension necessary for the ending of sexism.[22] One issue with this focus on individual discriminatory attitudes as the core of sexism, which is remedied by individual conversion, is that it draws attention away from social and cultural patterns of evil. A Catholic who is not conscious of individual evil thoughts and feelings about vulnerable women may conclude the following: I do not have conscious sexist attitudes. Therefore, I have no moral responsibilities to deal with sexism.[23]

The strong point that is preserved in each of the drafts is the recognition that sexism is experienced in different ways in the lives of different women. Each of the drafts includes helpful material about the intersection of racism and sexism within the society.[24] This may be a reflection of work in feminist theology that has more consistently considered racial and ethnic diversity as a crucial human difference. In addition the bishops say clearly, "Faced by obstacles to justice, women of color call upon the church to reaffirm its teachings on the dignity of every person."[25] This human dignity is not conferred by society and, hence, is not revocable by society. The human dignity of women (and men) of color is permanently rooted in their status as women and men sharing in the image and likeness of God.

On another matter, the bishops recommended in "Partners in the Mystery of Redemption" that priests and bishops commit themselves to working more collegially with women in the church. The writers also said if seminarians displayed "an incapacity to deal with women as equals, [this] should be considered as [a] negative [indication] for fitness for ordination." The second and third drafts repeat this point using the same language.[26] The fourth draft makes no comment on whether the abilities to respect women as equals and to work cooperatively with them have a bearing on fitness for ordination.[27]

Beginning with the second draft, the bishops emphasize a Roman Catholic conception of men and women as equal in human dignity but as created by God with certain inherent sexual differences. Thus, the bishops asserted that men and women have separate sexually associated traits and predispositions but are equal in fundamental human worth. This insistence on an inherent array of traits and qualities belonging to men or belonging to women is called complementarity. The bishops tried to be nuanced in their treatment of sexual differences. They acknowledged that not every man or woman displays each of the qualities associated with sexual complementarity. Nor do the bishops ever quite say that any area of human activity should be the sole province of one sex or the other. Sometimes, in their discussions of the role of women as mothers, they seem just about to proclaim that fathers can never raise young children as adequately as mothers. However, their statements never become that blunt.

Church authorities who insist upon sexual complementarity hold in tension two beliefs regarding the divinely ordained differentiation of human beings as members of the male sex or the female sex. On the one hand, "women and men have the same nature, a common humanity, fundamental equality." On the other hand, "women and men are different because their identical natures are embodied in different ways."[28] The bishops assert explicitly that complementarity of the sexes does not necessarily imply the superiority of either sex nor does it imply or justify one sex's rightful domination over the other sex.

The first draft of the pastoral letter on women recognized that many women were uncomfortable with the firm reaffirmation of the church's opposition to any artificial means of birth control. This had been reaffirmed by Paul VI in 1968 in *Humanae vitae*. The drafting committee for the letter on women's concern acknowledged social science findings that the vast majority of sexually active American Catholic women were not complying with the teachings of *Humanae vitae*. In the second draft, it similarly, although more briefly, acknowledged that the majority of Catholic women had not accepted the norm that any use of artificial means of contraception is morally wrong. Still the drafters of the second version firmly reiterated the Vatican position on birth control. The reader is left with a sense that there will not be an ongoing dialogue between women and the bishops about birth control, nor will there be any reassessment of theological thinking on the subject.[29] By draft three, the teaching on birth control was upheld emphatically using a key traditional moral standard. "The marital act cannot be separated from openness to life."[30] There was no acknowledgment in any of these drafts—nor has there been in other documents from the hierarchical magisterium, up to the present time—that this core objection to artificial birth control is fundamentally inconsistent with present-day scientific knowledge about female human biology. From a woman's perspective, the requirement that morally licit sexual intercourse must always be an expression of love *and open to the conception of new life* is nonsensical. A woman is fertile for two or three days during her approximately month-long menstrual cycle. Even a woman who is attempting to become pregnant will probably engage in more marital acts that are *not* "open to life" than marital acts that are. Getting together a group of female moral theologians might be a start toward developing a new teaching about procreation that takes the female body, as God created it, into adequate account.

By 1991, Vatican officials and Pope John Paul II became uneasy with the American Catholic bishops' work on a pastoral letter on women's concerns. The chair of the ad hoc committee on women's concerns along with other officials of the Conference of Catholic Bishops had a meeting in Rome where content and procedural issues involved in writing the pastoral letter were discussed. The third draft clearly incorporated some requests for revisions from the Vatican. There is a strengthened emphasis on female–male complementarity. In the third draft, material about the full human dignity of women and material about the God-given sexual differentiation between men and women are held together. The description of men and women as different but as sharing equal human dignity was moved to the beginning of third draft.

In the fourth version, references to some of women's specific discontents with the Catholic Church were sharply reduced. For example, the frustration that women have almost no direct access to decision making and policy setting in the church was not grappled with in a serious way. There is a reminder that, since 1983, women have been eligible to serve as judges for marriage tribunals or to be chancellors of dioceses. But there is no imaginative thinking about new church structures that would allow Catholic women to share authority equally with men, even though women are refused ordination. Despite these limitations, the final version of the US bishops' pastoral letter stated clearly, "We pray that this pastoral letter will strengthen our common efforts to assure the true dignity and rightful equality of women and men created in the image of God and redeemed in the blood of Christ."[31] However, note that the wording is *true* dignity and *rightful* equality. This probably means equality and dignity as understood from a complementary perspective. That understanding would be consistent with other places where the drafters of version four say women and men "are different, yet equal."[32]

Conclusion

In 1975, before the American Catholic bishops as a group responded to the Women's Movement or feminist theologians, Bishop Carroll T. Dozier challenged the people of his diocese to work for Women's Liberation. He said, "Let us hear, then, those voices that vocalize woman's determination to assert her equality and profess her competence." He issued a prophetic warning to the church as an institution: "Heedless institutions must inevitably pay the costs of indifference."[33]

Catholic feminist theologians were virtually unanimous that the final version of the pastoral letter on women's concerns was not acceptable. The way in which the bishops, as early as draft two, pulled back from empathic listening to the 75,000 Catholics who participated in the discussions of the 1980s was one root of the collapse of the pastoral letter. P. Francis Murphy, a bishop who had been on the drafting committee for the pastoral letter, hailed the initial nationwide consultation with diverse women. In his words, the bishops paid attention to "the experience of many [women] whose talents and aspirations are unjustly overlooked, especially in the church. It brought this listening process into the public domain and opened a dialogue that cannot be dismissed or ignored."[34] As a feminist moral theologian, many times it seems to me that Bishop Murphy was too optimistic. Many Catholic women—feminist theologians and others—have been losing hope of being invited to share their experiences and ethical insights with the leaders of the Catholic

Church. Social sin is a persistent phenomenon, and the church shows few signs of repenting the sin of sexism or of performing actions that confirm that the church has a firm purpose of amendment where sexism is concerned.

Notes

1. Richard A. McCormick, "Notes on Moral Theology, 1965," in *Notes on Moral Theology 1965 through 1980* (Lanham, MD: University Press of America, 1981), 38–52. See also "Notes on Moral Theology, 1966," 108–16; "Notes on Moral Theology, 1967," 164–68, "Notes on Moral Theology, 1968," 208–15.

2. Betty Friedan, *The Feminine Mystique* (New York: Norton, 1963).

3. Mary Luke Tobin, S.L., "Women in the Church since Vatican II," *America,* November 1, 1986, 243.

4. Mary Daly, *The Church and the Second Sex* (Boston: Beacon Press, 1968). Reprinted in 1975 with a "Feminist PostChristian Introduction."

5. Mary Daly, *Beyond God the Father* (Boston: Beacon Press, 1973).

6. Some examples include Rosemary Radford Ruether, *Sexism and God-Talk: Towards a Feminist Theology* (Boston: Beacon Press, 1983); Elizabeth Johnson, *She Who Is: The Mystery of God in Feminist Theological Discourse* (New York: Crossroad, 1992); Catherine Mowry LaCunga, ed., *Freeing Theology: The Essentials of Theology from a Feminist Perspective* (San Francisco: HarperSanFrancisco, 1993); Elisabeth Schüssler Fiorenza, *Discipleship of Equals: A Critical Feminist Ekklēsia-logy of Liberation* (New York: Crossroad, 1993).

7. *Roe v. Wade*, 410 U.S. 113 (1973).

8. *Lumen gentium*, no. 5.

9. Given the brevity of this essay and its focus on sexism, I may create the false impression that I think that women are morally superior to men. I do not. First, women can be and are complicit in forms of sexism. Second, I insist that any "assumption that *all* women (or some select group of women) as women have higher moral sensitivities is dangerous" because it obscures women's moral obligation to resist multiple and intersecting forms of social sin. That was an aspect of my thinking on theological anthropology in 1986. That is still my position now. Barbara Hilkert Andolsen, *"Daughters of Jefferson, Daughters of Bootblacks": Racism and American Feminism* (Macon, GA: Mercer University Press, 1986), 107–10, 113–16.

10. National Conference of Catholic Bishops, "One in Christ Jesus: A Pastoral Response to the Concerns of Women for Church and Society," *Origins*, April 5, 1990, 115.

11. National Conference of Catholic Bishops, "Partners in the Mystery of Redemption, First Draft of U.S. Bishops' Pastoral Response to Women's Concerns for Church and Society," *Origins*, April 21, 1988, 28.

12. Ibid.

13. Ibid., 224.

14. NCCB, "One in Christ Jesus: A Pastoral Response," 21.

15. Ibid., 31.

16. National Conference of Catholic Bishops, "Third Draft of U.S. Bishops' Proposed Pastoral Response to the Concerns of Women for Church and Society: Called to Be One in Christ Jesus," *Origins*, April 23, 1992, 16.

17. National Conference of Catholic Bishops, "One in Christ Jesus: Fourth Draft of U.S. Bishops' Response to the Concerns of Women for Church and Society," *Origins,* September 10, 1992, 44.

18. Ibid., 51–52. Emphasis mine.

19. Ibid., 28, 38–39.

20. Ibid., 41.

21. Ibid., 31.

22. NCCB, "Third Draft of Proposed Pastoral," 50–51.

23. Bryan Massingale makes a very similar point with respect to racism. As long as a Catholic, who believes she or he personally has good will toward black persons, fails to recognize that racism is embedded in cultural and institutional racism, she or he will ignore her or his moral responsibility to work to transform racist social structures into more just ones. See *Racial Justice and the Catholic Church* (Maryknoll, NY: Orbis Books, 2010), 25–42, 64–70.

24. NCCB, "Partners in the Mystery of Redemption," 147–52.

25. Ibid., 152.

26. Ibid., 229; NCCB, "One in Christ Jesus: Proposed Pastoral," 123; NCCB, "Third Draft," 124.

27. NCCB, "One in Christ Jesus: Fourth Draft." See comments immediately at the end of the bishops' document in *Origins.*

28. NCCB, "One in Christ Jesus, Proposed Pastoral," 25.

29. Compare NCCB, "Partners of Mystery of Redemption," 71–75, with "One in Christ Jesus," 72–78, and NCCB, "Third Draft of Proposed Pastoral," 77–79.

30. NCCB, "Third Draft of Proposed Pastoral," 78.

31. NCCB, "One in Christ Jesus: Fourth Draft," 7.

32. Ibid., 23.

33. Carroll T. Dozier, "Woman: Intrepid and Loving," *Catholic Mind,* November 1975, 59–64.

34. "Let's Start Over: A Bishop Appraises the Pastoral on Women," *Commonweal,* September 25, 1992, 11.

DIGITAL LOCALITIES, THE CHURCH, AND ETHICS

Jana Marguerite Bennett

As Catholic theological ethicists consider the local context of the church and the moral implications of living in those various localities, we must also consider our digital localities. I discuss digital localities more below, but as an opening definition, I name "digital localities" as social media–based ways for Catholics to be connected, or in Pope Francis's words, to "encounter others" and the gospel. Pope Francis suggests, "The internet, in particular, offers immense possibilities for encounter and solidarity. This is something truly good, a gift from God."

Digital localities might occur in social media networks, such as Facebook, Twitter, or Instagram, or be part of blogging communities, as at Patheos.com. They may be part of virtual reality platforms online such as online labyrinths. These localities are not necessarily *dedicated* to discussion of theology or participation in Christian practices online, but they are groups that allow for such discussion and participation even in a loose way. For example, a group of Twitter followers who occasionally engage each other in conversation about theology is a kind of digital locality, as are blogs dedicated to discussion of Catholic life and theology.

While some scholars still debate the nature of online discourse by asking whether the church ought to be online, for many people, there is no debate. Digital technologies are so much a part of life that it makes little sense to debate the point! Catholics already participate in blogging discussions and social media conversations, engage with prayer and other Christian practices online, read papal encyclicals, participate in intentional communities, and make theological arguments about Catholic teachings online.

This essay explores the possibilities present in these spaces for encounter and solidarity. I will spend the first half of this essay detailing some key characteristics of these digital localities. That discussion of characteristics then enables me to consider some of the ethical questions that arise.

Characteristics of Digital Localities

In this section, I lay out some of the characteristics that digital localities hold in common. Digital localities are quite diverse, as I alluded to in the introduction. Yet I do think there are commonalities across our diverse ways of engaging digital localities, whether that engagement involves YouTube channel subscriptions and discussion, or participation in private church-related Facebook discussion groups, or more public debates found on blogging forums.

Tools

One common characteristic of digital localities is that they are accessed via apps or websites on tablets, smartphones, computers, and similar contemporary technologies. This is significant because these technologies are multifaceted, enabling people to carry out a range of activities almost simultaneously. A person might use her smartphone to map a route to a new restaurant, text her friends that she'll be arriving for drinks a bit late, and also click on a friend's article linked on Twitter that directs her to a quiz about what kind of Christian she is. It is necessary to recognize this multifaceted nature of technology use because there are ranges of ways people use technological devices, and not all of those purposes will raise the same kinds of ethical questions. For example, some of the uses of smartphone apps are instrumental, enabling people to complete certain tasks like getting from point A to point B.

"Technologies as tools" can literally bring people closer together, as in the GPS example above, or have a negative, isolating effect, just as offline tools like hammers can be used for good (e.g., helping build a Habitat for Humanity house) or evil (e.g., as a weapon to inflict harm). While some theologians have rightly called into question the degree to which we can and should see contemporary technologies as *tools*, seeing technology as a tool does remain one significant way to identify human uses of technologies, and as we shall see in the second section of this essay, technology-as-tool raises important moral questions.[1]

Communication Tools

A second and quite related characteristic of digital localities is that they are tools *of communication*. The Catholic Church's documents relating to "technical devices" as important and even godly tools of communication stretches back far before the rise of social media. In a 1957 document, Pope Pius XII observed, "From the drawings and inscriptions of the most ancient times down to the latest technical devices, all instruments of human communication inevitably have as their aim the lofty purpose of revealing men as in some way the assistants of God."[2] For Christians, tools of communication are important because they are means of conveying God's own Word, the gospel, to the world.

This midcentury document also connected our technological tools of communication to Thomas Aquinas's metaphysical understanding of natural and artificial things. The pope states, "As Aquinas says: 'But it is natural to man to come to things of the understanding through things of sense; for all our knowledge has its origin in a sense.'"[3] We humans are part of natural substance that tends toward God, and as such we apprehend God through our senses that are taking in the world around us. Artificial things—those things we humans create via our art—enable us to make use of our world in order to know God. In using this kind of reasoning, Pope Pius XII discussed the importance of radio, television, and motion pictures in relation to God's salvation history. Technologies are not separate from divine life, and this point remains important in an age of digital technologies. So Pope Benedict XVI wrote in his 2013 World Communications Day address, "Believers are increasingly aware that, unless the Good News is made known also in the digital world, it may be absent in the experience of many people for whom this existential space is important."[4] The link between communication tools and the Gospel remains crucial for how Catholics and Catholic hierarchy understand the importance of digital localities.[5]

Culture

Yet the current characteristics of digital localities are not only instrumental, even inasmuch as the tool-based nature of technologies may be linked to friendship with God. Communication is also part of *culture*. Heidi Campbell and Stephen Garner, both scholars of religion and technology, describe the cultural importance of technology. They argue, "Technology has a significant sociocultural dimension—it is *human* technology—that wraps it in a network of relationships, values and histories, and makes technology dynamic."[6] Technology is, quite simply, the "environment in which we live."[7] Both Pope Francis and Pope Benedict were able to see this cultural aspect of digital localities to an extent, though it is clear that their main connection to digital localities is as tool for communicating.[8] Yet as Pope Benedict notes,

> The digital environment is not a parallel or purely virtual world, but is part of the daily experience of many people, especially the young. Social networks are the result of human interaction, but for their part they also reshape the dynamics of communication which builds relationships.[9]

The importance of understanding digital localities as cultures is to recognize that, digitally, local culture forms us in ways that we don't necessarily see. Because we use them all the time, it is easy to miss the ways digital localities shape our world, just in the way that other nondigital technologies also shape our culture. Doorknobs offer one nondigital example. Their shape and placement are culturally dependent (some cultures favor doorknobs in the center of doors, or prefer handles over knobs) to the point that when we encounter doors, we reach out to hold them in particular ways.[10] When we were small children, we had to think about how to move our bodies physically so as to appropriate those tools, but as adults we usually don't have to think about it. Yet the placement of doorknobs is important: they can be placed to be exclusive of people with disabilities, for instance.

In addition, it is important to note how technologies and cultures shape Christianity. Campbell and Garner use a historical description of the Protestant Reformation to discuss this interconnection.[11] The printing press was one key technology that facilitated the Reformation, since the printing press enabled larger volumes of books—especially the Bible—to be printed. The ease of printing in turn made it more possible for laypeople to have access to books, and to read the Bible themselves. Martin Luther and other reformers emphasized laypeople reading the Bible as one way to critique Catholic readings of scripture.

Yet not only did the printing press enable people to read the Bible on their own, it also facilitated particular kinds of Protestant Christian cultures to flourish. For example, "Printing allowed bureaucracies to develop through the social and institutional standardization brought about by using text";[12] thus, the printing press enabled a denominational structure that presumed ready access to scriptures as well as printed tracts and sermons. One example might be Methodism's bands and societies, the formation of which relied on the written rules that transferred quickly and easily via mass-printed rulebooks and guides.

While the Protestant Reformation and its various denominational forms were indubitably shaped by the printing press, Catholics can similarly recognize the ways in which their own ability to be Catholic was shaped and formed by the printing press. It is difficult to imagine Catholic life in the contemporary period without attention to Ignatius's *Spiritual Exercises*, which rises to prominence in part because of the printing press, or to the prayer cards and other printed memorabilia that constituted many pious Catholic homes in the nineteenth century.[13]

In a more contemporary vein, it is difficult to imagine some versions of Catholicism without also recognizing that Catholic Answers (Catholicanswers.com), Patheos, and vatican.va comprise part of Catholic culture. For example, in the US American context, Catholic Answers is a digital locality that has also fueled debate about democracy, voting, and Catholic life—to an extent that goes far beyond the simple webpages of Catholic Answers itself. Catholic Answers devised the term "the five non-negotiables,"[14] an idea that has shaped American Catholic ideas about voting since 2004. This voting guide, it should be said, does not have a stamp of approval from a bishops' conference or other hierarchical body. Indeed, the US Catholic bishops' own voting guide, Faithful Citizenship, offers counterpoints to Catholic Answers.[15] Still, Catholic Answers is likely more well known, identified as "Catholic," and used than the bishops' own site.

Additional aspects of digital localities that impact Catholic life include "mashability" of digital content. That is, people can take lots of different media content (video, music, texts), and break those down to create new media content. Digital localities also enable constant and instantaneous access to communication; indeed, such access is often expected, similar to the ways we expect doorknobs simply to be present. To use media psychologist Sherry Turkle's term, we are "always on"[16] and always needing the Internet in order to do everything from simply tool-based tasks like getting an address or phone number to commenting on a friend's latest blog post.

Communities

One final and important characteristic of digital localities is that people encounter them as *communities*. Sometimes theologians have complained that social media does not offer opportunity for "real" community (which usually seems to mean embodied community). Craig Detwiler, author of *iGods*, suggests, for example: "All that time spent online is a step away from human contact."[17] One of the concerns is that the people one meets online are people we don't necessarily know in "real" life. People can and do create fake online personas.[18] Moreover, even if we are encountering real people, we can ignore these online people at will. Too, we can use our online "friendships" to ignore the real and pressing needs of the flesh-and-blood offline people who live with us.

All that said, digital localities are not usually abstract faceless communities of people that will never meet. Rather, social media research suggests that most of the people we engage with online are also offline friends. Indeed, our participation in digital localities often serves to shore up our offline friendships.[19] Many of us do also "friend" people online whom we have never met "in real life," yet there is a strong likelihood that we will eventually meet many of our digital friends "in real life."[20] Thus, in the past, we might have made a strong distinction between online and offline relationships, but that kind of distinction is less and less people's experience.

One further aspect of digital communities is that "the individual rather than institutions is now the central node or media hub within networked communication."[21] That means that communities in which we participate are communities that we choose, communities that represent our own personal interests. We are able to be more selective of our relationships and our communities, which, as I suggest below, generates particular moral concerns in both positive and negative ways. It is to those ethical considerations that I now turn.

Ethical Considerations in Digital Localities

In his 2013 World Communications Day message, Pope Francis offered a moral vision for our digital lives:

> It is not enough to be passersby on the digital highways, simply "connected"; connections need to grow into true encounters. We cannot live apart, closed in on ourselves. We need to love and to be loved. We need tenderness . . . The world of media also has to be concerned with humanity, it too is called to show tenderness. The digital world can be an environment rich in humanity; a network not of wires but of people.[22]

In his message, Pope Francis is clearly concerned with ensuring that we consistently recognize each other as human beings, regardless of where we meet. His vision suggests Catholics are called to be people who are engaged with others in ways that enable us to love more. We need to see the people who are part of the technology, rather than merely seeing the smartphone or the computer screen. This is a statement that gets to the heart of our Catholic faith. We are a people who believe that Jesus is the God-made-human whom we encounter in the bread and wine we use at the Eucharistic celebration; we who become Christ's body offer many opportunities for encountering the risen Christ in our daily lives, including online.

So, how do we best form spaces that enable us to encounter each other as humans as well as God-with-us? In this section, I take the characteristics of digital localities from above and make observations about ethical considerations, especially about how to encounter each other in our humanity.

Tools for Inclusion or Exclusion?

One of the operating assumptions about tools is that they are neutral, but can be used for good or ill depending on the intent, will, and action of the user. Our tools can, indeed, bring us closer together, as in the example of the GPS app above, yet we can also use these tools to deliberately separate ourselves from others. We can become so engaged in using the tools—the computer, the smartphone—that our tools overtake our relationships.

Digital apps are common online tools people use. For Catholics, there are numerous apps that have been developed as tools for praying the rosary and the divine office, making an examination of conscience before receiving the sacrament of reconciliation, and doing the readings for daily and Sunday Masses, among other things. Usually, these tools enable users to participate more fully in some aspect of Catholic life. For example, we can use online prayer apps instead of paper copies of the daily office. Indeed, online apps facilitate use of the breviary, because they present the whole text without the user having to hunt and search for the different parts of the prayer across four volumes. Some of the apps also feature podcasts of the prayers or audio versions of the prayers, which are an aid to people who cannot see or who otherwise receive spoken words better than visual words.

So in some ways, the online app and the paper book version of the breviary are interchangeable, as they both have the words of the same prayers. Yet in other ways, the different aspects of each version might make one tool more appropriate than another, depending on circumstances. Our use of both online and offline tools (as with other kinds of tools) depends in part on our right use of practical wisdom. When we pray together, choosing the kind of prayer tool that most benefits our neighbors would seem to be the best moral choice. It is also possible to use either the online prayer app or the paper breviary as isolating tools that we use only for ourselves, so that we fail to encounter others.

*Care or Efficiency as Underlying Values
in the Use of Communication Tools?*

There are additional ethical concerns that arise when we consider the specific nature of tools for communication.

As one simple example, consider the prevalence of texting, which many now prefer over telephoning in order to communicate.[23] Those who prefer texting suggest that speaking on the phone is perceived as putting too much pressure on others to take time to speak with a voice and to have an extended conversation. Texting can be done in quick bursts, at times that are most convenient. Indeed, a person can ignore some texts and answer others in ways that might appear rude in phone conversations. Thus, texting seems to be a way of demonstrating that we care about other people's time and conversational preferences and, hence, that we care about our neighbors. Texting also enables good communication with those who are deaf; indeed, texting as a medium arose out of a desire to create more and better means of communication with the hard of hearing. Texting thus seems like a good activity, a way of being concerned about others' welfare, and even a way of being inclusive of others.

It would *seem* that, as with general technological tools, our chief ethical consideration in using our communication tools is right use of practical wisdom. We need to have care about when, where, how, and with whom we choose to use our technological tools. Perhaps Great Grandma needs a telephone call because she does not text, while a good friend who is busy with small kids and a full-time job would most appreciate texting.

Yet there are other ethical considerations for our communication tools, which actually show the insufficiency of seeing our technologies as communication tools. That is, communication is not simply a matter of conveying a message. Marshall McLuhan is credited with the common phrase, "The medium is the message,"[24] which means that the message we want to offer to others operates in tandem with the medium in which we choose to convey that message. Medium and message inform and shape the kind of information we receive and perceive.

When we use our communication tools, we are not simply picking up and putting down our tools; we are shaping a worldview. In the above example, I suggest that texting shapes even our very sense of time. Most of us wouldn't notice, in our daily use of our communications tools, how differences in texting and telephoning privilege the particular timeliness of contemporary life. A desire to respect others' time via texting may presume "time is money." Respect for others' time in this particular digital way supports a particular view of global capitalism that rewards efficiency.[25]

Such an understanding takes us further into critique of the medium. Christians are concerned with who and what gets left out when efficiency is our primary virtue. Saint Pope John Paul II described efficiency as one of the key aspects of a culture of death:

In reality, what might seem logical and humane, when looked at more closely is seen to be senseless and inhumane. Here we are faced with one of the more alarming symptoms of the "culture of death," advancing above all in prosperous societies, marked by an attitude of excessive preoccupation with efficiency and which sees the growing number of elderly and disabled people as intolerable and too burdensome.[26]

Our penchant for texting may in fact mean that we leave out some people with disabilities, people who live in cultures that have very different concepts of time, and people who have little or no access (or do not wish to have access) to these same kinds of digital localities. We may thereby be demonstrating little regard for human encounters with our neighbors.

Technologies as communication tools thus present complex ethical concerns. On the one hand, communications tools can be used for good or ill. On the other hand, we ought to be very aware of the limits of seeing our technologies as tools.

Transcendence of Geographical Spaces and Its Ethical Impact

Considering texting and time shows how quickly the idea of "technology as tool" bleeds into "technology as culture," to the point that it is difficult to distinguish the two. Our technological cultures shape and form many other quotidian aspects of life. In the first section, I mentioned that digital culture involves instantaneous access to communication and being always "on." Those aspects of digital culture raise additional concerns about technology and time such as that our technologies create a space where we always seem to be at others' beck and call. This is especially an ethical concern for workers who are required to be constantly connected to their jobs and have little or no effective vacation and Sabbath time.[27]

Perhaps even more crucial to consider is the way digital localities interplay with geographical spaces. Both a blessing and difficulty of online engagement is that we lose a sense of geographic place. For example, I have been part of a small Christian community online;[28] this small group featured members based in Nairobi, and other, smaller towns in Kenya, as well as from other countries like Tanzania (and the United States). In that community, we read the week's lectionary together and each offered online commentary for each other. I, for one, encountered readings of scripture that I could not likely have encountered in my own geographical location.

Thus online life can mean that we can relate to people we might otherwise never have known, and offer help, even from far-flung places. There are websites devoted to offering microloans and grants to people in need of funding. The church, of course, has been both supportive and at the forefront of online giving and attempts to help people from around the world encounter each other.[29]

The globality of the Internet makes geography disappear in troubling ways, too. It matters little online whether one is in a desert climate, or living near floodwaters, or watching the ice caps disappear in Greenland; our geography online is defined by pixels and computer codes. This disconnection to physical geography is frequently named as one of the benefits of online life. Mountains and untraversable deserts do not constrain online life. Yet we also do not see that our very use of electricity to charge our online devices drives some climate change that contributes to disappearing ice caps. We do not see that our collective use of technological devices contributes to drought.

Our social media habits of sharing stories usually involves sharing globally interesting stories about global cities, rather than stories from one's local town or county. That means that social media users can miss out on important local ways of encountering their neighbors.[30] Additionally, website and app algorithms can operate "filter bubbles" according to users' preferences, which means our Google searches and other online interactions are tailored to our own ideals and patterns of thought. This means that we lose sight of our neighbors who have different preferences than us. Surely this is a problem for Christians who are asked to treat all as neighbors.[31]

The constraints of digital localities also mean some are left behind. We do not see the people who do not have access to online space.[32] And, while people who are poor are also often connected online—that is the nature of our global capitalist world—we do not necessarily see that poverty. We fail to encounter others' humanity. Christians making use of digital localities need to be consistently attuned to the fact that their digital localities do not tell the whole story.

Online Communities as Enclaves

As I noted above, digital localities are often communities for the people who participate. I have myself observed Catholics saying that a particular Facebook community or digital prayer platform helps sustain faith life.

Yet Catholics are also guilty of failing to sustain these online communities. Vatican public relations officials have called out Catholic bloggers for generating a "cesspool of hatred, venom and vitriol, all in the name of defending the faith"[33] in their online debates. This is especially important for ethicists, since the vitriol usually appears in relation to intense moral questions about life and death, politics, and other common ethical concerns.

Blogger Elizabeth Scalia suggests that there are online Catholic "collectives" of people who only see themselves and a small group of followers as correctly following and reporting the faith. In Scalia's view, these enclaves are troubling because they actually prevent the kind of community that could be enriching for both the faith and the world in general. She writes, "The cyber-world is teeming with intellectual and spiritual dead ends, and that is what makes a Catholic presence within it so imperative. Those collectives will over time prove themselves a bigger challenge to online Catholic evangelization than the doubters and secularly inclined ever could be."[34]

One of the reasons blogging vitriol exists is surely due to the questions of time and space that I mentioned. Geographical and temporal blurring means that digital localities are very flexible. People can very easily move in and out of online communities. This kind of flexibility is already an aspect of local offline parish life: people do not pay attention to geographical parish boundaries, and very easily move from parish to parish where there are many options for Catholic Masses. Yet this flexibility is heightened in online communities, to the point that perhaps many avoid, or give up on, spending the time it takes to create and sustain communities—especially in the midst of heated arguments. I don't think that sustaining online communities is necessarily more difficult than sustaining offline communities, but I do think that the problems of space and time I've mentioned above take on particular characteristics in our digital localities.

In conclusion, in a world where people simply "are" connected online, we Catholics would do well to keep fostering better localities online. We need to pay attention to the several ethical concerns our digital localities raise, and most especially make each other aware of the people and places that we cannot or do not see when we are online.

Notes

1. See Brian Brock, *Christian Ethics in a Technological Age* (Grand Rapids, MI: Eerdmans, 2010); Brad Kallenberg, *God and Gadgets: Following Jesus in a Technological Age* (Eugene, OR: Wipf and Stock, 2011). I raise similar concerns in *Aquinas on the Web? Doing Theology in an Internet Age* (New York: Bloomsbury, 2012). Yet I have found that to omit "tool" from consideration of how technology works in our lives has the disadvantage of cutting out a primary way that people describe themselves as engaging with technologies, so I do include it here.

2. *Miranda prorsus*, no. 24. I am grateful to the work of former University of Dayton graduate student Katherine Schmidt, who examined some of the several church documents related to technology and the contemporary age in her dissertation. See especially chapter 2 of her unpublished dissertation, "Virtual Communion: Theology of the Internet and the Catholic Imagination" (PhD diss., University of Dayton, 2016).

3. *Miranda prorsus*, no. 41.

4. Pope Benedict XVI, "Message of His Holiness Pope Benedict XVI for the 47th World Communications Day," May 12, 2013, http://w2.vatican.va/content/benedict-xvi/en/messages/communications/documents/hf_ben-xvi_mes_20130124_47th-world-communications-day.html.

5. See, additionally, Pope Francis a year later, "Message of Pope Francis for the 48th World Communications Day," http://w2.vatican.va/content/francesco/en/messages/communications/documents/papa-francesco_20140124_messaggio-comunicazioni-sociali.html.

6. Heidi A. Campbell and Stephen Garner, *Networked Theology: Negotiating Faith in Digital Culture* (Grand Rapids, MI: Baker, 2016), 23. Emphasis theirs.

7. Ibid.

8. The papal Twitter feed is a prime example, since it involves tweets related to the pope's homilies, addresses, speeches, or simply messages the pope wishes to convey about Christian life. Yet it is a one-sided message; the pope does not cultivate the broader community

of Christians who read, retweet, and comment on his tweets. Those Twitter followers frequently engage in dialogue and response to the pope's tweets, not only in online conversation but in offline engagement. A person reading the pope's tweets might be inspired to head to a soup kitchen, or to turn off their air conditioning, or other practical offline activities.

9. Pope Benedict, "Message of His Holiness Pope Benedict XVI for the 47th World Communications Day."

10. I am grateful to Brad Kallenberg for providing this particular reference, in a face-to-face conversation about engineering ethics.

11. See especially Campbell and Garner, *Networked Theology,* 26–29.

12. Ibid., 28.

13. Robert Orsi deftly describes similar kinds of Catholic artifacts in *Between Heaven and Earth: The Religious Worlds People Make and the Scholars Who Study Them* (Princeton, NJ: Princeton University Press, 2005).

14. The non-negotiables are seen as pro-life issues; the idea is that if candidates supported these non-negotiables, Catholics could not vote for them. The non-negotiables are: abortion, embryonic stem cell research, cloning, same-sex marriage, and euthanasia.

15. See the most recent version here: https://www.catholic.com/audio/hm/72. The US bishops' guide is here: http://www.usccb.org/issues-and-action/faithful-citizenship/.

16. Campbell and Garner, *Networked Theology,* 52–55. See also Sherry Turkle, *Alone Together: Why We Expect More from Technology and Less from Each Other* (New York: Basic Books, 2012).

17. Craig Detweiler, *iGods: How Technology Shapes Our Spiritual and Social Lives* (Grand Rapids, MI: Brazos Press, 2013), 15.

18. One of the most well known is Manti Te'o's made-up girlfriend. See http://www.vanityfair.com/culture/2013/06/manti-teo-girlfriend-nfl-draft.

19. Pew Research Forum data, cited in "Is Technology Making People Less Sociable?," *Wall Street Journal,* May 10, 2015, https://www.wsj.com/articles/is-technology-making-people-less-sociable-1431093491.

20. Pew Research Forum, "Social Media and Friendships," August 6, 2015, http://www.pewinternet.org/2015/08/06/chapter-4-social-media-and-friendships/.

21. Campbell and Garner, *Networked Theology,* 56.

22. Message of Pope Francis for the 48th World Communications Day, http://w2.vatican.va/content/francesco/en/messages/communications/documents/papa-francesco_20140124_messaggio-comunicazioni-sociali.html.

23. Neil Howe, "Why Millennials Are Texting More and Talking Less," *Forbes,* July 15, 2015, https://www.forbes.com/sites/neilhowe/2015/07/15/why-millennials-are-texting-more-and-talking-less/#751256e05975.

24. Marshall McLuhan, *Understanding the Media: The Extensions of Man* (Berkeley, CA: Gingko Press, 2013).

25. See Neil Postman's incisive book *Technopoly: The Surrender of Culture to Technology* (New York: Vintage Books, 1993).

26. *Evangelium vitae,* no. 64.

27. Leslie A. Perlow, *Sleeping with Your Smartphone: How to Break to the 24/7 Habit and Change the Way You Work* (Boston: Harvard Business School Publications, 2012).

28. See http://www.smallchristiancommunities.org/.

29. See https://www.kiva.org and Catholic Relief Services at https://www.crs.org.

30. Michael Tiboris, "The Two Cities: Inequality in Global Cities," *Chicago Council on Global Affairs*, June 14, 2016, https://www.thechicagocouncil.org/blog/global-insight/inequality-global-cities-chicago-forum.

31. Eli Pariser, *The Filter Bubble: How the New Personalized Web Is Changing What We Read and How We Think* (New York: Penguin, 2012).

32. Adam Taylor, "47 Percent of the World's Population Now Use the Internet, Study Says," *Washington Post*, November 22, 2016, https://www.washingtonpost.com/news/worldviews/wp/2016/11/22/47-percent-of-the-worlds-population-now-use-the-internet-users-study-says/?utm_term=.132a11ea418a.

33. Catholic News Service, "Vatican PR Aide Warns Catholic Blogs Create 'Cesspool of Hatred,'" reported in Cruxnow.com, https://cruxnow.com/cns/2016/05/17/vatican-pr-aide-warns-catholic-blogs-create-cesspool-of-hatred/.

34. Elizabeth Scalia, "Catholics Online: Cogs in a Divine Whirligig," *Institute for Church Life* (Winter 2012), http://liturgy.nd.edu/assets/96847/scalia_catholicsonline_winter2012.pdf.

SHEPHERDING THE LOST (AND FOUND) SHEEP IN A SECULARIZED CONTEXT

Struggles, Challenges, and Opportunities for Working with(in) Civil Society's Catholic Organizations

Ellen Van Stichel

Teaching and studying theology means living on a frontier, one in which the Gospel meets the needs of the people to whom it should be proclaimed in an understandable and meaningful way [. . .] We must guard ourselves against a theology that is exhausted in the academic dispute or watching humanity from a glass castle.

—Pope Francis

I Have a Dream . . .

- of an inclusive, participatory society and world where every person's dignity is respected and his/her invaluable contribution to the good of us all is recognized;
- of a theology in general or a theological ethics in particular that supports and sustains such societies and thus is relevant for the public sphere;
- of an academic theology that invests in and is based on the reciprocal relationship between reflection and experience and thus validates the efforts and undertakings at the service of civil society done by theological ethicists as part of their core business;
- of a church that cherishes and fosters the dynamic between the universal and the local church (beyond structures, but including grassroots movements embodying its inclusive ideal) so that Catholic social teaching (CST) and Catholic social thought can become really cross-fertilizing and equal dialogue partners;
- of theological ethicists who help the church in this process and thus are the intermediaries between these various levels of reflection and praxis;

- of a public theology that engages with the secular world in an appropriate language, is also ecclesial, enhances human flourishing and is utopian and keeps the hope alive for a better world.[1]

It is this dream that drives and motivates me, that makes me get out of bed every morning. It is this dream that is challenged by my very particular context: being a theological ethicist in a secularized Belgium that influences Catholic movements and thus also theologians involved in them.

Ninety-Nine Lost Sheep:
Analysis of the Belgian Context

In a striking reversal of Jesus's parable on the lost sheep (Luke 15:6), we could say that with regard to religious life in general and Catholic life in particular in Belgium, rather it is the case that one sheep was saved, while ninety-nine others were lost.[2] Inquiries show that about 5 percent of Belgium's population can be called "practicing Catholics," implying that those people attend Mass "regularly."[3] However, people still participate in sacraments like weddings (26.2 percent) and baptisms (57.6 percent),[4] and 40 to 50 percent identify him/herself as Catholic.[5]

Hence, the individual and institutional aspects of the secularization are self-evident. At the individual level, there is a waning interest in the Catholic faith and tradition, implying a diminishing public support for the church. This was not in the least influenced by the recent pedophilia crises, although the pontificate of Pope Francis was able to change the tide slightly with a renewed openness of Belgians for the church so long as it proves itself to be authentic. Institutionally, the role of the church has changed from one of the most powerful players in society half a century ago to a very small minority with a hardly hearable public voice.[6] It goes without saying that Catholic organizations within civil society—once very strong and powerful in Belgium—are put under a lot of pressure because of these developments. And there is more.

The analysis of some culture sketches the bigger picture and helps us to grasp the emergence of a new social paradigm, which seems to replace the former, religiously rooted worldview. In his analysis, the Belgian psychoanalyst Paul Verhaeghe wonders what is today's society's "grand narrative," which shapes our identity?[7] He summarizes the current dominant narrative in three elements. First, "scientism": in the aftermath of the Enlightenment, rationality became the criterion, and under the influence of the success of the natural sciences, the belief was fostered that everything can and should be controlled accordingly. Research (evidently considered value-neutral) should focus on factual measurements that are objectively processed in figures in order to come to universal standards, dissociated from any context. Everything is manageable and predictable, and can be fixed in protocols and procedures, which always work and lead to general agreed knowledge. Second, the ideology that the individual is responsible for his/her own success: "you have to make *yourself*, and you have to make *it*." It is our own responsibility, and if we are not succeeding, we fail and feel guilty. And because we all have to make it, society consists merely of competitors. The criterion of success is economic prosperity, which brings us to the third element, which Verhaeghe calls "the neoliberal ideology." Until recently, the spheres of politics, religion, culture, and economy all balanced each other out, because they stood on equal footing. At the end of the last century, however, the economy became the superpower, imposing its "meritocratic model," in which in all (aspects of) our lives, the worth of individuals is measured by their productivity, a quality that can be measured in figures and data, thereby resulting in competition among each other for success.

We notice the symptoms of this dominant narrative at different levels and in different spheres. The fact that this quality is measurable through figures has not only influenced the academy (with its focus on "output" and even the proposal to increase tuition for university degrees that have no connection with businesses whatsoever), but also, for instance, the health care system (which has clearly described protocols of how many minutes a nurse can spend with a patient, how many days a patient can stay in the hospital for this or that treatment, etc.). This paradigm is also reflected in policy making, as for instance our very tolerant and "progressive" bioethical legislation shows: after twenty-five years of legalized abortion and fifteen years of legalized euthanasia, the public opinion is in general convinced that these laws are "normal," as if we follow tendencies in the rest of the (Western) world, while the truth is that Belgium has some of the most exceptional and pioneering foregoing legislation on these beginning- and end-of-life issues. The symptom that is most interesting for the scope of this essay, relating it back to the question on religion and theology in the public sphere, is the effect of this dominant narrative on an individual's identity. Absorbed by this economic model, individuals shift from being citizens to being customers, constantly asking themselves and others, "What's in it for me?" Such individualism evidently threatens a sense of community and the commitment to solidarity. If still willing to commit oneself, one often chooses loose and temporary commitments—always under scrutiny, with self-development as the main criterion.

What If the Laboratory of the Scientist Is Imploding?

These two factors, namely, secularization and the dominant neoliberal narrative, challenge the church, Catholic organizations, and thus also theology.

Worldwide, Belgium is known for its very well-developed Catholic organizations in civil society. *Rerum novarum* had hardly begun to be promulgated when the Catholic Labor Organization was founded; it not only focused on acknowledgment of the worker's rights (including the establishment of a Catholic health insurance system) but also on their formation (in law, politics, and even culture). Inspired by the social teachings of the church, figures like the Dominican George Rutten (1875–1952) and Joseph Cardinal Cardijn (1882–1967) further expanded the scope of Catholic action, including not only the Catholic Labor Union but also youth movement and women's movements, and farmers' and employers' organizations. In the 1960s, motivated by the urgent call of the Second Vatican Council and *Populorum progressio*, Catholic nongovernmental organizations (NGOs) fighting global and local poverty and exclusion originated. Traditionally, schools and hospitals had also been Catholic and were part of this civil society. These organizations' alliance to the church varied, but all of them had priests as chaplains and members of their board. Hence, the link with the official church was structured and guaranteed. Moreover, politically the Christian-Democrat Party was very influential and dominant as it was part of all governments for more than five decades between 1947 and 1999 (with the exception of 1954–58). At the level of the individual, one's life was ordered according to adherence to the Catholic faith with the Catholic organizations providing support with regard to education, health care, leisure time, social rank, sports, culture, etc. This also applied to social-democrats, liberal-democrats, and, to a smaller extent, Flemish Nationalists, who had their own political party as well as labor unions, youth movements, and health insurance. Since the majority of the population was Catholic, however, it goes without saying that the Catholic structures and institutions were immensely strong and well developed.[8]

Consequently, membership in these organizations used to be self-evident and automatic: if you were Catholic, you would participate in the Catholic organizations at the different levels and domains of your life. Nowadays, however, growing flexibility, on the one hand, and the reduced Catholic faith, on the other, imply that these organizations are insecure about the number of members and have to fight for their "market share" in civil society. Significant in this regard is the recent trend in which these organizations fail to speak about "members," but rather address their audiences as "customers." Moreover, since our population is less and less Catholic, the same is true also among their members and staff.

As a consequence, within these organizations the alliance to the church or Catholic faith is externally and internally openly questioned. Many of them struggle with what we could call an "identity crisis": Are we still Catholic? Do we still want to be Catholic? If so, what does this mean? In his analysis, theologian Lieven Boeve distinguishes so-called survival strategies and protection strategies. While the former focuses on the continuity between Catholic faith and context (looking for connections between these organizations and culture), the latter takes the discontinuity as its starting point and aims at "shielding the Catholic identity from threats from the context."[9] Taking this to its extreme, an organization can either choose to return to (mostly a strict interpretation of the) Catholic tradition and teachings (the so-called reconfessionalization, a form of organizing of, by, and for Catholics), or it can choose to embody the secularization institutionally in becoming "neutral" (often with the consequence of silencing any religious discourse) or "pluralistic" (open to all religions without a clear stance on itself).

Currently, most Catholic organizations have found themselves on a middle ground in which the only option is to translate the Catholic identity and tradition into secular terms. A significant "sign of the times" is the fact that in the last decade a lot of those organizations explicitly have chosen to change their name so as to get rid of the reference to the "C" in Catholic. Then the next question becomes, do we want to get rid of any reference to the Christian tradition? For indeed, in Belgium we see the very peculiar phenomenon of distinguishing between Catholic and Christian, mostly in order to distance ourselves from the official church that has lost credibility and relevance. As many individuals would indicate, "I'm a Christian, but not a Catholic," organizations are faced with the same question. When changing names and logos, the question then becomes how are our traditions referred to in our mission statement: Refer to "roots"? Or to "Christian identity"? Or "Christian values"?[10] Or rather leave out also the reference to "Christian," in order to not give the impression of being too close to the church—which might scare potential members/customers? For those who want to keep a reference to their Catholic tradition, in name or at least in inspiration, some questions arise: To what extent do we want to be Catholic? On what conditions? To what extent do we want to relate to and be identified with the church and its teachings? Or do we keep the values as our guiding principles? And if so, which values? Do we continue to have a staff member working on spirituality (not even theology)? If so, what exactly is his/her job?

These organizations are facing a double stretch. On the one hand, they are still too Catholic for the secularized audience of our society. This may lead to internal problems with their own staff members (who may want to work for these organizations, but do not want to be questioned about being part of a Catholic organization) but also in terms of recruiting members and volunteers or procuring subsidies from the government. In this position, they represent a tension between the local and universal church: these organizations are almost constantly—if not by themselves, then by outsiders—questioned on the credibility of the universal church, or issues going on within the local church (i.e., the pedophilia crisis). On the other hand, they are sometimes considered to be not Catholic enough for the church hierarchy, and many practicing Catholics feel that these organizations have "sold" their soul to society's demands and expectations.

These developments challenge not only the organizations within civil society but also the *theological ethicist* for whom this civil society is his/her laboratory where experience and reflection meet, cross-fertilize each other, inspire, and feed one another. As a theological ethicist who thrives on being relevant for society, I am faced with existential questions: Do these organizations still need me? If so, why? And how? For instance, they used to have priests as chaplains; now there are hardly any left. In the best-case scenario, they still have a staff member working on "spirituality," but even they say that they are the "last of the Mohicans." So I am left wondering: what could and/or should my role as a theological ethicist be?

At a more concrete level, the questions an ethicist is faced with by these organizations are as follows: Why should we still be Catholic? What is the point? What is the added value? And, maybe most importantly, what is the difference between a secular school or hospital and a Catholic one? And if you, as a theologian, are not able to explain this, maybe it does indeed not matter. Here I am questioned in my theological expertise. I notice that many theologians are struggling with these questions, and efforts have been made to answer these questions in relation to education and health care.[11] In general, however, I believe that these attempts are too fragmented and that we seriously have to reflect on this, together with Catholic organizations in civil society. For sometimes the water between academy and society/church seems very deep. Maybe theology and theological ethics are not occupied enough with questions and issues that matter for people on the street, let alone for those in the organizations. Probably the same goes for the local church. Ironically enough, the migration crisis of a few years ago had a positive impact on people's appreciation of the church for its immediate caring response toward the refugees. But when it comes down to explicitly taking a stance with regard to certain governmental policy measures or support for certain movements and networks that fight exclusion, the church is often silent. This being the case, I wonder whether faith-based organizations do not feel left alone by the church and theologians in their struggle for a more inclusive and participatory society. It would be all too easy to blame the organizations for the developments they are going through, without taking a look at the responsibility of the church and theologians.

Theological Expertise Engaging with Faith-Based Organizations

"The good theologians, like the good shepherds, smell of the people and of the road."[12]

Although this cultural environment is, to say the least, challenging for Catholic organizations, their struggle with their relationship with the church and Catholic faith are sincere and are to be taken seriously. At the same time, we also notice within some organizations more openness for reflection on their Catholic identity, roots, and tradition—unsurprisingly, openness that is inspired and motivated by the pontificate of Pope Francis. Broederlijk Delen (literally: Sharing Brotherly) is such an NGO in which I as a theological ethicist have been involved for several years.[13] It is the closest I come to being a shepherd who smells of the people as Pope Francis directs us to.

In 1961, Broederlijk Delen started as emergency aid, initiated by the Catholic Church in Belgium during a Lent campaign to address a very specific need, namely, the food crisis in the Congo.[14] Inspired by *Populorum progressio*, it later focused on the structural causes of poverty and inequality. To tackle these structural problems, the NGO gradually realized it had to work on three levels: the local level in the south to help them to help themselves, the local level in Flanders to raise awareness on these issues and foster global solidarity, and the political level of advocacy to change the rules of the games that create inequality and poverty.

The NGO is thus connected to the church, without being a direct clerical organization; it is "mandated" to participate in and contribute to the north–south solidarity movements from within the church. As a Catholic organization, it faces the challenges sketched above. In our secularized context, these organizations have to be bilingual in order to speak to both the secular and church-based audience. Not all of their staff is Catholic, and maybe not even religious at all, while its inspiration and roots lie in the Catholic faith. It can be critiqued from two sides, as either being too Catholic or not Catholic enough. The former is the case when applying for government subsidies: Should it not rather turn to its Catholic community for its subsidies, instead of also relying on the government? If not, how can it translate its ambitions and goals in a way that transcends religious language? The latter was certainly the case under the pontificate of Benedict XVI. His encyclical *Deus caritas est* (2005) focusing on charity as the "*opus proprium* of the church" (no. 29) raised some discussion on the identity of Broederlijk Delen as well: was its focus on structural development not in line with Catholic teachings and thus not "Catholic enough"?[15] Currently, under Pope Francis, a stronger justice discourse prevails with a focus on inclusion and participation to fight exclusion and deprivation (e.g., *Evangelii gaudium*, nos. 53ff.)—a discourse that goes back to CST's tradition of the 1960s and 1970s with the encyclical *Populorum progressio* and the Synod of Bishops' document *Justice in the World* (1971). This turn makes Broederlijk Delen again more comfortable with the (dynamic) tradition of CST, since Pope Francis brings them back to their original inspiration of a justice-based organization working for structural changes.

Nowadays the organization considers the "Christian inspiration" as the "common thread and thus informs the choices made." Starting from an integral view of the human person, spirituality is considered an important part of being human.[16] Though not always mentioned explicitly, this spirituality may be the basis of their work. Without focusing exclusively on Catholics, this spirituality makes them focus on some crucial values that can be found in the Christian tradition in general and CST in particular: "the preferential option for the poor" and "community building," as well as solidarity, inclusion, and participation.[17]

Inspired by liberation theologies' preferential option for the poor, the strategic choice to work with rural communities, with a focus on farmers, native people, women, and youth, is not coincidental; they are some of the most impoverished and suffering people in our world. In opposition to a juridical–justice approach, this theological account of justice is not blindfolded, for it takes the perspective of particular peoples, those in poverty, as its starting point. Nor is it abstract or buried in bureaucratic schemes and procedures, for it starts exactly with the concern for concrete people whom it gets to know only through proximity. It is charity inspiring justice, aiming at inclusion and participation, as its new slogan, "Until everyone is included," indicates.

Also, its methodology speaks of this focus on inclusion and participation; it is not about projects, but rather partnerships and thus relationships. Broederlijk Delen does not develop its own projects for regions in the south, but rather merely supports partner organizations that know the needs and struggles as well as the opportunities and networks of their communities. Theologically this is grounded in a relational anthropology that starts from a fundamental awareness of heteronomy and interconnectedness, aims at fostering and incarnating this relationality through dialogue and mutual commitment, and is convinced of the mutual change it will bring to both parties. The people in poverty are not "objects of help" nor merely "subjects of their own history." Rather, they are subjects of our common history that we have to write together. Hence, Broederlijk Delen's approach embodies and represents the idea of *justice in the world* when the bishops stated that "every people, as active and responsible members of human society, should be able to cooperate for the attainment of the common good on an equal footing with other peoples" (sec. 71c). So it is not just *their* self-development or common good that is at stake; it is *our* global common good we are constructing—together—in this way.

Applying CST's notion of participation in this way, to enhance inclusion and integral development, is countercultural. For applying participation not only as a goal of development but also as the process to achieve it requires the ability to live with an open end—which is exactly the opposite of the scientistic tendency sketched above. While our society looks for certainties and control mechanisms, expressed in the (ab)use of fixed procedures that are supposed to help streamline the process between ideas, action, and results, participation implies not knowing beforehand what is going to happen, what the exact end result may be. Nothing can be more against the current dominant neoliberal paradigm than this view. Participation is letting go of the false belief in manageability, control, and protocols. Applied to Broederlijk Delen, it is not about ready-made procedures established in an office in Brussels to be executed in the whole of Europe, but rather investing in partners instead of projects, in long-term relationships instead of clearcut but top-down results. It requires daring to take risks, for it is "living from what is coming"[18] and "space for the unexpected."[19] Indeed, it might happen that a partnership appears not to work and has to end. The results are not always foreseen and predictable. But is this not exactly where we believe that God's actual presence reveals Godself?

Against this background, the main challenge for theological ethics I see myself faced with is this one: The discourse of participation and inclusiveness, crucial in my theological work, relates very well to what the staff members of Broederlijk Delen want to achieve within their organization but also in society as a whole. I am challenged by how to apply this participation and inclusiveness more practically in my theological work. In other words, how do I make sure I am not just informing them about theoretical theological concepts but also making participation and inclusion into a methodological tool so that what Broederlijk Delen is doing informs my theological reflection and the development of CST in general? Both theologians and practitioners consider Catholic movements and organizations to be not only *executors* of CST but also *contributors*. As Kristin Heyer puts it, "In mutual dialogue with praxis, CST can remain fully theological and fully public, open to ongoing conversion by the suffering and resilience of those in need, rather than triumphalistic in its possession of truth or static in its formulations."[20] The idea that movements should inform CST from their "social witness," and already do so, is self-evident. The question that remains unanswered, in my opinion, is what the task of theological ethicists should be.[21] As a theological ethicist I consider it my task to support this vision and to foster this mutual dialogue between the two levels of Catholic social thought. The only question I am puzzled with is how. How can we bridge the gap between reflection and experience? How do we translate people's experiences appropriately into our theoretical discourse? And if we have already gotten this far, how do we bring it to the fore of official Catholic social teaching?

Lost in Translation?

A theological ethicist in this country seems to be faced with a twofold language barrier—a barrier that requires translation. One the one hand, secularization implies that people question the relevance and presuppositions of theological language—even within organizations that have a long tradition with Catholic faith. Talking about faith and the value of the Christian message for these contexts is a huge challenge, and it seems we need new theological language to make the translation. On the other hand, we need to find ways to translate the message and particular understanding of CST arising within faith-based organizations, such as Broederlijk Delen, to link it with academic and official CST discourse, so that these organizations can become not only executors but also contributors to CST, and thus bridge the gap between experience and reflection, as well as the gap between local and universal church.

Although taken from a very particular context and limited experience, I believe that this relates to challenges theological ethicists face around the world in similar and different contexts. How do we as ethicists, then, foster a mutually enriching dialogue between those different levels and spheres of discourse?

I am afraid I raised more questions than I gave answers. Rather than an ending point, I view this contribution as opening up the discussion among theological ethicists to see how it works in other contexts: How are our roles with grassroots movements and NGOs shaped? How do we link experience and reflection? My hope is that the theology we develop reflects and changes reality and makes a difference so that we can avoid the pitfall mentioned in *Laudato si'*:

Many professionals, opinion makers, communications media, and centers of power, being located in affluent urban areas, are far removed from the poor, with little direct contact with their problems. They live and reason from the comfortable position of a high level of development and a quality of life well beyond the reach of the majority of the world's population. This lack of physical contact . . . can lead to a numbing of conscience. (no. 49)

How do we avoid this as theological ethicists? How do we translate the sincere and authentic commitment for a more inclusive world inspiring our theological reflection into real contact and dialogue with people in poverty and in the margins, and the organizations working with them, based on the conviction that our theologies will always be lacking without their contribution?

Notes

1. See, for this definition of public theology, Duncan B. Forrester, "Working in the Quarry: A Response to the Colloquium," in *Public Theology for the 21st Century,* ed. William F. Storrar and Andrew R. Morton (Edinburgh: T&T Clark, 2004), 431–38.

2. This reversal is not new, as I heard someone using it more than fifteen years ago. Also Pope Francis used it at the beginning of his pontificate in a talk on an ecclesiastical congress in the Rome diocese in June 2013. Reference to this speech was made by Phil Lawler, *The Key to Understanding Pope Francis: The 99 Lost Sheep*, September 20, 2013, https://www.catholicculture.org/commentary/otn.cfm?id=997.

3. Nele Havermans and Marc Hooghe, *Kerkpraktijk in België: Resultaten van de zondagstelling in oktober 2009—Rapport ten behoeve van de Belgische Bisschoppenconferentie* (Leuven, Belgium: Centrum voor Politicologie, KU, 2011). Although dating back from 2009, these are the most recent research-based figures. Estimation, based on polls, is that church practice nowadays is about 3 percent.

4. For the sake of comparison: in 1967, participation in baptism and weekly church attendance was, respectively, 93.6 percent and 52 percent. See ibid.

5. Maybe, after the sexual abuse scandal of 2010, these figures are overestimated. (Take into account for instance that in 2010 only 13 percent of the population had confidence in the church as an institution. It is rather unlikely that the popularity of Pope Francis was able to change this considerably, although this has to be investigated.) For the research on church participation and confidence in the church in the aftermath of the pedophilia crisis of 2010, see Jaak Billiet, Koen Abts, and Marc Swyngedouw, *Evolutie van de kerkelijke betrokkenheid in Vlaanderen tijdens de voorbije twee decennia en het verlies van vertrouwen in de Kerk in het bijzonder tussen 2009 en 2011* (Leuven, Belgium: KU, IPSO, 2013).

6. Although the institutional church has lost power and influence, this is not to say that religion is completely disappearing in the public domain. In this regard, Lieven Boeve chooses to define this context as a "post-secular" society, which takes into account the changed way of dealing with religion as well as its pluralization. See Lieven Boeve, *Theology at the Crossroads of University, Church and Society: Dialogue, Difference and Catholic Identity* (London: Bloomsbury T&T Clark, 2016), 42.

7. Paul Verhaeghe, *Identiteit* (Amsterdam: De Bezige Bij, 2012). A similar analysis is found in the writings of another highly estimated culture critic, the psychiatrist Dirk De Wachter. In his book *Borderline Times* (Leuven, Belgium: LannooCampus, 2016), he comes to a very similar analysis, when applying the nine characteristics of borderline as described in the *Diagnostic and Statistical Manual of Mental Disorders* (the internationally accepted manual for psychiatry) in our society.

8. For an analysis of the origins of this so-called pillarization and its gradual disappearance while still being important, see Lieven Boeve, *Interrupting Tradition: An Essay on Christian Faith in a Postmodern Context* (Leuven, Belgium: Eerdmans, 2003), chap. 2.

9. Boeve, *Theology at Crossroads*, 151.

10. Besides "reconfessionalization" and "institutional secularization," Boeve mentions this focus on the Christian values as a way to bridge context and tradition, since it enables a consensus and common ground. The question is whether the specificity of Christian faith is then not sacrificed. Moreover, in practice it appears then that one easily shifts from talking about "Christian values" merely as "values" and thus losing any reference to roots.

11. See, for instance, the work of Lieven Boeve, *Theology at Crossroads*, who is also developing and implementing a fourth model of "dialogue" to "reprofile" Christian faith in dialogue with our pluralist context.

12. Pope Francis, Letter to the Theological Faculty of the Pontifical Catholic University of Argentina, March 3, 2015.

13. Since my passion for theology is connected with public theologies that focus on human flourishing, I find it self-evident that my research ties in to the work of NGOs and organizations. Hence, over the years, I have cooperated (through lectures, consultancy, etc.) with NGOs such as Broederlijk Delen (but also Caritas Europe, for instance) and with other organizations within civil society, like Beweging.net, one of the major overarching Catholic movements in Flanders. However, despite these connections I feel my experience is rather limited and I realize that colleagues in other countries are much more suited to write about the role of theological ethicists for NGOs. Hence it is with humility I am just offering some reflections here.

14. Quoted from their website, until mentioned otherwise: http://www.broederlijkdelen. be/over-ons). Since it is in Dutch, the quotations are my own translation.

15. See, in this regard, my analysis in "Movements Struggling for Justice within the Church: A Theological Response to John Coleman's Sociological Approach," *Journal of Catholic Social Thought* 10, no. 2 (2013): 281–94.

16. See the strategic document at http://www.broederlijkdelen.be/sites/default/files/ downloads/de_doelstellingen_voor_2014-2021.pdf.

17. The first two values are explicitly mentioned in relation to the Catholic tradition, while through the description of their goals and methods, the others appear. For the sake of the argument, I will merely focus on their development work, not advocacy and formation.

18. Title of the recent book of Dutch theologian Erik Borgman, *Leven van wat komt: Een katholiek uitzicht op de samenleving* (Utrecht, the Netherlands: Meinema, 2017).

19. Title of my recent Dutch book, coauthored with Katrien Ruytjens, *Ruimte voor het onverwachte* (Leuven, Belgium: LannooCampus, 2016).

20. Kristin Heyer, "The Social Witness and Theo-Political Imagination of the Movements: Creating a New Social Space as a Challenge to Catholic Social Thought," *Journal of Catholic Social Thought* 10, no. 2 (2013): 338.

21. See for instance the special issue of the *Journal of Catholic Social Thought* "Social Movements in Context" (10, no. 2 [2016]), where theologians reflect on the role of movements and their contribution to CST. Interestingly, the question on the role of theologians in general or ethicists in particular is not touched upon.

Epilogue

The Emerging Vocation of a Moral Theologian: Commonalities across Contexts

Lindsay Marcellus

The twentieth century witnessed extraordinary changes in the field of moral theology with respect to its scope, method, sources, setting, audience, and participants. Accompanying these changes have been changes in the self-understanding of the moral theologian. What does it mean to be a moral theologian or theological ethicist today?[1] So far, no consensus has yet been reached regarding the theological ethicist's role or vocation.[2] What themes are emerging? To what extent is the role or vocation of a moral theologian dependent on his or her specific context? How might one think through one's vocation as a moral theologian in light of the insights from theologians from other contexts?

At the turn of the twenty-first century, Peter Black and James Keenan traced the changes in the understanding of moral theology over the course of the twentieth century and indicated how these changes have also begun to change the self-understanding of the moral theologian.[3] In these pages, I aim to expand upon this study by focusing more explicitly on what contemporary moral theologians engaged in "contextual theologies" are writing about their roles and vocations. This essay will proceed in four parts. First, I offer a brief overview of what I mean by vocation. Second, I trace the self-understanding of the moral theologian over the course of the twentieth century, from the moral manualists to the revisionists. Third, drawing on the work of John Mary Waliggo, Laurenti Magesa, Christina A. Astorga, Vimala Chenginimattam, and Bryan Massingale as representative, I identify common elements of this vocational understanding of the moral theologian. These commonalities include the need to learn from others, the need to be deeply affected by the suffering and challenges faced by others and to allow the experiences of others to influence the ethical agenda, and an increased emphasis on action on behalf of others, particularly those who are poor, oppressed, or vulnerable.[4] Fourth, I conclude with some reflections about what such an understanding may mean practically speaking for moral theologians writing in the context of the United States.

Moral Theology as a Vocation

The authors cited in this essay frequently use the terms "role" or "vocation" in their descriptions of the moral theologian or theological ethicist. Since not all authors clarify their use of the term "vocation," it is worth spending a little time at the beginning of this essay doing so. I see three potential sources of confusion.

First, there is a danger of equating vocation simply with one's job or career choice. In the United States, we frequently speak of vocational training or schools or counseling. In his development of the Protestant doctrine of vocation, Douglas J. Schuurman begins by noting that "The most common understanding of vocation today is the secularized one where vocation refers to one's paid work."[5] Unlike a century ago, US moral theologians and theological ethicists tend to be affiliated with universities, and moral theology is pursued as an academic discipline.[6] With the shift to the university setting, there is the risk of forgetting that moral theology "exists in the service of the church."[7] To collapse the vocation of moral theologians into a description of the roles they are paid to fill does not adequately take into consideration either the "vocation" of moral theology as "the search for moral truth in an ecclesial context"[8] or developments in Catholic understanding of the universal Christian vocation.

A second potential source of confusion regarding the meaning of the word "vocation" is the tendency within the Catholic Church to identify vocations with priesthood and religious life.[9] While Catholic teaching since the Second Vatican Council has emphasized the many ways in which human beings participate in the ongoing, creative work of God, it bears remembering that this understanding represents a significant shift. In one of the most widely read and translated moral manuals of the twentieth century, Heribert Jone recognized three states of life in the church: clerical, religious, and lay. Holiness of life was considered a special obligation incumbent upon members of the clergy but not upon the laity, unless the layperson had taken vows as a religious.[10] The fourfold framework of vocations still used in parish settings (i.e., priesthood, religious life, marriage, and single life) builds on Jone's outline of the three states of life by bifurcating the third state of life (laity) according to marital status. This fourfold framework raises questions regarding whether the single life, if not freely desired, is in fact a vocation.[11]

A third potential difficulty with understanding pursuing moral theology as a vocation relates to the universal Christian vocation to holiness. After being forced to leave the field of biblical scholarship due to a controversy involving the incorporation of historical consciousness, Fritz Tillmann brought the biblical understanding of the Christian as a disciple of Christ into the field of moral theology in his 1934 work, *Die Idee der Nachfolge Christi*, and his more accessible text *Der Meister ruft* (*The Master Calls*), published in 1937. His contribution to the field of moral theology is enormous. For the purposes of this essay, I simply wish to highlight that he understood that all are called to be disciples of Christ, that Christian discipleship is founded on the sacrament of baptism, and that the call to discipleship is a call to pursue perfection. These themes would be incorporated into the teaching of the Second Vatican Council in the idea of the universal call to holiness.[12] All Christians have the same vocation to holiness, but this vocation is realized in a variety of ways.[13] Following the Second Vatican Council, understandings of vocations to the priesthood and religious life were put in the context of this more fundamental, universal Christian, or even human vocation.[14] Any vocational self-understanding of a moral theologian will also seek to identify the ways in which the Christian vocation to holiness is realized in a particular way in the life and work of moral theologians without identifying such a vocation too narrowly with the paid work that they perform.

The Self-Understanding of the Moral Theologian in the Twentieth Century: Thomas Slater to Bernard Häring

Given the changes in the Catholic understanding of vocation during the twentieth century, it is unsurprising that the term does not appear in relation to the self-understanding of the moral manualists writing before the Second Vatican Council. Consideration of the prefaces of the manuals of Thomas Slater and Heribert Jone, the authors of the first English manual and of one of the most widely read manuals of the twentieth century, respectively, shows that their intent was to offer technical assistance to fellow priests to help them prepare for parish work, and especially to hear confessions. The priests who wrote the manuals saw themselves as meeting a specific need in the church experienced primarily by other priests but also potentially by educated members of the laity who might be helped "in solving such questions as might occur in their everyday lives."[15] Yet while today we can understand the moral manualists to have been engaged in the "vocation" of moral theology understood as "the search for moral truth in an ecclesial context,"[16] they did not seem to see their role as moral theologians as integrally related to the living out of their call (as priests and religious) to pursue perfection/holiness.[17]

The deficiencies of the approach of the moral manualists of the first half of the twentieth century are well noted.[18] Indeed, moralists themselves began a self-critique of this methodology in moral theology and to search for a new way of going forward, especially following the Second World War. The result was profound changes in the understanding of moral theology itself. As Black and Keenan argue, the location of moral truth shifts significantly over the course of the twentieth century: "Whereas in the beginning of the century moral truth appears in the utterances of moral theologians, by today moral truth is found in the lives of Christians."[19]

Yet over the same period, bishops and the pope started writing more frequently on moral issues, and several features of the moral manualist period continued in these writings. Black and Keenan conclude, "Not surprisingly, just as for those centuries moral truth is identified with the utterances of the manualist, now in the twentieth century, with this emerging moral magisterium, moral truth becomes identified with papal and episcopal utterances. Furthermore, many bishops and parish priests assume again the middle-man role of espousing and explaining, this time, the papal and curial utterances on morality."[20]

Hence, it came to be that in the same year in which *Lumen gentium* was promulgated, in which contemporary scholars such as Mary Ann Donovan would locate the outline of the vocation of the theologian,[21] John C. Ford and Gerald Kelly offered a much narrower view of the role of the moral theologian. While all the faithful, including theologians, have the duty to "give the religious assent required by papal teaching," the "distinctive function of the theologian goes much beyond this acceptance of the papal teaching; as a theologian he must study the papal pronouncements and incorporate them into his teaching and his writing."[22] For Ford and Kelly then, moral theologians were to listen to and interpret the voices of the hierarchical magisterium, not "the many voices of our times" as presented in *Gaudium et spes*, no. 44.

Given the development of an increasingly moral papal magisterium during the twentieth century, it was perhaps inevitable that the self-understanding of moral theologians would be largely thought through in terms of their relationship to the magisterium. Ford and Kelly represent one way of thinking through this relationship. Despite subsequent and vehement disagreement, in many ways, these two theologians set the agenda for debates surrounding the self-understanding of moral theologians for decades to come. Perhaps most famously in the United States, Charles Curran came to a very different conclusion: the possibility of legitimate dissent.[23] In 1990, the Congregation for the Doctrine of the Faith published their *Instruction donum veritatis: On the Ecclesial Vocation of the Theologian*. A full quarter of this document is devoted to the "problem of dissent," indicating that the Vatican was also thinking through the vocation of theologians largely in terms of the relationship between theologians and the magisterium of the church's pastors, particularly surrounding the issue of dissent.[24]

Also writing in 1990, Bernard Häring saw the moral theologian as a "learner–teacher" who has been entrusted with the mission and ministry of a mediator. According to Häring, "The mission and ethos of the moral theologian (who is at the same time both learner and teacher) are those of a very alert mediator within the community of Christ's disciples—a mediator who is a member of the community of theologians, and a learner and fellow-pilgrim along with all the redeemed."[25] In keeping with the passage from *Gaudium et spes* quoted above, and far from Ford and Kelly's vision of moral theologians primarily concerned with explaining papal pronouncements, Häring viewed moral theologians as mediators of the biblical message for the contemporary context as well as the tradition. As learner–teachers, moral theologians must recognize that knowledge is not unidirectional, and that their ability to teach is dependent on their ability to learn to become "better students as disciples of Christ who are docile to the Holy Spirit, and as co-disciples in the faith community which extends even beyond the boundaries of the Roman

Catholic Church."[26] Häring goes on to say that "We cannot be genuine Catholic moral theologians if we confine our learning and teaching efforts to one stream of the Christian tradition, to one culture, or even to what the Holy Spirit has brought forth as the fruit of love, peace, and justice within Christianity."[27]

This emphasis on learning from others is a theme in contemporary, contextual theologies. Yet unlike more recent accounts of the vocation of the moral theologian from Africa, Asia, and less-privileged social locations within the United States, Häring is still explicitly concerned with the relationship of moral theologians with the magisterium, dedicating four pages to the topic. Yet his exploration of the magisterium includes the magisterium of "the little ones" as well as of the merciful and those in need of mercy. According to Häring, "Moral theologians who live in economically powerful societies as well as those who live among the poorest peoples of the third world cannot be true to their vocation and ethos unless they allow themselves to be deeply touched by these situations."[28] Furthermore, like the pope and bishops, moral theologians must be pastorally minded and ought to "give voice to 'voiceless,' marginalized people."[29] For Häring, theologians do not have a magisterium, but rather a ministry (a *diakonia*) that benefits the people of God. In short, the role of moral theologians is to speak and do the truth in love.

This section has traced how moral theologians at the beginning of the twentieth century wrote technical manuals primarily for other priests, how much of the method of the moral manuals was reappropriated by the Vatican, and, especially after *Humanae vitae*, prompted sustained reflection of the role of the moral theologian in relation to the hierarchical magisterium of the Roman Catholic Church, and yet how the role of the moral theologian was also increasingly thought through in terms of the universal Christian vocation to holiness. Häring's insistence on the necessity of learning from others, on being deeply affected by the challenging situations of others, and on both speaking and *doing* the truth in love has continued in the self-understanding of moral theologians and theological ethicists in the twenty-first century. These themes are the focus of the following section.

Common Themes in the Contemporary Self-Understanding of Moral Theologians Engaged in Contextual Theology

The Need to Learn from Others

As we have seen, in the work of the moral manualists in the first several decades of the twentieth century, knowledge was unidirectional. As the methodology employed in moral theology shifted dramatically, the pope began to fill this role of definitive moral authority. The Second Vatican Council called both pastors and theologians "to listen to and distinguish the many voices of our times and to interpret them in the light of God's word" (*Gaudium et spes*, no. 44) but did not specify what the relationship between the pastors and the theologians engaged in this task would look like concretely. Unsurprisingly, tensions arose between pastors and theologians, and attempts to understand the role of the moral theologian vis-à-vis his (and later his or her) relationship with the magisterium of the church marked the self-understanding of many moral theologians for much of the rest of the twentieth century. As a result, there was the risk of restricting "the many voices of our time" to which theologians were called to listen to the voices of the magisterium (often but certainly not always understood in terms of the magisterium of the pastors of the church) or to the voice of one's own conscience.

Today, moral theologians and theological ethicists emphasize the need to listen to a much wider variety of voices. Rather than imparters of knowledge of moral truth, contemporary moral theologians have affirmed Häring's concept of theologians who are mediators and codisciples in a wider faith community. For example, in the United States, Margaret R. Pfeil writes, "Called in baptism to a life of discipleship as a member of the People of God, the theologian responds in a particular way by offering herself or himself as a conduit."[30] In the same volume, Christopher P. Vogt emphasizes the need for the theologian to be a member of a wider faith community as a theologian by drawing attention to the lack of practices which promote sustained interaction with the church.[31]

Liberation theologies from South America have insisted, among other things, upon listening to the voices of the poor. In the United States, attempts to articulate theologies that listened to the experiences of women and black people began in the 1960s.[32] Today, more moral theologians are writing from non-Western contexts, and thanks to collaborative and networking efforts, more of their work is accessible to theologians working in Western contexts.[33] Along with these questions about doing contextual theology come questions about how one understands oneself as a moral theologian. Moral theologians around the world stress the need to listen to others, especially those who are vulnerable.

Writing from Uganda, John Mary Waliggo argues that "moral and ethical experts need a New Pentecost to attentively listen to the poor and the vulnerable."[34] He explicitly attempts to write "from the perspective of the majority poor and vulnerable peoples of Africa whose cries against the negative aspects and consequences of globalization must be heard by the theologians of the world."[35] In Tanzania, Laurenti Magesa sees theologians as needing to become "better voices for the voiceless and better representatives of the 'wretched of the earth.'"[36]

Vimala Chenginimattam, the first woman Catholic moral theologian in India, asserts that woman theological ethicists must prioritize the problems of women "who are voiceless, helpless, and victimized due to poverty, powerlessness and pollution."[37] Quoting Lúcás Chan, Chenginimattam also emphasizes that in order to do Catholic theological ethics in Asian contexts, theologians need to listen to all Asian women, and not just Asian women trained in theology or who are Christians. In a context where moral issues concerning women and the poor are relegated to the back burner as "women's issues," listening to women and the poor and prioritizing the problems they experience will help women theological ethicists relocate these moral issues as "human problems."

Christina A. Astorga, who is from the Philippines and currently teaches in the United States, challenges her readers to listen to the "triple cries" of the poor, women, and the earth that are caused by the connection between the domination of women and the domination of the earth.[38] In the United States, Bryan Massingale offers the understanding of the theologian as a fellow disciple who is "a thinker for the church" and whose tasks include listening "to the stories of the contemporary community and the world in which we live," and putting these stories "into dialogue with the larger tradition of the faith witnesses who have preceded us."[39]

Being Deeply Affected

A second element of Häring's self-understanding of the moral theologian that has been affirmed by theologians writing from different contexts is his insight that a moral theologian must be deeply affected by the challenging situations of others. Immediately after signaling the need for a New Pentecost so that moral and ethical experts can listen attentively to poor and vulnerable persons, Waliggo argues that such experts need "to feel and form unity with the poor and the victims in what is happening in their lives."[40] He asks if moral theologians "can develop a *holy anger* in denouncing this humiliation and ill treatment of God's poor people."[41] Being deeply affected in this way is a necessary prerequisite for true solidarity. Magesa laments that so far African theologians have not "integrated themselves enough into the lives of the people."[42] In his caution against theologians becoming too "academic," we see an affirmation of the need to be deeply affected by the challenges affecting others.

Chenginimattam proposes specific areas in which women theological ethicists need to make contributions. For example, health care is one area that requires much more theologizing from the experience and vision of women theological ethicists precisely because such women ought to be affected by the impact that abortion has on women, and the problems that pregnant women face in trying to be healthy mothers and raise their children. Other areas of concern include marriage and family, gender justice, the social security system, education, and the commercialization of women. Being deeply affected by the challenges experienced by women in India will bear fruit in the sense of a revised ethical agenda that more accurately reflects the truly critical issues of the time.

Massingale challenges theological ethicists, especially white theological ethicists in the United States, to be deeply affected by the racism with which the church and Catholic theological ethics have been complicit in the "systematic erasure" of the black- and dark-skinned body in Catholic theological ethics.[43] In proposing a way forward, Massingale is wary of offering concrete proposals that could "lead Catholic ethicists into an intellectual 'promised land'" at the expense of bypassing the "'gut' level" and "visceral" engagement of racism.[44] Instead, he offers the practice of lament, which "engages a level of human consciousness deeper than logical reason."[45]

Citing Massingale's understanding that "Lamentation is a cry of utter anguish and passionate protest at the state of the world and its brokenness," Astorga also calls for lament as a response to the triple cries of the poor, women, and the earth.[46] The cry of the poor must deeply affect us. Astorga writes, "The cry of the poor must be our cry. For only then can the numbness of our indifference be pierced and the callousness of our insensitivity be broken."[47] Lament also provokes a response of compassion, which "is entering into the pain of another and making it as one's own, that one may act together with the other to alleviate and transform the pain."[48]

In the writing of these five theologians, we find the expectation that moral theologians or theological ethicists will not only listen to others, particularly those who are considered "other" within their society, but also that they will be personally affected by this listening. They offer examples of how moral theologians in diverse contexts might draw upon their "access to Christian narratives and practices that provide pathways to the *conversion* of the *imagination*, the *emotions*, and the *moral dispositions*."[49] Moral theologians cannot be entirely impervious to the very real struggles experienced by members of the people of God. Yet moral theologians or theological ethicists are also unlikely to share fully in those struggles, which raises questions about what listening to others and being deeply affected by others' struggles means concretely. Writing in different contexts, both Astorga and Massingale offer lament as one appropriate response for theologians who theologize from relatively privileged social locations.

Speaking and Doing the Truth in Love

Häring titles the third section of his reflection on the role of the Catholic moral theologian "Speaking and Doing the Truth in Love." In this section, he argues that moral theologians ought to be forceful witnesses to the truth and have the "courage of the provisional" so that they can "be content to raise helpful questions instead of asserting final solutions."[50] Moral theologians have both a prophetic and healing role, and their approach must include the central concern of helping "Christians (by means of an attractive vision) to gain deep knowledge of the loftiness of their vocation in Christ, and its dynamic to bear fruit for the life of the world (Vatican II, *Optatam totius*, n. 16)."[51]

This essay has referred to many changes in moral theology over the course of the twentieth century. Yet one constant in moral theology over this same period has been its concern for moral truth. Nonetheless, there has been a significant shift in what it means to seek the truth, with greater attention coming to be paid to the place of suffering and praxis in theological ethics.[52] Although the ways in which contextual theologies have responded to this concern for suffering and the need for solidarity have differed, contemporary moral theologians place more emphasis on linking their search for the truth with other forms of action aimed at not only identifying but also at least partially instantiating that moral truth.

One common theme is that of prophecy, which is linked to liberative action. Waliggo writes that "Any theologian, particularly, the Catholic theologian, is and should be the contemporary and *vibrant prophet* who *critically, professionally,* and *objectively* analyzes society and humanity in a holistic manner and in God's name gives support to positive values and trends, while courageously denouncing negative ideologies, evils, and injustices in society and humanity."[53] Magesa sees theologians as needing to be "advocates for the sufferings of the excluded humanity" who teach by example and meet the need in African society "for prophecy in its double role of denunciation and affirmation."[54] In the face of the triple cries of poor, women, and earth, Astorga offers three responses in faith, including "prophetic lament," which "holds the power to bring those who benefit from injustice to penitence and conversion."[55]

A second theme is great attention to the practical aspects of *doing* moral theology or theological ethics. Moral theologians are agents of change.[56] Magesa identifies two challenges to African theologians: to influence church leaders and "to engage directly in the process of change themselves," particularly by participating in small Christian communities.[57] He argues that current theological education programs, which largely occur in seminaries, do not give sufficient attention to the practical side of theology. Waliggo expects African theologies to "become a social movement exerting noticeable impact on policy, giving a new direction in economic development that can eradicate poverty and resist the negative aspects of globalization."[58] Prophetic action does not end with denunciation but includes influencing policies and laws. According to Waliggo, one of the roles of the Catholic theologian is that of "effective advocacy."[59] The way forward requires unity and solidarity between theologians and ethicists. Networking is necessary in order to share information.

Astorga identifies gender resistance and ecological kinship as the other two responses in faith. Gender resistance is primarily exercised by women, who must reclaim their agency. Gender resistance through organized movements of women may be more forceful, but women can also resist effectively in their everyday life, whether through the subversive practices of a subculture or a fundamental, interior refusal of subjugation and dominance in the mind and heart, "where it is fractured by daily struggle and dissent, until it is subverted."[60] Ecological kinship requires a new relationship between human beings and the earth founded on interconnectedness (which requires a rejection of dualism). Although Astorga does not explicitly draw implications for the vocation or role of the moral theologian, some results would seem to include women speaking up in male-dominated spaces where possible (and men enabling women to do so), promoting a theologically based "alternative vision to a hegemonic belief system," and exploring what Pope Francis's vision of "ecological kinship as the rightful order of our relationships with the earth, and all of creation" would mean in practice.[61]

Chenginimattam argues that the role of women theological ethicists is to "deconstruct the age-old oppressive perceptions and to restructure moral theology in consideration with human problems—particularly women's problems who are voiceless, helpless, and victimized due to poverty, powerlessness and pollution."[62] More than the other authors cited here, Chenginimattam seems to envision the changes that women theological ethicists are called to enact in terms of setting the agenda of moral theology so that the field takes seriously "women's issues," which are, after all, human issues. She does not seem to question that teaching and writing will continue to be the primary ways in which women theological ethicists in India will impact the field of moral theology.

In his exploration of the vocation of the black Catholic theologian, Massingale notes that many black Catholic theologians consider "activism on behalf of the black Catholic community a constitutive part of our 'scholarly' work, so much so that many of us would rather describe ourselves as 'scholar-activists' (as opposed to the 'teacher-scholar' designation typical in today's colleges and universities)."[63] However, this call to action on behalf of others is not unique to black Catholic theologians. Massingale argues that "the calling of the black Catholic scholar provides an alternative model and/or needed corrective for understanding the role of the Catholic theologian in the church and society."[64] Specifically, the vocation of the black Catholic theologian challenges all Catholic theologians to rethink the ways in which they measure success. At the close of his book, Massingale relates a personal anecdote of the reaction of his grandmother when he graduated from college:

> She glowed with pride after the ceremony as I showed her my degree. She took the folder in her hands, stared at it with a little awe, and she said: "Look at that! This sure is something." Then turning to me, with love and pride and affection and wisdom, she asked: "Now who are you going to help with it? Who are you going to use it for?"[65]

Massingale offers these final two questions, "Who are you going to help with it? Who are you going to use it for?" as "*the* vocational questions, not only for black Catholic theologians, but for us all."[66]

There are several other elements worth noting about recent reflections on the self-understanding of the role and vocation of moral theologians and theological ethicists. I would like to mention two. First, theology as speaking and doing the truth in love is increasingly viewed in terms of solidarity.[67] Solidarity and networking are not limited to people and communities who are poor, oppressed, or otherwise vulnerable but also extend to relationships between theologians and ethicists.[68] Hence, the question of the vocation of the moral theologian is linked to questions about our understanding of solidarity and how to practice it. Second, the ethical agenda proposed by theological ethicists from Africa and Asia repeatedly includes the challenges of globalization, poverty, gender, and ecology.[69]

It is also worth noting that a concern for the relationship of the theological ethicist with the magisterium of the pope and bishops is not often found in these accounts. Chenginimattam, Waliggo, and Astorga do not mention potential or actual conflict between theologians and the magisterium. When concern for such a relationship is found, it is not as central a theme as it was in the self-understandings of Ford, Kelly, Curran, and Häring. For example, Magesa concludes his reflection with a reference to the contributing problem of "too much control of theological imagination and thought by church authorities, so that many African theologians can be called 'court theologians.'"[70]

Yet several theologians are concerned with the connection between the theological ethicist and his or her ecclesial community. In the United States, Vogt draws attention to the lack of practices that promote sustained interaction with the church and suggests that, as a corrective, bishops invite lay theologians to regularly preach in a parish community.[71] Massingale offers a different perspective when he notes that "black Catholic theologians find ourselves involved in the so-called 'pastoral' life of the faith community to a far greater extent than most of our white colleagues."[72] Once again, social location influences the role and vocation of moral theologians.

Conclusion: Implications for a
White Moral Theologian Writing in a US Context

This essay has explored how the self-understanding of moral theologians has changed over the past century and identified three common themes that are emerging from theologians engaged in contextual theologies. This exercise has been personal as well as academic. After seven years working for a religious nonprofit organization, I experienced my return to graduate school for theology as a response to a call. Yet such a response would not have been possible for me less than one hundred years ago, when Catholic moral theologians were not only all men but also members of the clergy.[73] Furthermore, we are likely on the verge of more changes in the makeup of theologians in the United States, as more doctoral students and junior theologians struggle to balance theologizing and parenting.[74] As a white, married woman and mother living in the United States, I wonder what it means to live out the vocation, and not just career, of a Catholic theological ethicist well into the twenty-first century. So in conclusion, I would like to suggest a few connections that I think can be made between the self-understandings of moral theologians writing in different contexts and the self-understanding of moral theologians, particularly white moral theologians, living and working in the United States.

First, it strikes me that our self-understanding as moral theologians or theological ethicists will profoundly affect our "stance," which Curran argues is the most fundamental consideration in moral theology. Our stance or horizon or perspective is "the way in which moral theology looks at the reality of the Christian moral life and structures its own understanding of moral reality."[75] Our understanding of our vocation affects our point of departure, how we understand fundamental issues in Christian ethics, the issues we choose to prioritize, the sources we consult, and the general direction of our theologizing. How we do theology will depend on how we understand ourselves as theologians.

Second, I would like to suggest that moral theologians, especially those writing from privileged social locations, need to seek explicitly to develop the virtue of humility, understood both epistemologically and as knowing one's place in the world. In theological ethics, the language of virtue has proven to have cross-cultural appeal. In 1990, Häring challenged moral theologians to have the "courage of the provisional" and to welcome the "grace of doubt." Margaret Farley argues that the grace of self-doubt "allows for epistemic humility, the basic condition for communal as well as individual moral discernment."[76] While not all self-doubt is grace, the grace of self-doubt fights the temptation for certitude by helping one keep one's mind open. In the United States, the grace of self-doubt is needed for white theologians to hear the message of the historical and ongoing complicity of the US Catholic Church, including Catholic theologians, in racism and the systematic erasure of black- and dark-skinned bodies. The courage of the provisional will help us respond to this message, recognizing that such a response will be an ongoing process.

Lisa Fullam argues that humility is an epistemological virtue that is other directed and so "calls us to look outside ourselves to appreciate the gifts of others, not to denigrate our own gifts."[77] In the case of white theological ethicists in the United States, pursuing the virtue of humility will certainly require us to be open to appreciating the gifts of our black- and dark-skinned colleagues. It will also require us to be open to appreciating the gifts that contextual theologies developing on other continents offer the church, and so challenge us to think through what such appreciation will look like in our daily lives.

Similarly, if theological ethicists are going to live out their vocation as fellow disciples who serve as mediators between the biblical message, the tradition, and the concerns and struggles of real people, then they will need to have a good understanding of their own place in the world.[78] Yet part of how we learn our place in the world is through others. White theologians in the United States cannot have an adequate understanding of our place in the world if we do not even begin to face the reality of white privilege. Similarly, listening to theologians writing in different parts of the world can help us learn our place in the world in relation to critical issues such as ecological degradation and the impact of globalization.[79] In turn, a better understanding of our place in the world will help us better respond to these ethical challenges within our own context.

Lastly, when thinking through our vocation as moral theologians or theological ethicists, we would do well to remember that the pursuit of moral truth did not always take place in universities and colleges. While Curran argues that the transition of moral theology into an academic context has been largely positive, he notes four possible dangers, including forgetting that moral theology exists in the service of the church and downplaying the role of the public intellectual in both the church and in society.[80] Thinking through our vocation as moral theologians challenges us to examine critically how we spend our time as well as how the structures of our workplaces affect our vocations, positively or negatively. Given that there are already tensions emerging in the academy between the ideals set for theological professionals and the demands of family life,[81] perhaps maintaining this historical awareness of the contingent nature of the academy as the setting for moral theology will help us think through and respond to these challenges in more constructive ways, haunted by Massingale's questions: "Who are you going to help with it? Who are you going to use it for?"

Notes

1. While I recognize that distinctions have been made between moral theologian and theological ethicist, I use these terms interchangeably throughout this essay. Both terms appear in the writings of the contemporary authors I cite.

2. Dionisio M. Miranda, S.V.D., "What Will You Have Me Do for You? The Theological Ethics Agenda from an Asian Perspective," in *Catholic Theological Ethics in the World Church: The Plenary Papers from the First Cross-Cultural Conference on Catholic Theological Ethics*, ed. James F. Keenan (New York: Continuum, 2007), 184.

3. Peter Black and James F. Keenan, "The Evolving Self-Understanding of the Moral Theologian: 1900–2000," *Studia Moralia* 39 (2001): 291–327.

4. I choose to focus on these five theologians precisely because I have less familiarity with African and Asian contextual theologies as opposed to Latin American contextual theologies, and because I have less familiarity with black theology in the US context than with other contextual theologies, such as feminist theology.

5. Douglas James Schuurman, *Vocation: Discerning Our Callings in Life* (Grand Rapids, MI: W. B. Eerdmans, 2004), 1. As Schuurman observes, the term "avocations," which refers to activities other than paid work, illustrates our cultural tendency to identify vocation simply and narrowly with paid work. Such an understanding of vocation omits any religious context in addition to eclipsing relational spheres outside of paid work.

6. One of the most significant shifts in moral theology during the twentieth century was the shifting of the professional setting from seminaries to colleges and universities. Charles E. Curran, *Moral Theology at the End of the Century*, Père Marquette Lecture in Theology 1999 (Milwaukee, WI: Marquette University Press, 1999), 34–41. Nevertheless, this shift was not absolute. Some scholars, such as Black and Keenan, have identified the emergence of two tracks of moral theology, with bishops' advisors participating less frequently in the professional activities, such as conferences, of moral theologians who pursue moral theology in an academic setting. Black and Keenan, "The Evolving Self-Understanding of the Moral Theologian: 1900–2000," 307. It is worth noting that, in some countries, the setting of moral theology is still seminaries and formation programs for religious.

7. Curran, *Moral Theology at the End of the Century*, 41.

8. Black and Keenan, "The Evolving Self-Understanding of the Moral Theologian: 1900–2000," 294.

9. For example, Schuurman cites the entry for "vocation" in the *Catholic Encyclopedia*, which only includes "Ecclesiastical and Religious Vocation." Schuurman, *Vocation*, 2, n.I.

10. According to the third English edition of Jone's moral manual, published in 1946, "Clerics should lead a spiritual life more holy than the laity to whom they should be an

example of virtue and the upright life." Heribert Jone, *Moral Theology*, rev. in accordance with the 16th German ed. and contains additions that will appear in the 17th (Westminster, MD: Newman Press, 1960), 288. All religious, though they may be laypersons or clerics, also have the obligation to strive for perfection (ibid., 294). Jone paid little attention to the lay state of life. While the sections on the duties and rights of clerics and religious take up a few pages each, Jone is content to offer one short paragraph on each with respect to the laity and to refer the reader to other related sections concerning specific stations in life, such as "laborer" or "physician" (ibid., 300–301).

11. For a recent reflection that treats this topic, see Jessica Keating, "Celibacy at 30 Is Not Just an Empty Holding Pattern," *America Magazine*, September 8, 2016, http://www .americamagazine.org/faith/2016/09/08/celibacy-30-not-just-empty-holding-pattern.

12. See *Lumen gentium*, nos. 39–42. In the development of this document, there was discussion of to what extent the gifts of the Spirit were given to all of the baptized, as evidenced in the disagreement between Cardinal Suenens and Cardinal Ruffini. For more on this topic in the context of baptism, charism, and vocation, see Mary Catherine Hilkert, "The Vocation of the Theologian," *Horizons* 27, no. 2 (September 2000): 43–44. The call to holiness is a call to pursue perfection, to "the fullness of the Christian life." See *Lumen gentium*, no. 40. "The Lord Jesus, the divine Teacher and Model of all perfection, preached holiness of life to each and every one of His disciples of every condition. He Himself stands as the author and consummator of this holiness of life: 'Be you therefore perfect, even as your heavenly Father is perfect.' . . . Thus it is evident to everyone, that all the faithful of Christ, of whatever rank or status, are called to the fullness of the Christian life and to the perfection of charity; (4*) by this holiness as such a more human manner of living is promoted in this earthly society."

13. *Lumen gentium*, no. 41, "The classes and duties of life are many, but holiness is one—that sanctity which is cultivated by all who are moved by the Spirit of God, and who obey the voice of the Father and worship God the Father in spirit and in truth. These people follow the poor Christ, the humble and cross-bearing Christ in order to be worthy of being sharers in His glory. Every person must walk unhesitatingly according to his own personal gifts and duties in the path of living faith, which arouses hope and works through charity." The paragraph goes on to discuss the particular situations of priests, other ministers, married couples, and Christian parents.

14. For example, in a 1970 piece, Enda McDonagh places the theology of vocation in the context of an understanding of human vocation, writing: "Human existence is a matter of becoming a human being; it is a call to become this particular human being." Enda McDonagh, "The Theology of Vocation," *The Furrow* 21, no. 5 (1970): 293. After addressing the vocations associated with the word and sacrament, McDonagh goes on to say, "These are the two particular kinds of vocation to which we are accustomed, but they are vocations which simply specify the basic Christian vocation. Within these two, there can be a great many different varieties. You can have a teacher priest, a worker priest, as well as a parochial priest. You can have any kind of priesthood, as long as the ministry is given a clear relation to word and sacrament. Similarly, in regard to the religious life, you can have a vast variety. But I think that every kind of vocation must always recall that the basic vocation of the Christian is, within the community of the Church at large, to bring the word of God to mankind and to celebrate the meaning and unity of mankind in the sacrament."

15. Jone, *Moral Theology*. See the very first page, "Author's Preface (to the First Edition)."

16. Black and Keenan, "The Evolving Self-Understanding of the Moral Theologian: 1900–2000," 294.

17. While it would be anachronistic to attempt to interpret the self-understanding of moral theologians who were writing before the Second Vatican Council in terms of the universal Christian call to holiness, it is worth highlighting the profound changes in the understanding of vocation and holiness that occurred in the twentieth century. Moral theologians writing before the Council were priests, and thus understood themselves to be obligated to strive for perfection. Yet Jone, for example, did not understand the holiness of life of the cleric in relation to the exercise of specific priestly ministries such as hearing confessions (toward which the moral manuals were primarily directed), much less in relation to contributions to moral theology. Rather, for Jone, clerical holiness was understood primarily in terms of specific spiritual practices such as daily meditation and frequent confession, visitation of the Blessed Sacrament, recitation of the rosary, and examination of conscience. Jone, *Moral Theology*, 288. Similarly the striving for perfection incumbent upon members of religious life was understood in terms of not violating one's vows or offending against religious discipline and observance (ibid., 294).

18. Moral manuals did not address growth in discipleship but only the avoidance of sin. Thomas Slater famously wrote in the preface to the first moral manual to appear in English that the manuals of moral theology "are not intended for edification, nor do they hold up a high ideal of Christian perfection for the imitation of the faithful." Thomas Slater, *A Manual of Moral Theology for English-Speaking Countries,* 6th and rev. ed. (London: Burns Oates & Washbourne, 1928), v. Furthermore, while the authors intended to deal with matters related to everyday life, the scope of ethical concern was limited and did not address the really important issues of the day. For example, Keenan draws attention to the fact that moral manualists writing during the Second World War gave more attention to girls' dresses and sperm than to atomic weapons. James F. Keenan, *A History of Catholic Moral Theology in the Twentieth Century: From Confessing Sins to Liberating Consciences* (London: Continuum, 2010), 30.

19. Black and Keenan, "The Evolving Self-Understanding of the Moral Theologian: 1900–2000," 293.

20. Ibid., 305.

21. Mary Ann Donovan, "The Vocation of the Theologian," *Theological Studies* 65, no. 1 (2004): 3–22, doi:10.1177/004056390406500101. In this article, Donovan examines sections of both *Lumen gentium and Gaudium et spes.*

22. John C. Ford and Gerald Andrew Kelly, *Contemporary Moral Theology I: Questions in Fundamental Moral Theology* (Westminster, MD: Newman Press, 1964), 28–29.

23. Dissent is a theme that pervades Curran's work. The legitimacy of dissent is a "most significant debate in contemporary moral theology." Charles E. Curran, *Toward an American Catholic Moral Theology* (Notre Dame, IN: University of Notre Dame Press, 1987), 18. He recognizes that dissent may be exercised either responsibly or irresponsibly. He believes that dissent done responsibly on the part of theologians can play an important and constructive role in the church as part of "the ongoing process by which truth is sought within the church." Charles E. Curran, *The Living Tradition of Catholic Moral Theology* (Notre Dame, IN: University of Notre Dame Press, 1992), 125. Curran also identified the dissent of many moral theologians, such as Richard McCormick, as the "most significant ecclesial aspect of moral theology in the post–Vatican II period." Ibid., 88. Significantly, the aftermath of *Humanae vitae* formed the historical context for these debates over dissent and the rela-

tionship of theologians with the teaching authority of the hierarchical magisterium. Keenan notes that after *Humanae vitae*, "Moral theologians had a protracted battle with hierarchical authority about the competency of the moral magisterium." Keenan, *A History of Catholic Moral Theology in the Twentieth Century*, 141. Curran sees the issue of dissent as related to broader themes about the exercise of conscience of the believer and the question of diversity within Roman Catholicism. See, for example, Charles E. Curran, *Directions in Fundamental Moral Theology* (Notre Dame, IN: University of Notre Dame Press, 1985), 257–78.

24. Congregation for the Doctrine of the Faith, "Instruction on the Ecclesial Vocation of Theologian," http://www.vatican.va/roman_curia/congregations/cfaith/documents/rc_con_cfaith_doc_19900524_theologian-vocation_en.html. Ten of the document's forty-two paragraphs are addressed to "The Problem of Dissent." In terms of word count, dissent occupies closer to a third (32 percent) of the document. It is noteworthy that even though by 1990 several women had not only completed doctorates in theology but were also recognized as theologians in university contexts, the Congregation for the Doctrine of the Faith assumes that theologians are male.

25. Bernard Häring, "The Role of the Catholic Moral Theologian," in *Moral Theology: Challenges for the Future: Essays in Honor of Richard A. McCormick*, ed. Charles E. Curran (New York: Paulist Press, 1990), 32.

26. Ibid., 34.

27. Ibid.

28. Ibid., 37.

29. Ibid., 38.

30. Margaret R. Pfeil, "Transparent Mediation: The Vocation of the Theologian as Disciple," in *New Wine, New Wineskins: A Next Generation Reflects on Key Issues in Catholic Moral Theology*, ed. William C. Mattison III (Lanham, MD: Rowman & Littlefield Publishers, 2005), 71.

31. Christopher P. Vogt, "Finding a Place at the Heart of the Church: On the Vocation of a Lay Theologian," in *New Wine, New Wineskins: A Next Generation Reflects on Key Issues in Catholic Moral Theology*, ed. William C. Mattison III (Lanham, MD: Rowman & Littlefield, 2005), 46–50.

32. Feminist theology is generally dated to Valerie Saiving (Goldstein)'s 1960 article "The Human Situation: A Feminine View," *Journal of Religion* 40, no. 2 (April 1960): 100–112. Susan A. Ross, "Feminist Theology: A Review of Literature," in *Feminist Ethics and the Catholic Moral Tradition, Readings in Moral Theology*, No. 9, ed. Charles E. Curran, Margaret A. Farley, and Richard A. McCormick (New York: Paulist Press, 1996), 11. The term *black theology* appeared in the United States in the mid-1960s. M. Shawn Copeland points out that while the emergence of black Catholic theology is often dated to 1978 (with the first meeting of the Black Catholic Theological Symposium), this date reflects convenience more than actual history, as there were "other black Catholic attempts, in the early 1970s, to articulate a theology adequate for our particular pastoral and social needs." M. Shawn Copeland, "Method in Emerging Black Catholic Theology," in *Taking Down Our Harps: Black Catholics in the United States*, ed. Diana L. Hayes and Cyprian Davis (Maryknoll, NY: Orbis Books, 1998), 124. Initially, these two approaches to theology did not greatly influence each other or the wider theological context. For example, most US theologians ignored the insights of black theology. For the few exceptions to this general trend, see ibid., 124–25. Similarly,

early feminist theology was undertaken from the departure point of the experiences of white women. Black and Latina women constructively critiqued feminist theology and offered womanist and *mujerista* theology as correctives. Today, more attention is paid to the differences in experiences of women from different backgrounds. Ross, "Feminist Theology: A Review of Literature," 18–21.

33. For example, the first intentionally cross-cultural conference on Catholic theological ethics was held in July 2006 and resulted in an edited volume. See James F. Keenan, ed., *Catholic Theological Ethics in the World Church: The Plenary Papers from the First Cross-Cultural Conference on Catholic Theological Ethics* (New York: Continuum, 2007).

34. John Mary Waliggo, "A Call for Prophetic Action," in *Catholic Theological Ethics in the World Church: The Plenary Papers from the First Cross-Cultural Conference on Catholic Theological Ethics*, ed. James F. Keenan (New York: Continuum, 2007), 254.

35. Ibid., 253.

36. Laurenti Magesa, "Locating the Church among the Wretched of the Earth," in *Catholic Theological Ethics in the World Church: The Plenary Papers from the First Cross-Cultural Conference on Catholic Theological Ethics*, ed. James F. Keenan (New York: Continuum, 2007), 55.

37. Vimala Chenginimattam, "Through Her Eyes: The Role of Women Theological Ethicists in Terms of the Future Development of Moral Theology," in *Doing Asian Theological Ethics in a Cross-Cultural and an Interreligious Context*, ed. Yiu Sing Lúcás Chan, James F. Keenan, and Shaji George Kochuthara (Bengaluru: Dharmaram Publications, 2016), 311.

38. Christina A. Astorga, "The Triple Cries of Poor, Women, and the Earth: Interlocking Oppressions in the Christian Context," in *Doing Asian Theological Ethics in a Cross-Cultural and an Interreligious Context*, ed. Yiu Sing Lúcás Chan, James F. Keenan, and Shaji George Kochuthara (Bengaluru: Dharmaram Publications, 2016), 250–62. In this chapter, Astorga presents these triple cries in an Asian context.

39. Bryan N. Massingale, *Racial Justice and the Catholic Church* (Maryknoll, NY: Orbis Books, 2010), 157–58.

40. Waliggo, "A Call for Prophetic Action," 254.

41. Ibid., 258.

42. Magesa, "Locating the Church," 55.

43. Bryan Massingale, "The Systematic Erasure of the Black/Dark-Skinned Body in Catholic Ethics," in *Catholic Theological Ethics, Past, Present, and Future: The Trento Conference*, ed. James F. Keenan (Maryknoll, NY: Orbis Books, 2011), 108–16.

44. Massingale, *Racial Justice and the Catholic Church*, 113.

45. Ibid.

46. Astorga, "The Triple Cries of Poor, Women, and the Earth: Interlocking Oppressions in the Christian Context," 257.

47. Ibid.

48. Ibid., 258.

49. Lisa Sowle Cahill, "Moral Theology: From Evolutionary to Revolutionary Change," in *Catholic Theological Ethics in the World Church: The Plenary Papers from the First Cross-Cultural Conference on Catholic Theological Ethics*, ed. James F. Keenan (New York: Continuum, 2007), 225.

50. Häring, "The Role of the Catholic Moral Theologian," 39–42.

51. Ibid., 44.

52. Keenan, *A History of Catholic Moral Theology in the Twentieth Century*, 197–99. With respect to Latin American liberation theology, Keenan argues that despite several setbacks, "concepts like option for the poor, structures of sin, critical reflection on praxis, liberation, and the overall call of theology to respond to the irruption of suffering into theology, are now constitutively foundational to theology in general and moral theology in particular." Ibid., 203.

53. Waliggo, "A Call for Prophetic Action," 255.

54. Magesa, "Locating the Church," 55.

55. Astorga, "The Triple Cries of Poor, Women, and the Earth: Interlocking Oppressions in the Christian Context," 257–58.

56. In the introduction to *Catholic Theological Ethics: Past, Present, and Future: The Trento Conference*, James Keenan argues that one of the primary lessons learned concerned the vocation of theological ethicists. This vocation includes working for the transformation of church and society: "our vocation is based on the promise that we are needed because things are not as they could be. As the critics and reformers of society and church, we seek to practically bridge the gulf between who we are and who we can be."

57. Magesa, "Locating the Church," 56.

58. Waliggo, "A Call for Prophetic Action," 259–60.

59. Ibid., 255.

60. Astorga, "The Triple Cries of Poor, Women, and the Earth: Interlocking Oppressions in the Christian Context," 260.

61. Ibid., 259, 261.

62. Chenginimattam, "Through Her Eyes: The Role of Women Theological Ethicists in Terms of the Future Development of Moral Theology," 311.

63. Massingale, *Racial Justice and the Catholic Church*, 165–66.

64. Ibid., 173.

65. Ibid., 173–74.

66. Ibid., 174.

67. Waliggo, "A Call for Prophetic Action," 255. For example, Waliggo argues that theologians need "meaningful networking, unity, solidarity" in addition to prophetic witness and effective advocacy.

68. Ibid., 260.

69. Although this chapter has explicitly focused more on contextual theologies from Africa and Asia, these themes are not limited to theologians from these contexts, as even a quick glance through two volumes in the CTEWC series reveals. See *Catholic Theological Ethics in the World Church: The Plenary Papers from the First Cross-Cultural Conference on Catholic Theological Ethics* (New York: Continuum, 2007) and *Catholic Theological Ethics Past, Present, and Future: The Trento Conference* (Maryknoll, NY: Orbis Books, 2011).

70. Magesa, "Locating the Church," 56. Shaji George Kochuthara identifies "Bridging the gaps between the authority and theological ethics and between people and theological ethics" as one challenge for theological ethicists. Shaji George Kochuthara, "Context and the Future of Theological Ethics: The Task of Building Bridges," in *Catholic Theological Ethics: Past, Present, and Future: The Trento Conference*, ed. James F. Keenan (Maryknoll, NY: Orbis Books, 2011), 292.

71. Vogt, "Finding a Place at the Heart of the Church: On the Vocation of a Lay Theologian."

72. Massingale, *Racial Justice and the Catholic Church*, 165.

73. St. Mary's College in South Bend, IN, was the first US university to offer a doctoral degree in theology to women. Prior to then, only the Catholic University of America offered doctoral degrees in theology. Curran, *Moral Theology at the End of the Century*, 36.

74. Florence Caffrey Bourg, "The Dual Vocation of Parenthood and Professional Theology: How Are We Doing? Where Are We Headed?" *Horizons* 32, no. 1 (2005): 26–52.

75. Charles E. Curran, "Method in Moral Theology: An Overview from an American Perspective," *Studia Moralia* 18 (1980): 109.

76. Margaret A. Farley, "Ethics, Ecclesiology, and the Grace of Self-Doubt," in *A Call to Fidelity: On the Moral Theology of Charles E. Curran*, ed. Walter J. James, Timothy E. O'Connell, and Thomas A. Shannon (Washington, DC: Georgetown University Press, 2002), 69. Farley observes that whether self-doubt is to be achieved or overcome is related to positions of power and suggests that the grace of self-doubt is "necessary perhaps especially for those who are in positions of power" (ibid., 68). Like Häring, Farley pairs doubt with courage, concluding that both the grace of self-doubt and the courage of conviction are needed in ecclesiology and ethics (ibid., 70).

77. Lisa Fullam, "Humility and Its Moral Epistemological Implications," in *Virtue: Readings in Moral Theology*, ed. Charles E. Curran and Lisa Fullam (Mahwah, NJ: Paulist Press, 2011), 251.

78. Keenan defines the virtue of humility as "knowing the truth of one's place." See Daniel J. Harrington and James F. Keenan, *Jesus and Virtue Ethics: Building Bridges between New Testament Studies and Moral Theology* (Lanham, MD: Sheed & Ward, 2002), 191.

79. For example, see Christiana Z. Peppard and Andrea Vicini, eds., *Just Sustainability: Technology, Ecology, and Resource Extraction*, Catholic Theological Ethics in the World Church 3 (Maryknoll, NY: Orbis Books, 2015).

80. Curran, *Moral Theology at the End of the Century*, 40–41.

81. Based upon the results of a 2003 survey of the College Theological Society, Bourg concludes, "With the shift from clerical to lay theology in the Catholic tradition, more parents (or, prospective parents) are entering a professional environment with performance ideals not designed to fit their lifestyle." Bourg, "The Dual Vocation of Parenthood and Professional Theology," 50.

CONTRIBUTORS

Anne Celestine Achieng Oyier-Ondigo is a Kenyan Franciscan Sister of St. Joseph-Asumbi. She completed her postdoctoral scholarship at Boston College (USA). She earned her PhD from the Nelson Mandela University in Port Elizabeth (South Africa) and two master's: in peace studies and international relations from Hekima University (Kenya) and in linguistics from the University of Nairobi (Kenya). She contributed to various edited volumes and published several peer-reviewed articles in international journals.

Barbara Hilkert Andolsen holds a PhD in religion from Vanderbilt University (USA). She is professor of Christian ethics at Fordham University in New York. She has authored three books, coedited a volume, and published numerous journal articles. Andolsen's writings include *The New Job Contract: Economic Justice in an Age of Insecurity*; "Agape and Feminist Ethics," in the *Journal of Religious Ethics*; "Elements of a Feminist Approach to Bioethics," reprinted in *Feminist Ethics and the Catholic Moral Tradition;* and "Social Justice, the Common Good, and New Signs of Racism," in *Interrupting White Privilege: Catholic Theologians Break the Silence.*

Antonio Autiero is professor emeritus of moral theology at the University of Münster (Germany). Between 1997 and 2011, he was also director of the research center in religious and theological sciences at the Fondazione Bruno Kessler in Trent (Italy). He is a member of the German Academy of Ethics in the Medicine, of the Stem Cell Research Governmental Ethics Committee, and of the Planning Committee of CTEWC. He has authored books, edited volumes, and published articles on fundamental moral theology and moral theory, and in applied ethics (i.e., medical ethics, bioethics, and research ethics).

Jana Marguerite Bennett is associate professor of theological ethics at the University of Dayton (USA). Her latest book is *Singleness and the Church: A New Theology of the Single Life* (Oxford, 2017). She is also the author of *Aquinas on the Web? Doing Theology in an Internet Age* (Continuum, 2012). She is a managing editor of the *Journal of Disability and Religion* as well as the blog catholicmoraltheology.com.

Pablo A. Blanco earned a master's in social doctrine of the church (Salamanca), a master's in public administration, and doctorates in higher education and political science (UBA). He is associate professor at the University of Buenos Aires, assistant professor at the Pontifical Catholic University of Argentina, director of the Public Administration Observatory (INAP), member of the executive committee of the Latin American Episcopal Council (CELAM), and member of the regional Latin

America committee of CTEWC. His main research interests are the intersection between moral theology, political theory, and social ethics.

Aldo Marcelo Cáceres, OSA, earned a doctorate in moral theology, maste's in the social doctrine of the church, in bioethics, and in religious sciences, and a bachelor's in education. He teaches at the María Reina Institute, the Padre Félix Varela Institute, and the Archdiocesan Seminary in Cuba. His most recent books are *Iglesia y globalización* (Bilbao, 2012) and *Una ética urgente: La defensa de la vida y de la dignidad humana* (Buenos Aires, 2015).

Grégoire Catta, SJ, holds a doctorate in sacred theology from Boston College School of Theology and Ministry focusing on the theology of Catholic social teaching. He is assistant professor of theology at Centre Sèvres, Facultés Jésuites de Paris, where he holds the Jean Rodhain Chair. He is also a member of the Center for Social Research and Action (CERAS) and contributes to the *Revue Projet*.

Daniel J. Fleming is group manager of ethics and formation for St. Vincent's Health Australia—a role that sees him leading ethics education, advice, and strategy as well as supporting formation across the St. Vincent's Health Australia network. Previously, he held the roles of academic dean and senior lecturer in theology and ethics at the Australian Institute of Theological Education in New South Wales. He holds a PhD in moral philosophy and theology from the Australian Catholic University.

Elio Gasda, SJ, earned a bachelor of philosophy, a PhD in theology (Universidad Pontificia Comillas, Madrid), and a postdoctorate in political philosophy (Portuguese Catholic University). He is professor and researcher of theological ethics at the Jesuit Faculty in Belo Horizonte (Brazil). He is a member of various research groups: among them, the group on the social thought of the Church of the Latin American Episcopal Council (CELAM) and the group on theology, ethics, and politics of the Latin American Council of Social Sciences (CLACSO). Among his recent volumes are *Christian Faith and the Sense of Work* (2011); *Labor and Global Capitalism* (2011); *Economy and the Common Good* (2016); and *Christianity and the Economy* (2017).

Maria Isabel Gil Espinosa is a graduate of the Pontificia Universidad Javeriana (Colombia) where she earned a PhD in theology, a master's in theology, and a specialization in bioethics. Currently, in the same university, she is a professor of moral theology. She is also a member of the CTEWC Latin America regional committee. Her research interests include fundamental moral theology, human rights, and bioethics.

Roman Globokar studied theology at the University of Ljubljana (Slovenia) and at the Pontifical Gregorian University in Rome where he earned a licentiate and a doctorate. He is assistant professor of theological ethics at the University of Ljubljana. Since 2005, he is member of the National Medical Ethics Committee, and since 2011 he joined the National Experts Council for General Education. He is a cochair of the CTEWC European regional committee and member of the CTEWC planning committee. He has published several articles on fundamental theological ethics, bioethics, and ecological ethics. In 2013, he published *Theological Ethics between Universalism and Particularism in Slovenian*.

Konrad Glombik is professor at the Opole University (Poland) and chair of the department of moral theology and spirituality. He is also director of the Opole University Press and editor in chief of the biannual *Theological–Historical Studies of Opole Silesia*. He is a member of the CTEWC European regional committee and authored several books and articles on the ethics of marriage and family, sexual ethics, and the sacrament of reconciliation.

Kenneth R. Himes, OFM, is professor of Christian ethics at Boston College (USA). He earned his PhD in religion and public policy from Duke University. A past president of the Catholic Theological Society of America, Himes is the author of four books—the most recent being *Drones and the Ethics of Targeted Killing* (2016). He also coedited the second edition of *Modern Catholic Social Teaching: Commentaries and Interpretations* (2018).

Mary Jo Iozzio is professor of moral theology at Boston College (USA). Active in the American Academy of Religion, CTEWC, the Catholic Theological Society of America, and the Society of Christian Ethics, she lectures, teaches, and writes on Catholic social thought, virtues, and liberation ethics at the intersections of disability, gender, and racial justice. In addition to many publications, she has edited or coedited the *Journal of Religion, Disability & Health*, the *Journal of Moral Theology*, and the *Journal of the Society of Christian Ethics*. Forthcoming is her volume on a theological ethics of disability.

Laurie Johnston is associate professor of theology at Emmanuel College and visiting scholar at the Center for Human Rights and International Justice at Boston College (USA). She holds degrees from Boston College, the University of Virginia, and Harvard Divinity School. Among her recent publications are two coedited books: *Can War Be Just in the Twenty-First Century?* (with Tobias Winright) and *Public Theology and the Global Common Good* (with multiple coeditors). She is also a member of the Community of Sant'Egidio.

George Kodithottam, SJ, is professor of moral theology at Gujarat Vidya Deep Regional Seminary at Vadodara, affiliated with Jnana-Deepa Vidyapeeth Pontifical Institute in Pune (India). He graduated in civil law and holds master's degrees in sociology and theology. He earned his doctorate in moral theology at the University of Innsbruck (Austria). Besides teaching moral theology, he worked in mission parishes in rural Gujarat (India) for over twenty years.

Laurenti Magesa teaches theology at Hekima University in Nairobi (Kenya). He is author of many articles and several books on African thought, most recently *What*

Is Not Sacred? African Spirituality (Orbis, 2013) and *The Post-Conciliar Church in Africa* (CUEA Press, 2016). His research interest is in African Christian ethics. He is a founding member of the Ecumenical Symposium of East Africa Theologians (ESEAT) and collaborates in the Ecumenical Association of Third World Theologians (EATWOT).

Lindsay Marcellus is pursuing her doctoral education at Boston College (USA) as a Flatley Fellow in Theological Ethics and Presidential Scholar. She holds an MTS from the University of Notre Dame. Her research interests include Christian environmental ethics, virtue ethics, the history of ethics, and how women's experiences help in articulating theological ethics.

Claudia Montes de Oca Ayala is a Bolivian theologian, married, and mother of a girl and a boy. She studied moral theology, ethics and intercultural citizenship, ethics and economics, and integral ecology. Her research interests are ethics, social ethics, eco-theology, ecumenical and interreligious dialogue, and feminism. She is versed in research, teaching, and publications on these topics. She also works in social and ecclesial contexts by promoting reflection and action with the laity, youth groups, and women's groups.

Anthonia Bolanle Ojo is a member of the Congregation of the Sisters of St. Michael the Archangel (Nigeria). She earned a doctorate in moral theology with specialization in social ethics from the Catholic Institute of West Africa in Port Harcourt (Nigeria). She presently lectures in the department of moral theology of the Good Shepherd Major Seminary in Kaduna (Nigeria).

Haruko K. Okano is professor emeritus and former president of Seisen University in Tokyo. She taught theological ethics, gender studies, and history of religions at the Hiroshima National University and Seisen University. She was visiting professor in Salzburg (Austria), Tilburg (Holland), and Frankfurt (Germany). She writes on feminist ethics, intercultural dialogue, and the history of religion. Her volumes include *Die Stellung der Frau im Shinto: Religionsphänomenologische und soziologische Untersuchung* (1976), *Women and Religion in Japan* (1998), and *Christliche Theologie im Japanischen Kontext* (2002).

Elias Omondi Opongo, SJ, is the director of the Hekima Institute of Peace Studies and International Relations at Hekima University in Nairobi (Kenya). Elias, a Jesuit priest, peace activist, and conflict analyst, holds a PhD in peace and conflict studies from the University of Bradford (UK) and a master's in international peace studies from the University of Notre Dame (USA). His research and publications focus on transitional justice and postconflict reconstruction, state-building, and on how to address religious extremism and radicalization.

Vimal Tirimanna, CSsR, teaches moral theology at the Pontifical Alphonsian Academy (Italy), the Pontifical College of St. Bede (Italy), and the National Seminary in Kandy (Sri Lanka). From 1997 to 2012, he served as representative of the Sri Lankan Bishops in the Office of Theological Concerns of the Federation of Asian Bishops Conferences (FABC) and as executive secretary (2002–2012). At present, he is a member of the Catholic delegation to the third phase of the Anglican Roman Catholic International Commission (ARCIC III).

Nhu Y-Lan Tran is a member of the Congregation of Notre Dame and of the Committee for the Doctrine of the Faith in Vietnam. A medical doctor, she earned her doctoral degree from Weston Jesuit School of Theology (USA). She teaches biosexual ethics and fundamental moral theology at the Jesuit Scholasticate and at the St. Joseph Major Seminary of the Ho Chi Minh archdiocese, as well as five other theology institutes in Ho Chi Minh City.

Ellen Van Stichel earned her PhD in Catholic social ethics at the Faculty of Theology and Religious Studies of the Katholieke Universiteit Leuven (Belgium) on the relationship between charity and justice in the debate on global duties. Her research interests include social and political philosophy, Catholic social teaching, alternative thinking and practices in economics, and Christian anthropology in relation to social issues. Currently, she is senior researcher at the Dominican Research Centre for Theology and Society in Amsterdam (the Netherlands).

Index

abortion, 199–202
  prenatal diagnosis and, 200–205
  selective, 200, 201, 203, 204–5, 208
  US law and, 260–61
accompaniment, 42, 45–46
  conscience transformation and,
    51–52
  features of, 51–52
  science and, 49
accountability, 216
ADA. *See* Americans with Disability
  Act
Adolfo, Eldridge, 224
Afghanistan, US bombings in, 241
Africa
  applied ethics in, 122–24
  Catholic ethical formation in, 124
  Catholic fundamental moral
    theology in, development of,
    118–20
  Christianity in, 118
  church in, as family of God, 127,
    129–31
  common good in, 228
  communitarian ethics of, 120, 122,
    127
  corruption in, 223, 228
  cultural values in, 119–20
  dehumanizing factors in, 228
  elder care in, 83
  electoral violence in, 222–31
  families in, 129–30

fertility in, 83
holistic approach in, 121
justice in, 123
marriage in, 83
missionary legacy in, 118, 122
nation-state in, 123
new social-ethical imagination for,
  123–24
SCCs in, 127–28, 130–31
solidarity and, 120
suicide bombings in, 242–43
terrorism in, 235–44
theologians' challenges in, 301
youth unemployment in, 229,
  239–40
Africae munus (Benedict XVI),
  119–20
African National Congress (South
  Africa), 238
al-Bashir, Omar, 238
Al-Qaeda, 235, 240, 242
Al-Qaeda in the Islamic Maghreb,
  235, 242
Al-Shabaab, 235–36, 239, 240, 242,
  243
Alston, Philip, 225
Ambivalence of the Sacred (Hoffman),
  238
AMECEA. *See* Association of
  Member Episcopal Conferences
  in Eastern Africa
Americans with Disabilities Act, 255

319

Catholicism in, private, 162
religious oppression in, 162

Zacchaeus, Jesus and, Luke's story of,
42–45, 51
Zarazaga, Gonzalo, 20

Zimbabwe
electoral violence in, 222, 226, 227
EMB in, 227
revolutionary terrorism in, 238
state terrorism in, 238